CITY

S0-BCA-946

Also by William H. Whyte

IS ANYBODY LISTENING?

THE ORGANIZATION MAN

CONSERVATION EASEMENTS

THE LAST LANDSCAPE

CLUSTER DEVELOPMENT

THE SOCIAL LIFE OF SMALL URBAN SPACES

WILLIAM H. WHYTE

CITY

REDISCOVERING THE CENTER

PHOTOS BY THE AUTHOR

ANCHOR BOOKS
DOUBLEDAY
NEW YORK LONDON TORONTO SYDNEY AUCKLAND

AN ANCHOR BOOK
PUBLISHED BY DOUBLEDAY
a division of Bantam Doubleday Dell Publishing Group, Inc.
666 Fifth Avenue, New York, New York 10103

ANCHOR BOOKS, DOUBLEDAY, and the portrayal of an anchor
are trademarks of Doubleday, a division of Bantam Doubleday
Dell Publishing Group, Inc.

City was originally published in hardcover by
Doubleday in 1988. The Anchor Books edition is
published by arrangement with Doubleday.

Small portions of this book appeared previously in
The Social Life of Small Urban Spaces by William H. Whyte,
published by The Conservation Foundation, Washington, D.C.

Frontispiece photo of the author by Margaret Bemiss;
photograph on page 215 by John R. Clark.

DESIGNED BY WILMA ROBIN

Library of Congress Cataloging-in-Publication Data
Whyte, William Hollingsworth.
  City.
  Bibliography: p.
  Includes index.
  1. Cities and towns.   2. City and town life.
  3. City planning. I. Title.
HT151.W55   1988   307.7′6   88-3977
ISBN 0-385-26209-4

Copyright © 1988 by William H. Whyte
ALL RIGHTS RESERVED
PRINTED IN THE UNITED STATES OF AMERICA
FIRST ANCHOR BOOKS EDITION: FEBRUARY 1990

For Jenny Bell and Alexandra

ACKNOWLEDGMENTS

The main work of the Street Life Project was done by a small band of observers, and I want to thank them for their diligence, their curiosity, and their eagerness to dispute my hypotheses. The principal researchers the first years were Marilyn Russell and Nancy Linday. They were joined by Fred Kent, who later was to found a successor organization named the Project for Public Spaces, and by Ellen Ascher, Margaret Bemiss, Ann Herendeen, and Elizabeth Dietel. Working with us on special studies were Beverly Peyser, Ellen Iseman, and Ann S. Roberts.

For their support of our research I particularly wish to thank The American Conservation Association and Laurance S. Rockefeller. Others who gave support were the Vincent Astor Foundation, the Fund for the City of New York, the Graham Foundation for Advanced Studies in the Fine Arts, the J. M. Kaplan Fund, the National Geographic Society, the National Endowment for the Arts, the New York State Council on the Arts, the Rockefeller Brothers Fund, the Rockefeller Family Fund, and the Arthur Ross Foundation.

In 1980 I worked up a "prebook." There was still a lot of research to be done, but on one aspect of our work it was well in hand. That was our study of plazas and parks. There were some clear lessons for architects and planners, and I thought it would be helpful to get them out sooner than later. Under the title *The Social Life of Small Urban Spaces* the manual was published in softcover in 1980 by the Conservation Foundation. For this and his continuing support I am indebted to President William K. Reilly.

As my film footage grew I resolved to incorporate it in a documentary covering the points of the manual and its title. This was distributed by the Municipal Art Society of New York; for this I am indebted to then Executive Director Margot Wellington and to the society's president, the late Doris Freedman, one of the reasons many New York spaces so delight the eye.

Thanks to the interest of station WGBH in Boston, the film got a second life. It was shown on the PBS network as part of the "Nova" science series, retitled *Public Spaces/Human Places*.

I want to thank the following individuals for their help: Kent Barwick, Laurie Beckelman, Daniel Biederman, Peter Bosselmann, Angela Danadjieva, David Dillon, Donald H. Elliott, James M. Fitch, Nelson Foote, Martin Gallent, Brendan Gill, Sally Goodgold, Samuel Hamill, Mark Hinshaw, Philip K. Howard, Con Howe, Allan Jacobs, Fred Kent, Don C. Miles, Boris Pushkarev, Genie Rice, Halina Rosenthal, Stephen J. Small, Gail Thomas, George Williams, and Conrad Wirth.

CONTENTS

CITY

1

INTRODUCTION

For the past sixteen years I have been walking the streets and public spaces of the city and watching how people use them. Some of what I found out may be of practical application. The city is full of vexations: steps too steep; doors too tough to open; ledges you cannot sit on because they are too high or too low, or have spikes on them so that undesirables will not sit on them. It is difficult to design an urban space so maladroitly that people will not use it, but there are many such spaces. On a larger scale, there are big blank walls, whole block-fronts of them, fortresslike megastructures; atriums; and enclosed malls. There are concourses underground and skyways overhead, made the more disorienting with illuminated maps that you cannot decipher. Small problems or large, there are practical ways to deal with them and I shall be suggesting some—including a definitive solution to the blank wall.

But there is much to be encouraged about too. The rediscovery of the pleasures of downtown has been made in city after city. To take just one index, there has been a marked increase in the number of people using center city spaces. This is in good part because there has been a marked increase in the number of spaces created. Some of them have indeed been maladroitly designed; but many are not, and a few are superb. My research group kept fairly precise count of key spaces and found that beginning in the early seventies the year-to-year increase in daily use of key spaces averaged about 10 percent. Supply was creating demand; not only were there more spaces each year, but more people were getting in the habit of using them. In time, spaces reach an effective capacity, one that is surprisingly large and is nicely determined by people themselves. Much has been learned about the factors that make a place work, and they have been applied to good effect in some stunning locations. (One of our principal findings: people tend to sit most where there are places to sit.)

There has been a proliferation of outdoor cafés. Not so long ago, the conventional wisdom was that Americans would enjoy alfresco dining on trips to Europe but were too Calvinistic to do so at home. Today a number of once-staid cities have an outdoor ambiance in spring and summer that is almost Mediterranean. Washington is an excellent example.

The rediscovery of the center seems to be a fairly universal phenomenon. In European cities, which have had a head start on ours in the provision of congenial spaces, there has been a widespread increase in the peopling of downtown. The outstanding example is Copenhagen. Thanks in good part to proselytizing by architect Jan Gehl, the center has been pedestrianized to dramatic effect. Gehl has kept detailed records, and they show a dramatic increase in the simple pleasures of downtown—strolling, sitting, window shopping. They also show great increases in planned and unplanned activities, even in winter. A new "tradition," started in 1982, is the Copenhagen Carnival, a three-day affair that has people samba dancing their way to the center.

A good part of this book is concerned with the practical, and in particular, the design and management of urban spaces. But my main interest has been in matters much less practical—or, as I would prefer to term it, fundamental research. Whatever may be the significance, what is most fascinating about the life of the street is the interchanges between people that take place in it. They take many forms. I will take them up in detail in the next chapter, but let me here note a few.

The most basic is what we term the 100 percent conversation—that is, the way people who stop to talk gravitate to the center of the pedestrian traffic stream. A variant is the prolonged, or three-phase goodbye. Sometimes these go on interminably, with several failed goodbyes as preface to the final, climactic one.

Schmoozers are instructive to watch. When they line up on the sidewalk, along the curb most often, they may engage in an intricate foot ballet. One man may rock up and down on his feet. No one else will. He stops. In a few seconds another man will start rocking up and down on his feet. A third man may turn in a half circle to his right and then to his left. There seems to be some process of communication going on. But what does it mean? I have not broken the code.

Another source of wonder is the skilled pedestrian. He is really extraordinary in the subtleties of his movements, signals, and feints. I will analyze some instant replays of crossing patterns and averted collisions as testimony.

Let me tell briefly how all this got started. In 1969, Donald Elliott, then the chairman of the New York City Planning Commission, asked me to help its members draft a comprehensive plan. It was an enjoyable task, for Elliott had gathered together a very able group of young architects, planners, and lawyers. Moreover, the thrust of the plan was unusually challenging: it was concerned with the major issues of the growth and workability of the city and its government rather than with specific land-use projections and the kind of futuristic projects typical of such plans. There was also a strong emphasis on urban design and the use of incentive zoning to provide parks and plazas. New York was doing the pioneering in this area, and the text was properly self-congratulatory on the matter.

One thing I did wonder is how the new spaces were working out. There was no research on this. There was no budget line for it, no person on the staff whose job it was to go out and check whether the place was being well used or not, and if not, why. It occurred to me that it would be a good idea to set up an evaluative unit to fill the vacuum.

I got a break. Under another innovative New York program, I was invited to Hunter College as a Distinguished Professor. (What a splendid title! Translation: no doctorate; here only one year.) Through Hunter's estimable sociology department, I was able to put the arm on some students to do studies of particular places. Some of the studies were excellent. They were also a demonstration of how the times can color perceptions. This was during the period of campus unrest—the president of the college was regularly hung in effigy—and the students' studies of spaces in and around the college tended to indicate that the whole place was a lousy plot. Nearby Madison Avenue was viewed as a hostile place, and with some justification. Whatever the subjective factors, however, some of the students proved very good at observation, and this fortified my belief in the viability of a small evaluative group.

I applied for grants to set up a unit. One of the first applications was to the trustees of the Research Division of the National Geographic Society. The gist of my application was that they had supported observational studies of far-off peoples and far-off places, so why not the natives of a city? They thought it a bit cheeky, but they did like the argument. They gave me a grant—an "expedition grant" actually—the first domestic one they had made. (I had to submit an expedition-leader form as to whether the members had been inoculated against likely tropical diseases.)

A word about methodology. Direct observation was the core of our work. We did do interviewing, and occasionally we did experiments. But mostly we watched people. We tried to do it unobtrusively and only rarely did we affect what we were studying. We were strongly motivated not to. Certain kinds of street people get violent if they think they are being spied upon.

We used photography a lot: 35mm for stills, Super 8 for time-lapse, and 16mm for documentary work. With the use of a telephoto lens, one can easily remain unnoticed, but we found that the perspective was unsatisfactory for most street interchanges. We moved in progressively closer until we finally were five to eight feet from our subjects. With a spirit level atop the camera and a wide-angle lens, we could film away with our backs half turned and thus remain unnoticed —most of the time.

Our first studies were concerned with density. They had to be. In the late sixties and early seventies the spectre of overcrowding was a popular worry. High density was under attack as a major social ill and so was the city itself. "Behavioral sink" was the new pejorative. The city was being censured not only for its obvious ills but for the compression that is a condition of it. Fifth Avenue through a telephoto lens: eight blocks of people, tense and unsmiling, squeezed into one; on the soundtrack, jackhammers, sirens, and a snatch of discordant Gershwin. This was the image of the city of the documentaries. Was there hope? Yes, a bright hope, says the narrator. A little child is shown running up a grassy hill in a new town. Back in the city, crews with hard hats and wrecking balls are shown demolishing old buildings. They are the good guys. As children look on, up go high, white towers, like Le Corbusier's radiant city. And they came to pass, these utopias, and with the best of intentions.

There were many studies on density. Notable was the work of Dr. John Calhoun of the National Institutes of Health. In experiments with rats and mice, he found that varying degrees of crowding correlated with neurotic and sometimes suicidal behavior. There were university studies on the effects on people of different space configurations, such as how twenty people in a circle in room A performed a task as compared with the same number performing the same task in a square in room B. Another approach was to monitor people's physiological responses as they were shown pictures of different spaces, ranging from a crowded street to a wilderness glade.

The image of the city of the documentaries: Fifth Avenue through a telephoto lens; eight blocks of people squeezed into one, tense, unsmiling; on the sound track, jackhammers and sirens, a snatch of discordant Gershwin.

Perch at Lexington and Fifty-seventh Street. We used a battery of cameras to track pedestrian flows, street corner encounters, and the daily life of the newsstand at right.

Some of the studies were illuminating. Taken together, however, they suffered one deficiency: the research was vicarious; it was once or twice removed from the ultimate reality being studied. That reality was people in everyday situations. That is what we studied.

The concern over high density was peaking just about the time it was becoming obvious that cities were not gaining people but losing them. Harlem, exhibit number 1 in the documentaries, experienced a severe decline, losing some 25 percent of its population between 1950 and 1970. It was not the better for it. There were so many burnt-out buildings and empty lots as to provide the worst of two worlds: not enough people in many areas to sustain the stores and activities that make a block work, but severe overcrowding in the buildings that remained. A block that did work was one we studied on East 101st Street, in Spanish Harlem. It had its troubles, but it functioned well as a small, cohesive neighborhood. Among the reasons was that there was only one vacant lot, and that was made into the block's play area.

The momentum of Title I redevelopment programs was still in force. The idea had been to empty out the blighted areas of the inner city and replace them with lower-density high-rise projects. Many of the areas were not truly blighted, but the expectation was self-fulfilling. Once an area was declared blighted, maintenance ceased, and long before yuppies came along, the displacement of people was under way. Sometimes the redevelopment phase never did come about. To this day, there are cities with swaths of cleared space in limbo: Boise, Idaho, which came near destroying itself, still has many blocks awaiting redevelopment.

Too much empty space and too few people—this finally emerged as the problem of the center in more cities than not. It had been the problem for a long time, but the lag in recognizing it as such was lamentably long. This was particularly the case with smaller cities; for many of them it still is.

It is a well-known fact that small cities are friendlier than big ones. Our research indicates that the reverse is more likely to be the case.

It is a well-known fact that small cities are friendlier than big ones. But are they? Our research on street life indicates that, if anything, the reverse is more likely to be the case. As far as interaction between people is concerned, there is markedly more of it in big cities —not just in absolute numbers but as a proportion of the total. In small cities, by contrast, you see fewer interchanges, fewer prolonged good-byes, fewer street conferences, fewer 100 percent conversations, and fewer 100 percent locations, for that matter. Individually, the friendliness quotient of the smaller might be much higher. As a former resident of a small town, I would think this to be true. It could also be argued that friendships run deeper in a smaller city than in a larger one. As far as *frequency* of interchange is concerned, however, the streets of the big city are notably more sociable than those of a smaller one.

It is not a question of the overall population, but of its distribution. A small city with a tight core can concentrate more people in its center than a larger one that sprawls all over the place. But most small cities do not concentrate; indeed, few have the concentration that they once had. Blockfront after blockfront has been broken up, the continuity destroyed by a miscellany of parking lots. Some cities have gone over the 50 percent level in this respect, with more area in parking than city.

When I visit a city, I like to take some quick counts in the center of town at midday. If the pedestrian flows on the sidewalks are at a rate less than a thousand people an hour, the city could pave the streets with gold for all the difference it would make. The city is one that is losing its center or has already done so. There are simply not enough people to make it work—not enough to keep the last department store going, not enough to sustain some good restaurants, not enough to make lively life on its streets.

It is sad to see how many cities have this emptiness at their core. It is sadder still to see how many are adopting exactly the approaches that will make matters worse. Most of their programs have in common as a stated purpose "relief from pedestrian congestion." There is no pedestrian congestion. What they need is pedestrian congestion. But what they are doing is taking what people are on the streets and putting them somewhere else. In a kind of holy war against the street, they are putting them up in overhead skyways, down in underground concourses, and into sealed atriums and galleries. They are putting them everywhere except at street level.

One result is an effect akin to Gresham's law: to make their substitute streets more competitive, cities have been making what is left of their real streets duller yet. One instrument is the blank wall. According to my rough computations, the proportion of downtown blockfronts that are blank at street level has been growing rapidly—most of all, in small cities, which are the ones most immediately hurt by suburban shopping malls and most tempted to fight their tormentors by copying them.

They do copy them, and it is self-defeating of them to do so. Cities for people who do not like cities are the worst of two worlds. As the National Trust's Main Street program has been demonstrating, the approaches that work best are those which meet the city on its own gritty terms; which raise the density, rather than lower it; which concentrate, tightening up the fabric, and get the pedestrian back on the street.

But it is the big cities that face the toughest challenge. Will their centers hold? Or will they splatter into a host of semicities? At the moment, the decentralization trend seems dominant. The demographics indicate that this is the case. So do the colonies of towers going up between the cloverleafs. Even within the city, suburbia is winning. Now coming of age is a whole new generation of planners and architects for whom the formative experience of a center was the atrium of a suburban shopping mall. Some cities have already been recast in this image, and more are following suit.

I am eschewing prophecy in this book. It is hard enough to figure out what is happening now, let alone what might or might not twenty years hence. But one can hope. I think the center is going to hold. I think it is going to hold because of the way people demonstrate by their actions how vital is centrality. The street rituals and encounters that seem so casual, the prolonged goodbyes, the 100 percent conversations—these are not at all trivial. They are manifestations of one of the most powerful of impulses: the impulse to the center.

And of the primacy of the street. It is the river of life of the city, the place where we come together, the pathway to the center. It is the primary place. As I hope to show in the chapters that follow, it has much to teach us.

In a kind of holy war against the street, cities are putting people up in overhead skyways, down in underground concourses— everywhere except street level.

2

THE SOCIAL LIFE OF THE STREET

It was a dandy hypothesis. How far, I had wondered, would people move out of the pedestrian flow to have a conversation? My hypothesis was that they would gravitate to the unused foot or so of buffer space along the building walls. It was a matter of simple common sense.

We focused time-lapse cameras on several street corners and recorded the activity for two weeks. On maps of the corners we plotted the location of each conversation and how long it lasted. To screen out people who were only waiting for the light to change, we noted only those conversations lasting a minute or longer.

The activity was not as expected. To our surprise, the people who stopped to talk did not move out of the main pedestrian flow; and if they had been out of it, they moved into it. The great bulk of the conversations were smack in the middle of the pedestrian flow—the 100 percent location, to borrow the real estate term. In subsequent studies we were to find the same impulse to the center in traveling conversations—the kind in which two people move about a lot but don't go very far. There is much apparent motion, but if you plot the

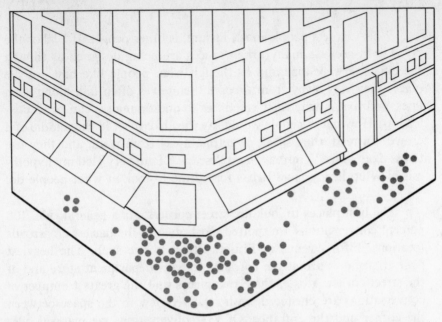

Location of street conversations lasting two minutes or more at Saks Fifth Avenue and Fiftieth Street. Cumulative for five days in June. Note main concentration at corner, secondary one outside entrance.

orbits, you will find that they are centered around the 100 percent location.

Observers in other countries have also noted the tendency to self-congestion. In his study of pedestrians in Copenhagen, Jan Gehl mapped bunching patterns almost identical to those observable here. Matthew Ciolek studies an Australian shopping center with similar results. "Contrary to 'common sense' expectations," Ciolek notes, "the great majority of people were found to select their sites for social interaction right on or very close to the traffic lines intersecting the plaza. Relatively few people formed their gatherings away from the spaces used for navigation."

Just why people behave like this I have never been able to determine. It is understandable that conversations should originate in the main flow. Where there are the most people, the likelihood of a meeting or of a leave-taking is highest. What is less explainable is the inclination to remain in the main flow, blocking traffic, and being jostled by it. This seems to be a matter not of inertia but of choice—instinctive perhaps, but by no means illogical. In the center of the crowd, you have maximum choice—to break off, to switch, to continue. It is much like being in the middle of a crowded cocktail party, which is itself a moving conversation growing ever denser and denser, occasionally ending up with everyone squeezed into a corner. It is a behavior universally deplored and practiced.

What attracts people most is other people. Many urban spaces are being designed as though the opposite were true and what people like best are places they stay away from.

What attracts people most, in sum, is other people. If I labor the point, it is because many urban spaces are being designed as though the opposite were true and as though what people like best are the places they stay away from. People themselves often talk along such lines, and that is why their responses to questionnaires can be so misleading. How many people would say they like to sit in the middle of a crowd? Instead, they speak of getting away from it all, and they use terms like "oasis," "retreat," and "escape." I am very glad my hypothesis blew up in my face. It has forced me to look at what people do.

The greatest urban spaces are street corners.

The best places to look are street corners. As a general rule, 100 percent conversations are spotted most often at the busiest crossroads locations. Fifth Avenue at Fiftieth Street is one such. The heaviest pedestrian flows are at the entrance to Saks department store and at the street corner. It is at these two places that the greatest number of conversations are clustered, with relatively few in the space between the corner and the entrance. Of 133 conversations we mapped over several days, 57 percent were concentrated in the highest-traffic locations. While there were no significant differences between men and women, men did tend to talk somewhat longer than women: 50 percent of male groups talked five minutes or longer, compared to 45 percent of female groups.

Lexington Avenue is more crowded yet—almost to the point of travesty between Fifty-seventh and Fifty-eighth streets. What with signs, floral displays, street vendors, its narrow, twelve-and-a-half-foot sidewalks are reduced to an effective walkway of five or six feet. At the peak of the lunchtime traffic, pedestrians have to walk single file. And it is then that the sidewalk is likely to be further blocked by conversation.

Pedestrians are surprisingly tolerant of the blockers. As an experiment, two of our researchers engaged in marathon conversation in the middle of the block. "Almost all of the pedestrians," one reported, "made an effort to avoid brushing against us even though this involved squeezing close to the displays or to the cars at the curbs. One woman did jostle me on purpose. A few made remarks under their breaths. But if the others felt resentful, they didn't show it. They were so polite that when they couldn't avoid brushing against us, they murmured apologies as they passed."

People waiting for people are interesting to observe, particularly so a few minutes after the hour. But most interesting of all are people who meet people they did not expect to. When I started observing street behavior, it was the high incidence of these chance meetings that struck me. But when you come to think of it, it is not chance at all. With about three thousand people an hour streaming past a spot, there is an actuarial probability that someone will see a friend, an acquaintance, or the familiar stranger you can almost place but not quite. The probability may be higher yet when you take shifts into account.

The postlunch groups heading back to the office around one o'clock look like junior and middle management people. The people you see around two are older, more expensively dressed, and apparently not in a hurry.

Of the street conversations we tracked, about 30 percent appear to have been unplanned. Some encounters were too brief to develop into a conversation—a quick hello and a wave of the hand. Some were awkwardly tentative, with neither party quite sure whether it would be right to pass on or stop. But many went on for three minutes or more. If one of the persons was with a group, the encounter sometimes involved a full round of introductions and handshakes.

It is difficult to gauge the value of chance encounters. Did the old friends meet for lunch as they said they would? Did the trade gossip turn out to be right? Possibly. But one thing is certain: it is at the crossroads that the chances are best. As we will see in the chapter on the outward move of corporate headquarters, chance is what they forfeit.

Most goodbyes are brief: a fast "ciao," "take care," a wave, and they're off. But a number are protracted, particularly so when they are an extension of a failed goodbye. It's a little like the people who hover in office doorways, forever on the verge of leaving, but never doing so. If people go through the motions of a goodbye and stop short at the point of consummation, a momentum is set up that can lead to progressively more emphatic goodbyes, up to the final resolving goodbye. It is fascinating to watch these three- and four-wave goodbyes and try to distinguish the real goodbye from the false ones. Don't be fooled by the glance at the watch. It is only premonitory. I have a wonderful film record of two men gripped in indecision in front of Saks Fifth Avenue. They just can't bring themselves to part. There are several rounds of goodbyes and looks at the watch, but it's not until a third party comes along that they finally break out of their impasse.

Best to watch are the postlunch goodbyes of the senior executives. Sometimes there is a note of irresolution about the leave-taking, as if the real business the lunch was supposed to have been about has not yet been broached. Finally, someone brings it up. The deal? The contract? Yes, yes, of course. How could they have forgotten? They now proceed to the business and as they do, their foot and arm movements tend to become reciprocal. This is an indication of people obliging one another, and soon the matter will be completed.

One of the most notable social rituals is schmoozing. In New York's garment district on Seventh Avenue, you will see groups of men lined up along the curb, facing inward. There are often so many of

Kiss, kiss.

Schmoozing on Seventh Avenue.

them that you have to go out into the street along with the handcart pushers if you want to make any headway. Sometimes the vehicular traffic slows to a near halt for all the gabbing.

"Schmoozing" is a Yiddish term for which there is no precise definition. But basically it means "nothing talk"—idle gossip, political opinions, sports talk, but not, so they say, business talk. But groups do tend to form up along occupational lines; salesmen, for example, tend to schmooze with other salesmen, and patternmakers, with other patternmakers. Some of the schmoozers are retirees who like to come back around midday to keep in touch. Almost all garment district schmoozers are men.

Physically, it's an awful place. It is without trees or graces, it is noisy and fume-ridden, and the traffic is so bad even cyclists try to give the place a wide berth. If you ask the schmoozers if they wouldn't prefer the plazas and open spaces further uptown, they will look at you as though you are crazy. Those other places: people don't *work* there. Kid stuff. This is the center of things.

In one respect, it most certainly is: in few places will you see such a clear demonstration of the relation between centrality and word of mouth communication. The schmoozing groups are anything but static. Some will last only ten minutes or so, dissolve, and then be

replaced by a new group. Other groups will constantly renew themselves, with newcomers joining as others leave. Then there are the people who roam. These are often senior men, to judge by the deference paid them. They work the block, stopping friends to chat for a moment or so, checking in briefly with the standing group. One man that we tracked talked with eighteen separate groups. He accosted them with a look of urgency, and they listened with interest. Whatever it was he was communicating, it was multiplied almost geometrically —and it wasn't "nothing talk" either.

Another great place for schmoozing is the diamond district, the single block on Forty-seventh Street between Fifth and Sixth avenues. Here Hasidic Jews play a large role. Schmoozing here is very much business, and many key transactions are carried out on the street. But there is a great deal of social schmoozing as well, and it carries on throughout the winter months.

Here there are ethnic factors to consider. You see a rich vocabulary of gestures rooted in the culture of the Orthodox Jews. In his remarkable study of gestures, David Efron compared those of the Eastern Jews in New York with southern Italians. The Italian gestures, Efron found, had a very specific meaning, and have had for generations. Reading old books on gestures (such as Andrea di Jorio's 1832 work on Neapolitan gestures), Efron found that gestures were the same as they were a century ago, for, indeed, in ancient Rome and Greece. Then as now, the gestures so well portrayed a particular

meaning that one could tell a story with them that others could follow and understand.

But this was not the case with the European Jews. When Efron compared their gestures with what they were saying, he found that the gestures emphasized and punctuated what was being said but had no symbolic meaning in themselves. Writes Efron, "To use an analogy, the Jew very rarely employs his arm in the guise of a pencil to depict the things he is referring to, but uses it often as a pointer to link one proposition to another, or to trace the itinerary of a logical journey; or else as a baton to beat the tempo of his mental locomotion." Efron found it to be especially characteristic of the Yeshiva type of Jew, who was accustomed to argumentation and syllogistic reasoning.

This is very observable on Forty-seventh Street. If you watch two men in a colloquy, you won't know what they are saying, but you will get a very clear impression of the *process* they are going through. It is the exercise of logic by reasonable, fair-minded men. The gestures sometimes indicate a dismay at the weak argument of the other, but generally these exchanges end up on an obviously friendly, or at least resolving, note.

Schmoozing is now to be seen all over, uptown and downtown, and while the intensity cannot match that of the garment district, the basic patterns are similar. Banks and corporations with large clerical staffs tend to have lots of schmoozers. These are also the kind of places that provide in-house cafeterias, recreation facilities, TV rooms, hobby clubs, and the like. But schmoozers want to get outside. They won't do much when they get there; generally they will form up abreast in a line. This is the most functional way to watch people go by. The schmoozers will sometimes exchange remarks on the passersby, but sometimes simply watch, bound in an amiable silence.

Schmoozers are fairly consistent in choosing locations. They show a liking for well-defined places—the edge of the curb, for example, or a ledge. They are also very pillar-tropic, obeying perhaps a primeval instinct for something at their backs. Rarely will they stand for long in the middle of large spaces.

Schmoozers are also consistent in the duration of their sessions, which will be either fairly brief or fairly long—fifteen minutes or even more. Some groups, as on Seventh Avenue, are of the semipermanent floating kind, and many last the whole lunch hour. The stayers dominate. If you add up the minutes spent by each schmoozer over an hour's time, you will find that the great majority of the total schmoozing minutes will be accounted for by the long-term schmoozers.

The most common form that street conversation takes is that of straight man and principal. For a while, one man dominates, while the other cooperates by remaining still and listening. Then there will be a shift—the onlooker can sense it coming—and the active man becomes the passive one.

Or should. Sometimes people will violate the tacit compact and keep on talking and gesturing beyond their time. Conversely, the straight man may fail to respect the pause during the principal's turn and jump in prematurely. When there are such failures of accommodation, there is a lack of symmetry in their movements. I have a film sequence of a long conversation on Fifty-seventh Street that is a catalog of discords. A cigar-smoking man has been long overextending his turn. This begins to be reflected in the gestures of the listener. He begins to look this way and that, as if for help and brushes lint off his lapels. He rocks up and down on his heels and then stops abruptly. He wheels to leave. The other man, still talking, grabs him by the sleeve and then finally releases him.

Soapboxers display cooperative antagonism in heightened form. About 1 P.M. they gather at Broad and Wall streets. Most are regulars; some are Henry George single-tax people, some specialize in world affairs, many concentrate on religion, interpretation of the Bible in particular. The proceedings will be highly adversarial, and that is why the soapboxers come—to dispute and be disputed. Some structure their discourse to be heckled and may be discomfited if they are not.

The classic form of their encounters is thrust and counterthrust. With a jabbing finger punctuating each point, one man advances on his adversary, who gives way at the same pace. After a climactic flourish, the first man stops, and his hands go limp. What more could possibly be said? The other man jabs out his finger. How could that be squared with Genesis? He advances on the other man, who gives way. The whole preceding scene is now acted out in reverse. Other soapboxers may egg them on. A man who is known as the Logician, a man with a spade beard and an incongruous tweed hat, may top off the session. Both men have missed the point.

The back-and-forth movements of street encounters have their parallel in speech. The pause is the crucial element. Professor Frieda Goldman-Eisler of the University College of London has found that in spontaneous speech 40 percent to 50 percent is silence and that the speed of speech is almost entirely a function of *not* speaking. Pauses have meaning: frequent ones indicate new thoughts, and few pauses, standard expression. When two people are talking, they show a tendency to match the rhythms of each other's pauses.

In their book *Rhythms of Dialogue,* Joseph Jaffe and Stanley Feldstein note the same phenomenon. Speakers tend to match the duration of each other's pauses and to space them at the same intervals. In his study of conversation, James M. Dabbs, Jr., of Georgia State University notes that each "turn" contained a number of pauses. These were of a continuation variety, not for interruption. The pause that concludes a turn, however, is a "switching" pause and is a clear signal to the other that he can take over. Distinguishing one kind of pause from the other takes art, and if one lingers on a continuation pause a half second or so too long, the other man is likely to grab the silence and run off with the conversation.

Gestures reinforce the speech and the pauses. A person may pause for effect and then add an "uh" or an "um" to signal that he's going to go on again. As he does he may signal the same message with a move of the hand. Gestures are especially important when one speaker does not play the game, jumping a pause, for example, or

Corner of Wall and Water streets: noon.

talking well beyond his turn. At such times, gestures are apt to be touching gestures—a hand on the other's sleeve, for example, as if to say, "I'm not finished yet."

Most touching gestures are friendly; the arm around another's shoulders is one of the more-common ones. But the purpose is often a measure of control. The one who does the touching is dominant—at that particular moment, at least—or seeking to be. When a man who is talking reaches out and touches another's arm, he is giving a command: Don't start talking again now, because I'm not finished yet. A more-open coercion is the grasping of another's arm to stay a departure.

Who touches whom? Men usually assume that women touch people more than men do. I assumed this and was rather pleased with some excellent examples I filmed of women picking lint from each other's coats and other forms of touching rituals. One of our researchers, a woman, took issue with my assumption, holding that typical male thinking was involved and that some systematic observation might be in order. She was right. In the street encounters we subsequently studied, we found that men did more touching than women. And the kind most frequent was men touching men.

Other studies have arrived at similar findings. Psychologist Nancy Henley found that touching correlates rather strongly with power and status. In the incidents observed, males did the most touching; males touched females more frequently than vice versa; and older people touched younger people more frequently than vice versa. Her analysis of touching in comics and TV movies showed men way in the lead. In fiction, as in life, the boss did the touching.

It is obvious enough that gestures help one person communicate with another. But there is a second function, and it may be the more-important. When one man is saying something to another, he may emphasize his points by gesturing with his hands. But the second man will be looking at his face, not at his hands. The gestures are as much for self as for the other person.

Some of the most interesting gestures are unseen by the other party. The man who's doing the gesturing often does it with his hands behind his back, out of the sight of the person for whom they're presumably intended. If you follow a traveling conversation, you will note that very often one of the group will have his hands joined behind his back and will show all sorts of finger and thumb movement, sometimes at variance with the placid mien he's showing his companion. (Occupationally I see a lot of these hidden gestures; when filming traveling conversations on the street, I find it much easier to film them from behind than from the front, and as a result, I've had to pay much more attention to these kinds of gestures than I otherwise might.)

Whatever the function of the gestures and movements, the street is a congenial place for the expression of them. They tend to be more expansive there than in internal spaces. You may see orbiting conversations in a building lobby, but out on the street they may cover far more space. Is there more room on the street? Not really; the highest incidence of encounters is in the most-crowded locations.

The street is a stage, and the sense that an audience is watching pervades the gestures and movements of the players on it. For example, are "girl-watchers" really looking at girls? They are putting on a show of girl-watchers looking at girls. The hard hats appear first and sit on the sidewalk with their backs propped up against the building wall. They are quite demonstrative, much given to whistles and direct salutation to the "girls." If there are several older men among them, the others may josh them, as though they were out of contention. They are a bit cruel: if a bag lady passes, they will hoot at her. White-collar girl-watchers stand or sit on ledges and are quieter. These are connoisseurs, amused and somewhat disdainful. They exchange comments on passersby and snicker and smirk. But it is machismo. I have never seen a girl-watcher make a direct pass at a woman. As our cameras have recorded, when a *really* good-looking woman goes by, they will be confounded, and they betray it with involuntary tugs on the earlobe and nervous stroking of their hair.

Attractive women can scare them. In an experiment to see how much room strangers would give each other as they passed, James Dabbs and Neil Stokes of Georgia State University recorded passing encounters. Among other things, they found that individual pedestri-

Girl watchers put on a show of girl watchers looking at girls. But it is all machismo. We have never seen a girl watcher make a real pass at a girl.

It doesn't take much to draw a crowd in New York.

ans would get farther out of the way for an oncoming pair than for a
single and would give more room to an oncoming male than a female.
But most interesting was the effect of beauty. Would people pass
nearer to an attractive woman than to a plain one? Both roles, by the
way, were played by the same woman. For one, she was wearing tight-
fitting clothes and attractive makeup. For the other, she used no
makeup, pulled her hair back, and wore sloppy clothes. Pedestrians
gave her a wider berth when she was attractive. It didn't make any
difference whether the pedestrians were male or female. They walked
noticeably closer to the unattractive girl, and in several cases, male
pedestrians made overtures to her. None did when she was attractive.
Dabbs and Stokes believe this behavior is best understood in terms of
social power, with a deference given to those further up the scale.

There are many other performers. The Three Jolly Fellows recur
so frequently that you would almost think they were an act put on by
street entertainers. Lovers are another example, fervently embracing in
the most heavily trafficked spots, oblivious of the crowd. But are they
so oblivious? I doubt it. Their display of affection may be quite genu-
ine, but it is a display. And they enjoy it very much.

Because I live in New York City, most of my initial research was
done there. I have been scolded about this, the city being deemed too
unique, too skewed, too much of a distorting mirror. There is some
truth to this. New York is a place that exaggerates things, no mistake.
But it is not necessarily any less informative for that. There one sees in
bolder relief patterns of behavior more muted in other places.

Our working assumption was that behavior in other cities would be basically the same, and subsequent comparisons have proved our assumption correct. The important variable is city size. As I will discuss in more detail, in smaller cities densities tend to be lower, pedestrians move at a slower pace, and there is less of the social activity in high-traffic areas. But the basic patterns are there. People are not all that different. Given the elements of a center—high pedestrian volumes, concentration, and mixture of activities—people in one city tend to respond like people in another.

One of the hardest tasks in observing a place is to find out what normal is. We spent a lot of time doing this in several small universes, among them a sleazy stretch of Lexington Avenue. As time went on and we got a better understanding of recurrent patterns, we broadened our field. We did comparative studies in other U.S. cities—in recent years, smaller cities in particular. We also did some observing in a number of major cities abroad. We were glad we did, for they provided more confirmation of basic patterns than did many in the United States.

Pedestrians in the great metropolitan centers act more like one another than pedestrians in smaller cities in their respective countries. Tokyo and New York are examples. The linear development characteristic of Japanese cities is quite unlike the grid pattern of American cities, and the cultural differences are enormous. But when you get people out on the street, the pedestrians of the two cities behave very much the same. They walk fast and aggressively, and cluster in the middle of the way. At Shinjuku Station, the busiest in the world, you will be struck by how much of the congestion is self-congestion. I prize a film record I have of two junior executives solemnly practicing golf swings at a Wall Street corner. But a better one is of three Japanese junior executives going through the same motions in Shinjuku Station in the very middle of the crowd.

Pedestrians in great metropolitan cities of the world act more like each other than like their compatriots in smaller cities.

In London you see the same recurrent patterns. In the City the financial people use their narrow sidewalks in the same ways New Yorkers do theirs. They block them. Alongside the Bank of England the sidewalk narrows at one point to about four feet, and that spot is favored for conversations. In other respects, people in the City behave very much like those in Wall Street, including the Three Jolly Fellows.

Schmoozers in Milan's Galleria tend to cluster in late afternoon rather than at midday, as in New York. But the basic rhythms are the same, with the schmoozing groups being constantly replenished as new people join and others drop out. Foot motions are as complex and indecipherable as in New York.

That the people of great cities should act alike is not surprising. They are responding to high-density situations and to a range of stimuli not found in smaller cities. It is at once the boon and the bane of smaller cities that they are not crowded. People in smaller cities do walk more slowly; they are not as aggressive and pushy because there is not much to be pushy about. Sidewalks are uncrowded, and there are fewer people blocking the flow.

But similarities of behavior between cities, large or small, are more significant than the differences. And this probably goes back in time. In the streets of the souk in the Old City of Jerusalem you see pedestrian behavior that probably differs very little from what it was centuries before. There are lessons in these old places. In considering plans for new civic spaces people often fret themselves into inaction over the thought of obsolescence. If we design for today's people, they ask, how do we know it will work a generation or so hence? You can't know, of course. But the fact is that spaces designed to work very well for their initial constituency usually work very well for later ones and, indeed, help define them.

3

STREET PEOPLE

Many people work the street. There are the regulars: cops, postmen, sanitation men, traffic directors, doormen, bus dispatchers. There are supervisors: transit authority people checking on bus dispatchers, traffic officials on traffic directors. There is even a man to check that the grate cleaners are doing their job.

Store owners can be street people. On a high-volume street with many small stores, some owners spend a lot of their time standing in the doorway. If a passerby stops to look in the window, they will start to sell him. There is very little they do not know about the street.

The irregulars are the most numerous: handbill passers, pushcart food vendors, merchandise vendors, messengers, entertainers, palmists, solicitors for religious causes, blood pressure takers. Then there are the odd people: Moondog, Mr. Magoo, Mr. Paranoid, Captain Horrible, Aztec Priestess, Gracious Lady, Tambourine Woman. Whatever the fantasies they have been acting out they make a beneficent presence on the street. Since the midseventies, however, their ranks have been swelled by scores of disturbed people released from institutions. There has been no outpatient support for these people and a number are on the streets who ought not to be. The bag ladies are a special category. They antedated the wave of released patients and endanger no one save themselves. They remain fiercely independent. There appears to be more of them on the street than before.

The underlife of the street has a rich cast too. There are the beggars, the phony pitchmen for causes, the three-card-monte players and their shills, the whores and their pimps, the male prostitutes and the Murphy Men, the dope dealers, and worst of all, the muggers in their white sneakers.

Bad or good, the variety of street people is astonishingly wide. To appreciate this, stand still. If you stay in one spot long enough, you will begin to see how many different kinds of people there are; how regular are their ways; and how many seem to know each other, even the ones you would assume to be adversaries.

If you stand in one spot long enough you will also become aware that they are noticing you. They have reason. You are not part of the routine of the block. You have no obvious business being there. If you write things down on a pad of paper they are more curious yet. Before long someone will come up to you and ask what you are up to. If you establish yourself as OK the word will get around. You will be accepted. People will say hello to you.

There is one regular you will find puzzling. He is the familiar stranger. You recognize him—you've seen him often. But you don't know who he is. He knows you. He nods to you. But who *is* he? He is out of context. He is not in uniform. He is not in the surroundings you usually see him in. Is he the assistant manager at Gristede's? The bartender at Gianni's? You need to *place* him.

The process works both way. The barber next door has been cutting my hair for fifteen years. But he always calls me Doctor. He thinks I'm a surgeon at the hospital down the block. I'm not going to tell him I'm not. It's too late. And it would not be fair to him. Calling me a doctor is part of our relationship and it is best let be.

Let us now take a closer look at the principal kinds of street people. Without drawing lines too fine we will go from good to bad.

Vendors

Street vendors sell everything. There are perennial staples: junk jewelry, watches, umbrellas, plastic raincoats, toys. But the vendors are always trying out new items and occasionally most of them will be riding one fad, or whatever the jobbers are loaded up with. Several years ago it was leather belts. So many vendors took to selling them that it looked like the point of saturation had surely been reached. But supply created demand, and the sight of all those leather belts on the sidewalks drove people to buy more leather belts. They are still buying them.

The vendors have been growing in number. They have been broadening the range of the merchandise sold. To the aggravation of merchants, they have also been staking out more of the sidewalk space, that in front of stores especially. They have been doing more selling in winter and more night selling. Some illumine their racks and tables with battery-powered fluorescent lamps.

Whatever the merchandise, the pitch is much the same. It's cheaper on the street. Ten dollars inside. One dollar here. Why pay more? The pitch is often made in a furtive manner, as if the deal were shady. Many vendors look shady. Many try to. It is to their advantage. There is a widespread assumption among knowing New Yorkers that much of the merchandise is stolen. Vendors do nothing to discourage this idea. As in a con game, the latent dishonesty of the customer is all for the good. He *wants* the goods to be stolen. That explains why he is going to snare a bargain. In actual fact, very little of the goods sold by vendors is stolen. They pick up their stuff from the jobbers in the Broadway–Thirtieth Street area who specialize in novelty merchandise. But if you ask the vendors where the goods came from, they may look at you slyly and wink.

Virtually all street vending is illegal. Under the statutes, food and merchandise vendors can be licensed, but that does not exempt them from all sorts of restrictions. Merchandise vendors are banned from the business districts; from areas zoned light commercial; from sidewalks less than twelve feet wide; from crosswalks; from bus stops; from places within ten feet of a driveway, or twenty feet of the entrance to a building. In other words, banned from almost anywhere.

The police do go after the vendors. But not very hard. Cops arresting vendors is one of the standard dramas of the street. Both parties know their parts and they play them cooperatively. When a cop comes up to a vendor and pulls out his summons book, he may say, I got a complaint—that is, this is not his idea. If any customers are still looking at the vendor's merchandise the cop may tell them it's OK to buy; it's going to take him some time to fill out the summons. The vendor won't be happy, but he knows that most judges think it is a to-do about little and will lay a fine of only a few dollars.

Confiscation of the goods is the ultimate sanction, and the police dislike it as much as the vendors do. Periodically the police will make a sweep, arriving on the scene with one or more vans into which they proceed to pack the vendors' stuff. These confrontations draw a crowd —from which come boos—and newspaper publicity. And that, to the chagrin of the Fifth Avenue Association, will be that.

Individually, some cops do go after vendors. One I used to see would sneak up on the traffic side of a line of parked trucks and then suddenly pounce on the unalerted vendors. A real mean bastard, they told me, not like the regular cops, who would approach them from the sidewalk.

Bank ledges on Fifty-seventh Street made fine all-purpose space.

An excellent podium for girl-watching.

A game of chess.　　　　　*Posing.*　　　　　*Sorting packages.*

The bank put in spikes.

Vendors used them as display racks.

There is another reason why vendors are not too unhappy about the police. The police thin out the competition. While vendors are fairly cooperative with one another—the regulars, that is—they don't like to be crowded in with a lot of amateurs. In a contest with the police, the amateurs have nowhere near the survival powers of the regulars.

Vendors are very adept at quick dispersal. This is particularly evident on blockfronts where a group of vendors has lined up. They will maintain one or two lookouts, usually a kid standing on a box at the street corner. Lately some groups have taken to using walkie-talkies. They are prepared for the getaway. They have determined which doorway they will use, which subway entrance, which parked van. Their displays are instantly collapsible and the merchandise can be thrown into one or two cartons. The racks they use for leather goods have wheels on the bottom and can be raced away.

The vendors also know the precinct lines. If a Midtown North patrol car is coming up, the vendors rush to the south side of Fifty-ninth Street. Now they're in the Seventeenth Precinct, and to hell with you, bud. If a car from the Seventeenth is spotted they rush right back again.

If the police do descend on them in force there will be shouts and whistles, and vendors racing this way and that. It takes about twenty to thirty seconds—I have timed these flurries—and then there will be no one except the police, and perhaps one hapless vendor who has been a bit too slow. Half an hour later the vendors will all be back. Teamwork is important in such situations. So is having a helper. They function not only as lookouts, but as extra salesmen and relief persons.

Many vendors, probably a majority, are recent immigrants. Until recently, Middle Easterners dominated merchandise vending, as Greeks did food vending. But ethnic patterns are shifting. Since 1983 there has been a strong influx of young men from Senegal, a former French colony on the west coast of Africa. From generation to generation street selling has been an honored tradition in Senegal. In recent years Senegalese vendors have become a fixture on the streets of Paris and from there they have spread to other European cities. Now they are in New York, over six hundred at latest estimate, and their numbers are increasing rapidly.

They are different from other vendors. They are polite, for one thing, even the police who arrest them note this. They speak little English, but they speak it with a soft French accent. They sell everything, but they are partial to gold trinkets and watches. Like other vendors, they buy from the jobbers.

They do not hawk their wares; they just stand silently behind their trays of goods. If they do address a customer, it is with a whispered question. Gold watches? Gold watches? Their serenity is disarming.

Other new arrivals are the book vendors. Some sell new books; some sell used ones. A few specialize in comic books. The most venturesome sell large-format art books and coffee-table gift books, usually at a discount from their high list prices. Spread out on the sidewalk, the large books make an attractive display and induce many a passerby to pause and look.

Unlike so many other vendors, the book vendors do not keep looking over their shoulders for cops. They are on to a secret. The cops can't arrest them. The selling of books comes under the protection of the First Amendment and cannot be prohibited by local ordinances.

Food vendors have been the caterers of the outdoor life of the city and their numbers are growing: from 3,400 licensed in 1978 to 4,300 in 1988. The bill of fare has broadened too. It used to be hot dogs, soft pretzels, soda, ice cream, and chestnuts. They are still the staples but to them have been added a host of dishes, many of them foreign, many cooked on the spot: souvlakia, falafel (with or without pita), Greek sausage, Italian sausage, bratwurst, omelets to order, Chinese beef, tacos, chili, quiche, stuffed Rock Cornish game hen. Another specialty is the juice squeezed to order from chilled fresh oranges.

The fare is surprisingly good. Is it safe as well? Merchants and officials are forever fretting over the possibility of contaminated food, airborne bacteria, and other such dangers. The record appears to have been quite good. Requirements for food carts in which cooking is done are strict; they must have hot and cold water, provisions for chilling as well as cooking, and hoods with filters and exhaust fans. The Health Department says there has never been a case of food poisoning traced to a food vendor.

Vendors can do very well. A good one with a good location can make as much as $40,000 a year. Consistency is important. The ones with the best clientele are the ones who are always in the same spot. One buys from them not just for the food, but to check in. There is Gus, for example, at the northeast corner of Fifty-second and Park. He has had his hot dog cart there for over fifteen years—every day, no matter what the weather. In winter he moves his cart directly over the cover of a steam manhole and traps the warmth with an awning. He is not very talkative but people like to stop by and say hello. He has put a son through college and graduate school from his earnings.

Food vendors are clearly functional and people appreciate this. Dealings with merchandise vendors tend to be adversary; with food vendors, agreeable.

Are there not lessons in the vendors' success? If these rascals thrive so, they must be providing something people like. It is the marketplace at its most basic—face to face, mano a mano, as it is and has been in alleys and souks and bazaars all over the world.

Merchants will keep up the fight against vendors—all kinds—but victory will continue to be elusive. It always has been. Over the years vendor regulations have fluctuated in degree of severity, sometimes leaning toward permissiveness. But these shifts do not make much practical difference. Even at their most liberal, the regulations are so full of nullifying stipulations that were they enforced to the letter there could be no more vendors at any place at any time. And this is not tenable.

Over time you cannot enforce a law that is against something people like. There is a parallel here to Prohibition. Authority is being refuted by the marketplace. People are told that food vending is bad for downtown business, bad for traffic, bad for them and their health. But people do not believe this. They like eating out-of-doors. They like the choices. They like the prices. They prefer a hot dog and a soda they can afford ($1.65) to a fuller lunch they cannot. So they buy. The vendors are providing what the established order is not.

There is a vacuum and it is of the city's own making. Take New York's Sixth Avenue. Once it was lined with places to eat: delis, cafeterias, Irish bars, coffee shops. New office building construction, spurred by incentive zoning, did away with these places. In their stead were plazas and bank windows. But no food. Not even a snack. Then vendors came. Then more. Today the sidewalks are full of them, lined up sometimes six to eight in a row. The revenge of the street.

Entertainers

Probably the finest street entertainer of our time is Philippe Petit. I was lucky enough to catch one of his first performances after he arrived from Paris. It was on upper Fifth Avenue at the Pulitzer Fountain. A gamin-like fellow with a battered high hat was stringing a tightrope between two trees. As a crowd began to gather, he got on a unicycle and pedaled around, simultaneously juggling some balls. He was obviously a master of the use of props.

The prop that he was to use best was a policeman. For the climax of his act, Petit got up on the tightrope, lit three batons, and proceeded to juggle them as he went across. The crowd applauded vigorously. Petit dismounted and made the rounds of the crowd with outstretched hat. At this point a friendly black cop who had been enjoying the show from the rear came forward. Petit looked stricken. He recoiled as if hit. "Don't hit him," someone shouted. The crowd was angry. Outraged at this display of police brutality, people pressed additional contributions on Petit, who had sufficiently recovered from his terror to make another round. As the bemused cop looked on, Petit mounted his unicycle, doffed his hat, and made his getaway.

Several weeks later, at seven-thirty in the morning, people around the World Trade Center looked up in amazement. On a wire between the two towers, 1,150 feet in the air, a figure was walking back and forth with a balancing rod. With an accomplice, Petit had gained access to a tower the night before and, with a crossbow, shot a rope and then pulled a metal cable across to the other tower. "When I see two oranges, I want to juggle. When I see two towers, I want to go across."

By quarter of eight a tremendous crowd had gathered. Traffic was stopped dead. For thirty minutes Petit performed. He would get down on one knee, get up, go back and forth; once he almost teetered into a fall. If there had been people on the street collecting for him, the take would have been a fortune. "I was happy," Petit recalled. "I was dying with happiness."

Petit was arrested. But the city government was rather pleased with the kind of publicity he generated. Petit was sentenced to give a special public performance. At street level.

Few street entertainers are in a class with Petit, but there are many talented ones. Some of them are professional; most are part-time —students, unemployed actors. One of the best ventriloquists in New York one summer was a Princeton philosophy major. The largest single category is "music students"; to judge by the signs, a large part of the street population is working its way through Juilliard. There are many musical groups, some pickup and some semipermanent—for example, the Fly-by-Night String Band, the Illusionary Free Lunch Band.

One way or another they all make a pitch for money. They pass the hat, they have someone pass it, or they have an empty instrument case or box in front of them. Propped up on it may be a hand-lettered sign with an admonition. People are very curious to see what it says.

"No credit cards please."

"Be a patron of the arts."

"Support live music."

"Send this weird boy to camp."

One black saxophonist had a sign that said "Send me back to Africa." He had done very well with it. "The blacks chip in because they want me to see their roots," he said. "The whites wish we'd all go back and figure it might as well start with me."

The donation and receiving of money is part of the performance. As with beggars, there is a strong domino effect; if two or more people stop to put in money there will likely be a rapid succession of givers. The entertainers usually acknowledge the donations with a smile and a thank-you. A musician may salute with a few high notes. The accepting, in sum, is done with grace. Rarely do entertainers express discourtesy to those who do not give.

Entertainers are a temperamental lot, many with large egos. But there is a good bit of occupational camaraderie among them. They are cooperative in settling territorial problems. On a busy afternoon they will work out a loose agreement as to who will play when at a key public space. At the steps of the Metropolitan Museum of Art, for example, there may be four or five acts waiting to go on but none will encroach on the one that is playing. While they are waiting, they serve as a volunteer claque and vigorously applaud the others' acts.

The same is true at London's Covent Garden and of the *ataliers* at Centre Pompidou in Paris. At both places there appears to be a tacit understanding that acts stay within a ten-to-fifteen-minute period. Both places have enough space to accommodate a number of concurrent acts, but entertainers dislike this kind of competition.

The size of the space is not the important factor for entertainers. They would as soon squeeze people in as not. What entertainers most look for is a place with a strong *flow*—a constantly self-renewing audience of regulars, such as office workers, and of tourists. Among the best places in midtown New York are the steps of the New York Public Library, the steps of St. Thomas Church, Grand Army Plaza, the mall in Central Park. Street corners can work very well. One of the very best is Fifty-ninth and Fifth. For individual musicians it is the closest thing to playing the Palace. The New York *Times*'s William Geist tells of listening to an excellent saxophonist there, Ray Peters. A woman put fifty cents in his case. "You're an exceptionally gifted young man," she said. "You'll make the big time someday."

"Madam," he called after her, "this *is* the big time."

In Boston the best space is in the Common at the Park Street station. In San Francisco one of the best places is Ghirardelli Square. It is so popular that entertainers must be auditioned by the managements before they can play there.

How do they like street performing? They are of several minds. Some say they do not like it; they feel that it is degrading, that there is no future in it. But most of them say that they enjoy it, the good parts at least. "It's terribly insecure," says one, "but I like the insecurity of it." Entertainers speak of free choice, the give-and-take with people, the honing of one's skills, the immediacy of the audience.

They also speak of what it is like when there is no audience, and of the humiliation of performing when no one stops to look or listen.

"I haven't yet hardened myself to the rejection and in this line of work there is rejection right and left," says a ventriloquist. Sometimes he talks to his dummy on a park bench for as much as twenty or thirty minutes—alone. It is a bitter wait. But then someone stops and listens, and then another stops. Soon there will be an audience.

Entertainers praise the toughness of street audiences and say that of all audiences, New Yorkers are the toughest. But also the most appreciative. If you can collect from them, they say, you've got to be good, which is to say that they are pretty good themselves.

It is interesting to watch people as they chance upon an entertainer. So often they will smile. A string quartet. Here at Forty-fourth! Their smile is like that of a child. For these moments they seem utterly at ease, their shoulders relaxed. People enjoy programmed entertainment, too, but not the same way. It is the unexpected that seems to delight them most.

It is interesting to watch people when they chance upon an entertainer. So often they will smile. A string quartet! . . . Their smile is like that of a child.

Street entertainers can have a strong binding effect on people. This is particularly the case when the entertainer is skillful in involving members of the audience in the act—like magician Jeff Sheridan, who borrows a businessman's coat and then appears to burn a hole in it; who gets a pretty girl to take off her straw hat, from which he produces a bottle of beer. How did he do it? Watch his left hand, someone says. No, it was up his sleeve, says another.

Sheridan is very skillful. But even a bad performer can unify a crowd. There is one magician who has a perfectly dreadful act and his patter is so corny that one almost has to say something about it. But he does get people involved and his inept performance provides a connection between them.

There is a communal sense to these gatherings and though it may be fleeting, it is the city at its best. I remember especially the end of a mime's act in front of Pulitzer Fountain at Fifty-ninth Street. The mime was making fun of people. He walked up to two junior executives and drew a square in the air over them. Everyone laughed, even the junior executives. Then a cop walked across the plaza with a side-to-side swinging gait. The mime walked behind with the same side-to-side swinging gait. The cop saw people laughing, looked over his shoulder at the mime, laughed, and then turned to the mime and shook his hand. The crowd applauded. It was a splendid moment, a very city kind of moment.

Historically, the police have warred against street entertainers, or, to be more accurate, have been made to war. Left to their own judgment, cops usually take a live-and-let-live stance. When one does move against an entertainer he may tell him he's sorry, but the captain has been on his back. And he has been so because the merchants have been on his back.

Merchants have been the main force against street entertainers. It is odd that people who champion the free market are against such a pure expression of it.

Merchants have been the main force against street entertaining, and it has been largely on their say-so that city councils have passed repressive ordinances against it. One feature of such ordinances is a prohibition against soliciting money. The vehemence of the phrasing in New York's old hurdy-gurdy law well conveys authority's attitude: "It is unlawful to solicit, ask, or request money in any way, shape or manner, directly or indirectly." The old statute was repealed in 1970 but the spirit lives on. Street entertaining is legal, but only if

1. not much noise is made.
2. the sidewalk is not obstructed.
3. there is no solicitation for money.

It is odd that people who champion the free market are against such a pure expression of it. What is so wrong about solicitation? The passersby are under no duress. They don't even have to stop. If they do stop they don't have to give. If they give, the amount is entirely up to them and their judgment of the worth of the entertainer. It is the latter who has taken the entrepreneurial risk. He should be entitled to some reward.

Merchants say that the entertainers have hurt their business and future inundations would make matters far worse. Michael Grosso, head of the Fifth Avenue Association, puts it this way: "If you allow one musician or peddler in, then you have to let them all in and they would take over the whole midtown area."

I wish I could say that our research proved that street entertaining is good for the merchants' stores. I think it is, but our research does not prove this. What it does prove is that there is a high degree of compatibility between a strong retail street and a lively street life. Merchants do not see this. They do not like much about street life anyway, except for customers coming in the door. Entertainers block them, the merchants complain, and block everybody else, to the point of endangerment. It is on this basis, pedestrian safety and amenity, that the merchants have mounted their legislative assaults on the entertainers.

There have been two federal cases. Both of them, fortunately, deal with physical situations that almost spectacularly belie the ordinances.

The first was *Davenport v. the City of Alexandria.* Lee Davenport was a music teacher who played his bagpipes on the streets of Alexandria. The city forbade him to do this. At the behest of merchants the city enacted an ordinance that banned street entertainers from performing on any of the sixty-one blocks of the central district and restricted them to certain designated park areas. Davenport did not want to play in the designated park areas. There were not enough people there. He wanted to play on the sidewalk, in particular the sidewalks of the two most attractive blocks of King Street. He sued to have the ordinance struck down. The case went to the U.S. District Court.

The city's case was based largely on assertion. Some merchants had been reported to observe instances of sidewalk blocking. The city manager said that once he had seen people pour out onto the street because of an entertainer. A check of the actual facts belied the claims of congestion. As a witness for Davenport, I was able to point out that the city's own counts and the measurement of the sidewalk showed there was an excellent balance between sidewalk space and pedestrian flows. In this respect, indeed, Alexandria was outstandingly well provided—not only the two blocks in question but the whole central district.

Judge Albert V. Bryan struck down the ordinance. Here are some of the reasons he cited:

> The court is unpersuaded that there is any actual safety endangerment, any real impediment of pedestrian traffic or any substantial interference with patrons of businesses even in the affected area . . . Furthermore, more persuasive testimony satisfies the court that, overall, pedestrian traffic is not congested—no more than 2.8 persons per foot per minute of passing pedestrians, a pedestrian "ease" level well below the standard for pedestrian comfort.

As to the designated park areas, the judge held that they were not an adequate alternative to the sidewalk:

> The exponent of the First Amendment expression is entitled to be "encountered" by those he wishes to receive his or her message. The sidewalk is a traditional place for such expression. Pedestrian flow and turnover is the "life blood" of the street performer.

The city appealed. The U.S. Court of Appeals reversed Judge Bryan's decision in part. It found that the ordinance was a reasonable regulation. It was not sure, however, that it was drawn "as narrowly as possible to maximize speech while securing the city's interest in public safety." It sent the matter back to the District Court, asking Judge Bryan to make explicit the factual reasons for holding the ordinance unnecessarily broad. How wide were the streets? What were the pedestrian flows? There was ample documentation on these points. By making them explicit, Judge Bryan re-established his original finding. There was plenty of room.

The second federal case was in Chicago. For quite a while the city had been hospitable to street entertainers. In the summer of 1979 Mayor Jane Byrne had the city hire a corps of young entertainers to perform at bus stops and transit stations during the summer. (Pay: ten dollars an hour.) People were delighted. STREET ARTISTS HELP CITY SPARKLE, said an editorial in the Chicago *Sun Times.*

But the merchants did not like street entertainers, anywhere. In 1982 they prevailed on the city council to pass an ordinance that would effectively ban them from the upper Michigan Avenue area— that is, the place most suited for them.

Guitarist Wally Friedrich initiated a class action suit against the city, and the American Civil Liberties Union joined in support. I served as expert witness on the pedestrian aspect.

The city's contention was that congestion on the sidewalk had reached drastic levels, and that entertainers added sorely to this congestion and should be banned, providing more room for pedestrian safety and amenity.

It was an extraordinary complaint. Of all the avenues in the United States, they could not have picked one with broader sidewalks than upper Michigan Avenue. They range between thirty and thirty-five feet in width. Pedestrian volumes were strong but did not tax them. My sampling counts and the city's counts jibed. The amount of space per pedestrian was very generous and provided a level of service that rated an A by anybody's computation.

There was, indeed, almost a surfeit of space. The city itself had judged there was so much space it had encouraged the withdrawal of large chunks of sidewalk space for roped-off planting beds. Were these grassy expanses converted back to sidewalk space, the level of service would be higher yet.

In *Friedrich v. Chicago* the court upheld the ordinance in part and denied it in part. The court found that the city was within its rights to curb street entertaining when it endangered the public safety. It also found that the ban was much broader than necessary. On Michigan Avenue all performances were banned on Saturdays and Sundays, and on weekdays from 11 A.M. to 2 P.M. and from 4 P.M. to 11 P.M. The court observed that the city had not done any homework to support these sweeping restrictions, and that its own records indicated that pedestrian flows diminished dramatically after 7 P.M. Rush Street was another matter. It is the city's disco, tavern, and café strip and gets lots of pedestrian traffic after dark, especially on Friday and Saturday nights. But this did not justify a ban starting at 3 P.M., the court found, nor one on Wednesday nights.

The most interesting part of Judge Marven E. Aspen's decision concerns break dancing. As in New York, so in Chicago break dancing surfaced as a fad in 1983. Everywhere one looked, it seemed, young blacks were staking out large swaths of sidewalk and doing acrobatics. Some were terrible—a few people jumping up and down to a portable tape player. But some were really quite talented and put on a show that attracted large crowds. It was these crowds, Judge Aspen noted, that caused most of the mischief.

But break dancing peaked in 1984 and is now performed only sporadically. This raises a question. If break dancing was the only major threat to public safety and if it has largely disappeared, why then the ordinance? In a section that could be subtitled "Much Ado About Break Dancing" Judge Aspen tackles the question:

> If it is true that breakdancing has gone the way of the hula hoop and is a faded fad, then perhaps the frequency of large audiences has substantially fallen . . . Thus, if the City chooses to renew the ordinance next year, it would be well advised to consider the passing of the breakdancing phenomenon in its evaluation. If it has passed, and if—as the evidence showed—most other performers attract only small crowds, the constitutional underpinnings of the ordinance may have vanished for future years.

Handbill Passers

For all the differences in people, times, and places, the rhythms of handbill passing and taking are surprisingly regular. If the passer makes any effort at all—that is, stands near the center of the sidewalk and actually offers handbills to passersby—the completion rate will run at least 30 percent or three out of every ten persons. The rate will vary according to pedestrian flow, character of flow, and time of day, but by far the most important factor will be the handbill passer himself and the assertiveness of his technique. Somewhat like the staccato patterns of donations to beggars, the taking of handbills tends to occur in bunches. In part this is due to the follow-the-leader tendency of the people who take handbills. But close analysis of the film record of

Like the staccato pattern of giving to beggars, the taking of handbills tends to come in bunches. Partly this is due to the follow-the-leader tendencies of the takers. But it is also due to the handbill passers' psyche. Success emboldens them. Their bearing becomes more assertive, their thrust more decisive.

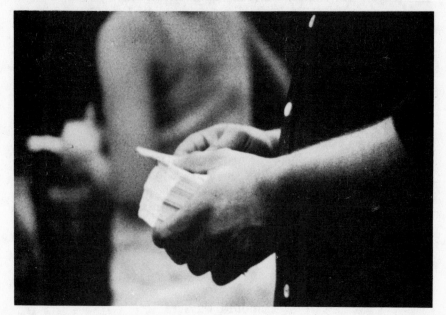

these occurrences shows that they are primarily due to the handbill passers. Success emboldens them. Their stance becomes more commanding, their thrust more firm. The passing and the taking become an end in themselves.

The best passer I've come across is Frank. With a face off an Etruscan coin, he works through persistence and a kind of genial intimidation. He uses a direct address; he will look at you straight in the eye with a look of amused disdain, often with a comment. I saved this for you. Here's one for you, honey. Sometimes a person will take a card, look at it disgustedly, and then hand it back. Frank will hand it to them again and this time it often sticks.

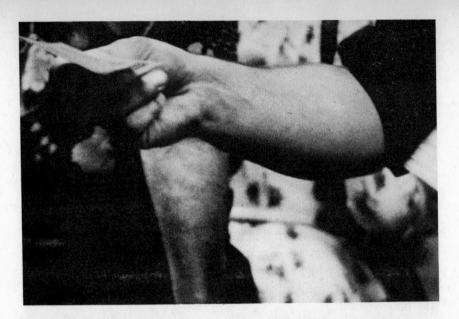

Handbill Frank: Fifty-ninth and Lexington, 5:10 P.M.

Frank seeks to dominate the encounter, and like most who do, he is responsive to the reception given him. At midday one August I filmed him at work from a fifth-floor window at Bloomingdale's. It was hot and muggy and people were moving more sluggishly than usual. Frank was doing all right, but there were some lulls. After two or three turndowns in a row, Frank would just stop and not offer handbills to anyone. In a minute or so, however, he would be at it again. In the half hour he spent, he averaged 50 percent completion to handbills offered.

I spoke to Frank later and told him about our midday count and how high his rate had been. He was pleased but said it was not a good time. We should get him when he's hot. Five o'clock. Rush hour. In front of the subway steps.

He was right. At five the southeast corner was a mass of people and in the middle, dominant, was Frank. The people were scarcely moving as they edged toward the curb or the subway stairs. But Frank was moving, making his own space. He was turning, first one way and then the other, and as the crowd swelled he worked faster and faster. Now he was giving a sharp flick to the cards at the end of the thrust. He was not smiling. He was staring intently, almost belligerently. There was no easy badinage now. He was giving commands. Take it, he would say, take it. And they did. It was six out of ten now. Frank was hot.

The only ones I've seen to match him were in Tokyo. Two young men were working the crowded alley leading to the Kannon Shrine. They were got up in ancient costume. One worked about twelve feet in front of the other and jiggled a sign up and down that told people to be sure to read the interesting message that was about to be given. The other handed out the message with a rate of completion similar to Frank's, about 55 percent. The message was for an eel restaurant several blocks away.

Handbills are a very important medium for places people pass by but do not see: places up alleys or up on a third or fourth floor. One of Frank's best customers is Sister Lane, a spiritual adviser and palm reader who has a third-floor room on the east side of Lexington. She has a neon sign in the window but is out of the pedestrian's line of sight. Handbills are a necessity for her.

Frank sometimes subcontracts. To handle some of the bill passing for Sister Lane he took on a young rascal named Eddie Leet. Eddie turned out to be almost as skillful as Frank; a film sequence I have of his hand motions and leering grin shows a master of insinuation.

Eddie broke with Frank and began dealing directly with Sister Lane. At the same time he took on bill passing for Mrs. Williams, another spiritual adviser, who had an upstairs room on the west side of Lexington. Eddie liked to work both sides of the street.

Another group of handbill passers was organized by Louis, the owner of a second-floor haircutting establishment on Lexington. He hired several personable young Puerto Ricans and showed them how to walk alongside women, give a quick spiel, and ask them to sign up for a 50-percent rebate on a hairdo. Right upstairs, they were to say as they drew abreast of the doorway.

It was a very effective technique. "A real bunch of hustlers," Louis told me. "And I really psych them up." But their interest flagged. What they liked to do most was to sit on the hoods of the cars parked out front and chat with their friends, of whom there seemed to be an ever increasing number. Louis would look down on them, like Fagin watching his brood, and rap sharply on the window to snap them to. At length he fired them. They went to work, carrying Louis' technique with them, for another haircutting establishment. Louis hired three of their friends as replacements. He said they worked harder and better than the others. A real hustle crew, he told me.

Eventually they were fired too. But they stuck around, joining that informal network of handbill passers, errand runners, vendors, lookouts, and the like that staffed that stretch of Lexington. They all seemed to know each other. One or two could usually be seen cruising from Fifty-seventh to Sixtieth and back, stopping to check in with a friend.

Let us turn to the handbill takers. Whether or not people accept a handbill has very little to do with content. People usually have no idea what is on them until after they have taken one. But people do read them. Some then immediately throw them away. But most hang on to them for a while. Some twist them. Some crumple them. Before they throw them away, some will walk a block or so clutching them, as if they were a kind of talisman.

Whatever the message, it will rarely be written with any style. The artwork will be bad. So will the paper and the printing. Advertising agencies, it would appear, would not touch the medium. And quite literally it is trash. No other activity generates so much of it or is harder to curb.

All this being the case, it would be fitting to say that the medium is also very inefficient. But it is not. For all the crudity of the form, it is an effective way of getting across a basic message—for example, come on up—and doing it close to the potential point of sale. And audiences can be targeted: some handbills for women only; some for men only. Costs are moderate, the labor supply inexhaustible. With a handbill-passing rate of no more than 40 percent, the cost per completed transaction will range between a half mill and several mills. There is a potential here that has not been touched. Thank heavens.

Mr. Magoo

The most compelling character on the streets of New York is Mr. Magoo. He is a man in his seventies, stocky, red-faced, and with a perpetually choleric expression. He dresses nattily, always with a flower in his buttonhole. In winter he wears a chesterfield and a black homburg.

Mr. Magoo directs traffic. On Fifth Avenue, his favorite, he will station himself in the middle of the intersection and with eloquent arm gestures direct the cars. Keep it moving is his idea. Taxis making slow right turns infuriate him. Taxis picking up people ten feet out from the curb infuriate him. He will go over and slam his hand on the hood. The drivers will curse. He will curse. A crowd will gather.

Mr. Magoo talks to the traffic, car by car. He calls their license plates. A woman in a car with Virginia plates is driving very slowly. "You're not in Virginia, honey," says Mr. Magoo, "you're in New York. Move! Move! Move!" The woman speeds up. To a white-haired lady who is jaywalking across the street: "Who in the hell do you think you are? Selfish bag, that's what you are." She is nonplussed.

All this delights the spectators, of whom quite a few will have gathered at the corners. Mr. Magoo plays directly to the gallery. He points to a New Jersey car making a poor turn. "New Jersey drivers: they're the worst," he says. The crowd laughs. "No, doctors are the worst," he says. More laughs. "No, no, New Jersey *doctors*—aye-yi-yi."

At the top of his form he is quite majestic. His gestures become more imperious. He stands taller. Cars are obeying him. The traffic is moving well—and it really does when he directs. People are listening to him and some are doing what he tells them to do. If it is a fantasy, it is a pretty good one to act out. And he *is* in charge.

He certainly gets people talking to each other. If you are at a corner watching him, someone is likely to ask you who in the world

Mr. Magoo on Fifth Avenue.

that guy is out there. Or tell you: that he's an ex-cop; that he scalps tickets at the Metropolitan Opera. One day a lady turned to me and in a confidential tone said that Mr. Magoo had made her day but that she wasn't sure why. We exchanged thoughts on this. Was it his arrogation of municipal authority, the individual against the system? No. He is strong for law and system. Should one feel sympathy for him? Hardly. Mr. Magoo is not a nice person. He's rude, a bit of a bully, and while he's funny about it he does treat people the way we'd like to but do not.

Let me add a methodological note. In filming street characters such as Mr. Magoo and the Witch, they are fully aware of the camera and I cannot say that is unobtrusive research. But there are usually other cameras pointed in their direction too, and they are obviously pleased to be photographed. The whole point of their performance is to be noticed.

Mr. Magoo affects great annoyance when he sees me filming with a camera. "You again," he says disgustedly and waves me away. I keep on filming, as he knows I will, and sometimes he sneaks a glance to see if I am.

Mr. Paranoid

There is a man who stands on street corners on Fifth Avenue. He wears a felt hat creased in the college style of the late forties. He stands at the curb, facing inward, and to no one in particular talks in a conversational tone of voice. If you pass by, you may hear the key words he keeps repeating: "FBI," "police," "IRS." What he is saying is that they're out to get him, the whole damn bunch of them. And they're out to get you too, he says, if you don't watch out. He is deranged, of course.

Tambourine Woman

She is a spare, middle-aged woman with frizzy gray hair. She walks quietly down the street until she comes to a prominent place, such as church steps or a department store entrance. She stops, takes a tambourine out of an airline bag she has been carrying, bangs it three times, and then begins a harangue. A crowd gathers.

What is she saying? It is hard to tell. As is so often the case with odd people, any one sentence is quite plausible. It is the lack of connections that is confusing. "I was Franklin D. Roosevelt's little girlfriend," she shouts, then goes on to say that Zionism is a plot. Suddenly, in midsentence, she stops, puts the tambourine back into the airline bag, and walks away, leaving the puzzled onlookers behind.

Knapsack Man

He was a handsome man who walked with a curious up-and-down loping gait. He wore a trenchcoat, no matter what the weather, and on his back was a knapsack. Fastened to it was a photograph of him and a card with a hand-lettered statement. It read ONLY MY FAMILY HAS THE RIGHT TO ASSAULT ME. IF YOU ARE NOT A MEMBER OF MY FAMILY PLEASE DO NOT HIT ME.

Passersby were fascinated by the sign and would fall in behind him, peering intently at the sign. But the up-and-down movement made the reading of it difficult. Sometimes there would be several people trying to read it and they would jostle each other for position. At street corners he would stop and then stand immobile with hands folded as if in prayer. The people who had been following him could now read the sign and soon would disperse.

The last time I saw Knapsack Man he still wore a trenchcoat but there was no knapsack or picture and he walked with a normal gait.

The Witch

She is a woman who looks like a witch. She has a long, pointed nose, black hair, eyes very far apart and one moving differently than the other. She dresses in black and usually has a folded *Wall Street Journal* under her arm. She hurls insults in a loud, rasping voice. Her targets are most often dignified people. At a St. Patrick's Day parade I watched her taunt a priest who was in charge of a parochial-school girls' band. She said she knew what he wanted, and then did a lewd bump and grind. The girls fell to giggling. The priest went up to a cop and bade him stop this terrible woman. "Sorry, Father," the cop said, "but she isn't breaking any law."

But she does spit at people she doesn't like. Children, for example. I have a splendid film sequence of her as a nice little boy and his mother walk by. The Witch rears back. "F—— you, you little bastard," she says, sending a cascade of spit hurtling his way. She is deplorable, but so are the onlookers. They exchange horrified glances. "Did you see that woman spit at that little boy!" But they are smiling, almost as though they are on her side.

The Witch plays the role of witch so convincingly and looks so much like a witch that quite likely she would have been burnt as a witch in earlier times. Many were, with far less fearsome appearance. But in these times she is good fun to watch, with vicarious malevolence, and she is pleased to have the audience. And I think she rather likes me. Whenever we pass on the street, she winks.

Shopping Bag Ladies

The toughest, hardiest of all the street people are the shopping bag ladies. They are disheveled and dirty, and their legs are often swollen. Their clothing is usually tattered. They carry two or three shopping bags—see-through plastic, mostly, filled with trash and bits of rags. Some wheel them in supermarket shopping carts. There are also a few shopping bag men. One, Cellophane Man, wraps himself in many layers of clear plastic.

Shopping bag people are very regular in their routes and stations. They tend to sleep in the same doorways or the same spots in Grand Central Station. According to the time of day, one shopping bag lady can be found at the southeast corner of Seagram Plaza, a doorway on Fifty-third Street, and the ledge of the Citicorp Plaza.

Where do they come from? Social workers find them baffling. Most shopping bag ladies are sustained by a grand fantasy of some kind, such as that they are very rich but the city is hiding their money. Another bag lady, whose beat is outside the Public Library, is working on a book that will save the world. One fancies she is still a pretty, coquettish woman and is grotesquely rouged. Most of these people come from a middle-class background. Some are well educated. There is one who is a Barnard graduate, was a Powers model with several magazine covers to her credit, and, completing the ideal of the All-American Girl, was a top-seeded tennis player in the Middle Atlantic Conference thirty years ago. I know this to be so because my wife roomed with her.

What they all have in common now is a fierce independence. In the city there are many homeless people temporarily out of the social service system; they may have lost their welfare check or have just been evicted from their apartment. But shopping bag ladies are different. They are totally outside of the system. What's more, they resist efforts to get them into it. If they are taken to an institution they are so confused, frightened, and upset at the intervention that they cannot meet the institutional rules for being helped. They won't say what their name is. They have no address to give. They refuse to take showers or be otherwise cleaned up. They cannot, in sum, qualify for the aid that would put them in shape to qualify.

The problems appear to be getting greater, not just for shopping bag ladies, but for disturbed people of all kinds. With their misplaced reliance on stabilizing drugs, New York State's mental hospitals put some fifty thousand people on the streets. There is much to be said for getting them out of hospitals, but the outpatient therapy that was supposed to be part of the plan has not been provided on any scale. For many people the result has been the worst of both worlds. The institutional experience conditioned them to a highly structured environment; for such people the freedom of the city can be a frightening experience. For some the only refuge is the single-room-occupancy hotel. But they are afraid of that too, and the people who might prey on them.

One of their few pleasures is sitting in the sun on the benches in the middle of upper Broadway. Older people of all kinds come there: some talkative, some rigidly silent. There may be a head-nodding junkie or two as well. But they are reasonably safe places and there is lots of life to see.

Beggars

Like handbill passers and entertainers, successful beggars are marked by centrality and movement. The best examples I have seen are the professional blind beggars who work Fifth Avenue. They are very consistent. They stay in one spot and it is almost always in the center of the sidewalk. At their side is a dog (not a true guide dog, but it looks like one). They wear a small sign that says something like "God bless the cheerful giver." They hold the traditional tin cup.

They move. One moves his body back and forth in a walklike motion while his feet stand still. All move the cup back and forth, occasionally giving it a sharp rattle. The fact of movement seems to be important. I found this out when one day by chance we had the equivalent of a controlled experiment. We had been filming time-lapse coverage of the beggar who usually stationed himself in front of St. Thomas Church. He was getting donations at his customary rate. Then another blind beggar appeared. He must have been truly blind, for he positioned himself about fifteen feet behind the first beggar. And he did not move. All he did was hold out the cup. He did not shake it. He just stood there, waiting for donations. There were not many. During a twenty-seven-minute period, the moving beggar received four times as many donations as the stationary one.

There is a pronounced domino effect in the giving of money. Donations tend to come in bunches—three or four in a row, quickly—and it is understandable that they do. Potential givers usually slow up about twenty feet away from the beggar and start fishing for a coin.

This appears to trigger any latent impulses to give in the people behind them. If they give too, there may be some congestion, and this may slow others and provide additional time to consider giving.

One hears stories about beggars being driven by chauffeurs in Rolls-Royces. I did see, on several occasions, one of the blind beggars being dropped off by a car at the Fiftieth Street entrance of Saks. It was an ordinary car. But they do not do badly. To get an idea of their take I charted the frequency of donations over considerable periods of time. The median interval between donations was twenty seconds. But because of the staccato nature of many donations and the slack periods, the average was one donation for every fifty seconds, or seventy-two an hour. The size of the donations, however, I could not determine. The beggars are always emptying small coins from the cup and leaving the big ones in. Assuming an average of 25 cents, their take would be about $18 an hour. Most of the professional blind beggars work about six hours a day. At the least they should average $100 to $150 a day—in all probability a good bit more.

These beggars are the regulars—same spot, same time, same props. Like members of a guild, their numbers have not increased materially. But begging in general most certainly has. I have taken no census, but I would estimate that the number of people begging on the streets of midtown has doubled since 1980. Much of this increase is due to the rise in homelessness. As a matter of fact, some of the most successful soliciting is for donations to the homeless. There is also a good bit of occasional and part-time begging, much of it by younger people, and with considerable aggressiveness. The Bowery bums who cleaned your windshield have been supplanted by teenagers who clean your windshield and are quite intimidating about being compensated for it. Some surprisingly well-dressed young women beg, usually for "fare money." One has a flaxen-haired baby with her and, whether rented or not, it draws very well. Most of the beggars, however, are without skill or stratagem. They are mostly winos and derelicts, too dazed to beg effectively or to defend themselves against predators. That there are so many of them at this time of apparent prosperity is not a good augur.

Pitchmen for Causes

Groups making pitches for religious causes range from the naïve to the fraudulent. Some, such as the Hare Krishna, are true believers in whatever they believe in. They may seem foolish, but so have a lot of groups over the years. And while their music and their saffron robes make an odd sight, it has been a friendly one. They are not to be seen so much anymore and many people rather miss them.

A group that is not missed is a rock group of young men and

women who dressed in black monks' robes and hoods and spoke as if they had all gone to Harvard. They looked like some kind of satanic cult but they said they were in the fight against drugs. They were ambulatory operators, like Louis' handbill passers, and while walking along with you would invite you to purchase their publication and made a donation. They made a point of saying they accep ed checks. An odious bunch.

A jaunty fellow with a tweed cap stands beside a small table. On it is a clipboard and writing pad. A sign fixed to the table says SAVE THE PORPOISE! As people go by he says to them, please join the fight and sign the petition for the porpoises. Many people stop. Just sign here, he says, extending a pen. As they sign up he suggests that a small donation would help. Overhead. Printing expenses. He is giving his time free. Most of those who stop, sign, and most of those who sign, give.

He came upon this modus operandi some years ago. I first saw him when his sign read SAVE GRAND CENTRAL. This was in 1975, when many citizens were quick to give for this estimable cause. The Municipal Art Society was most upset to have an impostor siphon away contributions, and it went to the police.

SAVE THE WHALES, the sign next read. A picture next to it showed small whales being clubbed to death. This appeal must have proved very lucrative, for he continued with it until the early eighties, when he switched to the porpoise.

Pickpockets and Other Crooks

Pickpockets usually work in pairs. They like crowds. If there is a street crowd watching an act, the pickpockets will work the "tip" of the crowd: they will be on the outer rank, looking in at the marks, and with a clear field behind them for the exit.

Pickpockets especially like crowds in confined places. Buses are ideal. I know, for I have been an easy mark. On two recent occasions I was fleeced while standing near the rear exit door. An older man standing near me dropped a package on the floor. I leaned down to help him pick it up. A younger man who had been standing next to me quickly lifted my wallet from my right rear pocket and vanished out the door. I looked around for the older man. He had gone out the front.

This was a standard operation, two top pickpocket detectives told me later. And I had been virtually asking for it, they added. There are many variants, but the crux is the quick, disconcerting move. Whether it is a shove, a jostle, a slight collision, it is a matter of only a few seconds and the two are off. My most recent encounter, again on a bus, was with a man who unfortunately got his hand mixed up with mine as we held on to the overhead straps. This time I was more alert. I disentangled and told him to cut it out. But he was gone, and so was my wallet. From my right rear pocket, unbuttoned.

You have to spot them beforehand, the detectives told me. Some of them they knew on sight; indeed, they had an almost friendly relationship with them. In most cases, however, it was a matter of observation.

I walked with them as they went back and forth over several crowded shopping blocks. I asked them what made them suspicious. Suspicious-looking people, they said. They were not being facetious. Pickpockets and other crooks are paranoid about the police, they explained, and are forever looking over their shoulder and darting their glance this way and that. When they spot a man doing this they can be sure they are on to something.

There is another thing to watch for, they said. Watch out for the guy who is moving around a lot but is not going anywhere. He keeps coming back, circling, like the predator he is. If he also is a teenager, black, and is wearing white tennis shoes he is likely to be taken as a mugger. This is not very fair to white tennis shoes, or teenagers, or blacks. While it may be true that most muggers wear white tennis shoes, most people who wear white tennis shoes are not muggers.

Watch for the man who is moving around a lot but isn't going anywhere. He keeps coming back, circling like the predator he is.

The key advice, to repeat, is to watch out for the guy who is moving but not going anywhere. And if he starts circling, move.

Three-Card-Monte Players

Three-card-monte players provide some of the best street theatre —and a demonstration of the lengths people will go to be gulled. They should be suspicious from the start. Two raffish young men, usually black, put a carton down on the sidewalk and play begins. The dealer shuffles three cards: two of them black, one red. Periodically he shows the red card face up. He taunts the player to bet which one it is. He has a chant:

> Red you win
> Black you lose
> It all depends
> On the card you choose.

The two are arguing very loudly. This attracts people and soon a crowd has formed. A second shill will join the crowd. He will probably be an older person, occasionally a woman, but in any event will be in disguise as an ordinary citizen.

The game is obviously rigged. The shill should be easy to spot. He

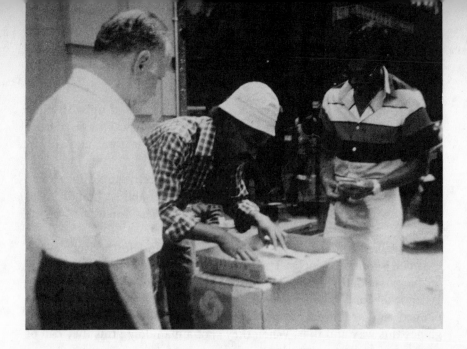

wins. But on the players come. There is a lot of ego here. The active players have a knowing look. They're on to this crook. He's met his match. As they win some small bets the dealer is visibly upset; he almost cowers. The player moves in for the kill and triples his bet.

In more cases than not, however, the dealer will be hostile and menacing and the game becomes an exercise in intimidation. The dealer shouts at the player. He glares malevolently at him. Put down the twenty dollars, he says. Put it down. Put it *down.* Why anyone should obey is a puzzle, but they do.

Sleight of hand and the law of averages are enough to assure that the dealer will win. And so he does, invariably. But to win big he has another tool. In the classic gambit of the con game, he uses the player's own taste for larceny. The sequence goes like this. A shill shouts "cop." The dealer goes off to investigate, leaving the cards lying on the carton. One of the onlookers picks up the red card; with a wink at the audience he slightly crimps one corner of the card and puts it back on the carton. The dealer returns. The onlooker puts a big bet on the crimped card. It comes up red. He wins. He bets again and wins. The dealer is furious. He tells the onlooker he can't play anymore. Leave. Onlooker does.

Now people are jostling each other to be first to get a big bet down on the crimped card. One man comes up with two hundred dollars and lays it on the card. The dealer turns it over. It is black.

> Red you win
> Black you lose
> It all depends
> On the card you choose.

Dope Dealers, Whores, and Pimps

I did a study on loitering for the police department and the Fund for the City of New York. The place was the West Forty-second Street area in front of the Top Bar and the store and boxing club in the building next to it. They were the key hangouts for the pimps and dope dealers of the area. What the police wanted to find out was the effect of the police presence on the activity. Were frequent sweeps better than fewer, longer ones? Were the usual two-man patrols a better use of manpower than three- and four-man patrols?

In a room on the fourth floor of an abandoned hotel across the street, I set up a 16mm camera and two Super 8 time-lapse cameras. As with most observational studies of a place, the first step was to find out what normal was. In the case of the Top Bar normal was a heavy flow in and out of the entrance and a forming and re-forming of groups on the wide sidewalk outside. Loitering, one might call it, but there was more purpose to it than that. Discussions were animated; there were greetings, with much hand clasping. Some of the groups were ambulatory, ranging from the bar area all the way to the corner of Broadway and back. The cast had many regulars, and they were easy to identify because they usually wore what they had been wearing before.

A recurrent event was the arrival of a red two-door sedan in midafternoon. After parking directly in front of the bar, the driver would open the hood and then unlock the trunk. He would be joined by several people. After about ten minutes of activity the driver would get back in the car and leave. This routine would take place two more times in late afternoon.

However illegal, the goings-on were satisfyingly regular. On a hot summer night the first test came. At 7:03 three cops walked up to the lamp pole in front of the bar. During the previous hour there had been five group sessions of about six to eight minutes. At exactly two minutes before the arrival of the cops the last group broke up. For the ensuing thirty minutes the cops remained by the light pole—loitering, you might say—and at one point were joined by a fourth.

At 7:33 the cops began to move east. At almost the same time, three of the regulars materialized. By 7:34 the cops moved out of the picture. We are back to normal again. The group activity continued unabated the rest of the evening. On subsequent occasions also we found that the activity that ceases with the appearance of the cops resumes within a few seconds of their departure.

We did a similar study of the loitering patterns around the Aristo

Hotel, a squalid old hotel in the Times Square area. Prostitution and dope peddling appeared to be its principal activities. As was the case around the Top Bar, the area of activity embraced the street corner and a half-block stretch beyond. There were usually four to five whores; they stood in doorways most of the time, spaced twenty to forty feet apart. If they walked it would be only as far as the next doorway or so and back. Customer behavior was equally regular. Potential johns would look in a shop window or just stand there for a while before approaching a whore. Another predictable occurrence would be the arrival of a big fat woman about every four hours to check on the whores. She would chat briefly, accept what appeared to be money, and go on to the next one. Late in the afternoon a pink Cadillac convertible would stop, and out would get a tall black man in a long fur coat. He was so much the archetypal pimp that one suspected he might be an undercover cop.

There were several other common denominators. There was a loose network of people and it included some street regulars. A guard at a nearby bank moonlighted on and off as a sort of messenger. There was a cooperative lookout system. We noticed that every once in a while a window shade on the third-floor front would be yanked up and down. Invariably, it signaled the approach of a police car.

Around Forty-second Street and Times Square it is hardly surprising to see people who look like criminals. Go down to the subway world underneath and there are many more—tough, mean, and dangerous. This is the national cesspool, and when people from other cities start talking about their undesirables the New Yorker has to laugh. They should see ours. Here are the *real* undesirables.

In view of this great concentration, what is remarkable is how safe is the adjoining business district. I have been keeping reasonably abreast of activity on its plazas and small parks, and as far as assaults on one's person are concerned, they have been largely trouble free. This needs some qualifying, of course: no street is safe at 2 A.M.; certain fringe locations are best avoided; white-collar drug traffic, while not dangerous, continues to be a problem. Similarly, prostitution waxes and wanes as a street phenomenon. In the seventies there were a lot of whores on the street, Lexington in particular; they have been less visible since but there are indications streetwalking is picking up again.

There is plenty of sin, in short, but not so much danger. Perceptions, however, are otherwise. In many cities the perception of crime in the center is considerably greater than the actuality. In Dallas, a poll of citizens indicated that most agreed that crime in downtown was a serious problem; quite a few added, however, that personally they had had no trouble. Statistics bear out the qualification. Of all the parts of Greater Dallas, the one with the lowest incidence of reported crime has been downtown.

So in other cities, the central business districts are among the safest of places during the hours that people use them. Conversely, among the most dangerous are the parking lots of suburban shopping malls.

But the image of crime is itself a force. Corporations seeking sanctuary in suburbia invariably cite crime on the streets as a reason for their move. It may, in fact, be a minor one. But the corporations are worried enough by the image that they build their new headquarters like fortresses.

I don't wish to be Pollyanna. There are dangerous places in the city, and dangerous times. There are dangerous people. But it is important to differentiate between kinds of people—between the mugger, say, and the vendor. Many businessmen and civic leaders do not differentiate. Being themselves insulated from the life of the street, they lump all its people as undesirable, and some leaders would be quite happy if they were eliminated altogether, a result that their policies in some cities are calculated to bring about.

They should be working in the other direction. The time to worry is when street people begin to leave a place. Like canaries in a coal mine, street people are an index of the health of a place.

This is not reflected in the kind of city rankings lately so popular: the ten best quality-of-life cities in the U.S., the twenty happiest communities, and so on. Cities like New York go at the bottom, the top going to communities that could also qualify as the highest on any blandness index. While one would not wish to add yet another spurious statistical exercise, it might be in order to come up with a city index of enjoyability—the number of street entertainers, food vendors, people in conversation, the number smiling. A silly index, perhaps, but there is a simple point to be made. Street people are not just a problem; they are the heart of the street life of the center. Its liveliness is the test of the city itself.

Good performers and good audiences. These are the stuff of a good street life. Its vigor is a test of the vigor of the city itself.

4

THE SKILLED PEDESTRIAN

On skinny old
lexington avenue
i speed up
to pass this man
so i can slow down
i take
great pleasure
in the exact size
of my steps

Robert Hershon

The pedestrian is a social being: he is also a transportation unit, and a marvelously complex and efficient one. He is self-contained, self-propelled, and moves forward with a field of vision about 100 degrees wide, further widening this with back-and-forth scanning movements to almost 180 degrees. He monitors a host of equations: two crossing patterns at left front, 290 feet a minute, three on the right, angle on the cars 30 degrees and closing, a pair abreast dead ahead, a traffic light starting to flash DON'T WALK. In fractions of a second he responds with course shifts, accelerations, and retards, and he signals to others that he is doing so. Think of the orders and computers it would take to match him! Transportation engineers are spending millions on developing automated people-mover systems. But the best, by far, is a person. Here, in a brief summary, are the chief characteristics of the pedestrian:

1. Pedestrians usually walk on the right. (Deranged people and oddballs are more likely to go left, against the flow.)
2. A large proportion of pedestrians are people in pairs or threesomes.
3. The most difficult to follow are pairs who walk uncertainly, veering from one side to the other. They take two lanes to do the work of one.
4. Men walk somewhat faster than women.
5. Younger people walk somewhat faster than older people.
6. People in groups walk slower than people alone.
7. People carrying bags or suitcases walk about as fast as anyone else.
8. People who walk on a moderate upgrade walk about as fast as those on the level.
9. Pedestrians usually take the shortest cut. In some pedestrian malls curving pathways have been outlined in the paving. Pedestrians ignore them. They stick to the beeline.
10. Pedestrians form up in platoons at the lights and they will move in platoons for a block or more.
11. Pedestrians often function most efficiently at the peak of rush-hour flows.

What is most impressive about the individual pedestrian is the skill with which he adapts his moves to the moves of others. The simple avoidance of collision, as Erving Goffman noted, is really a rather remarkable demonstration of cooperative effort. Consider, for example, the moves necessary in a simple passing situation. Up ahead the pedestrian spots someone advancing on him. When the two are about twenty feet apart, they will look at each other. This is a critical moment. By their glance they must not only convey the signal but see if the signal has been acknowledged. A few feet nearer they drop their gaze and make a slight shift in course—to use Michael Wolff's term, the step and slide. The course shift in itself is not enough for a full clearance but it will be enough if the other pedestrian makes a comparable move, as with few exceptions they do.

In ambiguous situations there may be a sharp look in the direction the pedestrian intends to take, a slight pointing motion with hand or folded newspaper. As the two pass, they will be looking directly ahead, heads slightly bowed, slightly forward, shoulders drooped.

Pedestrians have a number of ways of coping with crowded situations. They do not walk directly in back of someone. As with tailgating, this can lead to collisions, and if you do walk directly behind someone for a while, some sixth sense often stirs that person to turn

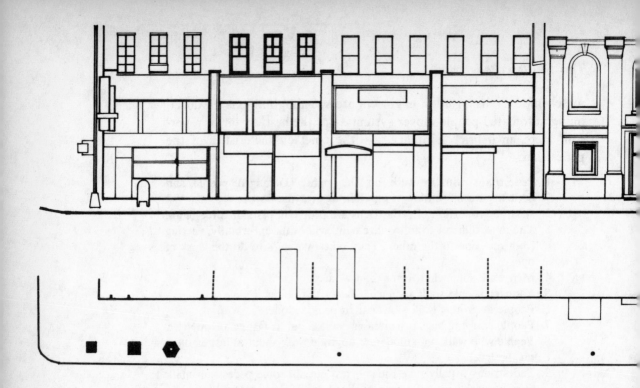

around and give you a sharp look. The good pedestrian usually walks slightly to one side, so that he is looking over the shoulder of the person ahead. In this position he has the maximum choice and the person ahead is in a sense running interference for him.

More challenging than simple passing patterns are the maneuvers needed when you are approaching people walking diagonally to your course, or perpendicular to it. In addition to the techniques of the simple pass, you now may instinctively use what could be called a retard—a slight, almost imperceptible slowing that will avert a collision course. In analyzing film that was shot at the regular cine speed of twenty-four frames per second, I found that the retard takes place within three or four frames—one fifth of a second or less. Just that fraction, however, will be enough to avert collision.

Some of the most challenging situations are cross flows at street corners. One of them that we have studied intensively is at the southwest corner of Fifty-ninth and Lexington. It has a subway entrance, usually at least one vendor at the curb, often one or two more on the sidewalk itself. At peak the pedestrian flow runs over five thousand people an hour, and it is a wonder the whole mess does not come to a dead stop.

But it never does and a great deal of skill and cooperative behav-

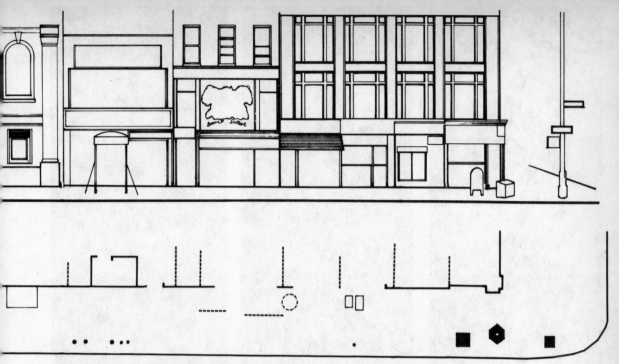

For recording where pedestrians did what and for how long, we made work-sheet maps of Lexington Avenue blockfronts. This is of the east blockfronts between Fifty-seventh and Fifty-eighth.

ior is the reason. In slow motion and regular, we have filmed scores of collision courses, crossing patterns, and passing maneuvers, and then plotted them on large-scale maps of the corner. Study any one encounter and you begin to appreciate not only how adroitly the participants managed, but how much the resolution of neighboring encounters made the success possible. It is a very complex web of movements.

There is guile, too. Pedestrians are not all saints and some would prefer to have others give way rather than give way themselves. They use feints and sometimes intimidate. Our instant replay of Fast Brown and Slow Blue is a case in point. Looking directly down at the Fifty-ninth Street corner, we see Fast Brown approaching from the left. He is big and he is walking fast—360 feet a minute. At the bottom of the scene appears Slow Blue. He is smaller and he is walking slowly. Both are on a collision course. Neither changes pace. Then, just at the critical point, Slow Blue slowly passes his left arm up by his head. This throws Fast Brown. He comes to a dead stop as Slow Blue glides on. Completely discomfited, Fast Brown wastes seconds in lateral foot movements before getting under way again.

Good tactics call for quick identification of the oncoming flow. Which are individuals? Which are moving in groups? It makes a considerable difference. A pair of men, for example, may force you to a

Of all pedestrians, New York's are the most skilled. They walk fast and they walk adroitly. With the subtlest of motions they signal their intentions to one another: a shift of the eyes, a degree or so off axis, a slight move of a hand, a wave of a folded newspaper.

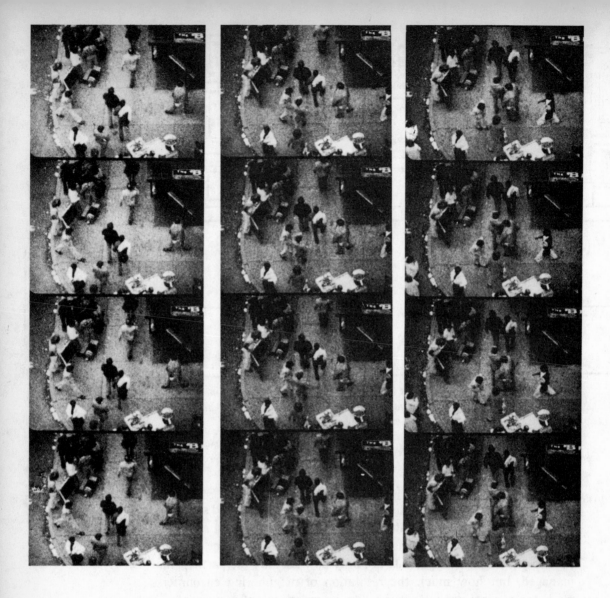

side step that you would not take if they were two individuals. Three-somes are more difficult yet. When they come at you in phalanx you can cleave the formation if you dare. But few do. Most people detour around the side. This is why natives can be so vexed by tourists. Sometimes they come four and five abreast.

It may be parochial of me, but I think that of all the pedestrians, New York's are the best. They walk fast and they walk adroitly. They give and they take, at once aggressive and accommodating. With the subtlest of motions they signal their intentions to one another—a shift of the eyes, a degree or so off axis, a slight move of the hand, a wave of a folded newspaper.

They bully cars if they can. When a driver slows to make a right turn they do everything possible to thwart him. They pretend not to see the cars. They make themselves hostage and force an impossible choice. Make way for me or kill me.

The New York *Times*'s Richard Shepard, a keen student of the street and himself a pedestrian, says that "the New Yorker walks with a special purposive gait, the foot locomotion of people who have a destination to reach and, as befits our municipal tempo, do not want to dawdle about it." Another explanation, much favored by New Yorkers, is that the city's pace is due to its attraction for ambitious, intelligent, aggressive people—that is, people such as themselves.

They resent constraints. Traffic signals are a particular vexation. They are, for one thing, timed to benefit cars rather than pedestrians. Take Fifth Avenue. You want to make time going north. At the turn of the light to green you start walking briskly. You have about 240 feet to go to reach the next light. You will reach it just as the light turns red. Only by going at flank speed, say 310 feet per minute, will you beat the light.

Whereas an out-of-towner by habit may wait submissively at the light, the New Yorker may not look at the light at all. He will look at the roadway to see what openings there may be. Well before the light goes green he will be streaking across.

New Yorkers are incorrigible jaywalkers. They may start out within the crosswalk but there is a strong tendency to veer off at an angle. Many jaywalkers elect to cross directly in the middle of the block, especially when the blocks are very long; Forty-second Street between Fifth and Sixth avenues is the prime example. At the morning rush hour, jaywalkers just about take over. When car traffic is slight enough, jaywalkers will often cut across a roadway on a long diagonal, sometimes traversing as much as two thirds of a block's length. It is dangerous, but there is some logic to it. By taking the hypotenuse, the jaywalker cuts the journey by as much as a third.

In some places the jaywalking is involuntary. There simply is not enough sidewalk space to handle the number of people. The Lexington Avenue sidewalk alongside Grand Central is a notable example. As I will detail in the next chapter, there is a threshold point, a fairly precise one too, and beyond it people turn very mean to cars. In such cases there are some reasons for the jaywalking. But most of it is foolish. There is a great deal of zigging and zagging between cars, almost as if the very danger of it was the attraction. And it is dangerous.

One's admiration for the bravado of the New York pedestrian must be tempered by his frequent extinction. Per 100,000 population, New York has been averaging 7 pedestrian fatalities annually, at the top of the list. (Chicago: 4.5; Los Angeles: 4.) Sixty-eight percent of those killed were men. One problem is the lack of any effective sanctions. People are not ticketed for jaywalking, and if they were, the fine is $2. Another problem is the drunken pedestrian. Of all pedestrians killed in New York City, one in seven has tested intoxicated.

A new danger for pedestrians is the rise of the messenger cyclists. Up until about five years ago most of the cyclists one encountered were people on their way to work. The messenger cyclists, however, are animated by money. They get paid for the number of deliveries they can make in a day, and true speed will net them around $100 additional a day, for a total take of about $250–$300. So they go fast, very fast—thirty to thirty-five miles per hour when possible; they go against traffic and they run red lights. They seem to hate pedestrians; they scowl and curse at them and yell and blow whistles at them to get them out of the way.

Pedestrians are still not acclimated to them or to their unpredictable ways, and instincts honed in the battle with cars ill prepares pedestrians for this newer contest. Before crossing a one-way street, the pedestrian normally takes a look in the direction the cars should be coming from. Then he steps out. But this could be a bad mistake. Out of nowhere, from the wrong direction, a cyclist may be upon him. Some cyclists periodically blow their whistles to alert people to get out of the way, but usually the approach is without sound until the whirr is upon one.

In 1986, 3 people were killed in pedestrian-cyclist encounters, 1,640 injured. But most encounters go unreported. The danger is underestimated in another respect. Walking has become much less enjoyable. Now you must crane your neck right, then left, watching for the defile between the cars. Two feet is all he needs. Danger has been further heightened by the way cyclists have been taking to the sidewalk. Here they wheel and circle and by their unpredictability enforce unpredictability on the pedestrian. Is he going to go to the right, or the left? The cyclist has been taking your course as a given. For you to adapt to his course now throws everything off. Out of these ambiguities can come some very nasty moments.

In documentaries on the plight of the pedestrian, a stock shot is a bunch of them moving together in the same direction, and fast. Actually, this is no bad situation. When there is a dominant direction, the flow makes the best of the walkway space available and moves at fairly high speed for that degree of congestion. There is, to be sure, an offset. If you are going with the flow, fine. If you are not, you had best be agile. At the Seventh Avenue, easternmost entrance to the Long Island Railroad concourse, some 14,000 people per hour stream out via a seventeen-foot defile during the morning rush hour. It is a remarkable feat. Unhappily for them, however, there are about 2,500 people who want to get *into* the station. (Some are commuting to a job in suburbia.) They fight their way in, tight against the wall.

The slower the vehicle traffic, the easier it is for the pedestrian to assert himself. Boston's pedestrians, for example, are another aggressive lot, and in part this is due to the narrow and winding streets of the old downtown. As the vehicle traffic on these streets increases and the speeds decrease, the balance of power shifts to the pedestrian. You will see Bostonians signaling with their arms for cars to get out of their way or stop, slapping their hoods when they don't, and frequently forcing them to a dead stop.

Another tough bunch of pedestrians are Montreal's. They have much to contend with. On Ste. Catherine, the principal shopping street, the sidewalks are as mean as Lexington's: twelve and a half feet. The sidewalk flows are prodigious: during the busy period, some 5,000 to 7,500 people an hour. Intersection behavior is understandably anarchic. Derek Drummond, director of the school of architecture at McGill University, has studied the pedestrians' patterns extensively. "The most striking feature of pedestrian traffic along Ste. Catherine Street," he reports, with some pride, "is that so many people pay no attention at all to the traffic lights."

Up to 60 percent of those crossing the street do so while the light is red. Drummond thinks they have reason to. "A light cycle insensitive to pedestrian movement results in the pedestrian arriving at an intersection just after the light turns red," he notes. "Montreal's light cycle is very long (100 seconds) with a 60-second green light for traffic on Ste. Catherine Street. It is little wonder that pedestrians sprint through any gaps in the vehicular traffic."

They keep coming back for more. Even in the coldest weather— say twenty below—the pedestrians are out in full force on the street. At such times the heated concourse of nearby Place Ville Marie draws only 30 percent to 40 percent of the flow on Ste. Catherine.

A tribute to Tokyo pedestrians is in order. In view of the wide cultural differences, they are remarkably similar to those of New York. They are also every bit as skilled, though noticeably more disciplined. They walk fast—about 300 to 320 feet per minute in the downtown centers. But they do run more. This is most noticeable just before the half-hour and hour marks of the morning rush hour. As they near the end of their journey, a number of people will break into a run. Many will laugh as they do it. And other pedestrians may laugh, too. Tokyo people see the comedy of the street, and they enjoy it.

While Tokyo's pedestrians are less anarchic than New York's, in their own way they make the crossing of streets something of a game.

Tokyo pedestrians are well disciplined; they almost always wait for the signal before crossing. At this intersection, loudspeakers broadcast cautionary announcements in a little-girl voice. It's almost the end of the WALK cycle, she says, so don't be childish. At this point, the final mad rush begins.

At the main avenue crossings they will form up what seem to be the most docile of platoons. After the light has turned red against them they will wait obediently. Lest they fail to do so, from nearby loudspeakers a little-girl voice will caution them. Don't be childish. Wait for the light. By now some pedestrians are impatiently toeing the white line. The light goes green. From each side the two platoons move out. At some crossings in the Ginza area, four platoons will cross diagonally from all four corners. It is quite a sight.

After about forty seconds of green, the little-girl voice says not to cross any more. From now on the pedestrian crossing is dangerous, she says. Let's cross safely at the next light. Now the pedestrians start streaking across. Again, as in the rush hour, there will be much laughing. Some people will start across at only a few seconds to red and will clear the middle of the avenue just as the cars start roaring across. People will begin to form up. The little-girl voice goes on again. Let's all wait for the light.

Pedestrian Speeds

Given a reasonably clear track ahead, people are fairly consistent in the walking speeds they choose. In general, men walk faster than women; younger people faster than older people; people alone faster than people in groups. Loads do not seem to slow people up; neither do slight upgrades. They put out a little more energy but they do not slow down.

In a big-city downtown, men will average about 5 feet a second; 290–300 feet a minute; 3½ miles an hour. Fast walkers will average about 4 miles an hour, and in passing situations they may accelerate to 5 miles an hour. How long people will sustain these speeds depends a good bit on the nature of the city. In the newer, auto-oriented cities of the Southwest, somewhere around three to four blocks is about as far as most people will walk. In New York City it is about five.

People in big cities walk faster than people in small cities. Just why this should be so no one has satisfactorily explained, but the fact of the difference does seem well established. Studies have shown that there is a rough correlation between the size of the city and the pace at which its pedestrians walk. The measurements are usually of people in free-flow situations; since such situations are rarer in big cities than small, the pace of big-city pedestrians might have been overstated a bit. But probably by very little. Our own tracking studies of pedestrians in varying situations indicate that the conventional image of city people as hustlers is rooted in fact. They do walk fast.

People in big cities walk faster than people in small cities.

Why are the big-city ones so fast? The Regional Plan Association's Boris Pushkarev believes they walk faster because they walk farther. Their time is valuable to them and so they compress the time of their trips.

Another explanation is the high density of people they must cope with. Psychologist Stanley Milgram saw it as a matter of overload. People in big cities are subjected to a very high volume of stimulation, he reasoned; they have a large number of people with whom to interact. The load is greater than the individual's capacity to process it, so in defense they seek to minimize it by walking fast.

I do not think this is so. If it is, it certainly does not follow from the data on pedestrian speeds. The pedestrian speeds, furthermore, were clocked in free-flow situations. They were not walking fast because they were crowded. They were not crowded. True, they may have become so habituated to crowds that they walked fast whether there was a crowd or not. But such conjectures are limitless.

As for overload, it is certainly true that people adopt various defensive mechanisms to cope with crowded situations: going limp on the subway, avoiding unnecessary contact with strangers, and so on. But is walking fast necessarily such an adaptation? One could as well argue that people do so to *increase* environmental stimulation.

In timing individual pedestrians, I have noticed that those going at a fast clip do not appear to be any more harried or tense than anyone else. They do appear to be getting somewhere, and the manner of their gait sometimes carries a touch of arrogance. It seems to say, I am an important, busy person and I am on my way. Most fast walkers,

It has been said that people walk fast to escape sensory overload. But the commonplace explanation may be the right one: They walk fast because they're in a hurry.

however, are not imperious, and the commonplace explanation might be the right one. They walk fast because they are in a hurry.

Like carrying capacity, the concept of overload is a sloppy one. It is pejorative and, by implication, treats a high degree of stimulation as something to be mitigated. But some of the most pleasurable streets to walk along are those that do have a high degree of stimulation. As I will argue in a later chapter, the best streets are sensory streets, and we cannot have them all good and no bad. On real-life streets the mix is inextricable, like the florist's display you like to touch but that too many other people do too.

But people are attracted to these streets. If they were not they would go elsewhere. They would go to the streets with a very low degree of stimulation: the streets that are lined with blank walls and are unencumbered with activities. Pedestrian counts show that people do not use such streets save for necessity. And when they do use them, they do not tarry.

What one is walking past influences how fast one walks. A pedestrian may start out at a brisk 290 feet a minute, then slow down to about 200 feet a minute as he goes past something—a shop window, a merchandise display—and he may sometimes stop for a few seconds. When he resumes he may go up to 340 feet a minute, as if impelled to make up the pause. Similarly, as he passes a bank or a blank wall, he may step up his pace a bit. Dull blocks are fast traversed.

Time of day affects pace. One of the best moments is just before lunch. While it is not measurable, there is an upbeat quality to the movement. There will be quite a few people in groups, younger executive types in particular, and they will be manifesting what appears to be very high spirits. This is when the Three Jolly Fellows are most likely to appear. There will be much joking and laughing. Expectations are high. Something good is going to happen.

After lunch the pace is slower, though occasionally someone will break into a run to get back in time. There will be many leave-takings as lunch groups break up. The key ones come late—around two, as befits the seniors. It's been a good lunch, their ambling gait seems to say. There may be a prolonged round of goodbyes, or a delayed resolution of the deal lunch was about. These casual moments can be quite climactic.

Rush-hour tempos are brisker. Of the two, the morning rush is the most purposive. This is a time when people really are intent on getting from A to B, and they manage it with considerable skill. Long before a decision has to be made, they will anticipate the placement of an escalator by shifting to the extreme right or left of the flow.

The evening rush hour is brisk too, but it is more sociable. There will be more people walking in twos and threes, more 100 percent conversations, more prolonged goodbyes, and more people just standing there. But it is an efficient flow nonetheless. And thanks to the phenomenon of the open door it may flow easiest at the very peak.

If there is a proper place for it, there will be a great dance. The best of the old railroad stations provided such places, and where these remain the movement is splendid. Stand on the balcony overlooking the main floor of Grand Central. At left, with three of the four escalators heading down, there is a mass of people going the same way. But only for a moment. They split into an infinity of directions. Some swirl around the information kiosk clockwise, some counterclockwise. Hundreds of people will be moving this way and that, weaving, dodging, feinting. Here and there someone will break into a run. Almost everyone is on a collision course with someone else, but with a multitude of retards, accelerations, and side steps they go their way untouched. It is indeed a great dance.

5

THE PHYSICAL STREET

If pedestrians are skilled, it is because they very well have to be. Almost every American city gives them the short end of the stick. Local transportation authorities usually have it written in their charter that transportation embraces pedestrians as well as vehicles and that they ought to plan for them. But they do not. They plan against them, defensively. Traffic signs addressed to pedestrians generally feature the words "prohibited," "no," "watch out for," or "don't."

Grade separation is another indicator. One of the most venerated of planning concepts has been the separation of vehicular from pedestrian traffic. And for whose benefit has this been? Vehicles. Pedestrian overpasses are an example. They are supposed to make things easier for pedestrians. But they are really meant for cars, so they can go faster and won't have to stop and let a bunch of pedestrians pass across the roadway. But pedestrians will take the roadway if they have a fair chance. They do not like to climb up and over the structures, and transportation engineers wouldn't either if they had to.

Traffic lights are rigged against pedestrians. In most cities the major avenues get more green time that the side streets. Since the avenues carry more vehicles, this would seem fair enough. The trouble is that the bulk of the people using the avenues are not in vehicles. They are on foot and the timing is not right for them. If you want to

One of the most hallowed of planning concepts is the separation of pedestrian from vehicular traffic. This is for the benefit of vehicles, so they will get the prime space.

cross North Michigan Avenue in Chicago, for example, you had better be off the mark the instant the light says WALK. Eighteen seconds later it will start flashing DON'T WALK. They let you have a bit more time but it is nervous time.

The discrimination is a waster of time. New York's Fifth Avenue provides an example. Each blockfront on the avenue is 200 feet long, building line to building line. If you start across at an intersection just as the light turns green and walk at a brisk pace, you will arrive at the next intersection just as the light turns red. A platoon of fellow pedestrians forms up. After idling fifty seconds, you start off again, and again reach the next intersection just as the light turns red. There is no flow for the pedestrian: instead, a series of staccato stops and starts that makes walking take almost double the time it should and maximizes the bunching of people into platoons.

But it is in the division of space and the rules for using it that the pedestrian gets the shortest end of the stick. In almost all U.S. cities the bulk of the right-of-way is given to the roadway for vehicles, the least to the sidewalk for pedestrians. New York's Lexington Avenue is a prime example, in particular the four-block stretch between Fifty-seventh and Sixty-first streets. It is the reductio ad absurdum of the U.S. city street—and by its very excesses it provides clues for its redemption.

In almost every U.S. city the bulk of the right of way is given to vehicles; the least, to people on foot. This is in inverse relationship to need.

As with many streets in U.S. cities over the years, Lexington's roadway has been made wider at the expense of the sidewalks. The roadway is now 50 feet, each of the sidewalks 12½ feet. The sidewalk pavement is cracked, buckled; at several places it slopes at an angle of about twenty degrees. It is full of holes and hollows, some with semipermanent puddles that are replenished by rain and snow in winter, and by the water trickling down from the air conditioners over store doorways in summer. The only level places are the subway gratings, which women avoid because their heels get caught.

The streetscape is so wretched that pictures of it are often featured in presentations on the decline of urban design. Along the curb is an ill-placed assortment of trash containers, mailboxes, newsstands, subway stairs, fire hydrants, signs, and poles, a number bent by trucks, some with nests of bicycles chained to them. Parts of the sidewalk will be in use for unloading and storage of boxes. There will be handbill passers, vendors displaying merchandise, cops arresting vendors—in all, so many obstructions that the effective walkway is no more than 6 or 7 feet. At times it will be reduced even more: when the merchants push their wooden billboards out as far as they dare, the passage will be narrowed to about four feet.

Now consider the load to be carried. Each day on the block between Fifty-seventh and Fifty-eighth some twenty-two thousand people traverse the east sidewalk, nineteen thousand the west—in total, forty-one thousand people. During this same time, twenty-five thousand traverse Lexington in vehicles.

The space is allocated in inverse relationship to the load: two thirds to vehicles, one third to pedestrians. This is so bad it's good. With that many people squeezed in so small a space, the leverage effect of a relatively small addition of space can be great. If, for example, one vehicular lane were eliminated, there would be 10 feet to divide up between the two sidewalks. That does not sound like much, but 5 feet added to each sidewalk would just about double the effective walkway. It would also widen the sidewalk past the minimum needed for good-sized trees and amenities like benches.

The width would seem much greater too. A good demonstration of this has been provided by the new Citicorp Building. On its Lexington blockfront it has added a 5-foot strip of space to the sidewalk, increasing it to 17½ feet. It seems like a boulevard.

Some of us floated a proposal to liberate upper Lexington with a reallocation of space. It fell flat. Most people thought it quite impractical. Even community-board people, for whom "pedestrian" is a holy word, shied off. Where would the vehicle traffic go? It was bad enough with five lanes. What would happen with only four?

If there was to be any action on pedestrian congestion, such ques-

The pass at Lexington Avenue and Fifty-seventh Street. This exasperating street had its sidewalks narrowed to twelve and a half feet. The effective walkway, however, ranges between four and six feet, depending on the placement of signs, floral displays, vendors' tables, and various impedimenta.

tions about vehicular traffic had to be answered. To this end, my group embarked on a study of traffic movement in the Lexington corridor, in lane-by-lane detail. Standard traffic counts record the number of cars passing over a counter cord stretched across a roadway. This is useful for getting gross figures but does not tell anything about the internal characteristics of the flow. To get at this we filmed the daily traffic with a series of time-lapse cameras aimed at two cordon lines. Then, frame by frame, we charted the passage of each vehicle: what type of vehicle it was—car, taxi, bus, or truck; which lane it was traveling in; the precise second it passed by. In addition we made spot observations to check vehicle occupancy, right-turn behavior, and the like. The result, I immodestly note, was one of the most thorough analyses of vehicular traffic made up to that time. (It was also exhausting; to chart twelve hours of actual traffic took six weeks of work, principally by researcher Ann Herendeen.)

We found out some things we did not expect to find:

1. When traffic is heaviest, between 7 and 8 A.M., it flows most rapidly —almost as fast as the traffic lights will allow. The parkers have not arrived yet.
2. The traffic follows a uniform saucer pattern. It is lightest at midday, just when the pedestrian flow is heaviest.
3. The traffic is badly distributed. The bulk of it is squeezed into only two of the five lanes.
4. The left-hand lane is rarely used for vehicle movement. In early morning, drivers don't need to use it; the rest of the day, they can't. Parkers have taken it over.
5. The right lane is not used much either. Bus drivers do stop in it, but for moving they like the middle lanes. With good reason: unless the right lane is exclusively for buses, drivers are chary of being mouse-trapped by a car at the curb.
6. Buses carry a disproportionately high share of the load. They make up only 4 percent of the vehicles but they carry 37 percent of the people.
7. Private cars carry the fewest. They average 1.6 occupants per car (including driver). The bigger the car, the smaller the number. In our checks, Cadillacs averaged 1.1 occupants.

The chart of the traffic on each lane shows just how badly distributed the traffic was. Lanes two and three carried 75 percent of the traffic. Lane one, the bus lane, had a very small flow; so did lane four, the double-parking lane. Lane five had practically no flow at all.

The key factor, clearly, is the blockage of a lane by parkers. We decided to do some close-up studies. How long did the parkers stay? What was the turnover? We took time-lapse films and from them made charts like player-piano rolls to chronicle a day's parking in several blocks. The charts demonstrated that a small number of long-term parkers accounted for over two thirds of the available parking time. They came early, they stayed late. In the few spaces that they did not hog, there was some turnover. But not much, and little of the kind that merchants like to think takes place.

Merchants like on-street parking because they believe it services a high turnover of shoppers. But it does not. Our studies showed that in-and-out parking accounted for only a small proportion of the double-parking time available. The bulk was accounted for by cars parked for hours or more—and they were much more likely to belong to the owners or employees of the stores than the customers.

Double parkers? We expected lots. In our minds' eyes Lexington was always jammed with double-parked vehicles. When we counted them, however, we found only one or two per block at any given time. It seemed odd that so few could do so much. But the number, we found, was not the critical factor. It was the amount of time a lane was out of action because of double parking. Just one vehicle per block is enough.

But the double parker is not the villain of the piece. Most often he has a truck with a delivery to make or he is on a service call. He double-parks because he has to and he does not tarry long. The real villain is the nonessential parker. He blocks access to the curb for those who really need it; he also slows down traffic in the lane outboard of him. Drivers do not like to skirt too close to a lane of parked cars: since they can expect abrupt pullouts they give it a wide berth, with the result that the capacity of the outboard lane is reduced by as much as one half.

Later we did a study of the entire midtown business district. With the help of sixteen graduate students of architecture from Columbia University, we did a sweep count of every block, plotting the location of each parked vehicle, its license plate, and any identifying cards on the windshield (for example, "Member Police Chiefs Association"). The pattern was the same as Lexington's, writ large. A relatively small number of vehicles were doing the congesting. On the 36 miles of street in midtown, we logged 4,031 parked vehicles; 2,000 were parked illegally; only 22 were ticketed. In every single block of midtown we found at least one lane interdicted to traffic—whether by cars parked legally or illegally, double parked, or standing.

There is an extraordinary dis-efficiency in all this. Once one lane is blocked, it takes only a few more elements to bring about a complete stoppage. Add a utility crew digging a hole in the street, a parked mail truck straddling two lanes as is their custom, a trailer truck caught halfway across an intersection—add just one more double-parked car —and the whole thing comes to a honking, cursing halt. You must

The balance of traffic is fragile. Block another lane; add a utility crew at a manhole, a trailer truck halfway across an intersection. Now add just one more double-parker and the whole thing comes to a honking mess. Is some malign mastermind at work? No. Chance alone does the trick.

The perverse economics of congestion: the Korean wig seller paid the store owner four hundred dollars a month in illegal rent for 4 square feet of sidewalk space on Lexington Avenue. The diplomat who habitually parked his Mercedes-Benz at the curb paid nothing for his 180 square feet. Had he paid at the same rate per square foot as the wig seller, he would have paid eighteen thousand dollars a month.

suspect that some malign mastermind was coordinating the vehicles from central control. No such mastermind, of course, is needed. Chance alone dictates the result.

The cost is great. It is not to be measured merely in congestion, lost energy, and time. More important are the positive benefits that are forsworn. By giving away land to parkers, or renting it for a pittance, cities are squandering some of the most valuable real estate that they have. There are much better uses for it than the nonmovement of vehicles. Its highest and best use is transportation: specifically, for pedestrians. They are the major component of center-city transportation. They should be given a larger share of the spaces and the city, and the city's merchants will be better off if they are.

For a clue from the marketplace, consider the case of the Korean wig seller. He used to pay a store owner on Lexington Avenue four hundred dollars a month for using 4 square feet of sidewalk for his wig stand. It wasn't the store owner's space to rent, of course; but as such charges go, it was reasonable, and the wig seller thought the business was worth it. In the curb lane adjacent, a diplomat used to park his Mercedes-Benz every weekday. And he parked it all day long. For using 180 square feet of space he paid nothing. If he had to pay at the same rate as the wig seller—one hundred dollars a month per square foot—he would have paid eighteen thousand dollars per month. Multiply that by the number of parked cars in the city, and New York's financial troubles would be over. The mathematics may be preposterous, but so is the situation.

To set matters right, we argued, it would not be enough to boot the parkers. The vacuum would soon be filled. If the space was not transferred to pedestrians, and quickly, it would be claimed by vehicles: the availability of the space would induce yet more traffic.

Several projects provided a vivid illustration. One was the Madison Avenue exclusive-bus-lane project. The two right-hand lanes were reserved for buses, the other three lanes for cars and trucks. The key was the left-hand curb lane. It had been posted against parking. Now the rule was enforced. "Don't even *think* of parking," the sign said. If people still didn't believe, several roving tow trucks made the point.

The result was a marked speedup of bus traffic. The other vehicular traffic, though now restricted to fewer lanes than before, moved more easily too. Lexington Avenue was speeded up. Traffic Commissioner, Samuel Schwartz was not only inventive but daring. He eliminated most of the privileged parkers from the left-hand curb lane that they had so long hogged—no easy feat in a city run by privileged parkers. Again, the provision of more space for vehicle movement spurred more vehicle movement. For so congested an area, the vehicles move with surprising ease and speed.

And therein lies the problem. A few more successes like this and the city will be further than ever from its goal of reducing vehicle traffic. More immediately, the city will be further than ever from making pedestrian traffic easier and safer.

The Lexington approaches to Grand Central Terminal provide a test. If we look at the total right-of-way, it is apparent that it is divided up as inequitably as was upper Lexington in the seventies. Of the people who traverse the right-of-way, 78 percent do so on foot, only 22 percent in vehicles. But the space is allocated the other way around: 66 percent for vehicles; 33 percent for pedestrians.

As a result, the sidewalk alongside Grand Central has become one of the worst choke points anywhere. At peak the rate reaches 7,500 people per hour, or 125 a minute. The space? The nominal width of the sidewalk is 12½ feet. The effective width is about 6 feet. This translates into a rate of 21 people per foot of walkway width per minute. This is off the charts. It is also dangerous. In clocking rush-hour flows, I have noted that when the rate reaches 90 people a minute some will edge out onto the roadway; when it reaches 100 a minute they swarm.

The simplest thing to do is widen the sidewalks. If this was coupled with the repavings that come up periodically, the cost would be moderate. New York proved this when a major overhaul of the Avenue of the Americas was being considered. The department of transportation, praise be, thought there would be some imaginative restructuring. The right-of-way was an unusually broad one, and parts of it were not very functional—traffic islands, parallel roadways that were little used, and odd bits and pieces of space. In the overhaul, these spaces were reworked into a series of parks and sitting areas. These were simply and nicely done and most have been very well used by the people of the neighborhood. The costs over and above the resurfacing: $400,000.

A number of cities have converted a stretch of their principal street into a transit mall. Unlike the all-pedestrian malls, these set aside one or two lanes for buses: in the case of Portland, Oregon, for streetcars. Some have worked very well—the buses providing not only better downtown access, but activity that pedestrian malls could use more of. Retailing is the crux; some transit malls have attracted the retailing needed to make them work, some are still struggling.

What has been most encouraging, however, is what has not happened: contrary to widespread prophecies, the closing of one strip of downtown to cars has not created jams on the others. Traffic has adjusted very quickly to what is available for it. As space for it diminishes, so does the traffic.

Transit malls are a promising approach. Unfortunately, however, most American cities have not yet gotten around to the more rudimentary step of widening their key sidewalks. Nor have they booted the parkers from the curb lanes. These approaches are not costly and they can be done incrementally.

But their sheer modestly is a disadvantage. Programs like this do not stir civic passions. Quantum leaps, or steps that promise quantum leaps, do stir passions. If a city has sidewalks that are too narrow it could meet the problem by widening them. But that is not something to get excited over. What would be is a multimillion-dollar project to add umpteen miles of sidewalks in underground concourses and skyways.

Cities should take a closer look at what they already have. Most of them are sitting on a huge reservoir of space yet untapped by imagination. They do not need to spend millions creating space. In their inefficiently used rights-of-way, their vast acreage of parking lots, there is more than enough space for broad walkways and small parks and pedestrian places—and at premium locations, at ground level.

How wide should sidewalks be? Studies by transportation planners have provided some useful guidelines—in particular the work of John J. Fruin of the Port Authority of New York. With cameras and counters, Fruin observed people in all sorts of high-density situations: bus cues, elevators, station corridors. From these studies he developed a level-of-service concept: that is, the amount of space per pedestrian that is needed for unimpeded movement, level A; for slightly unimpeded movement, level B; and so on up the degrees of crowding to the almost unbearable. For level A, walkways should have a flow rate of seven people or less per minute per foot of walkway width. This would involve some crowding at the busiest time but the going would be easy most of the time.

The Regional Plan Association of New York adopted Fruin's level-of-service concept in its influential study, *Urban Spaces for Pedestrians*. It went quite a bit further than Fruin. The planners felt that Fruin's standards were adequate for flows in terminals and concourses, which are apt to be unidirectional at peak times. For street situations, however, they believed more space was needed because of the cross flow and the tendency of people to bunch in platoons. Thus they applied a standard somewhat more liberal than Fruin's to platoons and crosswalks, namely, six people per foot per minute. This resulted in an hourly *average* flow of only two pedestrians per minute per foot of walkway width as their "unimpeded" standard A. Since this standard cannot be attained in a truly high-density urban environment, they are willing to settle for an average flow of four pedestrians per foot per minute on the busiest streets. That is equivalent to eight people per foot per minute in platoons. These are expansive standards, but the research behind them is impressive, and a number of cities have been adopting them for new-development areas.

I think Fruin was right the first time. The RPA standards are too expansive. They would provide much more space per person, and this would make for rather easy going even at the peak of the rush hour. The trade-off, however, would be empty space most of the rest of the time. This would be particularly likely in large-scale redevelopment projects where the designers have a fairly blank canvas to work with. Their inclination is to overscale in such situations. Giving them such an additional rationale would further confirm them.

The Regional Plan Association has done a service in raising standards for pedestrian space. Though I think they have gone a bit overboard on sidewalk widths, let it be noted that the provision of too much space for pedestrians is not a pressing danger. The problem is to get even a little extra space, and the RPA standards have been helpful in dramatizing how inadequate are our existing spaces.

Oversized spaces, however, are not desirable. They leave vacuums. One such was the sidewalk alongside the Exxon Building in New York. It was a prairie of a space, some forty-five feet wide. It was supposed to be an amenity but it proved so empty and dull that the management filled the void with some planter tubs and shrubbery.

Chicago's North Michigan Avenue is another case in point. For six blocks its sidewalks are a generous twenty feet in width; for the next six they are wider yet, thirty feet. There is so much space, indeed, that grassy plots with keep-off-the-grass chains around them have been introduced. One odd consequence is that the thirty-foot sidewalks have less walkway space than the twenty-foot sidewalks.

Another pitfall is the scanting of the social components of congestion. Formulas based on the pedestrian as a transportation unit are most applicable to transportation situations, such as getting from concourse exit A to gate B. But pedestrians are social beings too. Sometimes they stop and chat with someone—even on the concourse. They cluster in doorways. They pause to look at a shop window. In a word, they self-congest. The crowding and the pleasure are inextricably bound up. To put it another way, part of what attracts people to the street is a measure of the congestion the high standards would save them from.

A third problem in the formula approach is that it gives the same weight to one foot of walkway width as to another. But are they comparable? The first few feet of walkway width are absolutely critical. The walkway wouldn't be walkable without them. A tenth and eleventh would be nice to have. A twentieth might be quite marginal, if not too much—like the extra parking spaces of shopping centers that are only used several days in December.

Context is all important. How a walkway works depends very much on what is on either side of it. If it is hemmed in by walls it may feel narrower than it actually is. If it is bordered by open space, it may borrow some of the space and feel the wider for it.

Absolute widths are important too. A foot of walkway width on a narrow sidewalk is different from a foot on a wide one. Statistically, the pedestrian density might be the same. The walking experience, however, might be quite different. On the narrow sidewalk there will be less choice; on the wide one, more—more passing lanes, more opportunities for maneuver. Because formulas do not make allowances for such differences, they understate the case for adding width to narrow sidewalks and overstate it for wide sidewalks.

A wide sidewalk can tolerate obstruction better than a narrow one. On Fifth Avenue, for example, the effective walkway was abruptly narrowed to thirteen feet by two round benches outside of Elizabeth Arden. But there were few jams. In a kind of venturi effect, people anticipate a narrowing and adjust their gait accordingly, some accelerating, some making way. As they debouch from a narrower to a wider space, they may fan out from one or two files to three or four. For some people the required retards and accelerations and broken-field running are a welcome challenge. The point is, there has to be a field. On narrow Lexington there is hardly any to begin with; when merchants push their billboards out, there is none at all, and people have to veer out onto the street.

There is, of course, no one all-purpose optimum sidewalk width. But repeated observations do indicate that certain ranges work well in many kinds of situations and accommodate wide variations in flow. If I were forced at gunpoint to set a width for medium and large cities, I would specify a fifteen-foot minimum for most streets, twenty-five for major avenues. Even at peak, the sidewalks would be wide enough to handle the pedestrian flows comfortably—even New York's—yet narrow enough that there would be a pleasant hustle and bustle.

These are minimums. When in doubt it is probably best to err on the side of too much space. American cities have been paying a steep price for the sidewalk narrowings of the twenties and thirties. It would be in order to make up for them and then some. There would be more space for amenities, more space for future choices.

That said, too much space is to be avoided. This is a lesson current experience bears out. It is also a lesson of history. In the next chapter I am going to explore the street as a sensory experience and how, over many centuries and cultures, certain characteristics keep recurring in different forms: in souks, alleys, bazaars, fairs, and the like. They seem to be rooted in particulars unique to the place: the linear development of Japanese cities; the dimensions of wheeled vehicles in Rome. But there are common denominators as well, and the width of the street is one of them. For whatever reasons, there has been a congruity in the dimensions of the most celebrated of the ancient walkways. Most of them fall within a range of twelve to eighteen feet. Give people room, one lesson would be. But not too much.

6

THE SENSORY STREET

The street I have spent the most time on is New York's Lexington Avenue—specifically, the four-block stretch from Fifty-seventh to Sixty-first Street. The sidewalks are narrow and crowded; their pavements are cracked, full of holes and subway gratings; they are obstructed by a host of badly designed light standards, parking signs, mailboxes, trash containers; and much of the surface is in permanent use for temporary storage of crates, newspapers, displays of merchants, signs, and whatnot. Further obstructing the flow is a host of street operators: handbill passers, demonstrators, hustlers for second-floor establishments, pitchmen for stores, pushcart food vendors, knickknack vendors, beggars. There are all sorts of noises—the cries of the vendors, the blare of transistor radios. From food counters come smells—of pizza, knishes, hot dogs. At the sides and above is a miscellany of awnings, rickety marquees, flags, neon signs.

Why do people persist in using this street? Many have to; it's to and from a major subway station and their way to work. But if you track pedestrians, you will find that many of them could use less tacky or crowded routes if they wished. You will also find that on Lexington Avenue the side of the street with the most obstructions and slowest going is the side that attracts the most people. People love to hate Lexington, and they have terrible things to say about it. Some actually do avoid it, but it does appear that many of the people on Lexington are there because they want to be.

One reason is messiness. Wherever you are in the area, you seem to be on the edge of something else. There are no clear boundaries. On one side are the office buildings of the central business district; on the other, the apartment buildings and brownstones of the residential East Side. In between are department stores, savings banks, restaurants, bars, small shops. It is highly local, and a succession of service facilities such as cleaners, liquor stores, and delicatessens keeps repeating itself. The place is, in sum, a mishmash of activities—the kind that zoning was originally set up to prevent.

There are many shifts: commuters on their way to work, early shoppers, office workers going to lunch. The five o'clock crowds: late shoppers (Bloomingdale's open till nine), people lining up at the movies, people going to dinner. Most important of all, especially at night, are the people who live there. More than anybody else, they keep it alive.

On Saturdays, Lexington becomes a recreation area. You will see many family groups, with children perched on the fathers' shoulders. It is a time for shopping, browsing, eating, and looking at the crazies. The crowding reaches its peak in early afternoon, and it is of a different character from the weekday rush. The pace is slower, more amiable, and there is a lot of cruising back and forth. Puerto Rican teenagers come down from the Bronx and East Harlem to catch the action —and if you stay in one spot long enough, you'll repeatedly see the same ones passing up and down the street and across, stopping to greet friends, sitting on car hoods to watch the goings-on.

Many blind people know Lexington well. That admirable institution, The Lighthouse, has its headquarters a half block from Lexington and conducts its mobility training for the blind there. Because it is so congested, Lexington Avenue is an extraordinarily difficult challenge for the blind, but it is unusually rich in sensory cues. One who reads them with accuracy is Jerry, a young man recently blinded but with a great deal of self-confidence. Unlike the congenitally blind, he has a visual memory of the place, and he has learned to reconstruct it from touch and smell and sound. Approaching Lexington, he explains that the newsstand up at the corner is a smell cue. Newspapers have a very identifiable odor to him. Another cue is the voice of Bob, the man who runs the newsstand and who is always saying something to somebody. Ten feet further on, there is the smell of the hot pretzels of the vendor at the corner.

Now Jerry is on Lexington itself. There are many cues: the sound of water dripping from the leaky air conditioner over the door of the pet shop; the touch and smell of the flowers at Rialto Florist; the rush of warm or cool air in front of Alexander's doorway; the smell of beer from Clancy's Bar. (The smell of incense at the head shop had been a

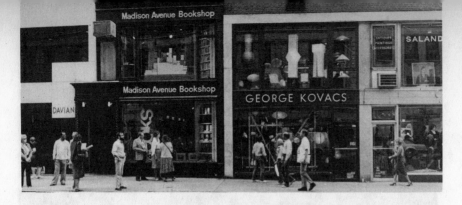

Madison Avenue, between Sixty-ninth and Seventieth: fine example of second storiness.

strong cue, but it was closed up.)

Lexington has so many cues, and some are so strong as to blot out others. The loudest is the loudspeaker at the record shop, playing rock. This kind of sound masks others that can be more helpful—such as the change in the pitch and reverberation of street noise as it is bounced off a building wall or canopy. For good reason Jerry keeps moving his cane from side to side, constantly testing.

Even Lexington's disadvantages can be helpful. The wretched topography of its pavement is a map to be read. Jerry knows every hillock and depression, the cracks and puddles, and he can tell from the angle of the pavement's slant exactly where he is. As Lighthouse instructors explain, Lexington is not a place for a "subtle traveler." Its cues are gross and blatant.

Second Storiness

Another reason Lexington works is its second storiness. There is still a good supply of brownstones along it, and in most cases the second story as well as the first is used for stores or restaurants. Along a three-block stretch one finds the following:

Dance studio
Palmist
Haircutting parlor
Doll hospital
Karate academy
Chinese restaurant
Nail studio
Mattress store
Record shop
Clock repair shop

Together they make a lively sight, especially at dusk and after. When the balance of light shifts to the interior, there is much movement silhouetted or spotlighted: dancing couples, hairdressers and cus-

tomers, couples eating at window tables. The scenes are an excellent argument for bringing back the double-decker bus.

The second storiness has a pronounced effect on the street level. Being a flight up, the proprietors must work hard to gain the attention of passersby. So they put out banners and flags—the haircutting establishments, which are fiercely competitive, are especially given to these. At the bottom of the stairs, signs are put out on the sidewalk. Sometimes a proprietor will station a pitchman there or send out a handbill passer. (One flight up, check us out.)

An outstanding example of second storiness is Madison Avenue in the Sixties and Seventies. It is now probably the finest specialty-shop street in the world, yet its basic elements are quite ordinary. The basic module is the five-story brownstone, twenty feet wide, ten brownstones to a block; and, while quite a few have been replaced by newer and higher buildings, the brownstone still sets the form and character of the street. With few exceptions, their first and second stories are used for stores, and the same is true with a number of the newer buildings that adjoin them.

New York's Madison Avenue is almost the reverse of the suburban shopping mall. It is a double-loaded street, with the basic module set by the twenty-foot brownstone.

It is not a good-taste street—not as a whole, at any rate. There is no uniform cornice line; the facades are a jumble of styles; so is the signage. But the scale is right for the pedestrian's-eye view; the ensemble is pleasing. Manifestly, the place works, and the rents bear witness. In the Lower Sixties, stores rent for about $300 a square foot, and half to a third of that on second floors.

What we have here is a double-loaded street—and a format almost the reverse of that of the suburban shopping mall. The latter also has two levels of shopping, often three. But it provides walkways for each level—and quite generously sized ones, too, some twenty to thirty feet across. Madison, by contrast, loads its two levels onto only one walkway, thirteen feet wide. This is squeezing things more than they should be—five more feet would help—but the sidewalk does work well. On Madison the load is still building. Cafés and delis have been putting out chairs and tables on the sidewalk, and on Saturday, Vanity Fair day, one has to thread one's way with care.

Window Shopping

In many cities window shopping would appear to be a dying activity. There are, for one thing, fewer windows to shop. More department stores have been closing downtown than opening up, and the new ones that have been built feature few windows at street level, if any, and none at all on their upper levels. Furthermore, that former adjunct to the window, the door, may be on its way out, too. Increasingly, access is from within the buildings, sometimes along replicas of shopping streets.

But the real thing still works. Where there are display windows, people window-shop, and the stores that have them enjoy a competitive edge greater than before. With an attractive window, even a small, twenty-foot-wide store can draw up to three hundred window shoppers an hour. How many become buyers is harder to tell, but the number of lookers and buyers does correlate with the number of pedestrians—with which figure, to the chagrin of retailers, rents correlate, too.

Window shopping is highly selective. As our tracking studies show, pedestrians tend to slow down or stop in certain places; they skip past others and speed up as they do. Most window shoppers are women and they are quite professional about it. The serious window shopper takes in the whole window in a kind of visual sweep and then looks down at any placard that might be there. If there are two women together, usually they will exchange comments. But it's all done very quickly. The median elapsed time is somewhere between forty and sixty seconds. There are many conversations that last longer and these are important in attracting more people, but the great bulk of window shopping is done with dispatch.

People on the inboard side walking to the right tend to look at the windows more than those outboard. But the close-up view has its drawbacks and the people on the outboard part of the sidewalk frequently get a better view of the displays. Many window displays appear to have been composed as though they were to be viewed from a perspective about twenty feet out in the middle of the street—somewhat like architectural renderings showing a facade from a point of view nobody could share because a building is in the way.

Window shoppers tend to come in bunches. Partly this is due to the fact that the pedestrian flow itself comes in bunches. The traffic light at the corner is a key factor but there are other reasons for bunching. Window shoppers attract window shoppers. One person stops, another stops, then a couple. They attract others. The domino effect is short lived, to be sure, and it may be followed by several minutes of nobody stopping at all. Then someone stops again.

Pauses lead to successive pauses. When a person has stopped to look at one attraction, he is likely to be more responsive to other stimuli in the same vicinity. The behavior of passersby at the Rialto Florist is an example. Almost always, there is a stand of forsythia, or pussy willow, or the like out on the street. As people pass by, some will brush up against the flowers; others will stop to touch them. These momentary stoppages may trigger similar touching by the people following behind—in much the same way that people putting money in a beggar's cup induce others to do the same.

This is good for the business of the florist; some of the touchers will go into the shop and buy something. But the stoppage is also very beneficial to the store next door. This is a store that features T-shirts with decals on them. People who come to a full stop because of the flowers get a much better view of the T-shirt store than do other passersby, and they are more likely to look at the windows. This in turn prompts a number to go on in through the door.

Stoppages are so effective at inducing spillover traffic that merchants might well consider it worthwhile to deliberately create them. One who did was Mr. Kadescu, a former Romanian musical comedy star who ran a fruit juice stand on Lexington. He used to stick a street sign out on the sidewalk advertising discount cigarettes; he was anxious to preempt business from a discount cigarette store two doors north. He soon saw that the really valuable function of the sign was obstruction. It reduced the effective walkway to about six feet and so constrained pedestrian traffic as to divert more of it to his counter. He began moving it farther out onto the sidewalk. Occasionally somebody would angrily move the sign back to the counter. But Mr. Kadescu would keep pushing it farther onto the sidewalk. I have a film sequence of him pushing it so far as to reduce the walkway to only four feet. It was bad of him and I certainly don't want to advocate such brigandage. As an example of the manipulation of space, however, it certainly was effective.

What draws people? The merchandise itself, of course, is the key. On Lexington Avenue women's novelty fashions and accessories are prime draws. Price is part of the attraction, and almost all of the pitches you hear emphasize the incredible bargain being offered, and how fleeting it will be. Today only. Everything half price. Today only.

But the very expensive attracts too. One display that we studied was of mannikins in very elegant skirts made from Chinese court robes. Though the prices were out of reach for all but a very tiny fraction of passersby, the particular window drew many more people than the location usually does, and many of the lookers were low-income people.

In this case, we found the display led to a significant number of sales. Ordinarily it is difficult to figure what correlation there may be between lookers and eventual sales. Some high-drawing displays do indeed induce many sales—some clearly do not. But one must not apply too immediate a yardstick. Whatever else it is, window shopping is entertainment. It sells the store and it sells the environs.

The merchandise that attracts most is the merchandise that is out front, on the street, where you can pick it up, feel it. Wherever store owners have put a display on the street there is a marked increase in the numbers of lookers and stoppers; the Argosy Book Store, with its inset entry and piles of secondhand books, is one of the best such places. Oranges, apples, junk jewelry, even a pile of remnants will draw a crowd. Watching them, one gets the feeling that the fingering of the goods is an end in itself.

So is the back-and-forth chatter. Among the reasons outdoor merchandise pulls well is that the merchant or one of his staff will usually be out there, too. If he is at all aggressive, the merchant is physically in the ideal spot to turn a looker into a buyer.

Movement attracts. Day in, day out, the best drawing display on Lexington Avenue is a pet shop with a window full of puppies and kittens. Live people do well too. Bloomingdale's windows often draw best when the window dressers are themselves the show, fussing around with mannikins and lights. A whole party of people can be better yet. One time Bloomingdale's staged a disco dance in a corner window and kept sending in relays of pretty girls and junior executive types to dance away. The crowds outside got so big that traffic came to a halt.

Around the corner is Fiorucci, a woman's specialty shop that frequently features live people in its windows—girls having their legs painted with tattoolike designs, for example, or a live person done up as a mime who's affecting not to be live.

But one of the biggest draws I ever saw was when a store displayed nothingness. Bonwit Teller covered several of its windows with brown wrapping paper and cut small eyeholes in it at tiptoe height. This drove people crazy. Before long they were queuing up to get a crack at the peepholes. There was nothing much to see when they looked, but this amused them, too, and they stuck around to see how others would react.

Light attracts. The raunchiest block on Lexington (Fifty-seventh to Fifty-eighth, west side) was notable for its lighting effects. One store, Icarus, featured blinking strobe lights and neon. The effect was so chaotic one would think that the adjoining store owners would object. They did not. They did not even object to the combination of displays and light at the Lexington Rap Club. A sign on the sidewalk said "Come rap with one of our six lovely conversationalists." At the bottom of the stairs leading up to the club a pitchman stood. Over one doorway, two red lights revolved slowly.

Sound attracts. Selling streets are noisy. On Lexington the pizza man rattles a cowbell when he sees a platoon of people approaching. With bullhorn or loudspeakers, salespeople shout at passersby that a sale is on. Everything half price! Check us out! Then there is the rock. Alan, the young man who ran a music shop, had a loudspeaker canted at just the angle to catch people full blast as they went by. He played the same hard-rock selection time after time before he changed to another tested favorite. Again, neighboring store owners were surprisingly tolerant. The police were not. Alan was hauled into court a number of times and fined one hundred dollars each time. He has since moved on, unrepentant.

Food and the eating of it is Lexington's major activity and most of it takes place right on the street. Many of the shops have open counters: the fruit juice and pizza places, for example; the soft ice cream shop, which for good measure pushes the freezer out onto the sidewalk in fair weather. Some food shops have folding fronts; when they are folded back it is hard to tell where the sidewalk ends and the shop begins, a distinction further blurred when the proprietors put out tables and chairs.

All of this, mind you, takes place on sidewalks twelve and a half feet wide. It is a use of public space that is either illegal or, in the view of municipal officials, should be. Most cities ban such a sidewalk purveyance of food; some go so far as to prohibit citizens from the eating of it. Necessary for public safety, you will be told, for sanitation reasons—for decent appearances.

But the marketplace is stubborn. Witness what happened to the Avenue of the Americas in New York. When it was Sixth Avenue and had the El running along it, it was full of food places—restaurants, Irish bars, cafeterias, coffee shops, delis, mom-and-pop soda canteens. Then it was redeveloped. The El went; so did the old buildings, and the shops and bars. In their stead went up a series of towers and plazas and windows of banks.

Then, slowly, the street took its revenge. A few food vendors came to fill the vacuum, then a few more. Business boomed. Today the sidewalk in front of the Exxon Building, the liveliest sidewalk on the avenue, is in good weather jammed with as many as two dozen vendors and their customers.

But one element is missing. There is no drinking fountain on the avenue. There are none on Lexington. There are none on any major avenue in the city. There are few in most other cities.

An exception is the fine system of Portland, Oregon. It goes back to civic leader Simon Benson. Many loggers and seamen used to come to town, and Benson thought it would be a good idea to make water so available they would be less tempted to other drink. He gave a city-wide system of fountains. There are 140 operating today.

This is no small achievement. In these technically advanced times, we seem to have lost the capability or repairing the simple faucet. To their shame, most American cities not only have failed to provide new fountains for their streets but have failed to maintain the few that still exist. (Worst example: New York's Lincoln Center. Its one outdoor drinking fountain went out of order in 1980. Since then the city financed a renovation of the open spaces at a cost of over $1 million. The repair of the drinking fountain was not included, however, and as of this writing it is still out of order.)

Way back in 1972 New York launched a trial pedestrian mall. For a two-week period the city closed a fifteen-block stretch of Madison Avenue to vehicles between noon and 2 P.M. We set up time-lapse cameras and recorded what happened.

Socially, the mall was a success. The number of people on the street more than doubled, going from nine thousand to nineteen thousand. And this was not at the expense of activity on neighboring streets. The flows there were about as high as they usually were. What was most interesting, however, was where the additional people on Madison congregated. Some used the middle of the roadway—in particular, people promenading three and four abreast. But the majority, 60 percent, were on the sidewalks. Since these remained their niggardly thirteen feet there was a larger degree of crowding than before. But it was clear this was a matter of free choice. The sidewalks were where the stores and their windows were.

The mall was shot down, with the taxi drivers the key opposition. But Tokyo planners were impressed. They decided to close to traffic a major avenue, Chuo-Dori, every Sunday. Thus was born "Ginza Paradise"—and another demonstration of the pull of the sidewalk.

Chuo-Dori's right-of-way is ninety-five feet wide, its sidewalks twenty-two feet each, and its roadway fifty feet—dimensions similar to Fifth Avenue's. On Sundays, pedestrian volumes about double. As on Madison, the additional people are not distributed evenly over the right-of-way. On a Sunday when we counted peak flows of thirteen thousand people an hour, only five thousand were on the roadway, versus eight thousand on the sidewalks. The sidewalks accounted for 46 percent of the space but 62 percent of the flow. The department

This traditional shopping alley leading to the Kannon Shrine in Tokyo provides a pleasantly tactile hustle and bustle. Many new streets do not.

stores did their best to seed activity in the middle of the roadway with tables and chairs and umbrellas. But the crowds were on the sidewalks, and so were the vendors and the fast food and the stores' sidewalk displays.

But the most fascinating of Tokyo's streets are its ordinary ones. Mile after mile, they are consistently more interesting than ours. There are many reasons: the linear progression of elements, ever repeating—the coffee shops, food places, lantern signs; the profusion of neon; the many people on the street and the obvious enjoyment they take in it. In the Shinjuku district there are more such streets to savor than in most U.S. cities put together, and for sheer sensory impact there is nothing to match its back alleys with their charcoal grills and smells and clouds of smoke.

The Japanese have been served well by tradition. Historically, the city was formed as a linear progression of shops and activities, and the widths were fairly narrow. An example, little changed, is the walkway leading to Tokyo's Kannon Shrine. It is about seventeen feet wide, and because of the open stalls on each side, the effective walkway is about fifteen feet. We were fortunate to be there on the day of the shrine's annual celebration and to see the walkway tested by some of the heaviest crowds of the year. The pedestrian flow was that of a downtown sidewalk—running at a rate of about four thousand people per hour in midmorning. The pace was slow. There was considerable self-conges-

Mile after mile, Tokyo's streets are consistently more interesting than ours. Mixture is one reason. The Japanese do not use zoning to enforce a rigid separation of uses, but instead encourage different uses, side by side and upward—shops, showrooms, pachinko parlors, restaurants piled on top of restaurants, four or five stories or more.

The Shinjuku redevelopment area has streets as sterile as any U.S. redevelopment area.

tion; people stopped frequently to look at the merchandise, reassemble their groups, buy something to eat. Two handbill passers stationed themselves in the middle of the flow. But it was a congenial kind of crowding, quite appropriate to the time and place.

The merchants of Osaka had similar streets. During the postwar reconstruction, the city considered replacing them with several broad Ginza-type avenues. The merchants finally decided this would not be a good idea. The traditional fifteen-to-seventeen-foot width would be better for business. They prevailed.

Kyoto has conserved a not dissimilar warren. The merchants have glassed over many of the streets, but in other respects they are still functioning as they always have.

The basic factor is mixture. This is the chief reason Japanese streets are consistently more interesting than ours, and it is true of the obviously modern ones as well as the old. Contrary to U.S. practice, the Japanese do not use zoning to enforce a rigid separation of uses. They encourage a mixture, not only side by side, but upwards. In the new buildings you will see showrooms, shops, pachinko parlors, offices all mixed together and with glass-walled restaurants rising one on top of another—three, four, and five stories up. By day the jumble can be garish. By night it is invigorating.

Sometimes the Japanese have done it the American way. In the Shinjuku district was a large reservoir that was no longer needed. For the planners it was an ideal site for redevelopment, and as usually seems to be the case with blank canvases, they laid it out with an Olympian scale. There is visual order and coherence. The streets are wide and straight. The buildings are set spaciously back from them. The sidewalks are broad and uncongested; above them are second-level walkways.

It is easy to walk here. There is little to slow one down—no bordering stores or coffee shops to cause one to tarry. Save for one good plaza, that of the Mitsui Building, there are few places to sit, and not much to look at if you do. In one of the liveliest urban districts in the world, the planners were unable to reproduce the factors that made it so.

There is another exception that proves a rule: the Kasumigaseki government district. This is the one area in Tokyo laid out most rationally by Western planning standards. It is a confined, single-purpose district, like the civic centers in many U.S. cities, and it is about as interesting.

But these are aberrations. In the Tokyo experience there are positive lessons and the foremost one is mixture. It does not lie so much in the mixture of uses of the ancient streets but in how the Japanese have carried this over into their newer ones, and not by accident but by policy. This is where we fail. We have some good streets, but we do not seem to conserve them. More often than not, they have low- and medium-rise buildings: Madison Avenue in New York, Newbury Street in Boston, Oak Street in Chicago, Charles Street in Baltimore. Such areas are very vulnerable. On Lexington, for example, one of the liveliest, if raunchy, blockfronts (west sides of Fifty-seventh and Fifty-eighth) is being demolished for two towers; on Madison between Seventy-fourth and Seventy-fifth, a row of brownstones and the Books & Co. bookstore are to make way for the controversial new addition to the Whitney Museum.

The old is not necessarily a great loss; it depends on what goes up instead. But in more cases than not the new construction prices out not only marginal uses but some basic ones too. New stores will have rents far higher than prevailed before; worse yet, unless the city mandates street level retailing, developers may leave out stores altogether. The pedestrian's-eye view will be of office windows or banks or blank walls.

Mixture is too vital to leave up to the developer, or to the presumably objective verdict of the marketplace. It seems rigged against the old and the diverse and the modestly scaled because it *is* rigged. Nor is there any discipline for reestablishing mixture in new buildings. But cities can change these imbalances, and in a later chapter I will suggest ways to do so.

Trash

One corollary of food on the street, unhappily, is trash on the street. There is certainly a great deal on Lexington. We spent some time studying where it comes from, where it goes, and, by time-lapse, just what happens, minute by minute, in the daily life of a trash container.

We found, among other things, that trash containers are badly designed; that they are badly sited, being spotted in the same proportion on blocks with high trash loads as on blocks with low loads; that the containers are very functional for a number of nontrash uses.

We also found that the citizen is maligned. The gist of public service advertising sermons directed to him is to stop being such a slob. But he is not, usually. He is good about litter *if* there is a place to put it. The problem is that too often there isn't.

We rarely saw anyone deliberately throw trash on the street. Indeed, when we followed people who had taken handbills, we were struck by how far they would carry the handbills to find a place to dispose of them. We were similarly impressed by people's behavior on plazas. Since there are usually a lot of food vendors alongside, there is a heavy load of trash generated. There are rarely enough containers to take care of it. Initially, people will be very good about carrying their trash to a container, even if it involves quite a walk. Once the containers start to overflow, however, discipline vanishes and some citizens become the slobs they are accused of being. The conventional wisdom is right: In a place that is tidy, people are tidy. In a place that is messy, they make it messier.

The clear thing we found was that the trash container can be a very useful piece of street furniture. When we did our study, New York was in the process of shifting from one kind of container to another. The standard wire basket had worked well, but so many of them were being stolen that the sanitation department decided to

Anti-litter public service ads tell people to stop being such slobs. But they are not, usually. They are good about disposing litter if there is something to dispose it in. But there are too few receptacles and they are rarely sited in relation to the trash load.

switch to something that would be too heavy to cart away. It settled on a concrete container weighing some 470 pounds. It was about three feet high and on top of it was a hinged metal lid with an opening for the trash. The sanitation people liked it so much they didn't bother to have a trial run. A complete supply was ordered all at once and the switchover was made.

It was a very bad trash container. The opening at the top was so small that much of the trash aimed at it fell on the lid, from which it would soon be redistributed to the street by the slightest breeze. Because of the small opening, furthermore, the trash that did get inside was not compacted the way it usually is, and a relatively small volume of trash would be enough to clog the opening. All subsequent trash people would place on the lid, now functioning as a litter dispenser.

Scavengers made the containers work better. Most scavengers follow a regular route, and in the course of a day they will call at many containers. On the average, we found, containers get about one scavenger visit per hour. With the concrete kind, the scavenger would reach under the lid, pull the release lever, lay back the lid, and then stick a hand down and start rummaging through the trash for something of value. As they did so, the trash was distributed more evenly, air pockets were eliminated, and the trash was reduced in volume. Scavengers would not take very much out—they are quite choosy—but when they were through, the container's capacity to receive more trash was considerably increased.

Passersby scavenge also. It is surprising how many well-dressed people can be seen rummaging through trash containers, and not surreptitiously, either. Newspapers are especially sought, and in our time-lapse studies of trash containers, we have run across instances of the same newspapers being transferred back and forth from one container to another in a small area.

As we watched people using these trash containers we began to appreciate how very useful they were. They were not very good for trash, to be sure, but they were highly functional in other ways. They were used for so many different purposes that they served as an indicator of what's missing in our street furniture.

There are two basic reasons for their utility. First, whatever their shape and size, they are objects, and objects attract people. Second, they are placed at street corners, adjacent to the 100 percent locations.

Here are some of the ways they served:

As a shelf for rearranging packages or sorting through handbags or briefcases.

As a table for sandwiches and fast-food snacks. (We once saw a group of four having lunch on one container.)

As a desk for documents for street conferences. (On two occasions we observed secretaries resting steno pads on the container while they took dictation.)

As a stand for vendors' merchandise trays.

As a footrest for people sitting on nearby car hoods.

As an object for schmoozers to lean against.

The shelf function seems to be the most important. The flat expanse that made it so useful in this respect is what made it bad as a trash container. But there are a number of models that could be modified to handle trash and still have shelf functions. Another thing designers might want to think about is a molding on the side of the container at a height suitable for tying shoelaces—twelve inches is about right.

Walkways

In an earlier chapter I held Lexington up as an extreme example of too little sidewalk space for pedestrians. Now I am going to look at the other side of the equation. I am not relenting on those sidewalks; twelve and a half feet is ridiculous for so heavy a load. But part of

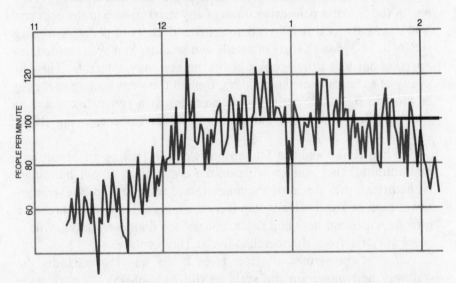

Here is the pulse of one of the worst choke points anywhere: the west sidewalk of Lexington Avenue at Grand Central Station. On this niggardly 12½-foot sidewalk, up to 4,000 people an hour walk off-peak. During midday buildup, when the rate reaches 100 a minute—or 6,000 per hour—pedestrians start veering out onto the roadway. At peaks of around 120 a minute, they virtually take it over.

Lexington's perverse attraction lies in the sensory experience of its walkways, and narrowness is a feature of them. Somewhere along the line, increasing width can work against a street. Defining a happy medium may be impossible, but it is not a bad goal to keep in mind.

At the opposite extreme from Lexington are the suburban shopping malls. Their walkways are wide—thirty feet or more. Originally, they were wider yet. The first regional malls had lots of green space, and their central walkways were as much as fifty to sixty feet across. When developers started putting roofs over malls, they reduced the walkways somewhat, but they were still an ample thirty to fifty feet wide. The spaciousness was considered a big psychological plus, an antidote to the crowding of downtown.

But mall developers began to see minuses. Quite aside from the cost of the extra space, when walkways are very wide, the stores on one side don't work well for the stores on the other; there is not the marginal friction you get in a tight shopping layout, nor the hustle and bustle.

The most dramatic contraction in walking width was in the Faneuil Hall Marketplace in Boston. The venerable old building was a given, and because of the placement of the pillars, the main walkway could be only eleven feet wide. Developer James Rouse and architects Jane and Ben Thompson thought the very narrowness would prove a virtue. So it has. The walking of it is an experience and it has attracted one of the heaviest pedestrian flows of any marketplace in the country. You edge past food displays, detour around knots of people sampling the food, and past all sorts of smells and sounds. You are crowded, no mistake, but it is a free-choice crowding and very tolerable. There is plenty of space outside the building, though the steps leading to it may be blocked by people eating lunch on them. It is somewhat messy at the most crowded times, but people do seem to be enjoying themselves.

When Rouse and the Thompsons went on to design Harborplace in Baltimore, they did so without the constraints of old buildings. Nonetheless, they designed the marketplace walkways to be even narrower than at Faneuil Hall—ten feet on average. They were careful to provide widenings here and there, but not too many or too big. One is never very far from the merchandise at Harborplace.

One of the virtues of street trees is the way they channel the walkway and moderate the scale of the right-of-way. A very wide sidewalk without trees is not a comfortable space. This proved the case with Chicago's North Michigan Avenue. Along one stretch the sidewalks were made thirty feet wide. This proved such a surfeit of space that it was decided to fill it up a bit. They put in trees and grassy plots with chains around them. They did this so expansively that the walkway width was narrowed to about ten feet.

A greater problem arises when the sidewalks are narrowed and the trees chopped down as well. In the cause of street widening, highway departments have destroyed many an alley of fine old trees. Paris, of all cities, has been guilty too. On the Boulevard Montparnasse, it eliminated one of the two rows of trees on either side and narrowed the sidewalk by about fifteen feet to make more room for cars.

The Selling Entrance

Doorways pose much the same challenge as walkways. To work at their best, they need to be broad, open, and congested. This is not a thought that most retailers would consider. Ingress and egress are the functions, and the concept that the doorway might also be a selling tool would seem farfetched to many.

If a selling doorway were to be devised, Lexington Avenue would be the place for it. Its two department stores are full of cues: one because its doorway is so good physically; the other because it is so bad.

One is Alexander's. It combines several features: The corner is mitered and provides an unusually spacious street corner area. The doorway, eighteen feet wide, has eight swinging doors. In fair weather they are open and function as an air door.

The entrance works very well physically; there is almost never a jam. It works even better socially. Many people stop in front of it to chat. People coming out of the store often will pause, as if to get their bearings, look about, and then move on. Some people just stand there —waiting for someone, or eating an ice cream cone.

The chart shows all of the people who stopped in the entrance area one day between noon and 1 P.M. Note that the greatest concentration of people is directly in the middle of the flow from the store. Note also that the invisible extension of the building line serves as a boundary of activity.

A block up the street is Bloomingdale's south entrance. It is a model of all that is bad in doorways. There are two revolving doors, one at either side, and between them are two swinging doors. The revolving doors do not handle the load well. When crowding is most intense, many a person will be confused by the pace, pause a fraction of a second too long, and miss a turn. If a man steps to the left to let a woman through the door first, he will find himself mousetrapped, with the line going through on his right. The two swinging doors take more effort and are much less used.

The total flow, if that is the word, is badly distributed. Of the four doors of the outer entrance, the revolving door at the right accounts for 83 percent of the people entering; the two middle doors, 8 percent

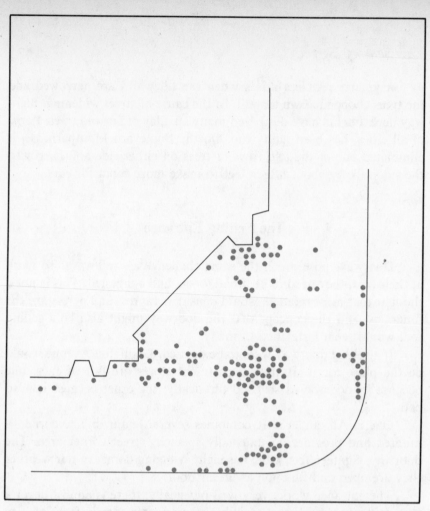

The doorway of Alexander's Department Store in New York is a great place for meeting people, conversing, or just standing. This cumulative record of where people stopped shows the tendency to cluster. Note how former building lines of chamfered corner seemed to act as an invisible boundary.

and 1 percent; the other revolving door, 8 percent. The people coming out show a somewhat similar maldistribution, skewed to the right.

That is the outer entrance. Inside there is another set of doors, plus a nun sitting on a chair. All the doors are swinging doors and they require considerable effort. As elsewhere, people queue up behind the open door rather than open one themselves. You often see someone try to open a door and then give up upon finding just how hard it is. Eventually, everyone gets in. It is a tribute to Bloomingdale's inner attractions that so many people go to so much trouble to do so. One wonders what would happen if it were made easy.

Whatever its difficulties of ingress, Bloomingdale's entrance is a very lively one socially. It has the highest densities I have ever come across at street level anywhere. Jamming at the doors is one reason, but much of the congestion is self-congestion. This is the case on

Saturdays, when Lexington becomes a recreation area. It is even more
so come Christmastime; Santa Clauses, Salvation Army people, beggars and vendors so swell the crowd that it becomes near stationary.

It is the vendors who have the greatest impact. In late afternoons
there will be a solid phalanx of them along the curb, with luggage and
leather goods and other displays directly in front of the main entrance.
On the side and around the corner will be a miscellany of minor items
—perfume, junk jewelry, marijuana wrapping paper, marked playing-
card decks for educational purposes only. There will be one or two
lookouts at one of the poles halfway up the street. The vendors are the
despair of Bloomingdale's and the police, and there are periodic
sweeps of them. There will be whistles and shouts and in less than
thirty seconds the vendors will have made off with their goods. A half
hour later they will be back.

Why do people buy from them? They offer no guarantee, no returns, and their patter virtually invites distrust. But this is the game.
The buyer feels put on his mettle. The larcenous aspect does not put
him off; it attracts him. Like the crimped card of the three-card-monte
player, it explains why he is going to get a bargain. He likes the idea of
no overhead, no sales tax. He even likes the idea that the goods might
be stolen. They are not—most are supplied by wholesalers who specialize in this provisioning—but the vendors encourage the suspicion.
(Vendor, winking: "A real steal, lady.")

But what may appeal most is the encounter itself—the fingering
of the goods, the give-and-take with the vendor. The interchanges tend
to be brusque and stimulating.

Woman: How much?
Vendor: Ten dollars.
Woman: TEN dollars?
Vendor: Ten dollars.
Woman: You gotta be kidding.
Vendor: In the store it's fifteen.
Woman: The clasp. There's only one clasp.
Vendor: Ten dollars you get one clasp. Take it, lady.
Woman: This is crazy. Gimme the brown one.

Customers stimulate other customers. I once saw a buying frenzy in
front of Bloomingdale's. Three vendors had spread out a pile of leather
handbags on the sidewalk. The usual portable radio was turned up full
volume, and over the din the vendors were shouting to people to grab
the bags before they were gone. A small crowd gathered. For a while
nobody bought. Then one woman bought a bag. Then another. More
pushed their way to the front of the crowd to see what was going on.

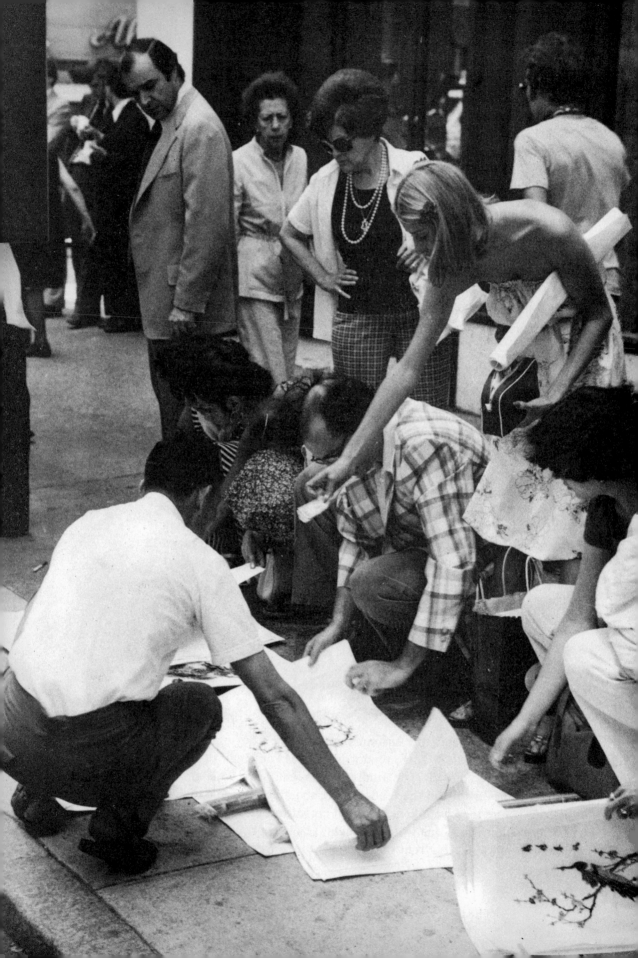

The tempo picked up. Suddenly almost everybody was thrusting dollar bills at the vendors.

Are there not some lessons? If these rascals thrive so, they must be providing something that people like. It is the marketplace at its most basic—face to face, *mano a mano,* as it is and has been in alleys and souks and bazaars all over the world.

Inside, stores may provide it. Bloomingdale's is full of models handing out cards and samples, people demonstrating appliances; the aisles are often partially blocked by stacks of goods; in the cosmetics department several pitchwomen will be at work. But all this is internal. The merchandising does not go beyond the doorways and this is true of most stores. U.S. merchants do not know how to use the street.

Japanese department stores do. For one thing, they beat the vendors at their own game. If you see street vendors hawking wares on the sidewalk beside the stores, you'll find that most of them are employees of the stores. The stores use them as come-ons. They merchandise outside to get people inside. A good example is Mitsukoshi. At its 100 percent corner in the Ginza there is a big, broad entrance that is very easy to wander into. To make it easier yet, staff people set up displays of merchandise on the street. They bring out boxes of impulse items—funny caps, sunglasses—and place them in racks just outside the door. A passerby pauses, looks at the merchandise, picks it up. A salesperson nods to the cash register just inside the store. As if enfolded by the tendril of a carnivorous plant, the passerby goes in and pays for his purchase. The first one.

Most department store doorways provide an either-or choice. You go in or you go by. There is no place for indecision, for halfway steps or second thoughts. The only transitional space usually leads to a second set of doors; save as a weather seal it is without function.

Open vestibule makes congenial tarrying place. Argosy Book Store, East Fifty-ninth Street, New York City.

A good entrance draws people—not just those who mean to go in, but those who do so out of impulse. It draws them not by forcing a decision, but by making a decision unnecessary. Let me cite Paley Park for an analogy. Its attractive paving and trees extend out to the curb. There is no clear line between park and street, and because the entry space is so broad, there is a full view of the activity within. Passersby look at it. Some will pause. Some will move a few steps closer, then a few steps more, and they are in, without having decided to be.

Store doorways should be similarly inducing. To this end the entrance should be broad and open so that it can be crowded. This is not the contradiction in terms it might appear to be. If entrances are physically cramped, there will be no slack to work with. If they are generously spaced, they will attract more social use: people holding 100 percent conversations, exchanging interminable goodbyes, just standing there. There also should be a number of people looking at their watches, waiting for friends to turn up. Entries can actively promote such use. Large, highly definable objects make ideal rendezvous points, such as the eagle at Wanamakers', or the lion at Mitsukoshi.

The merchandising should start out on the street. Instead of supinely letting vendors usurp the prime selling space, stores might put out their own displays, like Mitsukoshi. Displays flanking an entrance, especially those that invite touching, provide the kind of marginal friction that slows people down and makes them more likely to go in.

The transitional area between street and store should be selling space, not neutral space. If there is no such space, it can be created by recessing the entrance back into the store. Here, at the point of entry, is where the store should ply most vigorously its arts of lighting and display. The space should be a beckoning one, sheltered from the street and yet a part of it—easier to go into than to pass by.

The number of additional people a good entrance would attract is hard to estimate. But it would not take many to make an appreciable difference. Assume a store with an average hourly inflow of fifteen hundred people at its principal entrance. If only twenty more per hour were attracted, over a month that would add up to five thousand additional people. Most likely, more than that would be attracted.

Let me recapitulate the elements of the good street. They are as follows:

Buildings flush to the sidewalk.
Stores along the frontage.
Doors and windows on the street.

So far, not very novel. The description applies to many existing streets. But not all cities appreciate what they have in this inheritance. Nor do all planners and architects. A whole new generation has come of age for whom the norm is the suburban mall. To commend to them the basic street form, it is best to present it in entirely new terms. Speak of the multiple-access block, the continuous fenestration, the

Bookstalls on Fifth Avenue. They do busy up a sidewalk, but it is an amiable kind of congestion.

rhythmic repetition of entry points. The homely street will sound like a wonderfully fresh concept.

To continue with the list:

Second-story activity—with windows, so you can see it.

A good sidewalk, it should be just broad enough so it's slightly crowded at peak. On side streets, fifteen feet should be ample; on main streets and major avenues, twenty-five feet.

Trees. Big trees.

Seating and simple amenities.

Too many pedestrian malls and redone streets are over-designed. There's too much unified signage, too many award-winning light standards—too much good taste in general, or the pretension of it, and since many designers have the same good taste, the result is a bland conformity.

What's needed are simple benches, placed in relation to use; such basic amenities as clocks and drinking fountains, and trash containers that work. The Japanese are much more thoughtful than we are about such possibilities. In the spaces just outside department stores they are likely to provide such amenities as benches, large ashtrays, pay phones, and sculpture to meet at.

Some of the best spaces are accidental ones. My favorite has been the indented ledges of the Chase Bank at Madison and Fifty-seventh Street. They can be sat upon, albeit they're a bit high. They provide some wind protection and they still get some sun. There is usually a food cart at the corner and a good flow of passersby. The bank recently put spikes on the ledges. This has curtailed the sitting but has made the ledges more serviceable for vendors of books and pictures; they prop them up against the spikes.

Similarly, some of the most useful items of street furniture function more out of inadvertence than design. Trash receptacles with flat tops, for example, do not work well as trash receptacles but do work well as small tables. Fire standpipes are often the only sitting available on a block. Most such amenities are unintended. Why not intend them? They would cost little or nothing—a few lines on a plan—and if it's early in the game, they might be had for the asking. Here are some possibilities:

- A sitting ledge—about a foot deep, sixteen to twenty inches high.
- A shelf ledge for rearranging packages and sorting papers.
- Glass or steel walls—useful to women as mirrors for checking makeup, to men for checking trouser lengths.
- A ledge low enough to tie one's shoelaces on. Don't laugh. Watch how men use a fire hydrant.
- Chiming poles. People love to touch or rap on objects as they pass by, and if this makes an unusual sound, so much the better.

7

THE DESIGN OF SPACES

We began our research on spaces by looking at neighborhood parks and playgrounds. One of the first things that struck us was the lack of crowding in many of them. A few were jammed, but more were nearer empty than full, often in neighborhoods that ranked very high in density of people. Sheer space, it was obvious, was not of itself attracting children. But many streets were.

It is often assumed that children play in the streets for lack of playgrounds. But many children play in the streets because they like to. One of the best play areas that we came across was a block on 101st Street in East Harlem. It had its problems, but it worked. The street itself was the play area. The adjoining stoops and fire escapes provided prime viewing across the street and were highly functional for mothers and older people. There were other factors at work too, and had we been more prescient we could have saved ourselves a lot of time that we spent researching plazas. Though we did not know it then, this block had within it all the basic elements of a successful urban place.

As our studies took us nearer the center areas, the relative underuse of many spaces was even more apparent. There was much crowding, certainly, but most of it could be traced to a series of choke points—subway stations in particular. In total, these spaces are only a fraction of the center, but the crowding is so concentrated, the experience of it so abysmal, that it disproportionately colors our perception of the center. The space feels crowded, even when it is not.

By all odds, the center areas should have had many more pleasant spaces as relief. Since 1961 New York City had been giving incentive bonuses to developers who would provide plazas. If they did so, they could add twenty percent more floor space over the amount normally permitted by the zoning. So they did—without exception. Every new office building qualified for the bonus by providing a plaza or comparable space; in total, by 1972 some twenty acres of the world's most expensive open space.

Some plazas attracted lots of people. One, the plaza of the Seagram Building, was the place that helped give the city's planners the idea for the plaza bonus. Constructed in 1958, this austerely elegant place had not been designed as a people's plaza, but that is what it became. At lunchtime on a good day, there would be 150 people sitting, sunbathing, picnicking, and schmoozing. People also flocked in great numbers to 77 Water Street, known as "swingers' plaza" because of the raffish young crowd it attracted.

But on most plazas there were few people. In the middle of the lunch hour on a beautiful day the number of people sitting on plazas averaged four per thousand square feet of space—an extraordinarily low figure for so dense a center. The tightest-knit central business district anywhere contained a surprising amount of open space that went empty.

If places such as Seagram and 77 Water Street could work so well, why not others? The city was being had. For the millions of dollars of extra floor space it was handing out to developers, it had every right to demand much better spaces in return.

I put the question to the chairman of the city planning commission, Donald Elliott. As a matter of fact, I entrapped him into spending a weekend looking at time-lapse films of nothing happening on plazas. He felt tougher zoning was in order. If we could find out why the good places worked and the bad ones didn't and come up with tight guidelines, there could be a new code. Since we could expect the proposals to be contested, it would be important to document the case to a fare-thee-well.

We set to work. We began studying a cross section of spaces—in all, sixteen plazas, three small parks, and a number of odds and ends of space. I will pass over the false starts and the floundering, save to note that there was a lot and that the research was nowhere near as tidy and sequential as it can seem in the telling. Let me also note that some of our most logical theories turned out to be wrong; indeed, our research could fairly be termed a string of busted hypotheses.

The research continued for three years. The figure sounds impressive. But it is calendar time. For all practical purposes, at the end of six months we had completed the study. The city moves slowly, however. Adversaries appeared out of nowhere, and though our cause could have been assumed tantamount to mother love and the flag, we found we had to spend far more time communicating our findings than arriving at them. Eventually, in 1975, the city's Board of Estimate was to adopt the new zoning. This would be just in time, to get ahead of our story, for a new zoning crisis.

We started by charting how people used plazas. We mounted time-lapse cameras at spots overlooking the plaza—atop the Racquet Club for Seagram—and recorded the dawn-to-dusk patterns. We made periodic circuits of the plazas and noted on sighting maps where people were sitting, their gender, and whether they were alone or with others. We found we could do this in about five minutes—little more time than a simple head count would take. We also interviewed people and found where they worked, how frequently they used the plaza, and what they thought of it. But mostly we watched people to see what they did.

Most of them were young office workers from nearby buildings. Often there would be relatively few from the plaza's own building. As some secretaries confided, they would just as soon put a little distance between themselves and the boss come lunchtime. In most cases the plaza users came from a building within a three-block radius. Small parks, such as Paley and Greenacre, had a somewhat more varied mix of people—with more upper-income older people—but even here office workers predominated.

This uncomplicated demography underscores an elemental point about good spaces: supply creates demand. A good new space builds a new constituency. It gets people into new habits—such as alfresco lunches—and induces them to use new paths. It does this all very quickly. In Chicago's Loop there were few such amenities until the completion of the First National Bank Plaza. In only a few months it changed the midday way of life for thousands of office workers. Successes such as these in no way surfeit the demand for spaces. They show how great the unrealized potential can be.

Supply creates demand. A good new space builds its constituency—gets people into new habits, like eating outdoors; induces them to use new paths.

The best-used plazas are sociable places, with a higher proportion of couples and groups than you will find in less-used places. At the most-used plazas in New York, the proportion of people in twos or more runs about 50–62 percent; in the least-used, 25–30 percent. A high proportion is an index of selectivity. If people go to a place in a group or rendezvous there, it is most often because they decided to beforehand. Nor are these places less congenial to the individual. In absolute numbers, they attract more individuals than do the less-used spaces. If you are alone, a lively place can be the best place to be.

The best-used spaces have a high proportion of couples and groups. They also have a high proportion of women.

The best-used places also tend to have a higher than average proportion of women. The male-female ratio of a plaza reflects the composition of the work force and this varies from area to area. In midtown New York it runs about 60 percent male, 40 percent female. Women are more discriminating than men as to where they will sit, they are more sensitive to annoyances, and they spend more time casing a place. They are also more likely to dust off a ledge with their handkerchief.

The male-female ratio is one to watch. If a plaza has a markedly low proportion of women, something is wrong. Conversely, if it has a high proportion, the plaza is probably a good and well-managed one and has been chosen as such.

The rhythms of plaza life are much alike from place to place. In the morning hours, patronage will be sporadic: a hot dog vendor setting up his cart at the corner, a shoeshine man at the ledge, a messenger or two, an elderly pedestrian pausing for a moment, some tourists, a bag lady rummaging through her bags. If there are buildings under construction nearby, the hard hats will appear shortly after eleven with beer cans and sandwiches. Things will start to liven up.

Around noon the main clientele begins to arrive. Soon activity will be near peak and will stay there until a little before two. New York has an unusually long lunch period. In other cities it is closer to one hour than two, and in a few it is as brief as forty-five minutes. (Hartford, with its insurance companies, is one such. The city would like to see more outdoor life, but there just doesn't seem to be enough time.)

Some 80 percent of the people activity on plazas comes during the lunchtime, and there is very little of any kind after five-thirty. But this is par, and cities should not feel their downtown spaces are uniquely inefficient in this respect. Legitimate theatres operate only a few hours a day but are not the less functional for that. As we will take up later, there is much that can be done to extend the useful hours of downtown spaces. But one should not expect too much. What with, say, jazz for a late summer's afternoon, people will stick around for another hour or so. But by seven most will be on their way home.

During the lunch period, people will distribute themselves over space with considerable consistency, with some sectors getting heavy use day in and day out, others much less so. We also found that off-peak use often gives the best clues to people's preferences. When a place is jammed, people sit where they can; this may or may not be where they most want to. After the main crowd has left, however, the choices can be significant. Some parts of the plaza become empty; others continue to be used. At Seagram, a rear ledge under the trees is moderately but steadily occupied when other ledges are empty.

It seems the most uncrowded of places, but on a cumulative basis it is the best-used part of Seagram.

Men show a tendency to take the front-row seats, and if there is a kind of gate they will be the guardians of it. Women tend to favor places slightly secluded. If there are double-sided ledges parallel to the street, the inner side will usually have a higher proportion of women; the outer, of men.

Of the men up front the most conspicuous are the girl watchers. As I have noted, they put on such a show of girl watching as to indicate that their real interest is not so much the girls as the show. It is all machismo. Even in the Wall Street area, where girl watchers are especially demonstrative, you will hardly ever see one attempt to pick up a girl.

Plazas are not ideal places for striking up acquaintances. Much better is a very crowded street with lots of eating and quaffing going on. An outstanding example is the central runway of the South Street Seaport. At lunch sometimes, one can hardly move for the crush. As in musical chairs, this can lead to interesting combinations. On most plazas, however, there isn't much mixing. If there are, say, two smashing blondes on a ledge, the men nearby will usually put on an elaborate show of disregard. Look closely, however, and you will see them giving away the pose with covert glances.

Lovers are to be found on plazas, but not where you would expect them. When we first started interviewing, people would tell us to be sure to see the lovers in the rear places. But they weren't usually there. They would be out front. The most fervent embracing we've recorded on film has taken place in the most visible of locations, with the couple oblivious of the crowd. (In a long clutch, however, I have noted that one of the lovers may sneak a glance at a wristwatch.)

Certain locations become rendezvous points for groups of various kinds. The south wall of the Chase Manhattan Plaza was, for a while, a gathering point for camera bugs, the kind who are always buying new lenses and talking about them. Patterns of this sort may last no more than a season—or persist for years. A black civic leader in Cincinnati told me that when he wants to make contact, casually, with someone, he usually knows just where to look at Fountain Square. Some time ago a particular corner of a New York plaza became a favorite place for some raffish younger people. Since then there have been many changes in personnel, but it is still a favorite place for raffish younger people.

Standing patterns on the plazas are fairly regular. When people stop to talk they will generally do so athwart one of the main traffic flows, as they do on streets. They also show an inclination to station themselves near objects, such as a flagpole or a piece of sculpture.

They like well-defined places, such as steps or the border of a pool. What they rarely choose is the middle of a large space.

There are a number of explanations. The preference for pillars might be ascribed to some primeval instinct: you have a full view of all comers but your rear is covered. But this doesn't explain the inclination men have for lining up at the curb. Typically, they face inward, with their backs exposed to the vehicle traffic of the street.

Whatever their cause, people's movements are one of the great spectacles of a plaza. You do not see this in architectural photographs, which are usually devoid of human beings and are taken from a perspective that few people share. It is a misleading one. Looking down on a bare plaza, one sees a display of geometry, done almost in monochrome. Down at eye level the scene comes alive with movement and color—people walking quickly, walking slowly, skipping up steps, weaving in and out on crossing patterns, accelerating and retarding to match the moves of others. Even if the paving and the walls are gray, there will be vivid splashes of color—in winter especially, thanks to women's fondness for red coats and colored umbrellas.

There is a beauty that is beguiling to watch, and one senses that the players are quite aware of this themselves. You can see this in the way they arrange themselves on ledges and steps. They often do so with a grace that they must appreciate themselves. With its brown-gray setting, Seagram is the best of stages—in the rain, too, when an umbrella or two puts spots of color in the right places, like Corot's red dots.

Let us turn to the factors that make for such places. The most basic one is so obvious it is often overlooked: people. To draw them, a space should tap a strong flow of them. This means location, and, as the old adage has it, location and location. The space should be in the heart of downtown, close to the 100 percent corner—preferably right on top of it.

Because land is cheaper further out, there is a temptation to pick sites away from the center. There may also be some land for the asking —some underused spaces, for example, left over from an ill-advised civic center campus of urban renewal days. They will be poor bargains. A space that is only a few blocks too far might as well be ten blocks for all the people who will venture to walk to it.

People *ought* to walk to it, perhaps; the exercise would do them good. But they don't. Even within the core of downtown the effective radius of a good place is about three blocks. About 80 percent of the users will have come from a place within that area. This does indicate a laziness on the part of pedestrians and this may change a bit, just as the insistence on close-in parking may. But there is a good side to the constrained radius. Since usage is so highly localized, the addition of other good open spaces will not saturate demand. They will increase it.

Given a fine location, it is difficult to design a space that will not attract people. What is remarkable is how often this has been accomplished. Our initial study made it clear that while location is a prerequisite for success, it in no way assures it. Some of the worst plazas are in the best spots—General Motors' sunken plaza, for one, next to one of the great outdoor rooms of New York.

All of the plazas and small parks that we studied had good locations; most were on the major avenues, some on attractive side streets. All were close to bus stops or subway stations and had strong pedestrian flows on the sidewalks beside them. Yet when we rated them according to the number of people sitting at peak time, there was a wide range: from 160 people at 77 Water Street to 17 at 280 Park Avenue.

How come? The first factor we studied was the sun. We thought it might well be the critical one, and our first time-lapse studies seemed to bear this out. Subsequent studies did not. As I will note later, they did show that sun was important but did not explain the differences in the popularity of plazas.

Nor did aesthetics. We never thought ourselves capable of measuring such factors, but we did expect our research to show that the most successful plazas tended to be the most pleasing visually. Seagram seemed very much a case in point. Here again there was conflicting evidence. Clean, elegant Seagram was successful, but so was the "fun plaza" at 77 Water Street, which some architects looked on as pure kitsch. The elegance and purity of a complex's design, we had to conclude, had little relationship to the usage of the spaces around it.

The designer sees the whole building—the clean verticals, the horizontals, the way Mies turned his corners, and so on. The person sitting on the plaza may be quite unaware of such features. He is more apt to be looking in the other direction: not up at the other elevations but at what is going on at eye level. To say this is not to slight the designer's eye or his handling of space. The area round Seagram is a great urban place and its relationship to McKim, Mead, & White's Racquet Club across the street is integral to it. My personal feeling is that the fine sense of enclosure contributes to the enjoyment of using the Seagram Plaza. But I certainly cannot prove this with figures.

Another factor we considered was the shape of spaces. Members of the commission's urban design group believed this was very important and hoped our findings would support tight criteria for proportions and placement. They were particularly anxious to rule out strip plazas—long, narrow spaces that were little more than enlarged sidewalks, and empty of people more times than not. The urban design

It is difficult to design a space that will not attract people. What is remarkable is how often this has been accomplished.

group believed a developer should not get bonuses for such strips, and to that end it wanted to rule out spaces the length of which was more than three times the width.

Our data did not support such criteria. While it was true that most strip plazas were little used, it did not follow that their shape was the reason. Some squarish plazas were little used too, and, conversely, several of the most heavily used spaces were in fact long, narrow strips. One of the five most popular sitting places in New York is essentially an indentation in a building, long and narrow. Our research did not prove shape unimportant or designers' instincts misguided. As with the sun, however, it proved that other factors were more critical.

If not the shape of space, what about the *amount* of it? Some conservationists believed this would be the key factor. In their view, people seek open space as a relief from overcrowding and it would follow that places with the greatest sense of space and light and air would draw the best. If we ranked plazas by the amount of space they provided, there surely would be a positive correlation between space and people.

Once again we found no clear relationship. Several of the smallest spaces had the largest number of people, and several of the largest spaces had the least number of people. The latter, it should be noted, were not large at all by recreation standards, the four largest running around seventy-five thousand square feet. It is when civic spaces get really big that size begins to be a problem. Too much of it, unenclosed, is the bane of many a public space.

What about the amount of *sittable* space? Here we began to get close. As we tallied the number of linear feet of sitting space, we could see that the plazas with the most tended to be among the most popular. The relationship was rough. We did not weight the figures for qualitative factors; we counted a foot of concrete ledge the same as a foot of comfortable bench with back and arm rests. Had we weighted the sitting-space figures, there would have been a nicer conformance with the chart on usage. We considered this but decided it would be too manipulative. Once you start working backward this way, there's no end to it.

Nor good reason. No matter how many other variables we checked, one basic point kept coming through. We at last recognized that it was the major one.

People tend to sit most where there are places to sit.

This may not strike the reader as an intellectual bombshell, and now that I look back on our study I wonder why it was not more apparent to us from the beginning. Sitting space, to be sure, is only one of many variables, and without a control situation as a measure, one

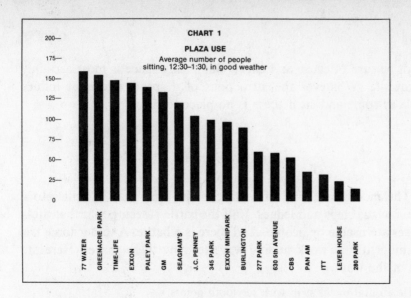

CHART 1

PLAZA USE

Average number of people
sitting, 12:30–1:30, in good weather

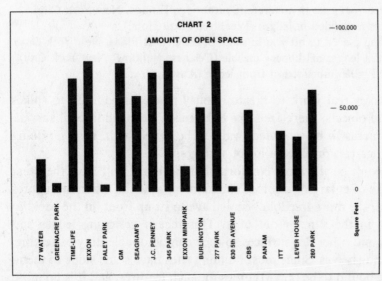

CHART 2

AMOUNT OF OPEN SPACE

Square Feet

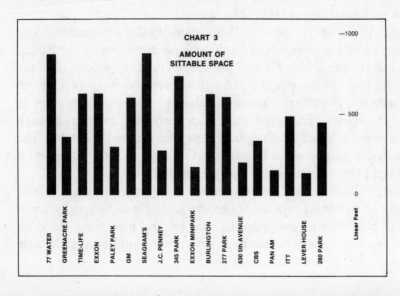

CHART 3

**AMOUNT OF
SITTABLE SPACE**

Linear Feet

cannot be sure of cause and effect. But sitting space is most certainly prerequisite. Whatever the attractions of a space, it cannot induce people to come and sit if there is no place to sit.

Integral Seating

The most basic kind of seating is the kind that is built into a place, such as steps and ledges. Half the battle is seeing to it that these features are usable by people. And there is a battle. Another force has been diligently at work finding ways to deny these spaces. Here are some of the ways:

> Horizontal metal strip with sawtooth points.
> Jagged rocks set in concrete (Southbridge Houses, New York City).
> Spikes imbedded in ledges (Peachtree Plaza Hotel).
> Railing placed to hit you in small of back (GM Plaza, New York City).
> Canted ledges of slippery marble (Celanese Building, New York City).
> Metal balls imbedded in front ledge (Austin, Texas).

It takes real work to create a lousy place. In addition to spikes and metal objects, there are steps to be made steep, additional surveillance cameras to be mounted, walls to be raised high. Just *not* doing such things can produce a lot of sitting space.

It won't be the most comfortable kind but it will have the great advantage of enlarging choice. The more sittable the inherent features are made, the more freedom people have to sit up front, in the back, to the side, in the sun, or out of it. This means designing ledges and parapets and other flat surfaces so they can do double duty as seating, tables, and shelves. Since most building sites have some slope in them, there are bound to be opportunities for such features, and it is no more trouble to leave them sittable than not.

This is one of the lessons of Seagram. Philip Johnson recounts that when Ludwig Mies van der Rohe saw people sitting on the ledges, he was quite surprised. He had never dreamt they would. But the architects had valued simplicity. So there were no fussy railings, no shrubbery, no gratuitous changes in elevation, no ornamentation to clutter the spaces. The steps were made easy and inviting. Though there was not a bench on the place, it proved eminently sittable. The periphery includes some six hundred feet of ledge and step space and it is just right for sitting, eating, and sunbathing.

Ledges, then, should be sittable. But how should this be defined? To stand up in zoning provisions there would have to be specific criteria as to how high or low ledges should be, and how deep. Since we could expect adversary proceedings ahead, we would need to be able to back up our criteria with facts.

Most ledges are inherently sittable. With ingenuity and additional work, they can be made unsittable.

The proceedings turned out to be adversary in a way we had not expected. The attack came on the grounds that our criteria were *too* specific, and it came not from developers but from members of a community board. Their park-and-open-space chairman said that it would be wrong to spell out the requirements in detail. Instead, the zoning should lay down a broad directive—for example, make the plaza sittable—and let the how-to of this be worked out in give-and-take across the table between developer, architect, and community-board people.

Let me pause to deal with this argument. It is a persuasive one, especially for laymen, and at the inevitable moment in zoning meetings when confusion reigns, someone will get up and say, let's cut through this crap and get down to basics. Much applause. Be done with zoning gobbledygook. Down with bureaucratic nit-picking.

But lack of guidelines is a much worse problem. If the homework has not been done beforehand, the specifics hashed out around the table will amount to spot zoning, and at its loosest. Firm criteria can become outdated; but so can building codes. The moral is to keep them up to date, not to do away with them.

Lack of guidelines, it was said, give architects more freedom to

Most incentive zoning
ordinances are very
specific as to what the
developer gets. They
are mushy as to what
he should give. You
must prescribe in
detail. And get it in
writing.

innovate. If this were so, the period after the passage of the 1961 zoning would have been a golden age for plaza design. There were virtually no guidelines. And very few good plazas were built. Lack of guidelines was a force for mediocrity. Developers wanted the minimum done, and done conventionally. And that is what they got.

Ambiguity as to what the developer must provide is an invitation to provide little. Most incentive zoning ordinances are very specific as to what the developer *gets*. The problem is that many are rather mushy as to what he should give—and mushier yet as to what will happen later if he doesn't. Vague directives, as a number of cities have learned, are unenforceable. You must prescribe in detail. And get it in writing.

Sitting Heights

One guideline we thought would be easy to establish was for sitting heights. It seemed obvious enough that somewhere around sixteen to seventeen inches would probably be the optimum. But how much higher or lower could a surface be and still be sittable? Thanks to slopes, several of the most popular ledges provided a range of continuously variable heights. The front ledge at Seagram, for example, started at seven inches at one corner and rose to forty-four inches at the other. Here was an opportunity for a definitive study, we thought; by recording over time how many people sat at what heights, we would get a statistical measure of preferences.

We didn't. At any given time there would be clusters of people at one height, fewer on another. But such correlations did not last very long. When we cumulated many days of observations, we found that people had been distributing themselves with remarkable evenness over the whole range of heights. We had to conclude that people will sit almost anywhere between a height of one foot and three, and this was the range that was to be specified in the zoning. People will sit lower or higher, of course, but there are apt to be special conditions—a wall too high for most adults to mount but just right for teenagers.

A dimension that is
truly important is the
human backside. It is a
dimension many
architects ignore. Not
often will you find a
ledge or bench that is
deep enough to be
sittable on both sides.
Some aren't sittable on
one.

A dimension that is truly important is the human backside. It is a dimension many architects ignore. Rarely will you find a ledge or bench that is deep enough to be sittable on both sides. Some aren't deep enough to be sittable on one. Most frustrating are the ledges just deep enough to tempt people to sit on both sides, but too shallow to let them do so comfortably. At peak times people may sit on both sides but they won't be comfortable doing it. They will be sitting on the forward edge, awkwardly.

Thus to another of our startling findings: ledges and spaces two backsides deep seat more people than those that are not as deep. Our recommended depth was arrived at quite pragmatically. The minimum-depth ledge we came across that was consistently used on both sides was thirty inches deep. (Front ledge, 277 Park Avenue). If a ledge is at least that deep and is accessible on both sides, the length of each side counts as seating.

For a few additional inches of depth, then, a developer can double the amount of his ledge-sitting space. This does not mean that double the number of people will use the ledge. They probably won't. But that is not the point. The benefit of the additional space is social comfort. There will be more room for groups and individuals to sort themselves out, more choice, and more perception of choice.

Steps work for the same reason. They afford an infinity of possible groupings, and the excellent sight lines make all the seating great for watching the theatre of the street. Steps are not very comfortable; they are cold, there is no real back support, and there is often not enough depth for comfort. With no sacrifice of their stair function, however, they could be made more comfortable. Landscape architect Paul Friedberg specifies a tread depth of at least fourteen inches for his steps; since this marries well with a low riser of, say, six or six and a half inches, the steps are also very easy going up and down on.

We decided not to credit steps as required sitting space. If they were, developers could have too easy an out, and some plazas would be mostly steps and little else. But steps should be planned with people's sitting tendencies in mind. This is especially the case with corners of steps.

To understand why, let us look again at the social life of plazas. The majority of the people who use plazas are in pairs or groups of three or more. Most sitting is linear. This is fine for individuals, all right for pairs, but not very good for three or more. Left to arrange things for themselves, as with chairs, people in groups will position themselves at angles somewhere around forty-five degrees. This is the most comfortable for talking, and the most comfortable for brown bag lunching.

Without knowing it, architects design for such groupings when they have step corners, and especially so with a ledge abutting at a right angle. Groups are attracted to these places. And so, not so paradoxically, are pedestrians on the move. Seagram is a classic example. People who are entering and leaving the building by the main Park Avenue doorways walk on the diagonal between the doorways and the step corners. In the process they bisect what are often the busiest eating and sitting spaces on the steps. Conflict? Theoretically, yes. Practically, no. For all the bustle, or because of it, the sitters don't seem to mind. Nor do the walkers. Sometimes tiptoeing, they will thread their way through the clumps of people rather than take long detours around them.

We found similar patterns at other places. All things being equal, you can calculate that where pedestrian flows bisect a sittable place, that is where people will most likely sit. And it is not so perverse of them. It is by choice that they do. If there is some congestion, it is an amiable one.

Circulation and sitting, in sum, are not antithetical but complementary. I stress this because a good many planners think the two should be kept separate. More to the point, so do some zoning codes. New York's called for "pedestrian circulation areas" separate from "activity areas" for sitting. People ignore such boundaries.

We felt that pedestrian circulation through and within plazas should be encouraged. Plazas that are sunken or elevated tend to attract low flows, and for that reason the zoning specifies that plazas be not more than three feet below street level or above it. The easier the flow between street and plaza, the more likely they are to come in and tarry and sit.

This is true of the handicapped also. If a place is planned with their needs in mind, the place is apt to function more easily for everyone. Drinking fountains that are low enough for wheelchair users are low enough for children. Walkways that are made easier for the handicapped by ramps, handrails, and steps of gentle pitch are easier for all. The guidelines make such amenities mandatory, specifying, among other things, that steps along the main walkways have treads at least 11 inches deep and risers no higher than 7.5 inches, and that ramps be placed alongside them. (Hindsight indicates we should have made the dimensions 12 inches and 6.5 inches). For the benefit of the handicapped, it is required that at least 5 percent of the seating spaces have backrests. These are not segregated for the handicapped. No facilities are segregated. The idea is to make all of the place useful for everyone.

Benches

Benches are design artifacts the purpose of which is to punctuate architectural photographs. They are most often sited in modular form, spaced equidistant from one another in a symmetry that is pleasing in plan view. They are not very good, however, for sitting. There are usually too few of them; they are too short and too narrow; they are isolated from other benches and from what action there is to look at.

Let's take the matter of size and placement. The social situation is more important than the physical. When there are few people around, the comfortable distance between strangers is fairly wide. If you are

Benches are design artifacts the purpose of which is to punctuate architectural photographs.

one of the few people sitting, and a stranger comes and sits on your bench instead of an empty one, there can be a strong feeling of intrusion. It's like sitting in a near empty theatre and having someone come and take a seat close to yours.

As a space fills up, social distances contract. Now one does not mind strangers sitting closer by. They have to, so it is in order. Crowding, in a sense, can make crowding more tolerable.

Watch how benches fill up. The first arrival will usually take the end of a bench, not the middle. The next arrival will take the end of another bench. Subsequent arrivals head for whatever end spots are not taken. Only when there are few other places left will people sit in the middle of the bench, and some will elect to stand.

Since it's the ends of the benches that do most of the work, it could be argued that benches ought to be shortened so they're all end and no middle. But the unused middles are functional for *not* being used. They provide buffer space. They also provide choice, and if it is the least popular choice, that does not negate its utility.

Small benches are mean. Sometimes they are purposely made small so they will be too short for undesirables to sleep on. Most times they are made small out of ignorance of their ordinary functions. Socially and physically, benches are best when they are generously proportioned. Wherever possible they should be at least eight feet long. Continuous lengths of benches, like ledges and steps, provide a satisfying range of sitting possibilities. The conventional park bench is often laid out in a continuous line along walkways, and it functions very well that way.

This is linear sitting and it has certain advantages in high-density situations. Because they are looking outward, a lot of people can sit quite close without impinging on others' privacy. With what Erving Goffman termed "civil inattention" one can note others' presence and leave it at that. What makes people uncomfortable is direct eye contact with strangers. True, people like to look at other people, but they don't like to be caught at it and they don't like to be looked *at*. In filming people's behavior in public places, I have found that cameras do not bother them. But if they see me looking directly at them, if only for a second or so, they are on to the game and they sometimes get quite annoyed. I do not blame them.

I noted earlier that when they have the choice, people in groups of two or more like to position themselves so that they are catty-cornered from each other—that is at an angle between forty-five and ninety degrees. It is easy to position benches to give such choice. Instead of stringing them out on a line, all that has to be done is to place some of the benches at right angles to others. Rarely is this done, or even considered. In the few cases where it has been done, the benches are apt to be too far apart for a comfortable social distance—like a coffee table that is just a few inches maddeningly out of reach of the sofa.

Benches placed at right angles should not be butted up against each other. Some space ought to be left. If people are to sit comfortably across from each other, there should be legroom and some social distance. How much? I have made a study of twosomes and threesomes in sitting situations and the nose-to-nose distances they elect. These were eye estimates, and not very precise: I had to forswear tape measures. But I found ranges fairly consistent. Eighteen inches is a workable minimum. Young lovers get closer than that but most people do not. A workable maximum is thirty inches. Between these limits the great majority of nose-to-nose distances will fall. The most important variable is noise. Outdoors in the city can be very noisy, and to talk easily—and hear easily—people inch themselves much closer in noisy places than quieter ones.

For bench placement, these figures indicate an arrangement such as this:

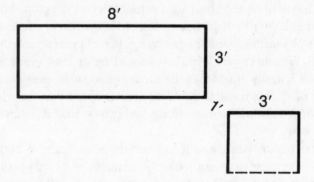

If the corner-to-corner distance between the benches is about a foot, they will be far enough apart to provide legroom but close enough for comfortable conversation. There will also be enough room for brown bags. Simply by shifting a few inches, people can easily adjust distances, as instinctively they do so well.

There is another advantage to benches. If it turns out they are not in the best locations, designers can move them to better ones. It is highly unusual for this to be done, however. It would call for firsthand observation of how the benches are working. Designers find it very difficult to do such observation, let alone recognize that the design is not working the way they thought it would.

This is why designers should be chary of too much concrete. If they freeze all their sitting spaces in concrete, they freeze their assumptions—that, for example, people want to sit facing away from the action. If it proves wrong there is not much that will be done about it.

This has been a problem with a number of pedestrian malls. All the design bets were made before the malls were completed. On opening day they were jammed and were proclaimed successes. When the bands stopped playing, however, and the crowds left, the malls were put to the test of normal usage. There were lessons—harsh lessons— but no easy way to heed them. And they were not heeded.

Designers should be especially careful of amphitheaters. Too many of those I have seen in use have an integral flaw: there is a large gap between the first rows and the performers. This makes difficult that arc of attention between performer and audience that is so critical. And it is not remedied by turning up the volume on the amplifiers. Watch a good street performer work a crowd. He beckons them closer. It's the people in the first two or three ranks that he concentrates on. Immediacy is just as important for small-group programs in parks and squares. For an audience of up to about 125 people just a plain space, grassy or paved, will serve admirably. If the audience is left to figure its own disposition it will probably gather around in a fairly cohesive pattern. People are quite good at this. For large events, such as a concert by the local symphony, much more elaborate facilities are in order: large portable stages, heavy duty amplifiers and equipment, and the like. Amphitheater seating can be fine, but a facility designed to meet loads of 1,000 or more people can be out of scale for the individual and small-group attractions that are the staple of the summer fare of public squares.

There ought to be more experimentation. The stock designs of the bench manufacturers come in all shapes and sizes and lend themselves well to different configurations. Small platform benches serve well as links between benches and are themselves eminently multipurpose. If designers want to try out a new layout, people will be very quick to let them know by their behavior whether it works or not. If someone looks. It would be most novel, and valuable, if there were a plan that countenances the possibility that the initial layout could be improved —that calls for postconstruction evaluation of the lessons, and action to make use of them. It would also help if the time lag was a year or less rather than a decade or more.

Chairs

We come now to a wonderful invention: the movable chair. Having a back, it is comfortable, and even more so if it has armrests as well. But the big asset is movability. Chairs enlarge choice: to move into the sun, out of it: to move closer to someone, further away from another.

The possibility of choice is as important as the exercise of it. If

People like to move movable chairs. Even though there appears to be no logical reason, they may move a chair a foot or more before sitting on it—as did this woman at Chase Manhattan Plaza.

you know you can move if you want to, you can feel all the more comfortable staying put. This is why, perhaps, people so often approach a chair and then, before sitting on it, move the chair a few inches this way or that, finally ending up with the chair just about where it was in the first place. These moves are functional. They are a declaration of one's free will to oneself, and rather satisfying. In this one small matter you are the master of your fate.

Small moves can say things to other people. If a newcomer chooses a chair next to a couple in a crowded situation, he may make several moves with the chair. He is conveying a message. Sorry about the closeness, but it can't be helped and I am going to respect your privacy as you will mine. A reciprocal shift of a chair may signal acknowledgment.

Chair arranging by groups is a ritual worth watching. In a group of three or four women, one may be dominant and direct the sitting, including the fetching of an extra chair. More times, the members of the group work it out themselves, often with false starts and second choices. The chair arranging can take quite a bit of time on occasion— it is itself a form of recreation—but people enjoy it. Watching these exercises in civility is one of the pleasures of a good place.

Fixed individual seats deny choice. They may be good to look at, and in the form of stools, metal love seats, granite cubes, and the like, they make interesting decorative elements. That is their primary function. For sitting, however, they are inflexible and socially uncomfortable.

Fixed individual seats deny choice. The designer is saying you sit here and you sit there. This is arrogant of him. People are much better at this than designers.

Social distance between people is a subtle dimension, ever changing. But the distances of fixed seats do not change and that is why they are rarely quite right for anybody. Love seats may be all right for lovers, but they are too close for acquaintances and much too close for strangers. Loners tend to take them over, propping their feet on the other seat so no one else will sit on it.

Where space is at a premium—in theatres, stadia—fixed seats are a necessity. In open spaces, however, they are uncalled for; there is so much space around them that the compression makes for awkward sitting. In theatres strangers sit next to each other without qualm; convention makes it tolerable. In open spaces, however, the closeness is manufactured. The designer has contrived it and he will brook no changes. Now, you sit here, the seating says, and you sit there. There is a manipulative cuteness about these groupings that makes some people balk. On one campus a group of metal love seats was cemented to the paving with epoxy glue; in short order they were wrenched out of position by students. The designer is unrepentant. His love seats have won several design awards.

Maintenance people are often hostile to chairs and before the fact will prophesy that most will be soon stolen. We could not mandate them in the zoning guidelines but we did build in an incentive. We credited chairs with thirty inches of sitting space, though most are only about nineteen inches wide. The city's building department objected. It objected to the idea of movable chairs at all. It had the responsibility of seeing that builders lived up to requirements. Suppose the chairs were broken or stolen and the builder didn't replace them? Whether the department would ever check up in any event was a moot point, but it was true that the fewer amenities there were to monitor, the easier the job would be.

Happily, the chairs stayed in. One reason was the documentation we could produce on the excellent record of the chairs at places such as Paley and Greenacre parks, and plazas such as 77 Water Street. There had been very little vandalism at any of them.

The record since then has been equally encouraging. The chairs have become a standard amenity at new places, and with few maintenance problems. Managements have been enlivening existing spaces and, at a number of them, adding considerably more chairs than the guidelines required. One reason has been cost. When we drew up the guidelines in the early seventies, about the cheapest chair available ran around $75, and the Bertoia chair, the new classic of chairs, about $150. Since then it would appear that every small city from Italy to Taiwan has been turning out white vinyl-coated steel-mesh chairs. The price is now down to under $10. There is really no point to stealing them.

The most generous provider has been the Metropolitan Museum of Art. On the spaces on either side of its front steps it puts out up to two hundred movable chairs, and it leaves them out, twenty-four hours a day, seven days a week. The Met figured it would cost less to buy replacements for lost or damaged chairs than to have the chairs brought in every night and put out every morning. The system has worked fine.

One of the pleasantest findings has been the beneficial effect movable chairs have had on ledge and benches. They provide linear seating —fine for individuals or twosomes but ordinarily not very good for groups. When there are three or four people, you will note that they often will improvise a group arrangement—with one or two standing, rather than sitting on the flanks.

This was particularly the case at Lincoln Center. Its clientele was heavily weighted with groups, and before matinees the travertine ledges of the tree planters would be very sociable planters. But even when there was extra room on the ledges, one or more members of a group would stand so that they all would be in a face-to-face configuration. The centerpiece would often be a bottle of wine and sandwiches on the ledge.

I recommended the provision of several hundred movable chairs. There was plenty of sitting space per se already, but I felt the best use of chairs would be as supplements to ledge seating. That is the way it worked out. There was much use of chairs as individual seating, but the most frequent use was to convert the ledges' linear seating to face-to-face seating for groups. We had a devil of a time getting the chairs out on the plazas—a key functionary was dead set against them—but once they were out, people helped themselves and did the chair arranging.

It was a convivial arranging, and the plazas never looked so pleasant or worked so well. As for vandalism, when the chairs were secured at night with wires and padlocks, there were no losses.

The battle was won; the cause was lost. Lincoln Center reverted. There are chairs down in the storage areas but they are not put out anymore. They might be stolen. If they are not put out, however, they will not be stolen. So they are not put out and there is no problem. Thus the institutional imperative.

A more successful trial took place on the plaza of the Dallas City Hall. The building was striking, but the plaza was near empty most of the time, and one factor was the seating. It was a series of concrete benches laid out in a modular pattern that had little to do with people flows or sun. Of thirty-four benches only three were sited so that they would be in the shade of a tree. There was considerable sentiment for demolishing the benches. If chairs were provided, however, the benches might prove useful in other ways—as tables, for example. So they did. But the most frequent use of the benches has been as footrests.

A salute to grass is in order. It is a wonderfully adaptable substance, and while it is not the most comfortable seating, it is fine for napping, sunbathing, picnicking, and Frisbee throwing. Like movable chairs, it also has the great advantage of offering people the widest possible choice of sitting arrangements. There are an infinity of possible groupings, but you will note that the most frequent has people self-positioned at oblique angles from each other.

A salute to grass. It is so adaptable; fine for sitting, napping, sunbathing, picnicking, and Frisbee playing. Like chairs, it provides a limitless choice of arrangements.

Grass offers a psychological benefit as well. A patch of green is a refreshing counter to granite and concrete, and when people are asked what they would like to see in a park, trees and grass usually are at the top of the list. The citizen groups that did the homework on the competition for the redo of Copley Square in Boston were united on one prime requirement: that it be soft and green. So it will be, with a common and lots of trees.

If there are some hills or slopes, so much the better for the grass, and if there are none they can be created. One of New York's most delightful new parks, Washington Market Park, was created on a flat

Dallas developer Harlan Crow converted the ground floor of a parking garage to several shops, a Chinese take-out place, and a gourmet delicatessen; planted a bosque of honey locusts; put out tables and chairs. The result is one of the most congenial spaces in town.

Addition of movable chairs at Dallas City Hall Plaza allows concrete benches to be put to highest and best use.

Washington Market Park, New York City. Favored seating here is grass.

site. Landscape architect Lee Weintraub had a hillock of earth created in the middle and planted it with grass. It has become a favored place for picnic lunches for office workers; off-peak, children take over. Another fine grassy place is the lawn of Bryant Park. The capacity is great; on a sunny day there will be clusters of people all over, and one must step carefully not to encroach.

How Much Seating?

A question we had to resolve for the guidelines was the amount of sitting space to be required. We spent a lot of time on this—much too much, I now realize—and I'm tempted to recount our various calculations to demonstrate how conscientious we were. The truth is that almost any reasonable yardstick would work as well as ours. It is the fact of one that is important.

This said, now let me tell you how conscientious we were. We measured and remeasured the sitting space on the plazas and small parks in midtown and downtown New York. As sitting space, we included all the spaces meant for people to sit on, such as benches, and the spaces they sat on though they were not meant to, such as ledges. Although architects' plans were helpful we did most of the measuring ourselves, with a tape, in the process stirring much curiosity from guards and passersby.

Next, we related the amount of sitting space to the size of the plaza. The square feet of sitting space on the best-used plazas ran between 6 and 10 percent of the total open space. As a ballpark figure, it seemed that somewhere around 10 percent would be a reasonable minimum to require.

For other comparisons we turned to linear feet. This is a more precise measure of sitting space than square feet, and a more revealing one. As long as there is some clearance at one's back, the additional square inches behind do not matter very much. It is the edges of sitting space that do the work, and it is the edges that should be made the most of.

For a basis of comparison, we took the number of linear feet around the total site. Since the perimeter includes the building, the distance is a measure of the bulk of the project and its impact on the surrounding environment. Amenities should therefore be in some proportion to it. On the most popular plazas, there were almost as many feet of sitting space as there were perimeter feet. This suggested that, as a minimum, developers could be asked to provide that amount of sitting space.

Even on the best plazas, the architects could have done better. To get an idea of how much better, we calculated the additional space that could have been provided on various plazas rather easily, while the original plans were being drafted. We did not posit any changes in the basic layout, nor did we take the easy way of adding a lot of benches. We concentrated on seating that would be integral to the architect's design.

In most cases it was possible to add as much as 50 percent more sitting space, and very good space at that. The Exxon Plaza, for example, has a large pool bordered by two side ledges that you can't sit on. With a few changes, such as a broadening of the ledges, the seating capacity of the plaza could have been doubled. All in all, these examples indicated, developers could easily provide as many feet of sitting space as there are feet around the perimeter of the project.

The requirement finally settled on was a compromise: one linear foot of sitting space for every thirty square feet of plaza space. It was to prove quite serviceable; indeed, with no changes it was adopted verbatim in the zoning regulations of many cities. By all accounts, developers have been meeting the requirement with no trouble.

It could be argued that the requirement should be stiffer. But the exact ratio is not as important as the fact of one. Once an architect and developer start considering ways of making a place sittable, it will be difficult not to surpass any minimum. And other things follow. More thought must be given to the probable pedestrian flows, the placement and pitch of steps, planting beds for trees, and the like. Embarked on

The formula for figuring the amount of sitting space required was a back-of-the-envelope compromise. It has been enshrined in countless zoning ordinances across the country, verbatim. It works fine.

such a course, it becomes almost easier to create a first-rate place than a mediocre one. One felicity leads to another.

Relationship to the Street

Let us turn to a more difficult consideration. With the kind of amenities we have been discussing, there are second chances. If the designers have goofed on seating, more and better seating can be provided. If they have been too stingy with trees, more trees can be planted. If there is no food, a food cart can be put in—possibly, a small pavilion or gazebo. If there is no water feature, a benefactor might be persuaded to donate a small pool or fountain. Thanks to such retrofitting, spaces regarded as hopeless dogs have been given new life.

What is most difficult to change, however, is what is most important—the location of the space and its relationship to the street. The real estate people are right about location, location, location. For a space to function truly well it must be central to the constituency it is to serve—and if not in physical distance, in visual accessibility. Monument Circle in Indianapolis and Fountain Square in Cincinnati are excellent examples.

The street functions as part of the plaza or square; indeed, it is often hard to tell where the street leaves off and the plaza begins. The social life of the spaces flows back and forth between them. And the most vital space of all is often the street corner. Watch one long enough and you will see how important it is to the life of the large spaces. There will be people in 100 percent conversations or prolonged goodbyes. If there is a food vendor at the corner, like Gus at Seagram, people will be clustered around him, and there will be a brisk foot traffic between corner and plaza.

It is a great show, and one of the best ways to make the most of it is, simply, not to wall off the plaza from it. Frederick Law Olmsted spoke of an "interior park" and an "outer park," and he argued that the latter—the surrounding streets—was vital to the enjoyment of the former. He thought it an abomination to separate the two with walls or, worse yet, with a spiked iron fence. "In expression and in association," he said, "it is in the most distinct contradiction and discord with all the sentiment of a park. It belongs to a jail or to the residence of a despot who dreads assassination."

Walls are put up in the mistaken notion that they will make a space feel safer. They make it feel isolated and gloomy.

But walls are still being put up, usually in the mistaken notion that they will make the space feel safer. They do not. As we will take up in the chapter on undesirables, they make a space feel isolated and gloomy. Lesser defensive measures can work almost as much damage. The front rows of a space—whether ledges or steps or benches—are the best of sitting places, yet they are often modified against human use. At the General Motors Building on Fifth Avenue, the front ledges face out on one of the greatest of promenades. But you cannot sit on the ledges for more than a minute or so. There is a fussy little railing that catches you right in the small of your back. I do not think it was deliberately planned to do so. But it does and you cannot sit for more than a few moments before your back hurts. Another two inches of clearance for the railing and you would be comfortable. But day after day, year after year, one of the great front rows goes scarcely used, for want of two inches. Canted ledges, especially ones of polished marble, are another nullifying feature. You can almost sit on them if you keep pressing down on your heel hard enough.

Another way to cut a plaza off from the street is to sink it or elevate it. A few feet either way will not make much difference, but once past three feet the space can become relatively inaccessible. It is not a physical matter so much as a psychological one. A space that is materially higher or lower than street level requires a decision. One plaza that people could be expected to use but do not is only a few feet higher than comparable ones that people do use. But it seems much higher. The steps are narrow, pitched at a sharp angle, and sharply defined by railings.

Sight lines are important. If people do not see a space, they will not use it. In the center of Kansas City was a municipal park just high enough above eye level that passersby did just that—passed by. It was a lost park until redone with a much more accessible street border. Similarly lost was a small plaza in Seattle. It was well located and enjoyed lots of whatever sun Seattle got. It would likely have been very popular if people could have seen it from the street. They never could. It was tucked away on a mezzanine level.

Unless there is a compelling reason, open spaces should not be sunk. With only a few exceptions, sunken plazas are dead plazas. You see few people in them. If there are any storefronts, some will turn out to have dummy displays to mask the vacancies. Unless the plaza is on the way to a subway, why go down into it? Once there, you feel as if you were at the bottom of a well. People look at you. But you don't look up at them.

A keen observer of spaces is the dancer Marilyn Woods. With her troupe, she has staged choreographic "celebrations" of public places across the country. The best places, not too surprisingly, make for the best performances and the most appreciative audiences. Seagram and Cincinnati's Fountain Square are at the top of her list. At the bottom are sunken plazas. They felt dead, she recalls, as if a wall had been put between the dancers and the audience.

What about Rockefeller Plaza? It has a sunken plaza in the mid-

Sight lines are important. If people do not see a space, they will not use it.

dle and it is a very successful place. So it is. But those who cite it as an argument for sunken plazas should take a closer look at how it works. The lower plaza is only a small part of a major urban space, and it is not the part where most of the people are. They are in the tiers of an amphitheater: many are at street level, on the space that slopes down from Fifth Avenue, or on the balconylike walks on either side of the plaza. Only about 20 percent are on the lower level. In a sense, they are shills for the place. In winter there is ice skating; in summer, an open-air café.

The plaza of the first National Bank of Chicago is also quite sunken—some eighteen feet beneath street level. This was to provide retail banking frontage, Illinois banks being enjoined from branch banking. Sunken or no, it has proved one of the most successful plazas in the country, with well over a thousand people on it at lunch on a nice day. It is successful because just about everything has been done to make it successful—there is plenty of sitting space, an outdoor café, a fountain, murals by Chagall, and usually music and entertainment at midday.

The First National plaza has an excellent relationship to the street. The broad sidewalks are part of its space and there is a strong secondary use of the plaza by the passersby. Many pause to look at what's going on. Some will drift down a few steps, then a few more. Like Rockefeller Plaza, it functions as an amphitheater, with several tiers of people looking at people who are looking at people who are looking at the show.

A good space beckons people in, and the progression from street to interior is critical in this respect. Ideally, the transition should be such that it's hard to tell where one ends and the other begins. You shouldn't have to make a considered decision to enter; it should be almost instinctive. Paley Park is the best of examples. The sidewalk in front of it is an integral part of the park and is paved with the same material, planted with the same trees and flowers. The steps are easy and inviting and on either side are curved sitting ledges. In this foyer-like space you can usually see someone waiting for someone else—it is a convenient rendezvous—and perhaps a group standing in the middle of the steps.

Passersby use Paley too. About half will turn their heads and look in. Of these, about half will smile. I haven't calculated a smile index—that would be much too solemn—but this vicarious, secondary use is important: the sight of the park, the knowledge that it is there, becomes part of the image we have of a much wider area.

I don't know of any way to quantify the benefits of such use but I think they might well be greater than the immediate benefits of the primary use. As passersby demonstrate by the expression on their

Paley Park is a delight to passersby as well as sitters.

faces, the visual enjoyment is real enough, and when these are multiplied by thousands of passersby over weeks and months and years, we have great benefits indeed.

Most of the people who enter Paley Park intended to go there; they make this clear by their course and stride. But there is a substantial amount of impulse use. As they come abreast, some people will do a double take, pause, move a few steps, then, with a slight acceleration, go on up the steps and into the park. Children do it more emphatically. The very young ones point to the park and tug at their mothers to go on in. Many of the older ones will break into a run just as they approach the steps, and skip up a step or two.

Watch these entry movements and you will appreciate how important are steps with low risers and deep treads. Those at Paley—five and fifteen inches respectively—almost pull you in. You don't have to come to a decision. You can stand and case the place, move up a step, pause, then another, and then, without having to make a conscious decision, step on in. The steps at Seagram and Greenacre Park are similarly inviting. Come on in, they say. And people do. They respond in kind; sometimes skipping up several steps, and businessmen too. The terpischore is the best part of the steps, and the measure of its grace.

8

WATER, WIND, TREES, AND LIGHT

I was fairly sure that sunlight would prove to be critical to the success of a space. For that reason I was greatly pleased with our first time-lapse film of the sun passing across Seagram Plaza. In late morning the plaza was in shadow. Shortly before noon, a narrow wedge of sunlight began moving across the plaza, and as it did, so did the sitters. Where the sun was, they sat; where there was no sun, they did not sit. It was a splendid correlation and I cherished it. Like the urban design people, I thought a southern exposure would be a necessity. Here was abundant proof.

Then something went awry. As we continued our time-lapse studies the correlations vanished—not only at Seagram but at other places we were charting. The sun still moved, but the people did not. At length, the obvious dawned on us. May had been followed by June. Earlier it was just chilly enough that one was not comfortable sitting unless he was in the sun. Now the temperatures were high enough that one could sit comfortably, sun or no sun. So people did. Sun, we had to recognize, was not the critical factor we had hypothesized it would be.

It was about this time that much of Paley park's sunlight was beginning to be cut off by an office building going up across the street.

From its scaffolding we focused time-lapse cameras on the park and recorded the progressive loss of sunlight and its impact on the park. The impact was surprisingly slight. People used Paley about as they had before. It is possible there might have been a net increase in their numbers had the sun not been curtailed; without an identical park as a control, one could never be sure. Unfortunate as the loss of sun was, we had to conclude, the park continued to function very well.

What attendance figures do not measure, however, is the quality of the experience. It can be greater when there is sun. For then you have choice—of sun, or shade, or in-between. The best time to sit beneath a tree is when there is sunlight to be shaded from. The more access to sun, the better, and if there is a southern exposure, it should be made the most of. The zoning guidelines that were later adopted required a southern exposure if at all feasible.

I do not think it should be mandatory. Our seemingly negative findings about sunlight suggest that places with little direct sun are not a lost cause. With adroit design, that little sunlight can be made to seem much more. As I will go into in detail in the chapters on sun and light, there are ways to snatch somebody else's sun and to get it bounced from neighboring buildings.

Warmth is just as important as sunlight. The days that bring out the peak crowds on plazas are not the sparkling sunny days with temperatures in the low seventies, good as this weather may be for walking. It is the hot, muggy days—sunny or overcast—that bring them out. You would think these are the days when people would want to stay inside and be air conditioned. But this is when the peak numbers are recorded. We must have some primeval instinct for the tropical.

The days that bring out the most sitters are not the sunny, sparkling days in the seventies. They are the hot, muggy days. We must have strong tropical instincts.

People do like warmth. In summer, they will generally sit in the sun as well as the shade. Only in very hot weather—ninety degrees or more—will the sunny spots be vacant. Relative warmth is important, too. One of the peak sitting days is the first warm day in spring. The absolute temperature may be what would ordinarily be considered on the cool side. It is the sudden change from cold that makes the difference. Similarly, the first warm and dry day after a stretch of cool or rainy weather will bring out the crowds.

I have related the counts of the number of people at various parks and plazas with the weather records. Most of the correlations are obvious enough: sun and warmth bring people out; rain and cold keep them away. It is the marginal days that are most interesting. They indicate that the difference between use and nonuse can rest on minor design features. For microclimates, to put it another way, slight causes can produce big effects.

Which brings us back to warmth. Of all the microclimatic factors, the ones with the greatest leverage are those that enhance warmth. Niches, for example. Given some sunlight and a place recessed from the wind, cool weather can be good for sitting. It is then that a space open to the radiant heat of the sun's rays can make the difference between sitting comfortably and not sitting at all. People will actively seek the sun, and given the right perches they will sit in surprising numbers in quite cold weather.

The more northern the latitude, the more ardently will they do so. Where the winters are long and the sun sets low in the sky, people cherish what sunlight there is. Jan Gehl's studies show that sitting and standing patterns in Copenhagen are very similar to those we have charted except for one thing. Copenhagen people are much more likely to orient themselves to the sun, especially in winter.

Within the United States, people in the North use outdoor spaces in the winter more than people in the South. I am undoubtedly a bit biased on this, being a Northerner, but I take some native pride in the hardiness of my fellow pedestrians. On really cold days you will see Bostonians and New Yorkers out schmoozing, sometimes without top-coats.

Southern cities have much better weather for this but do not use it very much. Dallas is a case in point. People there assure me that more good outdoor spaces would be provided were it not for a fearful handicap: the Dallas weather. In actual fact it is splendid most of the time, albeit a bit windy. July and August are awful, to be sure, but these months are academic. Nobody ventures out then if they can possibly avoid it. Once, it wasn't so bad. Along the main streets of the South and Southwest the sidewalks were shaded from the sun by canopies and awnings. In our hubris over air-conditioning, we have dispensed with such simple expedients.

We very much need to rediscover them, and if we do we can greatly improve the habitability of open spaces. On marginal days, for example, just the absence of drafts can make the critical difference. People like sun traps, and in this respect small parks bounded on three sides function very well. This is one of the reasons their relative carrying capacity is so high. New York's Greenacre Park has infrared heaters on an overhead canopy, but they are used only on very cold days. Because it offers both sun and protection from wind, the park is comfortable even on nippy days.

Out in Seattle it seems to be raining all the time, but it really isn't, and it's generally a light drizzle. One office building, 1111 Third Avenue, has a plaza designed to make the best of things. Two structures have been built on the edge of the plaza. One is a florist's store, the other a gourmet cafeteria; both function as windbreaks. The minute the drizzle stops, the people come out and sit at the chairs and tables on the plaza.

Indentations in building walls sometimes provide wind traps. If they also have the benefit of unobscured sun they can become good standing places. I know of no instance where such niches have been planned, though it would be good if they were. Some bus shelters have been designed with wind partially in mind. Most have not. New York's, open on two sides, give scant protection.

Closest to good prototypes are the wind baffles atop the roof of the World Trade Center. They group three glass panels around a bench. They do tame the fierce winds one experiences there, but not as much as they could. To this nonengineer's eye, the effective niche is too shallow. If you scrunch yourself all the way back, there is much less wind. If you sit on the front of the bench, there is too much. Inches, evidently, are a critical measure. With some tinkering, it ought to be possible to come up with a good module.

Drafts induced by buildings can make plazas unusable. At another Seattle plaza, that of the Seafirst Bank, the gusts are sometimes so fierce that safety lines have to be strung across the plaza to give people something to hang on to. Chicago has some outstandingly breezy places—not because of the local wind, which is not so very much stronger than in other cities, but because of the downdrafts from the John Hancock and Sears buildings. The drafts are often so strong as to prevent people from sitting on the plazas, even if there were reason to.

These effects are measurable and they are avoidable. Wind-tunnel tests are becoming routine for proposed towers, and there are design principles for taming the downdrafts of the free-standing structure. But the tests are used more to gauge the effects on the structure itself than on people. The tests for the World Trade Center determined stresses in the tower, and the steel necessary to cope with them. What the effects might be on the people down on the huge plaza below was apparently not a matter given much concern.

These problems are not technical, but conceptual. James Marston Fitch, an architect who has done more than any other to badger the profession into considering environmental effects, charges that it takes the easy way out. Architects simply ignore adverse effects. "The outdoor space," says Fitch, "is designed as if for some ideal climate, ever sunny and pleasantly warm." And this is a shame, he points out, for there are all sorts of ways we can greatly increase the habitability of urban spaces.

Technologically, one of the greatest is the tree. There are many good reasons for having lots of trees, but for climatic reasons alone we should plant many more of them—big ones, too—on the streets and spaces of our cities. In the open-space guidelines for New York we sharply stepped up the tree requirements: developers must provide a tree for every 25 feet of sidewalk, and it must be at least 3.5 inches in diameter and planted flush with the ground. For plazas, trees must be provided in proportion to the amount of space; for a plaza of 5,000 square feet, for example, there must be a minimum of six trees. At the hearings on the new guidelines, one developer testified that the standards were ruinously high and that the extra trees could bankrupt a man. In the ten years since then no developer has complained about the trees.

One reason is that we did not set the standards high enough. With the benefit of hindsight I now see that we should have specified a minimum diameter of at least 6 inches, preferably 8. There are ample precedents to invoke. One is the World Trade Center. With a very large plaza, it needs very large trees. Its initial plantings of London plane trees in the early seventies are now 40 feet or more high, and with large canopies to cast plenty of shade. The microclimate of the plaza is fierce, however, and they do lose trees. But when they replace them, they do not do it with saplings. They replant with trees of at least 8-inch caliper. Their reward is instant tree and it costs not so much more than a smaller one. The cost of an 8-inch-caliper tree runs around thirty-five hundred to four thousand dollars, but this is a reasonable sum for what is gained—about five years' lead time, for one thing, versus a small sapling.

The limiting factor is the volume of the planting bed. Increasingly, new urban spaces are the tops of parking garages, and instead of trees planted flush to grade, we have trees in above-grade planters or the ubiquitous urns. They do not have to be skimpy. At the World Trade Center, the London planes grow in rectangular planters providing, per tree, space 10 feet by 10 feet by 5½. (This is four times the cubic footage per tree in the planters at Lincoln Center. The difference in the trees is a strong sales argument for generous planters.)

It is important that the planting beds be specified in detail in the original plans. There are many sorry-about-that mishaps that can befall developers' tree plans. It might be the discovery that subsurface conditions will not permit a planting bed flush to grade. So they'll have to have tubs. And not very big ones. A decent-sized tree would require 500 cubic feet of well-watered earth, and this along with the tree itself adds up to a very big load. So, sorry, but the tree will have to be much smaller. There is also the problem of garage space. The additional bracing needed to support a tree load on the plaza above might be costly; worse yet, it might involve the loss of a parking space. They produce revenue. Trees do not.

In the cost-trimming phase of projects it may also be discovered that the architect doesn't really much want trees, big trees especially. At one large civic plaza the plan of the landscape architect for good-sized trees was overruled by the architect. He wanted smaller ones. These would not block the view of the architect's building and the statement it made.

At Lincoln Center the very early plans called for big trees on the plaza. Hugh Ferriss renderings make the plaza look downright luxuriant. During cost-pruning revisions by Robert Moses the plaza trees got left out. As subsequent experience has demonstrated, the loss was a great one. At night the main plaza is an exciting and colorful scene; during the day it is a glare box, sometimes a virtual oven, and with umpteen thousands of feet of travertine bouncing light, footcandle readings are extraordinary. What the plaza so badly needs is some handsome big trees, as the plans had it in the first place. In a study I did for Lincoln Center I made such a recommendation.

The reaction of some designers was one of pure horror. Even a landscape architect was aghast. Trees would mar the architectonic character of the plaza, he said. Some people thought the idea worth a try. Philip Johnson did sketches showing how several well-sited trees could enhance the lines of the place. In the eventual re-do of the plaza, however, the cost of the new granite floor was so great there was no money to be spared for the trees.

A city needs tree fighters. If there are any within the city government, all the better. One reason New York has a good number of trees is the nuisance that one of the planning commissioners repeatedly made of himself over projects' tree plans. He was not content with holding developers to minimum standards. He pressed them for more and bigger trees. He had no legal right to impose such higher standards. Still, it wouldn't hurt negotiations on other items if the developers went along. So many did. And the commissioner made it a practice to see, on the ground, if they planted what they said they would. There are many trees to see; for which a salute to Martin Gallent, former deputy chairman of the New York City Planning Commission.

Water is another fine element and designers have been doing very well with it. New plazas and parks provide water in many forms: waterfalls, waterwalls, rapids, sluiceways, tranquil pools, meandering streams, water tunnels. In only one respect is something lacking: access.

One of the nicest things about water is the look and feel and sound of it. I have always thought the water at Seagram looked unusually liquid, and I think it is because you know you can splash your hand in it if you are of a mind to. People do it all the time; they stick their hands in it, their toes and feet, and if they splash about, some

security guard does not come running up to tell them nay.

But in many places water is only for looking at. Let a foot touch it and a guard will be there in an instant. Forbidden. Chemicals in the water. Danger of contamination. Let people start touching the water and the first thing you know they will be swimming in it.

Sometimes they do. The big reflecting pool of the Christian Science complex in Boston makes a very handsome sheet of water. It also looks as though it would be great for wading or swimming. When it first opened, children flocked to it to do just that. It was with some difficulty that the pool was put off limits to such activity and restored to its ornamental function.

It's not right to put water before people and then keep them away from it. But this is what has been happening across the country. Pools and fountains are installed, then immediately posted with signs admonishing people not to touch. Equally egregious is the excessive zeal with which many pools are continually being emptied, vacuumed, and refilled, as though their function were to be emptied, vacuumed, and refilled. Maintenance, not use, is the first priority. The grand old Buckingham Fountain in Chicago's Grant Park, for example, was put off limits for repairs with a girdling fence "electrically protected."

Safety is the usual reason given for keeping people away. This is a legitimate concern but there are ways short of electrocution for handling it. At the Auditorium Forecourt Plaza in Portland, Oregon, there is a complex of sluiceways, rapids, and waterfalls that looks very dangerous. Landscape architects Lawrence Halprin and Angela Danadjieva designed it to look very dangerous. One consequence is that it is not dangerous. Teenagers have been clambering over it and there have been no serious mishaps. The design, for one thing, provides fail-safe positions; just when one thinks he has gone over the brink, he finds there is another ledge to go. Because of such reprieves and the care the design inspires, the place has worked out to be safe as well as fun. It is an affirmation of faith in people—teenagers at that—and says much about the good city of Portland.

Ice offers great possibilities. In the imagination of landscape architect Michael Van Valkenburgh, the waterwall at Paley Park conjured up the thought of magnificent ice walls. Could there not be all sorts of ice formations and in all sorts of places? To resolve the not inconsiderable technical problems, he has been experimenting with several prototype walls. One was in the quad of Radcliffe College in Cambridge. With the help of students, he rigged up a stretch of mesh wire and atop this he put a hose device to meter out water (just above freezing). As it froze on its downward course, the result was a dazzling wall of ice.

At some pools and fountains they don't want you to touch the water. Maintenance, not use, is its primary function.

The "beach" at Dallas City Hall Plaza. With truckloads of sand and some imagination, the city transforms a decorative pool and concrete into a popular beach resort.

The sound of water can be a great thing. When people tell you why they find Paley Park so quiet and restful, one thing they often mention is the waterwall. Actually, it is quite loud; close by, the noise level is about seventy-five decibels, measurably higher than the level out on the street. It is constant, however, whereas the sound on the street has the staccato rhythms of automobile horns.

Taken by itself, the sound of the waterwall is not especially pleasant. I came to this conclusion by accident. For the sound track of a documentary, I had been taping the sounds of various water features. One day, rummaging through the tapes, I picked up the wrong one. When I played it I realized it was probably one of the subway at the Fifty-ninth Street station. There was a near deafening sound of an express passing by. Then I heard my voice: "Noon. Six feet from east edge of Paley waterwall."

I have played the tape to a number of people and asked them to identify the sound. Most say either a subway or cars on a freeway. After I tell them it was Paley Park and play the tape again, they begin to hear it somewhat more appreciatively. In the park, of course, the sound is affected by the visual attractiveness of the place, the evident pleasure people take in being there. So you don't hear a loud, rushing noise. You hear a pleasant sound. It is white sound, too, and masks the intermittent honks and bangs of the street. It also masks conversations. Even though other people are close by, you can talk in a normal tone of voice and enjoy a feeling of privacy. On the occasions when the waterwall is turned off, the place seems nowhere near as congenial. Or as quiet.

9

THE
MANAGEMENT
OF SPACES

If you want to seed a place with activity, the first thing to do is to put out food. In New York, at every plaza or set of steps with a lively social life, you will almost invariably find a food vendor or two at the corner and a knot of people around.

Vendors have a good nose for spaces that work. They have to. They are constantly testing the market, and if business picks up in one spot, there will soon be a cluster of vendors there. This will draw more people and yet more vendors, and sometimes so many converge that pedestrian traffic is slowed to a crawl. Fifty-ninth Street off Fifth is a notable example. In front of Rockefeller Center one day during the Christmas holidays I counted the biggest concentration ever: fifteen vendors in a forty-foot stretch of Fifth Avenue.

The civic establishments of most cities deplore vendors. There are enough ordinances to make it illegal for vendors to do business at any spot where business is good, and if they are licensed, it is still illegal. The police don't like to bear down on vendors but the merchants are always getting on their back to enforce the ordinances. Sometimes there are sweeps, the police arriving with vans to haul the vendors' carts away. These confrontations draw big crowds, and they are almost always on the vendors' side.

By default, food vendors have become the caterers of the city's outdoor life. They flourish because they are servicing a demand the downtown establishment does not.

And well they should be. By default of others, the vendors have become the caterers of the city's outdoor life. They flourish because they are servicing a demand that is not being met by the regular commercial facilities. Plazas are parasitic in this respect. Hardly a one has been constructed that did not involve the destruction of luncheonettes and restaurants. The vendors fill this void, and how important they are can become quite clear when they are temporarily shooed away by the police. A lot of the life of the plaza goes away too.

New York City is less puritanical than many other cities. Some have ordinances that not only forbid the purveying of food outdoors but the eating of it as well. If you ask officials about this, they will tell you of the dreadful things that would happen were the restrictions lifted: the dangers of tainted food, the terrible litter problems, the bankrupting of cafés.

One of the most interesting hearings I have attended was before the Dallas City Council on a measure enfranchising food vendors. There was strong citizen support, mostly on the grounds that they would liven up the city's street life. The restaurant owners said it would be catastrophic. It wasn't just the danger of poisoning, or the swamping of the streets with litter, they said. A great moral issue was at stake. If this measure was passed, said the principal spokesman for the restaurateurs, it would signal the end of the free enterprise system as we know it.

The measure did pass. There was a marked improvement in the liveliness of the streets of downtown, including the beneficent congestion of two major street corners. The litter problem was reasonably well handled. The restaurant owners did not go bankrupt. For a number of reasons, more good new ones were opening up than ever before.

Outdoor eating has a strong shill effect—which is to say, food attracts people, who attract more people. We had an excellent opportunity to test this effect through a semi-controlled experiment at the rear plaza of the Exxon Building. At first, there was no food. There was not much of a crowd, either; usage was below par for the amount of space. At our suggestion, management put in a food cart. It was an immediate success. More people came. Soon a regular pushcart hot dog vendor set up shop on the sidewalk; then another. Business continued to pick up. Next, the management had one of its restaurant tenants install a buffet open-air café on the plaza. More people came, and yet more—and over and above the number who came to use the café.

The optical leverage of open air cafés is tremendous. For basic props nothing more is needed than several stacks of chairs and tables and some canvas. Put up the tables, bring on the waitresses and the customers, and the visual effect can be stunning.

The optical leverage in these things is tremendous. For basic props, nothing more is needed than several stacks of chairs and tables, and a canvas awning or two. Spread them out, put up the umbrellas, bring on the waitresses and the customers, and the visual effect can be stunning. If the café makes money, which most of them do, so much the better. But the cafés can be justified by their shill effect alone. It is hard to think of any advertising or promotional effort that could attract so many people at so little cost.

Paley and Greenacre parks are excellent models. Both feature pass-through counters, a limited but excellent bill of fare, good cake, good coffee, reasonable prices. Plenty of small tables are provided and people are welcome to bring their own food—wine too, if they like. From the street, the parks sometimes look as if a large party were going on. The line of people waiting to order food is a come-on too. Food, to repeat, draws people, who draw more people.

We proposed that the new zoning guidelines mandate the provision of basic food facilities at all new plazas and parks. Since most new buildings had been eliminating food facilities, it seemed only right that some restitution be in order. The planning commission demurred. It thought mandating food was too much to ask, but it did believe that the provision of it should be encouraged. As finally enacted, the guidelines favored food kiosks and other structures. Formerly, they were classified as obstructions; now they were amenities. Outdoor cafés were encouraged, and up to 20 percent of the open space could be used for them—so long as there was provision for brown bagging on the plaza as well.

The guidelines were made retroactive to stimulate provision of food facilities on existing plazas. One of the first retrofit operations was done by the city government. Next to the municipal building was a large windy space, St. Andrews Plaza. The then deputy borough president, Jolie Hammer, conceived the idea of using the plaza for a café featuring various ethnic concessionaires. She badgered some corporations into giving tables and chairs, and then lined up some bakeries and cafés and a clam house from nearby Little Italy to get things going. Later, she brought in some soul food and some Chinese concessions. The café was a hit from the beginning, with as many as six hundred people at the peak of the midday period.

Ms. Hammer also provided a lesson in space use. She did not distribute the facilities all over the large space. Instead, she bunched them and, with the tyrant's hand of a good hostess, grouped the tables close together. Waiting in line or weaving their way through the tables, people were compressed into meeting one another. Very quickly, the plaza became a great interchange for city government people and, by any index, one of the most sociable of places. I've never seen so many people striking up conversations, introducing people, saying hello and goodbye. If a check is ever made, it would probably show that many marriages and children could be traced back to a summer day at St. Andrews Plaza.

Farmers' market: Union Square, New York City.

The kind of food some people find most compelling is right off the farm. Displayed on the backs of trucks or in stalls, fruits and vegetables are proving to be a fine medium for enlivening public spaces. They are certainly a most sensory one: full of colors, inviting to touch and squeeze and sniff. The activity is also very sociable. There is a direct line from grower to consumer; the rules of the game for most farmers' markets require that the farmers be real farmers, not middlemen, and that they have grown what they are selling. This means more things to talk about, to query, and most of the farmers talk knowledgeably and well. There is also a good bit of interchange between the customers. City people who take to farmers' markets can be zealous in their conversion and they do like to display their newfound expertise.

There is no special price advantage; customers pay about the same for produce as they do in a supermarket. But there is a large quantitative difference. For sheer freshness and taste, farm-to-customer cannot be beat. The strong belief that this is so bonds the customers and is one of the reasons farmers' markets are so pleasantly gabby—about the Kirbys, for example, and how much better they are than regular cucumbers.

Another good thing that has been happening to urban places is the use of them for art. Public art used to mean generals on horseback

—no bad thing, let it be said; General Sherman at Grand Army Plaza is still a splendid sight. But as corporations have been turning to art they have shown themselves fairly eclectic. They incline toward big names, as they can afford to, and favor very big nonrepresentational works, in part because of the overscaled emptiness of some of the places they have to offset. But there is much excellent work, and not just as embellishment, but integral to the design—sculpture for sitting, for example.

Governments are now taking more of a lead. A number of cities and the federal government have set up "percent for arts" programs. Under these, up to 1½ percent of the capital cost of a government project is allocated for public art. San Francisco has gone a step further; it now requires a similar commitment for commercial buildings as well.

There have been fears that the kind of art chosen would be bland. Happily, public arts programs have been generating controversies, some of them quite fierce. Most usually, the charge is that a bunch of elitists is trying to ram some far-out art down the public's throat. Procedurally, the opponents claim, community people have not had enough say in the selection process; aesthetically, that the choice is ugly, unpatriotic, childish, something my little kid could do better.

The complainers are not always wrong. One of the more acrimonious controversies was over Richard Serra's *Tilted Arc* on the Federal Plaza in lower Manhattan. It is a forceful work badly sited: a big black steel wall on a big blank plaza that needs almost anything but a big black steel wall. The plaza is, in fact, a dog of a space—like so many government spaces, unfriendly enough to begin with.

But the overall record has been good. Indeed, considering how nonrepresentational and unsentimental most public art has been, the amount of popular support has been impressive. And time does help. In most cases, even art that initially stirred much hostility has become accepted, if grudgingly, and in time rather liked, sometimes cherished, as a beloved eccentricity.

Claes Oldenburg's sculpture on a plaza in Philadelphia is an example. It has a marvelous site: a crossroads space across the street from City Hall—which is no mean sculpture itself—and complemented by a line of food vendors at the curb. But a giant clothespin! In *Philadelphia!* Was this a joke? They are not radical in Philadelphia and this took some getting used to. But they did get used to it; they got to like it. They made it a fine meeting place—like the eagle at Wanamakers. It is well on its way to venerability.

Because our study of plazas was a continuing one, we had a number of opportunities to check the before-and-after effects of a work of

Bank of America Plaza, San Francisco. The sculpture is known locally as "Banker's Heart."

public art on people's behavior. In some cases it was considerable. Jean Dubuffet's *Four Trees* on the Chase Manhattan Plaza in lower Manhattan is one of the best examples. This is a very large space and it calls for a very large sculpture. *Four Trees,* twenty feet high, color white and blue, is handsomely large. It tames the size of the plaza and, in the process, seems itself eminently human in scale.

It draws people. Almost from the day it was installed, people have been walking by it, through it, around it, and as with so many successful places, holding prolonged conversations in the middle of it. They touch it; sometimes they rap on it, to see if it rings. (It doesn't.)

From afar it is a delight. Lying athwart the plaza's main axis, it beckons people to it—most strikingly around noon, when the first shaft of sunlight hits it. The passage through the sculpture is part of a larger processional experience that extends almost to the Hudson and affords some of the most vivid contrasts of sun and darkness, space and constraint, anywhere to be found.

Another example of a big sculpture working for a big place is Alexander Calder's *Pink Flamingos* on the Federal Plaza in Chicago. It has a very definite guiding effect on the foot traffic cutting across the diagonal of the plaza. (And it is not pink, but Calder orange-red.) On the huge plaza of the Dallas City Hall, a Henry Moore gives the space a needed anchor. It is also very easy to slide down and children love it —always a good sign.

But placement is critical. On another huge plaza, at the World

Street conversation: sculpture on Calgary pedestrian mall.

Trade Center, there is a fine Calder: just the size and color—red orange—this space could use. But the sculpture does not work too well here. It is scrunched up against the rear of the place.

The best demonstration I have ever seen of drawing power was a temporary exhibit at Lincoln Center. Atop a large empty bridge space between Juilliard and the rest of the center, the British sculptor Maurice Agis had placed his *Colorspace*. It was an inflatable, walk-through series of brightly colored vinyl tubes. It was great fun to walk through, or, in the case of children, run through. The light filtering through the vinyl was oddly pleasant, and so was the sound of the tapes of electronically synthesized music.

How Agis talked Lincoln Center into this I do not know, but I had a particular reason to be glad he did. I was studying the feasibility of using the small plaza and stair space adjacent for an outdoor café. The question was whether or not people down on the street could be induced to make the trip up. The tubes showed they could be. As soon as Agis pumped up the tubes in the morning, the top part of them became visible from the street down below—the red and blue tubes most vividly so. What were they? Up the people came. Word of mouth grew. By the end of the exhibit, people were coming in greater numbers during the day than ever they had before. That was in 1981. The sculpture has long since gone. The spaces have reverted to their emptiness.

Sculpture is not always the best draw for a space. Sometimes, as the Seagram Plaza indicates, quite a different solution is preferable. Phyllis Bronfman Lambert, who helped instigate the Seagram Building, tells how meticulously Mies van der Rohe studied approaches to sculpture on the plaza. Picasso suggested his *Bathers* be put in the pools; Constantin Brancusi, an enlarged version of one of his sculptures. Later, Mies turned to the possibilities of a Henry Moore. He had a photo of the sculptor's *Reclining Figure* blown up to different scales so he could study its relation to the plaza and building. As a next step, two full-size mock-ups were made and placed on the plaza so Mies and Moore could study them in place. This decided them. Better no sculpture on the plaza at all.

Moore felt that it would be out of scale with the plaza. Mies agreed. People would be the sculpture. As Phyllis Lambert puts it, "Seagram Plaza changes all the time. It looks wonderful when it is empty, then it changes as people go in and out of the building or just wander on the plaza. When people sit on the benches and walls, it again has another character."

As things have turned out, the plaza has been host to a number of temporary placements of sculpture. Most of these have been attention getters: Mark Di Suvero's semimoving structure; a huge head of the Easter Island kind; a large mound of what appeared to be yellow and white table-tennis balls. They have had a playful quality for which the serenity of the site seems to have been contrarily right.

In assessing public arts programs there are many factors to consider. Almost always, however, it comes down to a person. In New York it was the late Doris Freedman, a remarkable woman with a gifted eye for the mating of art and site and a great ability to marshal the troops. It was thanks to her imagination that the "City Walls" program turned blank walls of buildings into the canvas of artists such as Richard Haas. It was thanks to her campaigning that the city embarked on its "percent for art" program.

One offshoot is an "Arts for Transit" program. It is an exercise in perception. The idea is to get New Yorkers to believe that the subways are getting better, and thus to break the vicious cycle of declining

Bass player in Chicago subway station.

ridership and declining standards. The subways actually are getting better but this is not enough. People have to *think* they are.

To help them to this perception, the Metropolitan Transportation Administration has launched an "Adopt-A-Station" program to get public art in the stations. Some installations have been quite professional: at the Fifty-third Street station, for example, illuminated exhibits of the most interesting things to see up above. Some have been done by schoolchildren: at a Queens station some five hundred students did murals of the neighborhood.

Another program is for "Music under New York." For several years musicians have been playing in the subways—on the platforms too, not just on the mezzanines topside. But they had been playing illegally and, worse yet, passing the hat. In 1984 the transit police handed out 671 summons. The new program reverses course. Instead of banning musicians, the MTA encourages them. It has sixty on its roster and books them for eighteen active sites—most usually for peak times and the busiest places. The MTA does not pay them anything but lets them solicit contributions.

The program has been a popular success. People are surprised and delighted when they come upon a brass quintet down on a platform. Comments are laudatory, the most frequent one being that the music will calm down all those other uptight, nervous New Yorkers. The acoustics, surprisingly, are fairly good.

Other cities have had similar programs. Boston started its program in 1976; Paris followed suit several years later. In Chicago, then Mayor Jane Byrne sponsored a "Troubadours" program in 1982 for getting entertainers in the subways and on the streets. (As I note in the chapter on street people, the program was very successful with the public. But not with merchants and hotel people. They got the city council to pass an ordinance sharply limiting entertainers.)

Seattle, not surprisingly, has one of the finest public art programs in the country. It is distinguished by its strong emphasis on site—an approach its leaders trace back to the salvation of the Pike Place Market. The public referendum on the fate of the market was a referendum on more than the preservation of an old food market. In supporting it, the public was declaring what kind of city it wanted Seattle to be.

The Seattle Art Commission set up one of the earliest "1-percent for art" programs in the country, in 1973. As in other cities, the main thrust of the program has been on beautiful objects in parks and plazas. A later approach has been to site-determined art, in which the artist takes his cues from the site and its surroundings. In one example, a team of artists worked with architects on the design of a substation. Their fanciful art—"Whirligigs Garden"—was integral to the structure.

The commission decided to study all of the sites in the city and to conceive of downtown as itself a sculpture garden or art park. This concept proved impractical. It was too much of a set piece. "Instead of a static 'urban art center,'" says Richard Andrews, director of the commission, "it's clear that an arts plan should be based on the concept of the city as a network of primary public places in a constant state of flux." In defining these primary places, the commission has taken a leaf from the work of social scientist Kevin Lynch. In a very thorough inventory of sites it has identified paths, nodes, districts, and edges. It has also paid a lot of attention to human activity. Primary public places, it believes, should be socially functional and they should reinforce one's sense of place.

The commission people walked and walked, they surveyed every neighborhood, and they looked with opportunistic eye at the mating of grids: hillsides, alleys, the odds and ends of space produced by an ornery topography. The result is an extraordinarily thorough and imaginative agenda.

Here are some of the primary places they spotted and what might be done with them:

- The arcade on Western Avenue under the Pike Place Market: This is dark and looks awful. But it could be a good canvas and lightened up. (But a way to discourage pigeons must be found.)
- The triangular hillside shaped by Alaskan Way and Western Avenue is a state right of way. Its high visibility to both pedestrian and car traveler make it a very good location for public art.
- At the corner of First Avenue and Seneca is a small privately-owned parcel. Its location makes it an entry point to the city. It should be used for a temporary art project.

- At Second and Yesler is a lightly landscaped space on one side, an unusually large sidewalk space on the other. There should be a unifying design with shrubbery and landscaping.
- Seattle's older buildings used water tanks on the roof. Many of these or their platforms remain and provide ready-made structures for artworks. We saw one in Manhattan which was wrapped in gold lamé and it made a stunning transformation.
- Hill climbs to help pedestrians conquer the steeper streets will become more prevalent. With their small scale and pedestrian focus, they present opportunities for artists to become involved in their design.
- Parking lots and booths can be transformed into artworks by painting or manipulating the asphalt surface itself. Booths, many in disrepair, can be renovated with unexpected art.

The performing arts are another way to enliven public spaces. This is something American cities do rather well; they love the hoopla, the involvement of schoolchildren, the invention of new traditions to celebrate. And they do like music. The equivalent of the municipal band concert now is jazz, country, bluegrass, modified rock, even chamber music by woodwind or brass quintets, and, on occasion, municipal band concerts. There are also entertainments of various kinds: trampoline artists, mimes, magicians, and such.

As an itinerant observer I have a few observations to make. One is that the best place for presentations is a simple open space. The number of people a performing group will draw will be about 125–150 at the maximum; beyond that, people on the edge are too far back to enjoy the show, and there is a certain self-limiting factor at work. Symphony concerts and other large-scale events are another matter; they require large spaces and special logistics.

But the smaller, informal presentations are the bread and butter of programs. For that reason it is good to be chary of planning elaborate amphitheaters. They can accommodate large numbers, but they tend to be single-purpose facilities and are not well adapted to smaller groups. Too often the space between the performer and the first row of the audience is much too great, and since the amphitheater is frozen in concrete, there is not much that can be done about it. To repeat, keep it simple. A grassy lawn makes a fine stage, and if it slopes a bit, so much the better.

When it comes to equipment municipal governments are stingy. The people who stage the programs are forever scrounging around and borrowing equipment. What cities need is a good in-house supply of chairs, tables, demountable platforms, and amplifying equipment that actually works. Pittsburgh's program is one of the few that has a fair store of equipment, and that is one reason it is an outstanding program.

Another need is electricity. In the planning of plazas and parks, architects should be induced at gunpoint to provide several well-located 115- and 220-volt outlets. Very few spaces have been so provided, and as a result lines have to be laid in, covered with tape, taken up, laid in again. They are costly, ugly, and dangerous and add to insurance liability. Permanent lines accessible at a number of points allow the events people much more flexibility in staging events. They would also have more choices to make if original plans called for waterlines to be run in. If there are going to be festivals with food booths and such, water will be indispensable. Running it in after the fact is very costly, if done.

One of the finest examples of a well-programmed place is Pioneer Courthouse Square in Portland, Oregon. It had to be programmed to be built. A parking facility occupied the site, and many of the merchants and politicians would just as soon have kept it that way. An open square would attract undesirables, they said. A vigorous citizen effort won the day, however, and to capitalize on the momentum a great brick sale was launched. Within a year over 35,000 people had purchased bricks and other features for the plaza, raising much of the $7.8 million construction budget. Finding one's inscribed brick is one of the square's diversions.

Since then the series of events has been almost nonstop, and in a relatively short time a host of traditions has been established. The square is maintained by the city's park department, but the management of the space is handled by a nonprofit corporation set up for the purpose. It has a professional staff of eight, and it puts the arm on many citizen volunteers. It has a fine stock of equipment and lots of outlets. Annual expenditures: $300,000, plus $180,000 for maintenance, borne by the city.

The result is an astonishing variety of activities. Among those in 1986: tea dance for seniors; trick cycling demonstration; group aerobics sessions; brass quintet; woodwind quintet; Hester Street Klezmer Band; Chinese lion dance; Swiss Culture Day; mime; Portland Festival Symphony; Movies by Moonlight; Music from the 30's; square dancing; jazz quartet.

The corporation also rents out the square—all of it or parts, at reasonable rentals. Among other things, it pushes weddings. Here are excerpts from one of its flyers:

TIE A SQUARE KNOT

Want a wedding that's tied to tradition—with a twist of something new?
Rent Pioneer Courthouse Square for the big event.
The fee is $100; a refundable cleaning fee of $50 must also be paid.
A wedding site may be selected from among several areas: the am-

phitheater, close to Le Pavillon restaurant is one. Among the potted trees on S.W. Broadway is another. A very large event might want to utilize the curved stairs and ramp.

Call 223-1613 for details. And tie the knot in the square.

The corporation also rents space for commercial use; an eight-foot-square booth, for example, rents for $30 for eight hours. Lighting systems, sound systems, and portable staging modules are available. The corporation makes much of the stimulus to downtown retailing and is now merchandising a special "Square Deal" packet to people who pay the $15 membership fee. It contains $30 worth of coupons redeemable at neighboring stores.

The corporation is still selling those bricks.

With adroit scheduling, as the square has demonstrated, hours of use can be extended. Many American cities despair on this point. Their downtown spaces go dead when downtown goes dead, somewhere around five to five-thirty. Cities are right to be concerned but they should not be too discouraged. People come together in downtown to work together, and that is why they leave together. As with the perennial hopes for staggered work hours, hours of usage can be expanded somewhat but not greatly changed, at least not in the near term. Longer term, there are factors that could make a substantial difference: the creation of more downtown housing; more good restaurants and attractions to draw people to downtown or hold them there. The evolution of Dallas' West End warehouse district is an encouraging case in point. In relatively few years it has spawned a host of restaurants and beer-garden–type family places. It is fun to go to. Even if you do not, you feel better about downtown Dallas.

With the downtowns that are given, it is possible to extend the use of their public spaces. But not too much. Attempts were made by Rockefeller Center and Citicorp to schedule events so people would stay until eight o'clock or later. But not many did. The bulk of the office-worker clientele will eventually go home to dinner. But they can be kept till as late as seven—and in the dusk hours this is an accomplishment. Jazz for a late summer's afternoon, a glass of wine under the umbrellas: from such pleasures can some substantial shifts be created.

The exceptional example is what has happened to the demographics of Boston's financial district. Not so many years ago the place closed down at five and everybody was on their way out of town. Then came the Faneuil Hall Marketplace. Station yourself at one of the main street corners and you will see a massive trek of younger office workers head for the place. By six they are three deep at the bars, and they stay there until eight or nine or later. The South Street Seaport in New York is similar; at times you could mistake it for a gigantic singles party. Purists have complained that these places are frivolous; they are a bit, perhaps, but they may be a response to a social need that is not at all frivolous.

Triangulation

A sign of a great place is triangulation. This is the process by which some external stimulus provides a linkage between people and prompts strangers to talk to each other as if they were not.

We have gone over the principal factors that make a place work. But there is one more factor. I call it triangulation. By this I mean that process by which some external stimulus provides a linkage between people and prompts strangers to talk to other strangers as if they knew each other. There are, say, two women standing at a street corner. A well-dressed young girl sticks out her hand and solicits money from a man standing there. One of the women turns to the other. "Did you see that?" "Disgraceful," the other says. In the tone of voice usually reserved for close friends the two exchange thoughts on the decline of American values.

Street characters of a more positive sort stimulate much interchange. Mr. Magoo, as I have noted, can draw a crowd, and its members will start talking to each other about him. Street entertainers can have the same effect—even bad ones. One of the best of the bad ones I've seen is a young magician whose patter is so corny that you are virtually forced into conversation with your neighbor.

A virtue of street acts is their unexpectedness. When people form up around an entertainer—it happens very quickly, in a minute or so —they look much like children who have come upon a treat. Some will be smiling in simple delight. This is true recreation, though rarely thought of as such—certainly not by the retailers who try so hard to outlaw the entertainers. But there is something of value here.

The stimulus can be a physical object or sight. At the small park at the Promenade in Brooklyn Heights, there is a spectacular view of the towers of lower Manhattan across the East River. It is a great conversation opener and strangers often remark on it to each other. When you come upon such a scene it would be rude not to.

We have noted the strong social effects that sculpture can have. At the Federal Plaza in Chicago Alexander Calder's huge stabile has had a magnetic effect on the pedestrian flows. Before-and-after studies of the Chase Manhattan plaza in New York showed that Dubuffet's *Four Trees* has had similar effects. People are drawn to the sculpture and drawn through it. They stand under it. They touch it. They rap on it to hear the sound it makes. They talk to other people about it. What's it made of? Wood? Some kind of plastic maybe?

Another stimulus for triangulation is the universal expert. New York is full of him. He is knowledgeable on all matters and will volunteer his help. It's not wood it's made of. It's made of fiberglass.

10

THE UNDESIRABLES

The biggest single obstacle to the provision of better spaces is the undesirables problem. They are themselves not too much of a problem. It is the actions taken to combat them that is the problem. Out of an almost obsessive fear of their presence, civic leaders worry that if a place is made attractive to people it will be attractive to undesirable people. So it is made defensive. There is to be no loitering—what a Calvinist sermon is in those words—and there is to be no eating, no sleeping. So it is that benches are made too short to sleep on, that spikes are put on ledges, that many needed spaces are not provided and the plans for them scuttled.

One of the problems in dealing with undesirables is a failure to differentiate. For most businessmen, curiously, it is not muggers, dope dealers, or truly dangerous people that obsess them. It is the winos, derelicts, men who drink out of half-pint bottles in paper bags—the most vulnerable of the city's marginal people, but a symbol, perhaps, of the man one might become but for the grace of fate. When some people speak of these men they smile as if they were telling a dirty joke.

For retailers, the list of undesirables is more inclusive. There are the bag women, bag men, people who talk out loud in buses, teenagers, older people, street musicians, street vendors. On one occasion a retailer pointed out several for me: two young women in blue jeans

For most businessmen it is not the dope dealers or muggers who obsess them. It is the winos—a symbol, perhaps, of the man one might become but for the grace of fate.

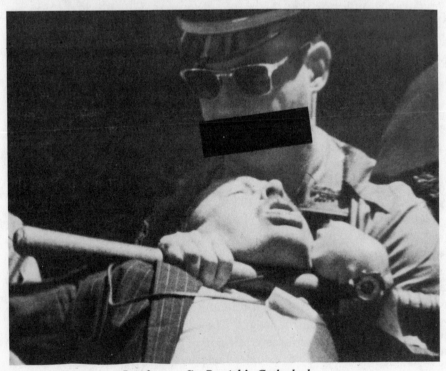

Incident at St. Patrick's Cathedral.

taking notes at the corner. "There are some of them," the retailer said. They were two of our researchers.

The preoccupation with undesirables is a symptom of another problem. Many corporation executives who make key decisions about the city have surprisingly little acquaintance with the life of its streets and open spaces. From the station they may have to walk only a few blocks to their office building, but once inside, some do not venture out again until it is time to head back to the station. So circumscribed is their territory that many spend a decade or so without straying more than a few blocks off their set pathways. If their office building has a plaza, they are likely to have seen it every day but not to have ever used it themselves. I showed a film to the brass of a large corporation on the life of their plaza. The plaza happened to be a successful one and the executives were fascinated by it—as if it were a far-off island place. They had never known it.

If it is a defensive plaza, few other people will have used it either. Places designed in distrust get what was anticipated and it is in them, ironically, that you will most likely find a wino. You will find winos elsewhere, but it is the empty places they prefer. It is in them that they look conspicuous—almost as if the design had been contrived to make them so.

Fear proves itself. Highly elaborate defensive measures are an advance indicator that the corporation may clear out of the city entirely. Long before Union Carbide announced it was leaving New York City for outer suburbia, its building said that it would. Save for an exhibit area, the building was sealed off from the city, with policelike guards with black uniforms and walkie-talkies. Outside were large expanses of paving and not a place to sit.

There still is not a place. Manufacturers Hanover Trust, which got the building for a song, put long, black, marble objects on the spaces with the name of the bank on them. But you cannot sit there; the sides are so steeply canted you slide off.

The best way to handle the problem of undesirables is to make a place attractive to everyone else. The record is overwhelmingly positive on this score. With few exceptions, center city plazas and small parks are safe places.

With few exceptions, plazas and small parks in most central business districts are as safe a place as you can find during the times that people use them.

They mirror expectations. Seagram management is pleased people like its plaza and is quite relaxed about what they do on it. It lets them stick their feet in the pools; it tolerates oddballs and even allows them to sleep the night on the ledges. The sun rises the next morning.

Good places are largely self-policing. Paley Park is an excellent example. It is courtly to people. Jackson Carithers and Jasper Green, the guards, are amiable hosts and rarely have to do much admonishing. If it is necessary—somebody throwing trash on the ground, for example—other guests are likely to do the admonishing. With its movable chairs and tables the park should be highly vulnerable to vandalism. But it is not. Here is the record of security infractions since the park opened in 1967:

1968	One of the flower units on the sidewalk was stolen by two men in a van.
1970	The "Refreshments" sign was taken from the wall.
1971	A small table was taken.
1972	A man tried to carve his initials on one of the trees.
1974	One of the brass lights at the entrance was removed.
1980	Snack bar broken into; new door required.
1983	Small refuse fire on sidewalk; probably accidental.
1967–1986	In entire period no movable chairs have been stolen.

In the sixteen years that I have been studying New York plazas and small parks, there has been real trouble in only three, all three of them badly designed and managed. In well-used places there has been no trouble.

Places that are designed primarily for security worsen it. For one thing, they feature walls. The idea is to keep out bad people. The effect can be the opposite. About ten years ago a corporation with a well-used small park was alarmed to note that some dope dealers were working the place at lunchtime. The management panicked. It took away half the benches. Then it had steel-bar fences put up along the two open sides of the park. These moves sharply cut down the number of people using the park—much to the delight of the dope dealers, who now had the place much more to themselves and their customers. Management decided to reverse course. Applying the recommendations of the Project for Public Spaces, it redid the park: it put in new food kiosks and chairs and tables and scheduled a series of musical events. The park has been doing well ever since.

The most striking example of a walled enclave is New York's Bryant Park. It should be one of the greatest of center-city parks. It is spacious—some nine acres—and it is in the very heart of midtown, just west of the Public Library at Fifth Avenue and Forty-second Street. And for over fifty years it has been a troubled place.

In the early thirties there was a design competition for a major redo of the park. The winning scheme was rooted in a firm philosophic premise. The park was to be a refuge from the city, free from the hustle and bustle of pedestrians. To that end, it was physically removed from the surrounding streets. It was elevated about four feet above street level, lined with an iron fence, and then, for good measure, given an additional separation from the street in the form of dense shrubbery. There were relatively few entrances into the park. Once there, one could not cut across the park. The idea was to discourage through pedestrian flows, not invite them, and beelines and shortcuts were blocked by continuous balustrades.

The intentions were the best. The basic design, however, rested on a fallacy. People may say they want to get away from the city, avoid the hustle and bustle of people, and the like. But they do not. They stayed away from Bryant Park. On fine summer days they would use the great lawn. In relation to its size and central location, however, the park remained very much underused.

Except by undesirables. A succession of various kinds dominated the park during the off-hours, culminating in the virtual rule of it by drug dealers in the late seventies. They even had people standing at the entrances, and when they walked down the pathways they walked in the middle. This was their place.

A coalition of civic groups and neighboring corporations has launched a large-scale effort to redeem the park. There are many elements in its program—a glassed-in grand café, for example; food kiosks, bookstalls, and the like. But the key aim is to open the park up to the street. Several new entrances are to be added; the labyrinthine internal layout is to be simplified to encourage through pedestrian flows. The shrubbery has already gone. Landscape architects Robert Hanna and Laurie Olin are dealing with a certified landmark and have had to be respectful of the original design. They have been adroitly so, however, and the result is a plan that looks very much like the old one but in function is the opposite of it.

Most well-used places have a "mayor" of sorts. He may be a building guard, a newsstand operator, or a food vendor. Throughout the day you will notice people checking in with him—a cop, perhaps, a bus dispatcher, various street professionals, and office workers and shoppers who stop by briefly for a hello or bit of banter. The mayors are great communication centers, and they are quick to spot any departure from the normal life of the place. Such as us. When we start observing at a place—unobtrusively, we like to think—the regulars spot us very quickly. We're not moving, for one thing. Before long, the mayor will drift over and try to find out just what we're up to.

One of the best mayors I've ever seen is Joe Hardy of the Exxon Building of Rockefeller Center. He is an actor as well as a guard and was originally hired to play Santa Claus, whom he resembles. Ordinarily, guards are not supposed to initiate conversations, but Joe is gregarious and curious and has a nice sense of situations. There may be an older couple looking somewhat confused. He will anticipate their questions and go up to them. Are they, by chance, looking for a reasonable place to eat? Well yes, that's what they were going to ask him. On another occasion there might be two girls taking turns photographing each other. Joe suggests maybe they'd like him to take a picture of the two of them. Yes, they would.

Joe is tolerant of winos and odd people, as long as they don't bother anyone. He is very quick, however, to spot incipient trouble. Groups of teenagers are an especial challenge. They like to test a place. The volume knob on stereo "blasters" is a favored weapon. Joe says you have to nip this kind of thing early or you've lost. One tactic he uses is to go up to the toughest-looking member of the group and ask his help in keeping things cool.

Another fine mayor is Debbie Day of the Portland, Oregon, Pioneer Courthouse Square. A young woman with a theater arts background, she was out of work when the square was opening up and applied for a job as guard. She has been a beneficent presence there ever since. A smiling, friendly person, she enjoys talking to people, such as the older people who come so regularly. She is especially good with teenagers. "If they have a problem with someone, they appreciate having me here," she says. "That's what I'm here for—to make people feel comfortable being here."

Guards are an underused asset. At most places they don't do much except stand. For want of anything to do, they tend to develop occupational tics. One might wave his arms rhythmically to and fro or rock up and down on his heels. Another may bend his knees at periodic intervals. If you watch him you'll get mesmerized trying to figure when the next knee bend will come.

The guard's job ought to be upgraded. The more one has to do, the better he does it, and the better the place functions. The two mayors at Paley are a case in point. It was originally expected that special security guards would be needed, in addition to several people to keep the place tidy and do painting and repairs. The two mayors were able to do all the jobs, and in a notably relaxed way.

There are antimayors. At one of our largest civic institutions, the head of the militia is a mean-looking fat man in a black uniform who cruises about in a golf cart. I have never seen him actually hit anybody, but he comes so close and at such speed you feel he really wants to. The guards under him are an agreeable lot, but the jobs are so dull they are bored to death. It is little wonder they sneak off to a nearby street to smoke pot.

The most bedeviling problem of access is the public rest room. Its numbers have been declining, and now, with the recent increase in the homeless, it is on the brink of disappearance. Failure to deal with one problem rationalizes the other. Provide rest rooms, it is said, and they

will be overrun by the homeless. This would attract yet more undesirables and stop downtown's revival.

This is very much like the argument for spikes on ledges. It is not
just the homeless who need rest rooms. Older people, shoppers, visitors to the city, and people in general need them too, and a policy that
withholds an amenity from all of them to withhold it from the homeless is a mean one indeed. The city has an obligation to provide such
facilities, and in providing them it may find that it is also acting in its
larger self-interest. Paris has come to this conclusion with its new
unisex toilets. So has Portland, Oregon. Its park department has been
putting individual unisex toilets in park areas and now has six in the
heart of downtown.

For any major downtown project in which zoning incentives are
involved—which is to say, most projects—provision of public rest
rooms should be required and so should their maintenance. What ca-
tastrophes would result? Precedents suggest none. At the Citicorp
atrium there are separate rest rooms for men and for women, and they
are well looked after. At the Whitney sculpture garden in the Philip
Morris Building a unisex toilet and lavatory is provided. It is tucked
away by the espresso counter, and you have to ask for it to find it. But
it's there.

In the gallery of the IBM Building there are attractive rest rooms
scrupulously maintained. There is also a checkroom for coats and
hats, with service on the house. Such internal spaces do not solve the
problem of the homeless—they are basically upscale in their clientele.
But they do meet a need and they demonstrate that it is practical to
press for more of them.

But there must be more public rest rooms in truly public places.
There used to be. There should be again. The rehabilitation of Bryant
Park may prove an indicator. One problem has been what to do with
the rather ornate structures that were originally provided as rest
rooms—one on the one side for men, another on the other side for
women. This use having been out of the question for some time, the
structures have been used as storage and tool sheds. Now a radical
proposal is being considered. Use them as rest rooms. If they work in
Bryant Park, it will be remarked, they will work anywhere. And there
is a very good chance they will work.

There is another problem with rest rooms and it is quite pervasive. At the very least, women's rooms should be half again as large as
men's. But they are not. The dimensions of women's rooms tend to be
the mirror image of men's rooms. The amount of space is the same in
each. The difference is in the fixtures: sometimes the women get an
extra toilet; sometimes not. The supply-and-demand factor is all out of
whack, a fact that is painfully evident when the facilities are taxed

with peak crowds. Intermission time at the theatre is a case in point. When the bell rings for the curtain, there still may be a queue of women outside the rest room, but no queue of men outside theirs. Space has been symmetrical; function has not been.

Cities have an opportunity to seize. Philadelphia is one. Through a design competition it has been canvassing ideas for the revitalization of the public spaces in and around City Hall. The basic aim is to make City Hall a meeting place for the workers and shoppers of downtown. There have been many excellent ideas: outdoor cafes, waterworks, laser beams, and such. But probably the best amenity of all would be good clean restrooms, for women especially, and for that overlooked constituency, women with children in tow. Such provisions would be much appreciated and all the more for the lack of them most anywhere else in downtown. And they are lacking in most every downtown.

There is a related question. How public are the public spaces? On many plazas you will see a small bronze plaque that reads something like this: PRIVATE PROPERTY. CROSS AT THE RISK OF THE USER AND WITH REVOCABLE PERMISSION OF THE OWNER. It seems clear enough. It means that the plaza is the owner's and he has the right to revoke any right you fancy you may have to use it. Whether or not a floor-area bonus was given, most building managements take it for granted that they can bar any activity they find undesirable. Their concept of this, furthermore, goes beyond antisocial or dangerous behavior. Some are quite persnickety. When I used a rule to measure the front ledges at the General Motors Building the security people rushed up in great consternation. This was not permitted, even though I was on the public sidewalk. If I wanted to measure I would have to secure written permission from the public relations department.

This is not a matter to go to the Supreme Court on, perhaps, but there is a principle of some importance involved. The space was provided by the public through its zoning and planning machinery. And the owner went along with the deal. It is true that the space falls within the property line of the owner, and it is equally true that he is responsible for the maintenance of it. But the legislation enabling the floor-area bonuses for such spaces unequivocally states that the space "must be accessible to the public at all times."

What does "accessible" mean? A commonsense interpretation would be that the public could use the space in the same manner that it uses any public space, with the same freedoms and the same constraints. Many building managements have been operating with a much narrower concept of access. They shoo away entertainers and people who distribute leaflets or give speeches. Apartment building managements often shoo away everybody except residents. This is a flagrant violation of the zoning intent, but to date no one has gone to court on it.

The public's right in urban plazas would seem clear. Not only are plazas used as public spaces; in most cases the owner has been specifically, and richly, rewarded for providing them. He has not been given license to allow only those public activities he happens to approve of. He may assume that he has license, and some owners have been operating on this basis with impunity. But that is because nobody has challenged them. A stiff, clarifying test is in order.

11

CARRYING CAPACITY

So far we have been considering ways of making city spaces attract more people. Now let us turn to another question. What if we were to succeed too well? Conceivably, so many more people might be attracted as to crowd out the values they came to enjoy. It has happened at national parks; it could certainly happen in the city. This possibility concerned the planning commission. Could our studies shed some light? Was there a way to gauge the carrying capacity of spaces? How many is too many?

To get at these questions we undertook close-up studies of five of the most intensively used sitting spaces in New York: a ledge alongside a building, a ledge at a plaza, and three sets of benches. First, we recorded the average number of people sitting at each place at peak and off-peak hours in good weather. It was immediately apparent that the number who could sit and the number who did sit were quite different. At the most heavily used places the number of sitters ranged between thirty-three and thirty-eight people per hundred feet of sitting space. These patterns are consistent enough to yield a rough rule of thumb: if you wish to estimate the average number of people who will be using a prime sitting space at peak periods, divide the number of feet in it by three and you will be close to a good figure.

This is not physical capacity. Were people to sit at the same relative density as they do on buses, the average could go as high as sixty people per hundred feet. In special situations, such as a marathon going by, the number can go to absolute physical capacity. That is about seventy people, though let it be noted you will never see seventy people neatly distributed along a sitting space like starlings on a phone line.

What we are concerned with is *effective* capacity; that is, the number of people who by free choice will sit at a place during normal peak-use periods. Each place, you will find, has its own norm, and this depends on many particulars—the microclimate, the comfort of the perch, what you can see from it, the attractiveness of the place.

Supply is another major factor. A lot of people have to pass by to provide a number of sitters, and thus there is bound to be a relationship between the number of sitters and the pedestrian flow. In his studies of Copenhagen, Jan Gehl found a strong correlation between the number of people sitting on benches along Copenhagen's main pedestrian way and the number standing or walking. The number sitting was a fairly constant fraction of those standing or walking.

Of all factors, of course, the sitters themselves are the most important. We concentrated on the north front ledge at Seagram for a minute-by-minute study of their behavior. From the roof of the Racquet Club across the street, we focused two time-lapse cameras on the ledge, and at an interval of a frame every ten seconds they recorded what went on from early morning to dusk.

The ledge at Seagram.

Projected, the film was fascinating to watch, most particularly the lunch period. One saw in speeded-up action a very heavy turnover of ledge sitters, and a seemingly random distribution of sitters and empty spaces. Yet the overall number of sitters at any one time remained fairly constant.

To understand why, I plotted the information in the film onto a horizontal chart and, in chronological order, recorded who sat where and for how long. I took an unconscionable amount of time doing it, I should add. The tediousness of this kind of analysis is one of the reasons few time-lapse-study programs last the course. They require many hours—about fifty hours in this case, spread over three weeks. I have since learned that speed and a measure of bravado is a necessity if there is to be practical use of time-lapse analysis.

Slow or not, I found the key to a puzzle. Each sitter was represented by a line, the length of which showed how long the sitter sat, and on what part of the ledge. Laid out in chronological order, the chart looked very like a player-piano roll.

The day at Seagram starts slowly. At eight-fifty, three people sit down; after a few minutes they leave. From then until about eleven-thirty use is sporadic, with the total number sitting at any one time fluctuating between two and five. The sudden upswing at ten thirty-five is caused by twenty-six school children who stopped to rest. Around eleven-thirty the tempo picks up; shortly after noon, the number of sitters is around eighteen. For the next two hours it will range between seventeen and twenty-two with the average around eighteen to nineteen.

Now let us look at the geographic pattern. When people start to fill up a space, they do not distribute themselves evenly across it, and they do not head for the emptiest places. They go where other people are, or reasonably close. At Seagram, the most favored spots are the corners of the front steps. This is where the buildup often begins.

You can see the same phenomenon at beaches. On a busman's holiday in Spain, I set up a time-lapse camera on a bluff overlooking a small beach. When the first comers arrived with their umbrellas and beach paraphernalia, most went to the front and center. As others arrived, they did not veer off to the empty spaces at the sides. Instead, in a sort of tic-tac-toe pattern, they located themselves about one or two spaces removed from other people. By noon the pattern was set. The beach umbrellas were spotted in three parallel rows and were so equally spaced that you would think they were laid out by a surveyor. The sides and the rear of the beach were still almost empty.

The dense areas got denser. Even in very-high-density places there is the same tendency to cluster. In an excellent study for the National Park Service, the Project for Public Spaces recorded the

When people start to fill up a space, they do not distribute themselves evenly across it. They go where other people are. The dense areas get denser.

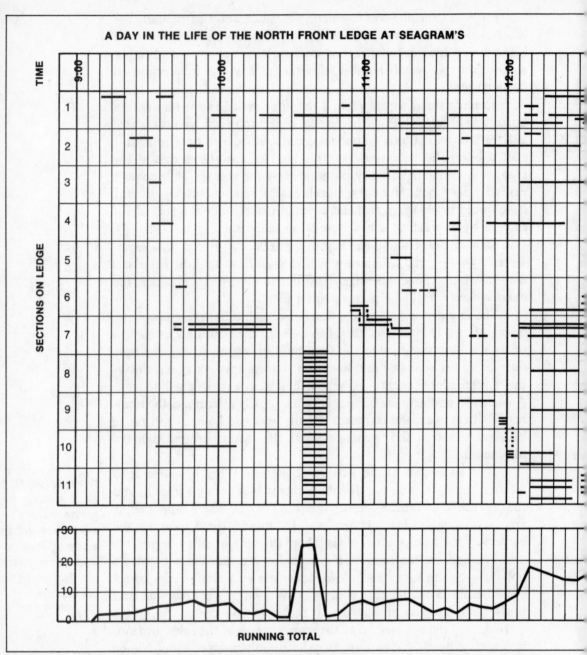

A DAY IN THE LIFE OF THE NORTH FRONT LEDGE AT SEAGRAM'S

How many is too many? This analysis of a day of sitting at the north front ledge of the Seagram plaza indicates that in their instinctive way people have a nice sense of what is right for a place. Plan view shows 11 sections of ledge at left. The lines going from left to right show on which part of the ledge each person sat and precisely how long. Morning activity is desultory. (The sharp upswing at 10:35 is due to 25 school children.) At noon, activity picks up

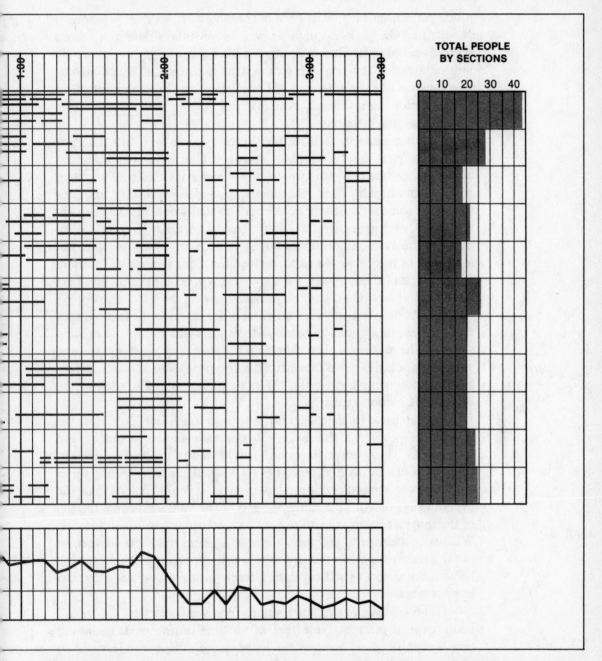

sharply and stays at a high level until 2:00. The turnover is heavy, but the number on the ledge at any time stays remarkably uniform—as running total at bottom shows, between 18 and 21 people. The number is not constricted by lack of space. Note that at the peak-use moments, there is plenty of space for more sitters. But they don't appear. In free-choice situations such as this, evidently, capacity tends to be self-leveling, and people determine it rather effectively.

beach patterns at Jacob Riis Park of the Gateway National Seashore in New York. On peak-use days as well as on others, the film record showed, people will cluster up front rather than fill up the relatively unused areas at the rear. This cannot be explained as a low-income phenomenon. At the other end of Long Island, at the Hamptons, there is much more sandy beach available per person. But the clustering tendency is much the same.

Another example is furnished by the people who use the IBM garden on New York's Madison Avenue. This large and attractive atrium space opened with twenty tables and sixty chairs. The tables were fixed into the floor; the chairs, however, were not, and this prompted some independent behavior. The staff would set the chairs at the tables, and generally the sitters found this OK. They would indulge in the usual minor moves but more or less stay at the table. But a number of people would elect to move the chair to another location. I kept track of these moves, for they were a good indication of where additional chairs might best be provided. As at the beaches, people's moves did not take them very far from other people. One favored spot was the base of a clump of bamboo trees just outboard of the existing seating. The staff man who tidied up the area was indefatigable and would periodically move the chairs back to the tables. Just as indefatigably, people would move the chairs to somewhere else, such as the base of the bamboo trees.

To get back to the Seagram ledge: as lunchtime proceeds, the number of people on the ledge will fluctuate between eighteen and twenty-one. This is surprisingly uniform in view of the heavy turnover. For two hours hardly a minute goes by without someone getting up or sitting down. Viewed as a time-lapse movie, it looks frenetic. But the overall range remains the same. Whenever the number reaches the top of the range at twenty-one to twenty-two, someone gets up and leaves. Whenever it drops to eighteen, there will be no more net leavers; to put it another way, enough new sitters will appear to make up for the leavers. Some sort of self-regulating mechanism, it would appear, has been at work.

Good spacing, one might assume. To a point, yes, but this doesn't really explain matters. Note that at no time during peak hours are people evenly spaced out over the ledge, nor do those who leave do so because they have been pinched in for want of space. In some places on the ledge there will be clumps of people sitting close together; elsewhere, people will have considerable space around them. This is true even at the three peak moments of this particular day: twelve-fifty, one twenty-five, and one-fifty. There is enough empty space on the ledge to take care of another half-dozen people easily.

But they do not appear. It is as if people had some instinctive sense of what is right overall for a place and were cooperating to maintain it that way, obligingly leaving or sitting down, or not sitting, to keep the density within range. Happenstance is at work too—the four friends who squeeze into a space left by three, the chance succession of three loners. Over time, happenstance can be quite regular.

Whatever the mechanism, there seems to be a norm that influences people's choices as much as the immediate physical space does. Thus is effective capacity determined. It is not static, nor can it be expressed only in figures. There are qualitative aspects to be considered—whether people are comfortable, whether they tarry or leave quickly—and these can be quite different for different people.

There even may be a music of sorts. On the ledge chart there is an up-tempo flurry of dashes around ten minutes before two. It is up-tempo on the ground, too; it is the last-minute return of the late lunchers. Since the chart looks so much like a player-piano roll I wondered what the sound would be if all the dots and dashes could be played. A composer friend was fascinated. With the right tonal scale, he said, the chart could be orchestrated and it would be music. I hope that one day it will be: *A Day in the Life of the North Front Ledge of Seagram Plaza, Vivace.*

The sitting chart of Seagram yields several other points worth noting. One is the uniformity with which the *total* number of sitters throughout the day is distributed on the ledge. At any one time there is little uniformity. By the end of the day, however, the cumulative totals for each of the ledge's eleven squares are similar. There is one exception: the square next to the steps. It has two edges and attracts double the number of sitters.

The log of the amount of time people sit is also revealing. Because of the high turnover, it is easy to assume that in-and-outers account for the bulk of the sitting done on the ledge. But appearances are deceiving. Over the day charted at Seagram there were some 266 sitters. As might be expected, the number who stayed for only a few minutes was greater than the number who stayed longer. Add up the total amount of time spent sitting, however, and you find that those who stayed longer logged far and away the most of it. Of the total— some 3,277 minutes—about three quarters was logged by people staying 11 minutes or more, almost half by those staying 21 minutes or more. A study of the south ledge showed similar results. Three quarters of the time spent during lunch periods was accounted for by people staying 15 minutes or more.

I have found the same pattern in other uses of space. Curbside car parking is one. As with ledge sitters, the activity seems to be dominated by the short-term users. Actually, it is the long-termers who

Capacity is self-leveling. People have a nice sense of the number that is right for a place and it is they who determine how many is too many.

dominate; out of proportion to their numbers, they account for the bulk of the available hours of use.

For the design of small parks and plazas, the density studies yield encouraging lessons. Capacity, to recapitulate, is self-leveling. People themselves determine the number that is right for a place, and they do it very well. Designers need not worry that they might make a place *too* attractive, too overrun by people. It is the reverse that they should be worrying about. The carrying capacity of most urban spaces is far above the use that is made of them.

The few that attract the highest density of people provide the most encouraging lesson of all. While they may in fact be the most crowded of places, they are perceived as the most pleasant, uncrowded of places. Sensitive design—and generosity of spirit—provide the anomaly.

Let me append a word about large spaces. My emphasis has been on small spaces. But this is not to scant the desirability of large ones. The question is sometimes raised as to whether it is better to have a Central Park or an equivalent amount of space in small parks. There is no comparability. Central Park is a magnificent space on a large scale, and it does something for the city that no scattering of small spaces could. Thanks to the eye of Frederick Law Olmsted and Calvert Vaux, Central Park is at once a large space and a host of small and distinctive ones, and it is experienced as such.

The fact is, however, that for a long time to come, the opportunities in the center city are going to be for small spaces. Costs are great; even when they are disguised in the form of incentives, tax abatements, and the like, space will come dear. But that is a consequence of centrality. Costs are high in the center because so many people will be served. Less costly places somewhere else can be a very poor bargain.

It is wonderfully encouraging to find that the places that people like best are the most replicable of spaces: relatively small—five thousand to ten thousand square feet—marked by a high density of people and an efficient use of space. They tend to be friendly places, with a high proportion of people in groups and much interchange back and forth.

I am not, heaven forfend, arguing for places of maximum gregariousness or for social directors. What I am suggesting, simply, is that we make places friendlier. We know how. With such details as some right angles in the seating, a recessed wind trap, and trees that catch the sun, we can create the conditions that lead people to mingle and meet. And to be comfortably alone, too. If one wishes to read or think or look, it is much better to do so in a place that others like than in one that is empty.

Some of the most felicitous spaces in a city are odds and ends, leftovers, niches: happy accidents that work for people, and of which there should be not so accidentally more. Bus stops should be inherently congenial and the reason so few are is a niggardliness of design which can be easily set right.

I am, in sum, advocating small, busy places. Too busy? I think not. Some fret that if places are made too attractive they will be overrun. This is a spectre that need not worry us. As we have seen, people have a nice sense of social distance and they manage it better than anybody else. They also have a nice sense of the number that is right for a place, and it is they who determine how many is too many.

They do not seek to get away from it all. If they did they would go to the lonely places, where there are few people. But they do not. They go to the lively places, where there are many people. And they go there by choice—not to escape the city, but to partake of it.

Planners sometimes worry that a place might be made too attractive and thereby overcrowded. The worry should be in the other direction. The carrying capacity of most urban spaces is far above the use that is made of them.

12

STEPS AND ENTRANCES

In the chapter on the sensory street I spoke of selling entrances—that is, entrances so inviting that people go in them on impulse. Let me now take up a more basic aspect: entrances that are easy to enter.

In most cities the biggest obstacles to pedestrian movement are the entrances to buildings. They are over-engineered, for one thing. Usually they consist of a set of revolving doors, flanked on either side by doors that swing open if you push them hard enough but that are very difficult to push open and that are not supposed to be used anyway. "Please use other door," a sign on them says. Sometimes the sign is mounted on a pedestal just inboard of the door and placed directly in its path, which does seem inconsistent for doors that may have to be used to get out of the place.

In any event, it is tough going. The revolving doors do not revolve, really; you revolve them and it often takes many foot-pounds of energy to do it. Some entrances use a set of swinging glass doors, and these are easier to manage. As with revolving doors, however, there is often a second set about twelve feet further inside. All this is necessary, engineers say, to keep cold or hot weather from coming in and, more important, to maintain an air seal so that drafts won't whistle up elevator shafts in a "stack effect."

Curiously, most building codes have nothing to say about entrances. You won't even find the word in their indexes. They have a lot to say about *exits,* however, and are very concerned with getting people safely from the inside to the outside. This is proper enough as far as it goes—enough doors for panic egress, doors wide enough, doors that swing in the exit direction. But there is no encouragement for making it easier to go from the outside to the inside, and one provision rules out the best kind of door there is.

For the clues to this door, watch a set of swinging doors as the rush hour builds. You may spot an oddity: as the number of people rises to a peak they go through faster and easier. I was first struck with this contradiction when I was studying the morning rush at the main entrance to Place Ville Marie in Montreal, one of the busiest entrances in the world. It has six swinging doors. At eight forty-five the flow was at a rate of six thousand people per hour. There was much congestion, with people queuing up behind one another. Ten minutes later the flow was up to eight thousand people per hour. But now the congestion was less. People were moving through easily and there was little queuing.

The explanation lies in the phenomenon of the open door. It is enormously attracting. Given a choice, people will head for the door that is already open, or that is about to be opened by somebody else. Some people are natural door openers. But most are not; often they queue up three and four deep behind an open door rather than strike out on their own.

An open door is very attracting. Given a choice, people will head for the door that is open or is about to be opened by someone else. Some people are natural door openers. Most are not.

As the crowd swells, more doors will be kept open. The people will be distributing themselves more evenly across the entrance, and finally, at peak, all the doors will be open and the people will be streaming through. The headway between the people going through the doors will be much shorter than is regarded as comfortable. But that is why they move so quickly. They don't give the doors a chance to close.

Thought: Why not leave a door open? Or two or three?

In New York City it would be against the law. The code says exit doors "shall normally be left in the closed position." Codes in other cities say the same. Then there is the stack effect to worry about, and the heat gain or loss. Fortunately, some building guards have not been properly indoctrinated about these dangers. I've noted a number of occasions when building guards propped a door open, even collapsed the leaves of revolving doors and left them open too. The building still stood. No overpowering drafts whistled through. The elevators continued running.

And the buildings were much easier to enter. Even at the peak of the rush hour the capacity of a few open doors is prodigious. A good example is the entrance to the RCA Building from the Sixth Avenue subway concourse. It consists of eight swinging doors. During the morning rush, the two doors on the right going in are usually open.

Lure of the open door: here at the busiest entrance to Montreal's Place Ville Marie, people queue up behind open doors. When flow is moderate, only a few doors are open, so there is considerable congestion. Later, when flow reaches peak, no door gets a chance to close, and everyone streams through.

That is because so many people are going through them. At the peak flow of eight thousand people per hour about two thirds of the people enter through these two doors.

Another high-traffic entrance is the west entrance of Grand Central Terminal on Forty-second street. It is a grubby-looking affair, with dimly lit vestibule. But it is very efficient. There are nine swinging doors, and a few of them do the job. One morning that I checked them, the flow rate at 9 A.M. was fifty-seven hundred people per hour. Three doors had been propped open, illegally but amenably. Of the people entering, 31 percent used these three doors; 42 percent went through a door that had been opened by someone ahead. Total open-door users: 73 percent. A similar set of nine swinging doors at the middle entrance on Forty-second shows the same open-door favoring. At the peak flows, the bulk of the traffic goes through three of the doors. Actually, it can be harder to enter in slack periods, when you may have to open a door yourself.

These precedents suggested the design for the entrance to a new building. For the Philip Morris Building across from Grand Central on Forty-second Street, architect Ulrich Franzen had designed an indoor sculpture garden to be operated by the Whitney Museum. The idea was to make the space as attractive as possible and the entrance easy and inviting. I recommended an open door. Franzen designed what could be called a mostly open door. The entrance is a twenty-foot-wide span of glass. In the center are sliding doors. In good weather they can be kept open to a width of six feet—quite enough for the normal flows. For overflows, and for confirmed door openers, there are swinging doors at either side. (Legislation was needed to make this setup legal. But the planning commission was delighted with the entrance, and the legislation was enacted.)

A small Bronx cheer is in order, however. The way the doorway has been managed considerably undercuts the welcoming intent of the door. For one thing, a moving TV surveillance camera is mounted atop the inside of the door. Slowly it revolves, sending its electronic image to a monitor on an upper floor—a rather redundant process inasmuch as the guards in the Whitney garden see better than the camera. Except as mobile sculpture it has no real function. A second Bronx cheer is for the doorway. Even in balmy weather when temperatures outside are the same as inside, the doors are not left open but are kept on automatic, to the frequent discomfiture of the people using them. As they approach the open door, they can be a bit taken aback as it starts to close on them; if they are resolute and keep advancing, the door will start opening again. But you can't tell until the last minute. It would make sense simply to leave the door open.

Open doors are good to have in interior spaces too. All too often, spaces within buildings are chopped up with unnecessary doors and partitions. This was the case with the underground concourse of Rockefeller Plaza. It was a revolving door manufacturer's dream: thousands of feet of concourse going this way and that, and wherever a concourse went under a building line or a street, there would be a set of doors to make visible the boundary.

A study of the concourse by the Project for Public Spaces showed that the doors accentuated climatic changes and drafts. As part of a major upgrading program, redundant doorways were removed, and in the freed-up space, sitting places were provided. As soon as the changes were made the pedestrian flows became much easier and less congested. The concourse became a more sociable place, particularly at lunchtime. Where previously groups had been broken up by having to go through the doors single file, they now ambled along. There was more schmoozing, more 100 percent conversations, more sitting and people watching.

(Another Bronx cheer: in a multimillion dollar improvement project the concourse area has recently been done over in white travertine—floors, walls, and all. This has made it much lighter and that is good. But there is no reading or sitting. All of the seating has been removed. Ledges that would otherwise be sittable have been interdicted with shrubbery and plants.)

For sheer ease of entry, to recapitulate, nothing beats an open door. For climatic and safety reasons, of course, doors cannot be open all the time. But they can seem to be. One way is to recess the entrance into the store. This provides a transitional area, and with the actual doorway at the rear the climatic change is moderated. An example is the Argosy Book Store on New York's Fifty-ninth Street. Its front is completely open to the street and, with tables stacked with second-hand books, functions as a browsing and come-on area. More cafés and restaurants are making a display of their fronts with French doors, or with foldable ones that can be retracted; the patrons at the front tables, in effect, are the window display.

I would nominate Bloomingdale's in New York as a prime candidate for such treatment. At the moment it has what is unquestionably one of the worst entrances anywhere; two sets of difficult doors, a narrow sidewalk, crowds backed up, vendors working the crowd. To make this a selling entrance instead, about 20 feet of frontage could be moved back into the store. About 12 feet in, there could be sliding glass doors, positioned open as much of the time as feasible. The transitional area would make for much easier access from the street. By being inviting, of course, the entry would induce more people to go in, but there would be room. There would also be room for Bloomingdale's to go to work on them. It does this now inside the store; you can't go 30 feet without somebody handing you a sample. But it's the vendors who get first crack out front. The store could do what Japanese department stores do so adroitly: have their own vendors in the entry area; put out high–impulse-appeal items. And have the purchases payable at a cash register just inside the entrance. Come into my parlor.

Steps

Steps are like entrances. They ought to be easy to negotiate and would cost little or no more if they were. The same is true of stairs that are safe. No new technology is needed. But observation certainly is. Little research on stairs has been done since that of François Blondel in Paris in the 1600s. His formulas govern U.S. building codes, and some updating might not be amiss.

Like entrances, most stairs are not easy. They are too steep, for one thing. To be easy to go up, stairs should have a pitch of under thirty degrees. Stairs with a 6-inch riser and a 12-inch tread would qualify, producing an angle of twenty-six degrees. But you will find few stairs in new office buildings that are this gentle. The recommended range in architectural practice is between thirty and thirty-five degrees. This is tolerable enough if there are not many steps in a flight. But if there are, the going up can be tiring.

For discomfort and hard going, one kind of stairs is in a class by itself: subway stairs. Most have risers of at least 7 inches and treads of no more than 11 inches. On the average, they have an angle of about thirty-five degrees. This steepness is rationalized as an efficient use of space. Steep stairs do not take up as much room as moderate ones. For similar reasons stairway widths are only 50 inches, 44 inches railing to railing. These are supposed to accommodate two people abreast, 22 inches each.

Such efficiency carries a stiff price. Going down is not bad, at slack periods at least. But going up can be tough going. This is particularly the case when there are no landings to break the ascent. Most building codes for commercial buildings require a landing after a rise of so many feet—eight in New York. But transit authorities make up their own rules. New York's now calls for landings, but some whoppers got through without landings. Possibly the worst stairway in the world is the one leading from the Lexington Line to the Grand Central Terminal concourse. Looking up, you see twenty-seven uninterrupted steps. The sight makes you tired even before you start the climb. Because the steps are so steep, people with shopping bags or suitcases

The formula for setting the dimensions of steps was formulated by Dr. François Blondel of the Royal Academy of Architecture of France in 1672. An updating might be in order.

The worst stairway in New York: twenty-seven steps and a gauntlet of beggars. Lexington line station at Grand Central.

slow down. Some stop to rest a few seconds. Quickly a knot of people will be backed up behind them. One lane may be blocked by a sleeping drunk.

At least these stairs are wide: about 17 feet. Negotiating the standard stairway is more difficult yet. They cannot handle counterflows well. When people going up are blocked by the slowness of people ahead of them, they will usually move to their left. But if there are people who want to come down in that space, it is just too bad. The dominant flow does not defer.

So the economy is a false one. A little space may have been saved in initial construction, but to what end? In time wasted, energy expended, discomfort, and incivility people have been paying for the meanness of these steps—day in and day out, year after year after year.

How much money is saved? Very little, if any. In the case of several new buildings, I have been able to compare the space requirements of the standard stairway they were going to build with those of a comfortable one they could build. The differential was only 6 to 8 feet of additional horizontal space. And the horizontal space would be there in any event; whether as a corridor space or as stairway space, the cost consideration would be minor. So it would be with many existing stairs. If you will check the floor space at the top or bottom of the stairs that you find steep, the chances are that there was quite enough space for a gentler run of steps. They were made steep by rote, not by necessity.

Most architects and developers do not give a hang. They show this in the way they handle subway station renovations. When these involve new office buildings there is usually a good bit of money available, the renovation being part of a bonus deal between city and developer. Attractive brick walls and flooring are installed; so is greatly improved lighting. If the city twisted the developer's arm enough there will be new escalators as well. But steps? There is no citizens' lobby for steps. Their pitch is a matter of indifference to the design people involved. The transit authority has liberalized its guidelines; it is no longer against the law to build comfortable stairways. But the old 7-inch–11-inch format is still permitted.

A number of studies have been made of the energy required to mount different step combinations. While the studies differ as to the exact number of foot-pounds, they do show that relatively small decreases in the angle of ascent make a big difference in the ease of the climb. The key is the riser. The small difference between the standard 7 inches and the much less common 6 inches makes for a whale of a difference, on long flights especially. Treads are important too, of course. The minimum depth should be 12 inches. If it is less, men have trouble fitting their feet to the space and often go down sideways, with crablike steps. Over a foot, additional inches of tread are nice to have, but they are less important than fewer half inches of riser.

Obviously, riser and tread must be in a satisfactory relationship. Unless they are, generosity of dimensions can fetch diminishing returns and, in some cases, danger. Some years ago at Lincoln Center, it was found that people were tripping on the steps in front of the Metropolitan Opera House. Railings were installed. Still they tripped. Architect James Marston Fitch of Columbia University investigated. He found that the trouble was an unusually shallow riser—3.3 inches— and an unusually deep tread—18 inches. The configuration did not match peoples' strides and threw them off balance. Lincoln Center eventually regraded the plaza and replaced the steps with a ramp.

There is a formula for risers and treads and it is found in some form in all building codes. Most commonly, it is expressed thus: the sum of two risers and a tread shall be not less than 24 inches or more than 25½. A lot of satisfactory combinations can be derived from this formula. But it does have a mathematical bias, however unintended. It favors generosity of treads. If you want a low riser—say, one of 5 inches—you must have a tread of at least 14 inches. The extra tread depth does not make much difference in comfort but might call for more lateral space than is available. Conversely, a 12-inch tread would marry nicely with a 5-inch riser, but it would not fit the formula. And the formula has never been changed.

Not since 1672, in fact. That was when it was formulated by François Blondel, director of the Royal Academy of Architecture of France. Blondel was a very resourceful man; he did a lot of walking and observing to determine normal strides. Two feet, he found, was about average. He then devised a formula to fit stairway dimensions to these strides. It stipulated that the total of the tread and two risers should be 24 inches.

In the ensuing 313 years people have grown taller, paces increased. But the formula lives on, unaltered. What has been lacking is a follow-up of the observational approach that led to the formula in the first place. But no more Dr. Blondels have come forward. The architectural profession should make up for the lost time by sponsoring fresh new inquiries. As Fitch observes, in addition to the step formula, most of the other rules of thumb for corridors and entrances and the like are quite arbitrary and are in conflict with each other.

Corridor and stairway widths are an example. They are usually set as multiples of 22 inches. This is the "body ellipse" and is presumed to include not only average shoulder width but an inch or so of buffer space. For a two-lane stairway, then, a width of 44 inches

Corridor widths are usually set at multiples of twenty-two inches— the presumed "body ellipse." That is not enough. People sway from side to side, as much as four inches.

should be enough. If everyone just stood, it would be. But when people walk they move beyond the ellipse. They sway.

J. L. Pauls of the Research Board of the Canadian Government has documented this phenomenon in an intensive film examination of behavior on stadium stairs. He found that people sway laterally as much as 3 or 4 inches from their straight-up position. In a study of ascents and descents of some 112 steps at one stadium, he found how very important are handrails—a feature often omitted in stadium designs, yet critical to safety.

Space needs for people going single file are underestimated; space needs for people going abreast are overestimated. One pitfall is to compute the disposition of people as though they were in a static situation; three people abreast on the right, three people in the opposite direction on the left—and all in a line at exactly the same frozen moment. Add it all up and you get six body ellipses in a row. But people do not walk that way. To be sure, if there is enough room ahead, three people will walk abreast and take plenty of space doing it. But when others approach them from the opposite direction, they close up a bit; next one or two of them will move back and slightly behind another. The lateral difference the three occupy may shrink from 6 or 7 feet to 4. Furthermore, they will slow down or accelerate so that the two groups of three will not come abreast of an opening in the traffic at the same instant.

By happenstance, I came across a test case of stair safety and the kinesthetic temptations of curved stairways. A large bank for which I had done a plaza study asked me to have a look at the main stairway of their new headquarters. They were very proud of the stairway. It was quite handsome, with two sets of straight steps joined by a graceful curve in the middle. It was well lit and had a dramatic view of the bank's conference center at the bottom of the steps.

But people were stumbling. About two thirds of the way down they would make a misstep. Only one person had suffered a bad fall so far, but the polished marble steps could make a slight fall a dangerous one. With dismaying frequency people were coming close. One could almost hear the law of averages clattering away.

It did not take long to find that the problem was inherent. The stumbles took place at the twenty-first and twenty-second steps. There was nothing wrong with the steps. The problem was the steps further up. They were bigger—bigger because they were curved. They encouraged longer strides and thereby set up people for the cross-up. At step twenty, the start of the straightaway, the steps were smaller. Suddenly so.

The best thing would be to tear down the stairway and replace it with a new one. But this would take time; the bank was going to be hosting a regional conference and could not tackle the redo for several months. Were there short-term measures that would help? We considered the possibilities.

"Guidelines for Stair Safety," published by the National Bureau of Standards, cited six major requirements: (1) consistency of riser and tread dimensions; (2) uniform lighting; (3) edge of treads clearly visible; (4) handrails; (5) no "rich" view to one side. (6) at least one landing for every eight feet of rise. The bank's stairs flunked on all counts save one. It did have handrails.

In a semicontrolled experiment some of the missing factors could be introduced one by one: marking the danger steps with white strips, carpeting the steps, changing the lighting, masking the distracting view at the bottom of the steps. For good measure, the bank stationed guards on the steps to individually caution people.

We learned some surprising things about stair behavior. The stumblers, we found out, tipped themselves off at the top of the steps. They did not grasp either of the handrails and look down at the steps below. Most people did. Older people, women especially, were most likely to do so. They took their time and all the way down continued to look at the steps with vigilance. Maybe that is why they had lived long enough to become old.

On stairways, younger people are the most likely to stumble or fall. They don't grasp the handrails and they don't look down. Older people do. That is why they have lived long enough to become old.

It was the younger people—the people with the most agility, the best vision, and the sharpest reflexes—who were most likely to be stumblers. They were least likely to grasp the handrail and look down. They went at a fast clip, some bounding down two steps at a time. The most confident of all were young fathers with children perched on their shoulders. I never saw one stumble, but it was unnerving to watch them.

I focused cameras on the key steps and recorded foot movements in slow motion. Whatever the depth of the tread, the films showed, people tend to place the foot as far forward as possible, with the front of the shoe a half to two inches beyond the edge of the tread. If the tread is increased in depth they push their foot that much further forward. Younger people are markedly more adventurous than older ones in this respect.

This toeing of the front edge of the tread looks dangerous, but ordinarily it is not. The fail safe is the metatarsal arch. As long as it is firmly supported by the tread, all will be well. Women, with their shorter strides, usually place their feet so that the front of the shoe is just short of the tread edge.

This presupposes that each stair will be identical to the next. This is a cardinal provision of all building codes, which specify that in any flight of steps the dimensions of the risers and treads shall remain constant. In the case of the bank, they did not. The reason was the marrying of a curve and a straightaway without an intervening landing.

As the stairway enters the curve, the treads assume a wedge shape and the wide side gets wider. This invites one to take bigger and bigger steps and to pick up the pace. As terpsichore it is rather fun. But a surprise is at hand. Just as one has become used to the rhythm of the wide tread, the stairs straighten and the wedges contract. The toe still pushes forward beyond the edge of the tread. But suddenly the edge of the tread is not there. The metatarsal arch meets air. So one stumbles.

Frequency? It was impossible to compute a statistically valid rate. Sometimes there would be three or four stumblers within an hour; other times only one, or none. Full falls were rarer, on the order of about one fall for every ten stumbles. One would expect that the number of stumbles and falls would run in some proportion to the number of people using the stairs. Volume, however, proved a misleading factor. During some periods, the higher the volume, the *fewer* the stumbles and falls. (Average daily volume: thirty-six hundred people in seven hours.)

As we observed with doorways, a large volume of people can be a discipline. On the stairs, an increase in the number of people slowed things down markedly. With both up and down sides of the stairs in full use, people would form up single file. They were more likely to take a handrail and look down—even younger people. There was no bounding down the stairs, and in the event of a fall, there were more people on the stairs to fall against.

There is nothing wrong with curved stairways. As long as curve and steps are constant, there is no cross-up. They do look more hazardous than straight ones but this is itself a safety factor. Spiral staircases, especially the kind with open risers, are scarier yet. But they are quite safe, in part because people treat them with unusual caution.

In experimenting with temporary measures we found that markings on the edge of treads do tend to alert people. We also found how valuable carpeting can be. The stair-safety people have mixed feelings about carpeting, being less impressed with its cushioning properties than with its susceptibility to tears and fraying. But we found carpeting of critical importance to safety. Not much research has been done on the life-and-limb aspect, the carpet manufacturers being curiously unresourceful on this product advantage. I know from personal experience, however, that those tufts provide the extra millimeters of give that make the difference between a spill and a bad accident. (I fell on a tile floor that usually was carpeted but wasn't when I fell. Instead of a bruise I broke a bone. All stairs and floors in our house are now carpeted.)

Not the least of carpeting's advantages is the way it demarcates the edge of treads. As the carpeting rounds over the nose of the tread, the fibers spread a bit and catch the light at different angle. This makes the edges look either perceptibly lighter than the rest of the carpet, or, in some cases, darker. Going up or going down, you see a series of highlighted edges.

We could not test each change by itself and thus could not assign precise cause and effect. But several points were clear. Of all the measures, carpeting was the most helpful. It did not stop falls but it made them much more tolerable. The other measures were of some help. But the stumbles continued, albeit at a somewhat reduced rate. Even the warnings of the guards were not much of a deterrent. The palliative measures, we had to conclude, were a minor counter to the flawed design. So we were back to where we started. Pay the two dollars.

The bank and the architect did it in good grace. A new stairway was designed incorporating the lessons learned. It had three straight-away flights linked by two generous landings. The stairway was entirely carpeted. It was handsome and nobody stumbled on it.

While the one landing of the original stairway was not a factor in the stumbles, there is some evidence that good-sized landings—and plenty of them—make stairs safer as well as easier to negotiate. If you see landings ahead, you know the going will be easier.

The new steps to the lobby of Carnegie Hall are a fine case in point. Architect James Stewart Polshek arranged the steps so that the next landing ahead would be visible. "That is an ancient and unobserved rule of graceful transition," he says. "You move up seven steps and come to a landing. Then you go up again until you come to the rear of the hall."

Such fine-tuning of stairs, it could be observed, is nice but rather pointless; for all practical purposes stairs have been superseded by escalators in the public spaces of most new office buildings and transportation facilities. Escalators have become so universal, indeed, that adjacent stairways are designed to the same pitch.

It is certainly true that the great bulk of people will take the escalator over the stairs. It is also true that one escalator operating near capacity—about seventy people per minute on the standard forty-one-inch width—can move heavy flows very efficiently. Even extreme choke points can be tamed by the adroit placement of an additional escalator or two. Penn Station's horrendous subway exits should soon be a demonstration.

But stairs are not yet obsolete. They are useful for taking care of the overflow at peak times for the escalators, and they are preferred by a small minority of confirmed stair climbers. More to the point, in low-volume situations, which means most situations, they remain the principal means of ascent and descent. They might as well be made safe and attractive and easy.

This is especially true of exterior steps. They are more used than interior ones, usually being the only way up and in. And they have more functions. One is ceremony. Architects do well with this aspect. Their steps for courthouses and government buildings and museums tend to be impressive, often more so than the buildings they lead to.

Another function of steps is to invite people into a place. The steps in front of Paley Park in New York City do this most elegantly. There are just four steps, with five-inch risers and fifteen-inch treads. People seem pulled toward them and they often go up them without seeming to have made any decision at all. The steps at Greenacre Park on Fifty-first Street function the same way. Both Paley and Greenacre were the work of landscape architects—respectively Robert Zion and Hideo Sasaki. For some reason landscape architects seem to have a special feel for steps.

Architect Mies van der Rohe, however, was responsible for the best steps of any major office building: those at the Seagram Building. He was always meticulous about the design of steps and it shows in both appearance and function. The steps up to the side entrance are both the easiest and the best-looking in New York City (five-inch riser, fourteen-inch tread). His steps in front of the plaza are inviting in the way Paley Park's are. They also discharge another function of exterior steps—they are fine for sitting—and the fact that the architect did not design them for that purpose does not detract from their utility as a model. The corners of the steps are particularly useful, for brown baggers especially, providing face-to-face sitting and a place for the food. The architect did not, as so many do, fussy up the corners of the steps with railings. In this case less has indeed been more.

The Seagram steps are so fine they are cause for dismay. The building was put up in the early 1950s; in fact it is now old enough to be declared a landmark. Its tower and plaza configuration have been enshrined in zoning codes and copied in countless office buildings. But not the steps. Day in, day out, for over three decades they have provided a model of a near ideal set of steps—easy, safe, elegant. In all that period no office building has incorporated steps their equal.

Another model has been provided by the steps to the subway entrances to the Citicorp Building. They have six-inch risers and twelve-and-three-quarter-inch treads. The vertical climb is nineteen feet but the pitch is comfortable, the landings generous. By contrast,

The easiest steps in New York City: New York County Courthouse, Foley Square. (Riser: four and a half inches; tread: eighteen inches.)

the standard subway steps cram their rise into fewer and steeper steps, resulting in far more expenditure of energy.

One of the most striking contrasts to experience is at Penn Station —specifically, at Tracks 17 and Tracks 18/19 of the Long Island Railroad. The steps to Track 17 are the standard. Those to 18/19, however, by some fluke or good deed were made quite humane. The difference in comfort and energy expended is dramatic.

The transit authority has liberalized its specifications for stairways. It now recommends a riser height of six and a half inches "wherever feasible" and a tread of eleven and a half inches. But it forbids risers lower than six inches or treads deeper than twelve inches —which is to say, steps as comfortable as Seagram or those of Tracks 18-19.

For sheer ease of climb this juror nominates the steps of the New York County Court House at Foley Square in Manhattan. They have risers only four and a half inches high and treads of eighteen inches, providing a remarkably gentle rise.

Some steps are designed for sitting. For Princeton's Wu Hall, architect Robert Venturi designed a staircase with oversized steps at one side. They were meant to be lounged and sat upon and so they are. Gund Hall at Harvard's Graduate School of Design has a set of oversized steps that are good for sprawling upon.

At the IBM garden the temporary stage put up for Christmas events turned out to be a popular sitting place. The steps, providing face-to-face right angles, were especially favored. We took our cue from the market and recommended a permanent temporary stage. A simple affair with several flat surfaces and steps, all comfortably carpeted, it functions day in and day out as a place to sit, read, and brown-bag. It's not a bad stage either.

Most steps are not particularly comfortable for sitting. The low riser that makes steps east to climb furnishes no back support. Step sitters tend to be younger people. But physical comfort is less important than sun and light, the angle of view, and the activity below—that is, it is not the comfort of the perch so much as what you see from it. In this respect, the two finest examples are the steps of the New York Public Library and of the Metropolitan Museum of Art. Both strike a nice balance: comfortable to negotiate, good to sit on and watch people from.

What makes a set of steps good for sitting is not the comfort of the perch so much as what you see from it.

Interior steps can be something else again. Going up to the Public Library, one ascends in easy stages—a few easy steps, a landing, some more steps, another landing, and so on up, easily. Once inside, however, monumentality is not so kind to you as it was outside. The steps to the second floor have a reasonable pitch—twenty-three degrees— but they make up for this by interminability. After ten introductory

A great niche: St. Thomas' steps, northwest corner of Fifth Avenue and Fifty-third Street.

steps, there is a landing, and then a left turn to face an uninterrupted flight of thirty-two steps. It's no easy climb up to the third floor either. John Merven Carrère and Thomas Hastings may have been fine architects but these steps are bad steps.

Some architects do not like landings and would not have them if the building code did not specify them. Some leave out landings anyway. The landings break the rhythm of the processional movement. To avoid landings, two sets of steps may be provided: one adhering to the building code; the other, to a higher aesthetic. Some architects are quite heartless on this score. And the building department lets them get away with it. (One loophole: a second set of stairs that conforms to the code in all details.)

Coming out foursquare for comfortable steps should not be a difficult stand to take. But it is a case that does need making. The fact is that most steps are nowhere near as comfortable as they should be, and they are so due to a number of outmoded or faulty rules of thumb. There are, for example, the least-energy riser tread formulas. They call for steps a bit on the steep side and rule out very low risers and very deep treads. The rationalization is that while each low-rise step is easy to take, more will be needed to negotiate the climb and this will cancel out the advantage.

It will not. There is a fallacy here. The least-effort equations scant the importance of time. More is indeed needed to go up, say, eighteen easy steps than fourteen steep ones. But that extra time is a boon. It spreads out the time in easier-to-take segments. At the end of climbing the very gentle steps of Track 18, one feels much less fatigued than at the end of climbing the more vertical steps of Track 17. I have not the apparatus to measure the relative exertions, but simple observation of the comparative flows leaves one in little doubt. People go up gentle steps more easily than steep steps.

There is enough knowledge in hand to warrant several major improvements. Step number one should be a revision of building codes to bring stair requirements out of the seventeenth century. Blondel's pioneering work needs updating. The standard two-risers-and-one-tread formula is too rigid, and it militates against low risers by requiring unnecessarily deep treads in compensation. Revised guidelines should not merely set forth the permissible range of riser and tread dimensions. They ought to take sides and come out for an optimum configuration—such as six-inch riser and twelve-inch tread at the very least; five and fourteen where feasible. These should also be incorporated in the guidelines of transportation authorities. Bureaucratic inertia being what it is, just changing those few figures would wreak major improvements, year after year.

Standards should be set for exterior steps. At present there are none. This has not been all to the bad; some of the finest exterior steps would have been forbidden had the formula for interior steps applied. The New York County Court House's exemplary steps would not have passed muster, nor would the steps of the Metropolitan Museum of Art. Conversely, for want of standards some steps were provided that should not have been—the handsome but trippable steps in front of the Metropolitan Opera House.

Exterior steps are in many ways more of a challenge than interior ones. They are more often a primary facility than an alternative; they carry heavy pedestrian flows; they serve as sitting and congregating places; they are a key element of the street and it is not a frill that they be elegant as well as useful. There is no dearth of good precedents. I conclude with my favorite: the steps to the side entrances of the Seagram Building:

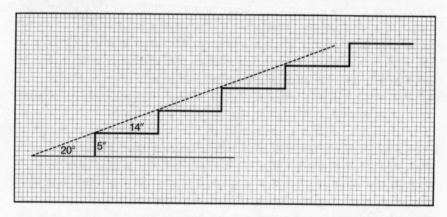

13

CONCOURSES AND SKYWAYS

The war against the street gains force. Not only have planners and architects been lining it with blank walls and garages; they have been leveling blocks of old buildings for parking lots, de-mapping streets for megastructures. Now they are going the next step. They are taking the principal functions of the street and putting them almost anywhere but on street level. They are putting them in underground concourses and shopping malls, in skyways and upper-level galleries. Ultimately, they may get the pedestrian off the street altogether.

The walkways and concourses we are going to discuss are the latest manifestation of one of the most venerable concepts of urban planning: the separation of vehicular from pedestrian traffic. From the Victorian era on, almost every utopian projection of the future has featured such separation, often in romantic terms—great bridges and tunnels in the sky, subsurface pleasure grounds and promenades, dirigibles and monorails, and, lately, computer-directed people movers.

All this is for the benefit of the pedestrian, it is said. The separation provides safety from cars, fumes, noise, and the like. In actual fact, the separation is for the benefit of vehicles. Who gets the prime space? Not the pedestrian. He had it once: ground level. The point of separation is to get him off it. So he is sent to the cellar, or upstairs. Vehicles get the prime space.

In principle, transportation departments plan for pedestrians as well as vehicles. But look at how they operate: federal, state, local—they are almost wholly concerned with maximizing vehicular traffic. The pedestrian is considered, to be sure, but as a problem, and not so much to be planned for as to be planned against.

One thinks of that ultimate declaration, the freeway cloverleaf, admitting of no trespass by pedestrians whatsoever. Where there are pedestrian facilities, they are apt to be both separate and unequal: the gigantic overpasses of Tokyo, for example—these are really for cars so they won't have to slow down for pedestrians. The latter sensibly avoid the climb if they possibly can.

The surrogate streets the most rooted in function have been the underground concourses. Originally, they came about as adjuncts to the underground rail systems. They were geared to the movement of great numbers of people in very short periods of time. They still are, and save for the introduction of escalators—pioneered by the London Underground—their physical characteristics have not changed very much. As a matter of fact new stations have not matched the design level reached by Grand Central and Pennsylvania stations. All that grandeur, we belatedly recognized, was rather functional: you knew where you were going; you knew where you were. The structure told you. The new Penn Station underground moves people adequately, but utterly without grace—and that is a form of inefficiency.

It was natural that there be an extension of underground rail concourses to nearby buildings. The concourse of Rockefeller Center was an early prototype. While it was primarily a transportation corridor, it featured shops along its spine and was connected with a sunken plaza at one end.

The next step was to see concourses as ends in themselves—connected with rail and subway stations, perhaps, but providing complete environments, with a range of shops and service facilities, restaurants and meeting places. Montreal's Place Ville Marie and the networks it spawned were influential precedents.

Of the benefits underground concourses provide, the most important is protection from bad weather. As one who has used the Rockefeller Center concourse for many years, I certainly would not scant that benefit. Nor the convenience shopping, the post office, the bootblack, the Greengrocers' take-out deli. The center is a true 100 percent location, with massive pedestrian flows concentrated along a clear axis from a major transportation facility.

Context is all important. What is troubling about the genesis of many off-street systems is how easily this factor is overlooked. Consider Minneapolis and Montreal. These cold-winter cities are the most

View from Minneapolis skyway to dullified street level.

copied models for off-street systems. The cities that do the copying are not necessarily cold-winter cities themselves. Some have splendidly mild winters. What impels them to copying is a feeling that their downtowns are too dowdy, too old-fashioned. A quantum leap is needed, and maybe some architectural razzle-dazzle might bring it about.

So the cities send civic delegations on pilgrimages to Minneapolis and Montreal. They like what they see. They like the skyways of Minneapolis. They like the concourses of Montreal. They note that both downtowns are successful. The syllogism completes itself.

So they go back to their cities with visions of concourses and skyways. What they do not go back with is the context that makes them work in Minneapolis and Montreal. They do not, for one thing, go back with eighteen degrees below zero. They do not go back with the high-density, 100 percent locations that Minneapolis has in the IDS Center, Montreal in Place Ville Marie, nor with the very heavy pedestrian flows that converge on these places. They go back to cities with low-density cores, light pedestrian flows, and little enough retailing at street level to begin with. What these cities sorely need are more people on the streets, not fewer people. But they put in the concourses and the skyways and they wonder why the streets are deader than ever.

Cities send delegations to Minneapolis and Montreal. They come back with plans for skyways and concourses. What they do not come back with is eighteen below zero.

Cedar Rapids, Iowa—Second Street.

If planners had to spend some time in their underground utopias they would become thoroughly disoriented. "You Are Here" say the illuminated maps. But where is here? In these symmetrical layouts there is no cue, no glimpse of sky or sun to hint at north or south.

How good is the substitute? If the planners had to spend some time in their underground utopias, they might have second thoughts. The underground spaces are, among other things, disorienting. Stay in one spot for a while and you will soon be approached by lost people seeking directions. There are signs around, but they do not help much. Nor do the illuminated maps, with their arrows pointing to YOU ARE HERE. People are puzzled by them. Where is HERE? That's a problem. HERE is a pillar or a wall like all the other pillars and walls, without uniqueness. There is no fixed point to sight on, no glimpse of sky or sun to suggest north or south.

The situation is compounded by architects' liking for symmetry. Concourses tend to be laid out so that north corridor A is the mirror image of south corridor B. Nothing is askew, as it is topside: no steeple, no dome, no eccentric building to get your bearings by. There are some clues. The pizza parlor means you're at the west end of corridor

A, not the east. That would be the card shop. But even the veteran can get confused. If I forget which side of the elevator bank I came down on, I can easily get myself turned around wrong and head north when I want to go south.

Les Terrasses, one of the newest shopping complexes in Montreal, was so confusing to people with its many levels and half levels that it was closed down for an extensive overhaul. As at the Bonaventure in Los Angeles, color coding was adopted to guide people to their various destinations. It is still confusing. The major problem is one that dogs so many complexes. You can't see out. You can't get your bearings from a known landmark. A new project, Complexe Desjardins, is much easier to read. At either end of the main space, large expanses of glass give a view of the buildings beyond. You know where you are.

Climatically, concourses are supposed to be a happy medium. But many are drafty, especially near entrances, and there may be abrupt variations in temperature from one section to another. There are not the extremes one finds outdoors, but that is itself a problem. An in-between climate can pose more difficulties if you alternate between outside and inside. What kind of clothes to wear? During a good part of the year it is too warm inside for the overcoat you need for the outside.

As shopping environments, concourses are fine for convenience items—newspapers, shoeshines, coin lockers, photocopies, automated teller machines, pastries and bread to take home. But they are not right for the top of the line. Basements are basements, whatever they are called, and the schlock quotient is usually high. This seems to be an international phenomenon; from Yaesu Square in Tokyo to Market Street in Philadelphia, concourses show a strong affinity for gift shops, fast-food counters, greeting card shops, and the like. The few concourses that do have some first-rate shops are apt to be part of a complex in which the street level has been dedicated to offices, bank windows, and blank walls rather than retailing. This provides a captive clientele for the retail shops down below and further confirmation of the rightness of undergrounding.

One underground environment that has had style and good shops is Montreal's Place Ville Marie. Its tenant mix is not as upscale as once it was. But it is still an outstanding prototype. Among the features visiting civic groups would do well to note is the site, like the IDS Center in Minneapolis, is a 100 percent location, lying between the railroad station and the main shopping street, Ste. Catherine. The site slopes sharply, and at its northern side it is entered at street level. Daylight has been brought into the complex through small courtyards leading to a broad plaza above. (The plaza itself, however, has lost key features, among them a cafe, now replaced by a computer facility.)

The winter climate is fierce. One winter day when I was filming Ste. Catherine Street, the temperature was so cold that my camera froze up. But this did not deter the shoppers, of whom there were many on the street—just as many per hour, indeed, as in the warm main corridor of Place Ville Marie.

The most praised benefit of concourses and skyways is that of system. They are not just an aggregate of segments, the point is made, but an encompassing network, with every building linked to every other—or soon to be, if all developers shape up. The dream is a graphic one, and the system is certainly impressive in maps of it. They do seem so complete.

But the completeness is not relevant to most pedestrians, nor is it perceived by them. If you check how people use a concourse, you will find that a few main segments carry the bulk of traffic. As you poke into the far reaches, however, the number of people drops markedly. So do the cost-benefit ratios.

It is nice to know that you can go from A to B and on to Z or Y or X. Old hands at Rockefeller Center, for example, know a way that takes them off the beaten track and, via innumerable twists and turns and right-angled passageways, ends them up at the Sperry Rand Building. But part of the pleasure of the route is that few other people know it. That particular escalator is not much used; sometimes several minutes go by without a person appearing. But the escalator keeps going, kilowatt after kilowatt—just as expensively as the escalators in the places where there are many people. This is not to gainsay the amenity of escalators. The point is that the advantages of completeness of system are vastly overrated, and costly to boot; it costs just as much to build the low-traffic segments, and as much to operate them.

The city that has done most to kill off its streets is Dallas. With extensive planning and strong civic support, it has embarked on the construction of an underground concourse-and-skyway system so complete that every building in downtown will eventually be connected with every other one.

They do not do things halfway in Dallas. It is to be *the* system, not merely a supplement. There is no namby-pamby sentimentality about pedestrian streets. One gathers that the proponents would be delighted if pedestrians could be eliminated from the streets altogether. This would decongest streets of people and make more room for cars. So in essence goes the rationale.

Here is how it has been put by Vincent Ponte, the planner who embarked Dallas on this course: "One of the chief contributing factors to traffic congestion," he says, "is crowds of pedestrians interrupting the flow of traffic at intersections." Because of this crowding, he points out, the structure of the core makes it impossible to widen the streets to accommodate more vehicles. There is not enough sidewalk space to cut down. How, then, to resolve the problem?

Get the pedestrians off the streets. "Studies show," says Ponte, "that downtown walkway systems, with their crosswalks and underpasses, draw pedestrians off crowded sidewalks."

The unstated premise is the primacy of vehicular traffic. But Ponte stops short of carrying the argument to its logical conclusion. If the pedestrians have been usurping street space to the hurt of vehicles, as Ponte indicates, why let them on the street at all? To be consistent, the city should make use of the underground level mandatory. If it did, it could reap a large windfall by recycling the now redundant sidewalk space. It could convert the space to additional traffic lanes for vehicles. In Dallas, that would mean two more lanes. Alternatively, the city could market the space commercially. It could move the building line out to the former curb line and sell or lease the extra space for retailing and office use.

Outrageous? Yes, but it does not beggar probability. There is a momentum to these projects that makes them self-aggrandizing. Once a number of buildings are linked to a concourse, there is mounting pressure on subsequent developers to join up with a link of their own. The provision of such a link, indeed, becomes something of a loyalty test, and it is a brave or foolish developer who abstains. Eventually, no pressure is necessary. Since so many other buildings are on the system, a developer will figure he has to join up if his property is to be marketable.

The biggest problem posed by surrogate streets is not that they fail to function but that they function too well. Dilution is the consequence. A downtown can support just so many stores and restaurants, and it is a lively downtown if there are enough of them on its streets. Add another level and something has to give. This is what happened in Dallas. Pedestrian crowding is notable for its absence. At the peak of the lunch period, sidewalk volumes are in the range of 1,400 to 1,800 people per hour, a very low figure for so highly dense a core.

Where are they all? Some are in the in-house cafeterias, others in the downtown clubs. A good number are in the salad bars and pizza places of the underground concourse system. In no one place are there very many people, and, while Dallas is a dynamic city, you would never guess it by its streets. Some crowding is just what they need. There are signs of vitality—street vendors have been licensed. But the undergrounding continues apace.

A city that has had second thoughts is Toronto. For many years it zealously pursued the goal of separation of pedestrian and vehicular traffic. It paid half the cost of underground segments and allowed

The biggest problem posed by skyways and concourses is not that they will fail to function but that they will function too well. A downtown can support just so many stores and restaurants. Add another level of them and something has to give.

builders to include basement space as a free bonus over and above the
floor space permitted by the zoning. As is usually the case, the pedestrians got the short end. They were given the basement; cars got
ground level. As time went on and more street-level retailers went out
of business, the city decided it had gone too far.

Toronto was becoming a city of moles, said head planner Steven
McLaughlin. "What we don't want is to have everyone use underground private streets, which close at 6 P.M., and leave the outdoor
streets empty of life except for a few brave souls dashing between
buildings from urban fort to urban fort under the eye of skyscraper
security guards." Toronto has now reversed course. It has withdrawn
the incentives for undergrounding and has followed New York's example of requiring retailing at street level in new buildings.

Skyways pose the challenges of system completeness as forcibly as
concourses. Once a few are built, the momentum for adding more
gathers force, and before long the civic goal is a complete system. The
best examples in the United States are the twin cities of Minneapolis
and St. Paul. The YOU ARE HERE signs you see in these cities show
comprehensive networks connecting virtually all of the principal
buildings of downtown.

The comprehensiveness is what most impresses visiting planners.
But it is a bit misleading. Those maps indicate a homogeneous network; they fail to show that the usage is concentrated near 100 percent
locations, and that it falls off markedly as one pokes out to the further
reaches. In Minneapolis, for example, the four skyways that feed into
the IDS Crystal Court have very heavy pedestrian volumes. On a cold
winter's day I clocked volumes at midday averaging 5,800, 4,800,
5,500, and 2,280 people per hour. As one moves away from the center,
the flows taper off rapidly. At an arcade a block and a half away, the
flow is around 1,100 people per hour. As with concourses, the capital
and operating costs of little-used segments are about as great as those
of the heavily used segments.

Aesthetically, skyways are a mixed bag. Most are poorly designed
and rarely in harmony with the design of the buildings they connect.
But some are handsome, not only for the view of them from the street,
but the view from them of the street. Most streets in our grid systems
never seem to have a stopping point; they recede off to infinity. A
pedestrian bridge can frame the scene, give it some closure, and bring
down the apparent scale of very large buildings. The bridge can also
provide vantage points and perspectives on the city that did not exist
before. The traffic below can be an interesting picture, especially at
dusk.

But bridges can mess up the townscape, too. St. Paul has a most
interesting topography, with lots of hillsides and different elevations.

The network of bridges—with so many at the same level—has a way of taming the topography and flattening the city.

Another city with topography to cherish is Seattle. Its city council has ruled against skyways, largely on aesthetic grounds. It was asked to make an exception in the case of a new complex that would link three stores. There was good economic justification for one and it was to be well designed. The city council would have none of it. Every day, said the chairman, she had to look at the two that were already built and they were awful. The other members agreed. Seattle had a fine compact core and attractive streets. The council reasoned that it should guard its blessings. The exception was not granted.

Why go up? Unless there is a clear reason, people resist. They are terrestrial. They like ground level and will often put up with difficulties at ground level rather than take a seemingly easier way up above. Those huge pedestrian overpasses in Tokyo are an example; sensibly, most Tokyo pedestrians prefer to wait for the light and cross the street rather than go up the overpass.

Baltimore's Charles Center was one of the earliest downtown renewal projects in the country and one of the most influential. It featured a large central plaza enclosed by old and new buildings—one by Mies van der Rohe—and with an elevated walkway system for pedestrians. The walkway system was considered a major advance in planning and inspired similar separation projects elsewhere.

But people did not use the walkways very much. In time, it was hoped, they would learn to. But they did not. The Charles Center people, a practical group, figured that the pedestrians probably were right. The walkways did not tie in with the main activity or with the stores; one stretch, for example, had not a doorway on it. The walkway also tended to make spaces beneath darker than they should be. In 1986, as part of an overall revitalization plan, it was decided to remove the major part of the second-level system and get the focus of activity back to ground level.

A few blocks south is another example, Harborplace. The waterside promenades and pavilions are a great attraction for people. They are somewhat hemmed off from the city, however, by a major highway. To make access easier for people, a large pedestrian bridge has been provided. Usage is much less than one would expect. Most people prefer to wait for the light and cross at grade.

At the University of Illinois' Circle Campus in Chicago, there is a two-level system: paved walkways on the ground and a duplicate set directly above them. It was hoped that the addition of the upper level would relieve pedestrian congestion and induce use topside by faculty and students. As it happened, there was no congestion to relieve and the upper level has been little used. Maintenance has been a problem, particularly in winter; the walkways, which are not covered, are wind-swept and difficult to clear of snow.

Mixed-use developments that spring up around interchanges are begetters of second-level systems. A case in point is the Crystal City complex in the Virginia suburbs of Washington. As in most such complexes, there is an enormous amount of superstructure used by not very many people. The problem is not that it kills off the street. There is no street to kill off. The problem is superfluity. In these complexes people do not walk much, whatever the level.

Some upper-level systems have been designed in the name of the street; that is, not to diminish its vitality but to relocate it. Several imaginative designs for high-rise housing have taken this approach. By stacking a tier of walkways vertically, they have given each floor its own street. The apartment units open directly onto it, as row houses do on the ground.

They have not worked very well. When you take a street away from street level you take away what makes it work. Remove the intricate mixture of people, the pedestrian bustle, the shops, and the traffic, and what you are left with is a corridor. It can be a very bleak one, too, as was the case with the ill-fated Pruitt-Igoe project in St. Louis.

The city that has done a good job of combining a lively street level with an upper-level skyway system is Calgary. It has reason for skyways; at latitude fifty-one degrees north, it has *average* daytime temperatures in winter of twenty-five below zero. In really cold weather it drops to fifty below. The sun shines a lot, but it sits low on the horizon and its shadows are long.

To make downtown more walkable in winter the city initiated the "plus fifteen" plan. Developers receive a bonus of extra floor space by providing walkways at the fifteen-foot level within their buildings and across the streets. Two additional levels, plus-thirty and plus-forty have been added. The design of the walkways is a cut above that of other cities: some are sited along the sides of buildings and are visually linked to the street. No blank walls here, but lots of see-through glass. Walkways open up into larger public areas, with snack bars and cafés.

But Calgary did all this without turning its back on the street. It has actively supported street activity as much as possible. Proportion-ately, its downtown blocks have more street-level retailing than most medium-sized cities, and the stores open directly onto the street. There are many places to sit, and while the office buildings are about par, there is one that is strikingly attractive. One of the principal streets has been turned into a pedestrian mall. In good and passable weather it is full of young people, and, while some citizens deplore the raunchiness of one end of it, it is an enlivening place. Calgary people make much

Housing project "streets in the sky" do not work very well. When you take a street away from ground level you take away what makes it work—such as the intricate mixture of people, the shops, the hustle and bustle. What you are left with is a corridor.

more of the sun and warmth they get than people who have a lot more of it.

There is, then, little dilution. In winter, people use the walkways to the fullest; in summer, the street.

Why not both approaches? As Calgary demonstrates, it is possible to have an upper-level system and a lively street level as well. Similarly, in the early stages, when there are as yet only a few skyways, cities can find that they complement the streets more than they compete with them. That will come later.

The coexistence will prove nettlesome. A large capital investment is riding on the off-street system, and so is civic judgment. To be vindicated, the off-street system must prosper, and to do this it must dominate. In most towns there is simply not the market to support two full levels of business. One or the other will suffer. And so will the city.

Several years ago Charlotte, North Carolina, had one main level. It was a good one. Downtown was compact, defined with a slightly eccentric grid (due, one story has it, to a drunken surveyor). There were stores along its main streets, fine old buildings and new ones, the most magnificent street trees of any U.S. city, a balmy climate, and an amiable citizenry.

But it was a bit old-fashioned. What it needed, a developer of suburban shopping malls believed, was a shopping mall. On a site adjacent to the center of town, he put up a mixed-use complex, combining a hotel, a bank and office tower, and, on the second level, a shop-lined concourse—the Overstreet Mall, it was called. The mall was soon connected by skyway to the city's new convention center across the street; next by another skyway to a department store; through it and thence by skyway to another store.

In a remarkably short time Charlotte had a second level—and without prolonged debate over the pros and cons. It was too late for that. Who would dispute success? The hotel did well; so did the bank and office building, and so did the shops on the second-level mall. Pedestrian traffic has been brisk; at lunchtime, counts on the main segment of the mall run around three thousand people per hour.

Street level has not done well. Comparable counts on the sidewalks of the key blocks average around one thousand people per hour. So much activity has been siphoned off to the upper level that ground floor space has gone begging. In one office tower the second-level retail space rented out quickly; it tied in with the mall. But the ground floor retail space remained unrented for several years.

The city's main street has been upgraded with benches and sheltered bus stops and other pedestrian amenities. What it lacks is more pedestrians. Of the few shops on the principal blockfronts, some are

Two-level downtown: Charlotte, North Carolina. Upper-level skyway and shopping mall for the affluent. Street level for bus riders.

excellent, and one arcade-and-alley combination is superb. But there is not the retail continuity there could have been. With a new central square to be provided at the crossroads of the two principal streets, pedestrian activity at ground level should pick up. But it will be from a low level.

There has been a social split. The second level is used by middle-class whites; the street level by blacks and by people who have to use the bus. In one way they get the best of it. They are the last street-level pedestrians. Thanks to them, the bus stops and benches are where most of the street life in Charlotte takes place.

Dallas has been similarly affected. David Dillon, architectural critic of the Dallas *Morning News* believes that the problem has been accentuated by the upgrading of the concourses that has been taking place. The newest complexes around one of the main intersections have provided some attractive food facilities. Most of the people using them are well-dressed young office workers. Most of the people up on the street are students, minority, and poor people. The only facilities for them are the bus shelters. "The social stratification is startling," says Dillon, "and it will only get worse as long as the underground system is treated as a kind of God."

A Gresham's Law is at work. To protect their investment in upper- and lower-level streets, cities are dullifying their street-level streets.

A Gresham's law is at work. The second-rate can fare better if there is no competition from the first-rate. Cities that go for off-street systems, accordingly, have reason to make the regular streets less attractive than before. To protect their growing investment in upper- and lower-level systems, they go along with the dullification of street-level frontages—most effectively, by sealing them off with blank walls that are now no longer inadvertent, but deliberate.

This has happened in Minneapolis. For quite a while the skyways complemented an active street level. The city's chief pride was the pedestrian mall along Nicollet. The IDS Crystal Court was attractively transparent and its street-level space a true meeting place. As the skyway system has grown, however, urban design at street level has taken a turn for the worse. Town Center, the newest link in the system, joins two department stores with a second-level walkway. Down below, most of the street scene is blank wall.

Another Gresham's law example is provided by Winnipeg. In the heart of its downtown is an underground shopping mall and concourse. Given the fierce weather up there, it is understandable that people use it. But they are a hardy bunch; even on the coldest days some people persist in using the sidewalks above. To induce them to go underground instead, the city has erected a concrete barrier on the sidewalk. This makes further passage at street level difficult, leaving the public stairway down to the concourse the alternative. Lest people evade this forced choice by walking across the street, police hand out tickets to those who do so.

The worst thing about dullification is the way people get used to it. They even get to like it. If there are no longer streets that are attractive to use, they will not use streets. They will forget there ever were any and, as in Dallas, say that culturally street life may not be suited to their city. So they take the choice that is given them: concourses and skyways. Like the blue cheese dressings of the salad bars, once you get used to them, you lose your taste for the real thing.

People adapt to the underground. It's like the simulated blue cheese dressing in the salad bars. Once you get used to it you lose your taste for the real thing.

14

MEGA-STRUCTURES

The ultimate expressions of the flight from the street are the mega-structures: huge, multipurpose complexes combining offices, stores, hotels, and garages, and enclosed in a great carapace of concrete and glass—such as Detroit's Renaissance Center, Atlanta's Omni International. Their distinguishing characteristic is self-containment. Intended for the salvation of downtown, they tend to be independent of it, and the design proclaims them so. The megastructures are wholly internalized environments, with their own life-support systems and with no obeisance to the streets—one of which, most likely, was demapped so the structure could be as big as it is. Their enclosing walls are windowless, and to the city they turn a blank face.

Smaller cities have been particularly vulnerable. They are the closest to the suburban malls and have felt the competition of them most keenly. They are tempted to fight the malls on the malls' own terms: to ask their chief tormentors to come to town and recast the instrument of their decline into the new boon. So they cooperate. They welcome the enclosed malls, the off-street streets, and they enforce the using of them by making the regular streets less attractive than before.

Megastructures are for people who have cars. Essentially, they are an extension of the freeway culture, and while they provide access to downtown, they also provide an almost closed circuit insulated from it. At Houston Center you can drive your car in from the free-

At Houston Center you can drive in from the freeway to the garage, walk through a skyway to one tower, thence to another, work, shop, lunch, work, and then head back to the freeway without ever having to set foot in Houston at all.

Detroit: People Mover and megastructure.

way to the center's parking garage, walk through a skyway to one tower and thence to another, work, shop, lunch, work some more, and then head back to the garage and the freeway without ever having to set foot in Houston at all.

And why should one? Save for vehicular portals, the street facade below is solid blank wall. The only activity is a drive-in bank. To the credit of Texas Eastern, builder of the project, it should be noted that the company has concluded that the separation from the street was a bad idea. For a future extension of the project they hope to have lively street spaces.

The resemblance to fortresses is not accidental. It is the philosophic base. "They do look a little forbidding," one proponent said to me, "But there is a reason. The hard fact is we're not going to lure the middle-class shopper back to the city unless we promise them security from the city."

To save the city, they would repudiate it. So, in spirit as well as form, the suburban shopping mall is transplanted to downtown, and security is raised to the nth degree. These complexes abound with guards and elaborate electronic warning systems. Ports of entry from the outside are few in number and their design is manifestly defensive. Where Renaissance Center faces Detroit, there is a large concrete berm athwart the entrance. It's a wonder there isn't a portcullis. But the message is clear. Afraid of Detroit? Come in and be safe.

Megastructures have an affinity for convention centers, sports

Megastructures have an affinity for convention centers and arenas, and via skyways can be mated into a closed circuit. The result is two cities: convention city and regular city, and with little intermingling between visitors and natives.

arenas, and merchandise marts. These are geared for visitors, and via skyways and concourses they can be mated into an almost closed circuit. As a result, some American cities are two cities: visitor city and regular city. There is not much intermingling between the two. As convention center experts would put it, there is little contamination.

These environments are so dull that even proponents concede something is missing. The street is what is missing, and to fill the vacuum, some managements are constructing facsimiles of streets. One example is the Georgetown-motif street in the White Flint Mall outside Washington, D.C. A further step will be a theme facility to give people the experience of the city without any of the dangers. One proposal I have seen would feature multimedia presentations of aspects of the city: striking visual images from batteries of slide projectors; high-fidelity tapes of street sounds, taxi drivers' colorful argot, and such. The walkways would be programmed with strolling actors done up as street people. One of them, to come full circle, would be a bag woman.

Which brings us to the issues of privatization. Malls screen out people. In suburban malls this is counted an asset. By keeping out undesirables, the malls' guards provide regular customers with a more secure and pleasant environment. They are public, but not *too* public.

A further self-screening factor is built into suburban malls. Since access is by car, people who don't have cars are less likely to go there. They may go by bus, but scheduled runs are infrequent. (If they do go by bus, furthermore, they may get a very small hello. At one mall in New Jersey, the bus waiting area provides no overhead cover and no place to sit.)

Much has been made of malls as the new town centers. They are not. Centers, perhaps, but not of the city. They reject many of the activities of a true center. They do not welcome—indeed, do not tolerate—controversy, soapboxing, passing of leaflets, impromptu entertaining, happenings, or eccentric behavior, harmless or no.

It is inconsistent of these presumed town centers to curb such functions. Whether it is illegal or not is another matter. Court rulings have been inconclusive. Some have ruled that malls are in fact public places and that the First Amendment rights of free speech should not be abridged in them. Other rulings have upheld the malls. The tilt, however, does seem to be toward the First Amendment rights.

With the move of shopping malls to downtown, the privatization issue has become more acute. Historically, the center of the city has been a place where all sorts of people are tolerated. For one kind, single men without means, it is the last refuge. Downtown can be especially important for older people. Though they may not live there, its congregating places are a key destination for them.

Suburban shopping malls are not the new town centers. They lack or forbid many of the activities of a center: soapboxers, controversy, passing of leaflets, impromptu entertainment, happenings, or eccentric behavior of any kind, including persistent non-buying.

Downtown malls' managements do not like such people. Some are quite overt about it. Guards are instructed to keep tabs on how long noncustomers have used a bench and, after a while, ask them to move on. In defense, older people learn to simulate shopping behavior. Some, for example, will take care to have a shopping bag (just one bag; with more than that and one crosses the line and is considered a bag woman).

Teenagers are a vexing problem. They have made suburban malls their favorite place to hang out and the malls have diverted them with game arcades. In the city, however, teenagers are more of an alien element, especially when traveling in packs. Guards monitor them carefully. They also keep a sharp watch for winos or people who look as though they might be winos. Malls also adopt preemptive measures, such as short benches not long enough for winos to sleep on. They say they do this to spare customers, but the latter seem more relaxed about it than the management. In one Canadian city the downtown mall started a major controversy by arresting as a wino a local character and having him exiled from the premises. It turned out that people liked him as a sort of landmark for downtown and thought the mall people heartless. But the mall people prevailed. They usually do.

In Toronto's Eaton Centre, police hand out trespass tickets for a fine of fifty-three dollars for undesirable behavior. In 1985 they forcibly removed about 30,000 people, mostly derelicts, teenagers, and other "undesirables." In one case, the ejectee successfully appealed. The court ruled that the center had allowed subway routes though its property and did not have the sole right to control access to it.

Sometimes even ordinary people can cause problems. Taking pictures with a camera is one of the most frequent of public-place activities, yet for some reason it upsets mall management. This has been an occupational hazard for me; I've found that even a small Olympus camera will bring up a worried guard in short order.

Some managements, let it be said, are quite openhanded. Citicorp in New York is an example. For such a hard-nosed outfit it has been notably hospitable. It has been providing an increasing number of chairs and tables for brown baggers and people who would like to sit and talk or read. Rest rooms are open to all comers and they are kept clean. Citicorp is tolerant of noncustomers and odd types as well. One, a bearded bag man, adopted the top of the main stairs as his favorite perch.

The IBM indoor garden in New York is another good example. Some executives worried that the garden would attract bag women and such. So it did. A recurring event in a time-lapse study I made of the daily life of the garden was the appearance of a young bag woman at about nine-thirty every morning. She would leave an hour or so

later. To the amusement of the guards, she would herald the departure
with several oaths and then be gone. This gave the nice matrons in the
place an interesting experience to talk about. While bag people have
been few, the clientele has been a diverse one and it has been very well
behaved, too—notably so in the disposal of trash. The guards are a
genial lot and have a fine, proprietary attitude toward the place and its
guests.

Such hospitality is rare. It should be the rule. In one form or
another, after all, managements have been given inducements to provide public spaces—tax write-downs, increased floor-area ratios, waiv-
ing of setback regulations, or the like. In return the city should require
that they provide public spaces that are public in fact.

The commitment should not be evaded because the original management sold to another one. The Crystal Court of the IDS Center in
Minneapolis is a case in point. Rightfully it was hailed as an indoor
space that was truly a center. In my film on the social life of urban
spaces, I showed how welcoming it was, illustrating the point with
shots of the older people sitting in the middle of the space—not buying
anything, just talking and sitting, and nobody hassling them to do
otherwise.

No longer. The place was taken over by new owners. They removed the public seating.

The key to the success or failure of an internal public space is its
relationship to the street. Milan's Galleria is constantly invoked and
its name borrowed for spaces that lack its basics. The Galleria is an
extension of the streets and spaces of Milan and has a fine 100 percent
location between the Duomo and La Scala. It does provide cover overhead but it is not a closed space; it is open at four great entries. It is
lined with stores and cafés on the street side as well as within. This
great place is a vibrant crossroads for Milan, not a refuge from it.

Almost without exception the best-used and best-liked inside
spaces in this country have a strong visual tie with the outside. You
can look out of them to the streets and buildings beyond; you can look
into them. They are their own come-on. Ulrich Franzen's design for
the Whitney sculpture garden in the Philip Morris Building is a good
example. It has large windows on both its Forth-Street and Park Avenue frontages. You know exactly where you are: right across from
Grand Central Station. The view from without is a good one too.
What are those crazy objects? What are those people doing? The open
glass doors beckon you.

The IBM garden is similarly open along its street frontages, and
for its good manners it is blessed with lots of afternoon sunlight falling
on it. The two best arcades in the country, the Cleveland Arcade

*The most successful
interior spaces in the
country have a strong
visual tie with the
outside. You can look
into them; you can look
out of them.*

The Crystal Court of the IDS Tower in Minneapolis, designed by John Burgee and Philip Johnson, is one of the best interior spaces in the United States. It has also been a hospitable place, with plenty of public seating—and well used by all

sorts of people, including older people of modest means. But no more. A new owner bought the building and removed the public seating.

(1888) and the Providence Arcade (1832), are eminently directional, with central spaces running through the block from one street to another, both streets are clearly visible. From almost any place within the arcades you comprehend the whole in a glance.

In a megastructure you cannot. All of the major factors that make for disorientation are present: little or no visual connection with the outside; mirror-image corridor layouts; misleading cues; lack of clear directionality. Until recently the acknowledged leader in this respect was Renaissance Center in Detroit. Legions of meeting goers have exchanged tales of getting lost in its circular mazes, ending up addressing the wrong audience, suffering a kind of jet-lag displacement of time and space.

A later example is Lafayette Place, a new hotel–department store complex in Boston. It has no visual access at street level, the space given over mainly to a parking garage, and no visual access from above, either. That is blank wall. The principal walkway is the ultimate in mirror images—a circle—and you can go twice around and more before you realize that you are where you were before.

If individual megastructures are disorienting, what happens when there is a whole downtown of them? Los Angeles is on the way to finding out. It wants to make downtown the center it once was, and, as the old two-reel comedies filmed there in the twenties show, there is a reason. It was a fine, compact downtown with strong retail continuity, excellent mass transit, and a year-round climate ideal for street activity.

Here and there a few elements of this past have been reclaimed. The Biltmore Hotel is a model of clarity and easy circulation with the street and its original floor plan is intact. (Another novel feature: elevators within walls.) The art deco Oviatt Building has been rescued from neglect and elegantly restored as an office building.

These buildings grace the street. Most of the development activity does not. It is in the other direction: toward buildings isolated from the street and the life of it; faced inward, their walls massively blank; in sum, toward a perverse denial of all the advantages of climate and site and Los Angeles.

Bit by bit, the street is being obsoleted. The heart of old downtown is still conventional, lined with stores. One new element is Broadway Plaza, a large structure enclosing a garage, a department store, and a hotel. It has been successful—internally. But it does little for its neighbors, to those on its sides it turns walls of brick.

Several blocks away is the big office-and-shopping complex of Atlantic Richfield. At street level there is a large plaza and a sculpture. But no shops or restaurants do you see. There are many of them

Bonaventure Hotel, Los Angeles. Since this picture was taken, management has cut a window into the wall.

but they are down below the plaza, in subterranean levels. In balmy Los Angeles.

By skywalk one can go next to the Bonaventure complex of John Portman. It consists of a large concrete base on which are placed four reflective cylinders. Within the base are many levels of shops, all facing inward. Down at street level there looms upward a gigantic slab of concrete, eight floors' worth of it. Originally it was unpunctuated by a single opening, but a window has been cut into it. It is still quite a wall.

The Bonaventure is also an outstanding example of disorientation. From the opening day it was full of baffled people seeking directions, and the layout was so complicated that the giving of directions sounded like a who's-on-first routine. To resolve the problem, the management figured out a set of directions and distributed them to visitors. They are worth repeating at some length:

> The Los Angeles Bonaventure, a Westin Hotel, welcomes you to downtown Los Angeles.***
>
> Noted architect John Portman has been responsible for some of the most elegant and innovative hotels in the country. Many feel that the Bonaventure is the pride of his fleet. Mr. Portman places a high priority on aesthetics in his hotels, and the Bonaventure is no exception.
>
> When you first arrive, the layout of this hotel can be a trifle overwhelming. This feeling is easily overcome with the knowledge of a few hints that will help you navigate among the five round glass towers that comprise the Bonaventure Hotel's guestrooms and the rectangular atrium lobby.
>
> As you face the Registration Desk, Figueroa Street is UP one level and to your left. Flower Street is on the Lobby Level and to your right. All buses stop at the Flower Street Drive.
>
> Each tower is color coded with a large DOT on the glass elevator shaft and a large vertical banner. With your room key you receive a map which shows you the basic layout of room numbers in each tower.
>
> Room number direction signs are clearly visible as you exit the elevators. Do not try to remember to turn right or left out of the elevator; you can get lost. Please look at the signs each time, then you'll have no problem. *Any* elevator will take you to your room.
>
> All meeting rooms except the California and Catalina Ballrooms are located on the Lobby Level, behind the YELLOW bank of elevators.
>
> The Lobby Level is considered level 1. Flower Street is on the Lobby Level. On the second level (one level above the Lobby), you will find the Figueroa Street Entrance, the California Ballroom, and the first of the retail shops, including the newsstand, ELSONS. Retail shops, from flowers to furs, can be found on levels 2 through 6.
>
> You can reach the TOP OF FIVE RESTAURANT and BONAVISTA LOUNGE *only* by taking the ORANGE elevators. These two facilities are at the top of the middle tower, which is taller than the other four towers.

Twenty miles away, in Disneyland, people pay good money to walk along a simulation of a regular, old-fashioned street, with stores and cafés and doors and windows.

They certainly will not find it in downtown Los Angeles. Now that the street is being deadened of most of its life, the next step could be the removal of pedestrians from it altogether. As in Dallas, the relegation of the pedestrian is being hailed as his emancipation. In a major design competition, Los Angeles has requested proposals for the creation of a grade-separated pedestrian system. One shudders to think of the hackneyed visions that will be unleashed: sidewalks in the sky, on pylons; cantilevered moving walkways; people movers; monorails; two and three levels of crisscrossing tubes—in a final, architectonic combination, I would wager, they will come up with downtowns that look like a very modern airport.

But there will be one matter that few proposals will tackle. Should there be such a system at all? A review of planning literature over the years shows that the grade separation idea goes way, way back and waxes and wanes in cyclical fashion, lying dormant for two or three decades until the failure of earlier schemes is forgotten.

Let me go back to the matter of context. The problem is not that megastructures in themselves are so awful. Against a background of older buildings they can look quite dazzling. Inside, there are solid attractions; whether or not one likes cocktail pods, or glassed elevators, or revolving bars on sky terraces, many people do. And there is no law that says the building has to be brutish on the outside. Portman's San Francisco Hyatt, for example, has a clear layout—a big triangle this time—and enjoys a fine waterfront setting.

Settings are the rub. Megastructures tend to go with the clean-sweep approach to downtown. Instead of remaining a singular element in their surroundings, they prompt comparable development and thus do away with their singularity. They become their own dullifiers.

Complexes derive urbanity from their surroundings. New York's Citicorp is an example. With its atrium, Citicorp could have seemed like a suburban mall. But it did not. It was surrounded by basic city: a lively mixture of new buildings and old ones, attractive stores, tacky stores, Irish bars, Gristede's, flower shops, and, at Fifty-third and Lexington, one of the most crowded, garish, and convivial newsstand-and-snack-counter places in New York City.

Bad taste can be a fine foil. Seagram never looked better than when the purple Harwyn Club and Al Schacht's Steak House were across from its plaza. We do not appreciate such counterpoints until they are gone. In the case of Citicorp the surroundings were ideal for this high-tech tour de force. The worst thing that could happen to it, some said, would be the building of a son of Citicorp. Unhappily, that is what happened, right across the street, and with a metallic skin to boot. Then another office building went up. More brownstones were cleared away. Two more office buildings went up. Then, at Fifty-third and Lexington, a very big office building with a mitered open space where the corner used to be.

The result is not quite an office park. Thanks to the no-blank-walls zoning requirement, developers have had to devote street level to

Fifty-third and Lexington: new buildings derive a sense of place from old ones—until the old ones are demolished.

If you want to know what fine feature is going to go next, look at the title of the newest development. It customarily is named for that which it will destroy.

retailing. And it is still a pedestrian district. But something of value has been lost. Mixture. The sense of continuity. The links with the past of a historic and vital avenue. It would have been good for the new buildings had there been, somewhere in those blocks, an anchor of landmark status. But there was not.

Real estate people would have been quick to advertise its presence. Characteristically, they lay claim to the graces of the neighborhood even as they are destroying them. Ads for very tall offices and condominiums in the East Fifties feature pictures of low buildings in the East Fifties. Lutèce and its brownstone is a favorite; so are the row

The worst thing that could happen to Citicorp would be son of Citicorp.

houses of Turtle Bay Gardens, and the gate and alley to Amster Yard. Up in my neighborhood, Yorkville, the behemoths that have been taking our sun away have a parasitic relationship with the five-story fire-escape buildings on the opposite side of the avenues. The kind of small stores that enliven the neighborhood can afford these old buildings, albeit just barely, and that's where most of the interesting shops and cafés have been going.

There is something about the internal world of the megastructures that inhibits people from venturing out of them. The idea was that their retail shops would stimulate the provision of more in the downtown around. It has rarely worked out that way. They have more often deadened competition than stimulated it. Stamford's Town Center has been so encompassing that a number of locally owned stores have fared poorly. "Our greatest planning challenge," says Stamford Planning Director Jon Smith, "has been to bring people out of that mall once they drive in."

A number of cities are forswearing the suburban mall model.

Broadway entrance to the Marriott Marquis Hotel: John Portman, architect. Passageway leads to vehicle unloading area.

This is where several generations of young people met under the clock at the Biltmore. (Now it is the Bank of America Plaza.) The clock was spared and is visible over the desk.

Oakland is one. It has two shopping complexes under way and both are street oriented. "We don't want a suburban solution," says Development Director George Williams. "We don't want to suck shoppers into a location where they never recognize that they are in an urban location. We want our downtown to be very street oriented." The rendering for one of the complexes, the Jack London Waterfront mall, does not feature the once inevitable atrium. It shows people walking on streets. Outside.

The old-line megastructure is beginning to look like a fossil. While shopping complexes may do well, the classic mixed-use megastructures have been in trouble and several have been close to bankruptcy. Simulated cities for people who hate cities, it turns out, is not such a tough-minded concept after all. People prefer the real thing and there is abundant proof in the marketplace. The most successful retail project in the country is the opposite of a megastructure: the Faneuil Hall Marketplace in Boston. A city street runs through the heart of it —open to the sky, uncanopied, not even air-conditioned or heated. And you know where you are.

Simulated cities for people who don't like cities, it turns out, are not such a good idea after all.

This is the question the megastructures cannot answer. They borrow a sense of place from their surroundings; they deny it within. Where, indeed, is *here?* And when? Is it night? Or day? Is it spring? Or winter? You cannot see out. You do not know what city you are in, or if you are in a city at all. Perhaps it is a complex out by the airport or at a new interchange. It could be on the West Coast. It could be on the East. It could be in a foreign country. The piped music gives no clue. It is the same music everywhere. It is the same place everywhere. You are in the universal controlled environment.

And it is going to date very badly. Forms of transportation have usually produced their most elaborate manifestations after they have entered the period of obsolescence. So it may be with the megastructures. They are the last, retrogressive expression of a freeway era that has crested, and they are a wretched model for the future.

15

BLANK WALLS

The dominant feature of the townscape of U.S. cities is coming to be the blank wall. I first noticed this in the late seventies. When I was sorting out the slides I had taken on my travels, it struck me that I had been favoring pictures of buildings with blank walls. Megastructures were the showiest examples, but there were many others, and they were all surprisingly photogenic: crisp verticals, clean horizontals, no fussy detailing to busy up the expanses. Just pure white space, like the kind in architectural models.

Since then I have been cataloging the many different kinds of blank walls, tracing their origins and, where possible, their effect on downtowns. I will not feign neutrality. I think the blank walls are bad for the city. But I must confess that I take a perverse pleasure in coming across newer and bigger blank walls—big not only in absolute dimensions, but in relation to what's left of the streetscape.

I have toyed with the idea of calculating a blank-wall index. It would be based on the percentage of blockfront up to the thirty-foot level that was blank. Compute this for all of the blockfronts of a downtown and you would have an objective rating applicable to all U.S. cities. Too much work. And it is not necessary. It is already clear which cities belong at the top of the list.

The blank walls here discussed are not inadvertent—the kind that are uncovered by the demolition of adjacent buildings. They are, rather, walls that were meant to be blank from the very beginning. And they have a message. They are a declaration of distrust of the city and its streets and the undesirables who might be on them.

World's tallest blank wall: AT&T's Long Lines building in New York City.

Small and medium-sized cities are the most susceptible. Big cities do have blank walls: New York, for example, has the biggest blank wall in the world; San Francisco, one of the most boorish. If one were to construct a blank-wall index, however, the highest readings would be found in smaller cities. They have been the most immediately hurt by the regional malls, and the most prone to throw in the towel and take an if-you-can't-beat-'em-join-'em attitude. The civic leadership is likely to be almost wholly suburban, in place of residence if not in spirit; the oncoming generation even more so. There will be few who have any memory of what a thriving downtown was like. The nearest thing to a center they have experienced is the atrium of a suburban shopping mall. This is often as true of architects as of their patrons.

The primary model is the suburban shopping mall. Out by the freeway interchanges the blank wall is functional. It provides more shelf space, and the absence of display windows is no problem. People already made the decision to enter the store when they drove their cars there. There is no need to beckon passersby. There are no passersby.

Now the mall is being transplanted to downtown. Here there are passersby and adjacent buildings and streets. But the form is little changed. Everything is internalized, as it was out in suburbia, with few or no windows. The one major difference is the parking; instead of being spread over acres of asphalt, the parking is concentrated in multilevel structures. Some add yet more blank wall, but a number have good, simple geometrics and are better to look at than the complexes they serve.

Another contributor is the convention center. They are big in big cities; they are big in smaller cities as well—great hulks of concrete stretching two or three blocks with scarcely a window in them. Convention center experts say that this sealed-box format is the way it has to be. Otherwise there would be "leakage," or "contamination"—that is, natives without badges mixing it up with the others. Thus the tight seal. Some experts would lock up the convention goers for the whole day.

The separation works. I've charted pedestrian activity on civic spaces adjoining some of these centers and found surprisingly little relationship between what's going on inside and what isn't outside. Within, there might be four thousand ophthalmologists, but on the sidewalk and benches of the adjoining spaces only a handful of people.

In some places the separation is so pronounced there are two cities: regular city and convention city. In the latter, the conventioneers follow an almost closed circuit: by shuttle bus from the convention hotels to the center and back. Spouses do get to shop, but they're segregated too, and on the whole there is little intermingling between

In some places there are two cities: convention city and real city.

Quakerbridge Mall, Route 1, New Jersey. Here the blank wall is functional.

the conventioneers and the natives. At night the separation is complete. The streets are deserted. Most restaurants have closed. The office work force has gone home. The only life is in the atriums of the hotels, conventioneers with other conventioneers.

The ultimate expression of the blank wall is the megastructure. As we noted in the previous chapter, the blank wall is ideologically necessary to it. The megastructure must acknowledge the dangers of the city around it and promise security from them. It must offer delights within but keep them carefully shielded from external view. A blank wall does all this, and the bigger and more declarative it is, the purer its expression of function.

But for whom? As it happens, most of the big megastructures have not been doing well at all. The marketing premise that people who come to the city want to be walled from it has been emphatically disproven. But suppose, for the moment, that the megastructures had been doing well financially. There would still be a larger question to be answered. How well have they been functioning for their neighbors, and for downtown in general?

They have been deadening it. Walk past one of these brutal hulks. Whatever is going on inside, there will be little going on outside. There will be few people on the sidewalks alongside and few on the blocks beyond. The blank walls, the lack of stores and activity have killed off the life that might have been.

Institutions like blank walls. Almost always there is a technical

Blank walls proclaim the power of the institution and the inconsequence of the individual, whom they are clearly meant to intimidate. Stand by the new FBI headquarters in Washington. You feel guilty just looking at it.

explanation: the wall space is needed for the stacks, for climate control for the computers, for lighting unvaried by natural light. But these are not the real reason. Blank walls are an end in themselves. They proclaim the power of the institution, the inconsequence of the individual, whom they are clearly meant to put down, if not intimidate. Stand by the new FBI headquarters in Washington. You feel guilty just looking at it. It is a truly menacing presence, yet, ironically, it is itself vulnerable, full of the kind of lurking spaces and dead ends and niches the wise person avoids.

Power and fear are conjoined. To judge by their design, one would gather that the institutions feel themselves under siege. TV surveillance cameras are everywhere. Signs abound telling you, redundantly, not to do this or do that. "These stalls for government cars only." "No admittance after 3:30." "Keep out."

Utilities go for blank walls, the elements of the Bell system especially. Even when they are in the heart of a downtown, they usually turn a blank face to the street. The outstanding example is AT&T's Long Lines Building in the Wall Street area. The expanse is absolutely breathtaking—about forty-plus stories of solid brick, surely the biggest blank wall in all the world. And at its base is a very small sign. It says "No Ball or Frisbee Playing."

What to do with blank walls? The one good thing that can be said of them is that they are so awful anything else looks good by contrast —against a background of opaque black glass, for example, a chromium fire standpipe looks rather elegant. These walls fairly cry for something to set them off—some enlightened graffiti, a "Kilroy was here," a touch of the vulgar. But this cannot be. These buildings are utterly without humor.

Regional variation? With my collection of slides of hundreds of blank walls across the country, I have tested peoples' perception of place. As part of a presentation on the blank wall, I show about sixty slides in rapid succession. They are arranged not geographically but in order of the number of saplings. For some reason audiences find this amusing, but on the matter of location they draw a blank. Regional cues? There are none. Nobody, myself included, has ever been able to discern any regional variation, or, indeed, any real variation of any kind. Close up, to be sure, you can see some differences—concrete striated horizontally on one wall, vertically on another. But from afar the differences in the walls disappear. They look like, well, blank walls.

The best thing to do with blank walls is to do away with them, or, at the very least, to prevent their recurrence. The way to do this is to fill the vacuum, or replace nothing with something—most particularly, street-level retailing.

The people of the city have an equity in this. An owner who lines

The walls fairly cry for something to set them off—some inspired graffiti, for example, a touch of the vulgar. But this could not be. These complexes are utterly without humor.

An owner who turns a blank wall to the street not only deadens his part of the frontage, he breaks the retail continuity of the block.

his frontage with a blank wall not only deadens his part of the street; he breaks the continuity that is so vital for the rest of the street. Stores thrive on the propinquity of other stores and the traffic they generate. Seal off a blockfront, interrupt a sequence of stores, and part of the line of the street is lost.

This was especially evident along the Avenue of the Americas. Where once there had been delicatessens and bars and shops, there were now plazas fronting on expanses of glass behind which were bankers sitting at desks. One of these buildings was bad enough; whole stretches of them, blockfront after blockfront, were stupefyingly dull. There was a true loss of amenity. These buildings took away far more in food facilities than they provided anew, and much of this was buried in off-street concourses.

Left to their own devices, developers would prefer to rent their ground-floor space to corporations—more rent, less trouble. But for providing these dull plazas, they had been getting very handsome floor-area bonuses. It seemed only fair that they liven up their frontages as a quid pro quo. We supported a provision requiring that at least 50 percent of the buildings' ground-floor fronts be devoted to retail uses. There were so many other provisions in the plaza legislation that this one went through with no fuss at all.

For the next five years there was no fuss. To repeat an observation: developers are a pragmatic lot, and once something is on the statute books, that tends to be that. Developers routinely provided the retail frontage, and the retail rents were apparently quite high enough not to be a hardship to them. When the midtown zoning code came up for a major overhaul, it seemed in order to raise the requirements to 100 percent of the frontages (less the entrance). This provision, furthermore, would be divorced from incentive zoning. Bonus or no bonus, it would be mandatory. Two other conditions had to be met: the stores would have to be accessible from the street; the glass fronts would have to be of see-through glass.

The legislation has worked unobtrusively and well. Some of the stores were wider than the planners had hoped they would be; they would like to see a greater number of the smaller frontages—twenty to twenty-five feet—so characteristic of good specialty-shopping streets. But in general the results have been good. The streets are certainly the livelier for the stores—and for the blank walls that were not put up but might have been.

Other cities are following suit. Bellevue, Washington, now requires ground-level retailing on designated streets. San Francisco does not specifically mandate stores in retail areas, but twists developers' arms to the same effect in project review. For its Sixteenth Street Mall, Denver gives incentive bonuses of extra floor space to developers for providing ground-level retailing. Shops must be directly accessible from the street and shopfronts be of see-through glass. No city has banned blank walls per se; it seems more effective to require positive uses. (For the text of the New York statute, see Appendix B.)

Cities would do well to have the discipline of a good statute. This is especially the case with smaller and medium-sized cities where the developers of downtown have lately arrived from suburban mall projects. In on recent center-city project the developer ruled out street-level stores, save a token or two. His leasing agent, he explained, told him that that kind of retailing wouldn't go in that location. As it most definitely will not, the design precluding it and a supine planning commission acquiescing.

Blank walls are tough to fight because no one is for them. There are no civic debates whether to have them or not. There is often no recognition that they have become a problem at all. Their growth is too incremental. They are the by-product of other causes, many seemingly good—separation of vehicular and pedestrian traffic, off-street circulation, and such. Given current momentums, the blank walls will continue to spread, even in the most exemplary of cities.

Such as St. Paul, Minnesota. It is the blank-wall capital of the United States. You would not expect it to be. It is a most habitable, attractive, and friendly city; it has one of the most resourceful and effective mayors in the country; its Lowertown redevelopment is of an eminently human scale and has a fine street presence. St. Paul also has one of the most complete skyway systems in the country, and it is probably the best designed of all of them.

It is paying a steep price. In a striking example of the Gresham effect, skyway level has led to the blanking-out of street level. The result is as drastic as if shop fronts and windows had been decreed illegal. There are few to see. The experience is so dull that to walk at street level is to do penance for not using upper level. Block after block, it is blank wall. Occasionally there is a break to indicate what might have been—like the trompe l'oeil windows on the wall of a parking lot.

It is not entirely farfetched to prophesy that one day St. Paul might embark on a rediscovery project to uncover its buried street level. Atlanta made a tourist attraction of its old underground streets; so did Seattle of its Skid Row. But prime shopping streets are a much greater treasure, and the fact that they have been concealed should make their reappearance all the more dramatic. Disneyland merchandises a simulation of a street. But cities have something even better: actual streets. Right under their noses.

16

THE RISE
AND FALL
OF INCENTIVE
ZONING

It seemed such a splendid idea. Developers wanted to put up buildings as big as they could. Why not harness their avarice? Planners saw a way. First, they would downzone. They would lower the limit on the amount of bulk a developer could put up. Then they would upzone, with strings. The builders could build over the limit *if* they provided a public plaza, or an arcade, or a comparable amenity.

Everyone would win. The developer would get his extra floors; the public would get an amenity it would not have otherwise; the city would get higher property assessments for its tax base; and all this would be brought about without spending an extra penny of public funds.

Thus, in 1961, New York embarked on incentive zoning. It worked. Over the next ten years it was to prompt the creation of more new open space in the center city than was created in all the other cities in the country combined. Other cities followed suit with similar programs. New York continued its pioneering by moving from across-the-board zoning to a flexible, case-by-case approach.

Case by case, developers would be pressing for bigger bonuses yet, and a number of imaginative zoning lawyers would help clear the way. Planners were to show similar resourcefulness in inventing new kinds of spaces to bonus: galleries, atriums, garden courts, through-block circulation areas, covered pedestrian areas, roof gardens. "Fine-tuning the zoning ordinance," this would be called, or "New York's sophisticated zoning." The euphoria was to run thick.

It should have been a warning. Things were about to go awry. Developers would soon be putting up buildings bigger than ever; shadows would be getting longer, even on the side streets where everyone pledged to keep buildings low. But developers would be unhappy; they weren't making enough money, they said. The planners would be unhappy, and unhappiest of all would be the civic groups. Debacle, they would cry, and at their behest a massive overhaul of the zoning would take place.

In this chapter I want to tell how this came about, and the lessons there are in the experience. They are not peculiar to New York, save in scale—New York's worst examples are so bad that one is almost proud of them. But the lessons are considerable pro and con, and those cities that are now beginning to adopt incentive zoning might well pay them heed.

Let us start with a look at the antecedents to incentive zoning. In its earliest form, zoning was for the provision of light. In eighteenth-century Paris the height of buildings was limited to a multiple of the width of the streets—low on narrow streets, higher on wide streets. When New York City instituted zoning in 1916, the same principle was applied. The recently built Equitable Building, which rose straight up from the street, was the symbol of what was to be avoided. The zoning specified that as buildings went upward they had to conform to a sky exposure plane. This was a specified angle slanting back from the street—sharply on narrow streets, less so on wide ones. If a building had enough setbacks in its lower portions, the tower could go straight up quite a ways. So a number of buildings did, most spectacularly the Empire State and the Chrysler Building. But the more customary result was the "ziggurat"—a building that looked like a series of successively smaller boxes put on top of one another.

By the late fifties it was evident that a comprehensive overhaul of the zoning code was badly needed. Over the years, the code had gathered some twenty-five hundred exceptions, in the process more than doubling in bulk. Most important, the zoning had been much too permissive on density. As horror sketches circulated by reform groups showed it, New York would be a solid mass of towers if building continued on to the legal limits. Clearly, some downzoning was in order.

Zoning landmark: the Equitable Building—which started the whole thing in 1916.

The planners thought so, and in the proposed new code they sharply reduced the allowable density. They did this through the device of the floor-area ratio. This was the multiplier the developer could apply to the number of square feet in his lot to get the total number of square feet in his building. For commercial districts this was set at a multiple of fifteen f.a.r. This meant that the developer could build the amount of square feet in his lot times fifteen. He could mass them in a squat building or go up higher with a tower that covered less of the lot.

There were no height limitations as such. In practice, however, the f.a.r. did impose a ceiling. Towers can become uneconomic as they

Inexpensive sun-study technique developed by Professor Brent Porter of Brooklyn's Pratt Institute. He takes a set of models out into the sun and cants them until the shadow of the stick (right) coincides with the mark for an hour of the day. Thus oriented, the models cast shadows as those actual buildings would.

poke up higher and slimmer. Given the size of most office-building sites, somewhere around thirty to thirty-two stories is the practical limit for buildings of fifteen f.a.r.

By eliminating the sky-is-the-limit feature of the old zoning, the floor-area ratio limited the bulk that could be put up in the city. But it would not unduly limit builders. Fifteen f.a.r. is a lot of building. Builders had been doing quite well putting up buildings of that size, and there was a good bit of empirical justification for setting it as the base limit. It was the median bulk of the office buildings put up since World War II.

There was to be a sweetener. To get the builders behind the new zoning, the planners offered in incentive bonus. The first application would be for plazas. The planners had been much impressed by the recently completed Seagram Building. It was handsome, introduced lots of space and light, and made possible a sheer tower far more elegant than the old set-back buildings. To prod builders into providing comparable spaces, the zoning offered them a deal: for every square foot of plaza space builders provided, they could add 10 square feet of office space. This would raise their total floor space by 20 percent, and the f.a.r. from fifteen to eighteen. The bonus, furthermore, would be as-of-right: if the builders followed the guidelines prescribed in the zoning, their plans would be assured of approval, and no special reviews or permits would be needed.

All in all, it was an attractive package, and builders took to it. There had been, of course, much opposition from builders to the proposed new zoning, but the bonus swung over enough of them to gain a critical margin of support.

There were doubters. Would not the exception beg the question of the rule? If fifteen f.a.r. was judged the right top limit, how could a higher one be right too? Planners felt the answer was in the offset. The extra density, they believed, would be more than compensated for by the extra amenity.

Others thought so, too. Civic groups saw the 1961 zoning as a great forward step and they were not inclined to nitpick over theoretical problems. Nor were the builders. Hailed on all sides, incentive zoning was off to a promising start.

The bonus proved almost embarrassingly successful. Over the next decade, with no exceptions, every developer who put up an office building took advantage of the plaza bonus. Between 1961 and 1973 some 1.1 million square feet of new open space was created that way—more than in all of the other cities of the country combined.

This should have been seen as an alert. When a building rents out very quickly, real estate people figure they might have set the rents too low. The planning commission might well have concluded that it had underpriced the bonus. It certainly seemed clear that the benefits for builders were great. Some suspected they might be scandalously so.

In a later cost-benefit analysis of incentive zoning, Jerold S. Kayden computed the construction costs, to the developers, of the plazas built between 1961 and 1973. They came to $3,820,278. In return for this, developers were able to put up 7,640,556 square feet of additional commercial space. Multiplying this by the average net capitalized value per square foot of $23.87—a conservative estimate— Kayden got a bonus value of $186,199,350. To put it another way, for each dollar he put out for a plaza, a developer reaped nearly $48 worth of extra space.

In many cases the developers' leverage was greater yet. Many were able to take advantage of various tax abatement incentives the city periodically offered. This was done to moderate building slumps; but cycles being what they are, the abatements tended to be consummated at the peaks of booms.

Were the developers getting too much? No, said the planners.

The larger costs of incentive zoning have been in the loss of sun and light. It is a loss rarely counted.

Both could argue that the presumed spread between cost and profit was only theoretical, and that in any event it was not a charge on the public. The extra space the developer got came out of the air—quite literally, with those extra floors—and did not cost the city anything.

The true costs, however, are not measured in cash outlays, or in land or construction costs. They are the sun and the light that are sacrificed, and the additional load of people on community facilities. But the offsetting benefits of a well-used plaza can go far beyond the direct costs of providing them.

Did any plazas do this? No one really knew.

The planning commission had set up an urban design group and had spun off similar groups to work in specific development areas. They were staffed with an outstanding group of young architects, planners, and lawyers, and they went about their work with imagination and élan. I had an opportunity to observe this, for at the time, I was working on the text of the commission's comprehensive plan for the city. In it, properly enough, there was a salute to the innovative approaches of the staff people and the new spaces they were creating.

But how well were the new spaces working out? There had been no mechanism for monitoring the program. In all that large staff, there was no one person who had the job of going out and checking up on the results. In a draft of the plan, I floated a proposal for setting up an evaluative unit. It got nowhere.

This was one of the reasons I set up the Street Life Project. As I recount elsewhere, I thought that observation of how people used city spaces would be useful for such specific matters as plazas and arcades. What I most hoped to demonstrate was the general applicability of the approach and the simplicity of the techniques involved.

It was obvious that a lot of the places were awful: sterile, empty spaces not used for much of anything except walking across. But a few were excellent. When I showed the planners time-lapse films of nothing happening on some plazas, lots on others, they agreed that further case-and-effect study was in order. Planning commission chairman Donald Elliott thought it could help frame new zoning standards. We struck a bargain. My group would try to determine what made good plazas work and bad plazas not work, and the reasons why. If these could be translated into tight guidelines, the commission would incorporate them in a new open-space zoning section.

That is what happened. Nailing down the guidelines was easy; getting them through the mill took some time. They were as-of-right, as most of the zoning guidelines to date had been, and spelled out in considerable detail what the rules of the game were—the maximum permissible height of the plaza, the amount of seating, the minimum number of trees, and so on.

Opponents argued that guidelines would cramp architects' freedom and dictate design by formula. The best rebuttal to this was made by the chairman of the local chapter of the American Institute of Architects, Herbert Oppenheimer. Testifying in favor of the legislation, he argued that tough guidelines would not mean less freedom for the architect, but more. Without guidelines, he said, the developer would call all the shots. If there were no requirements for seating, for example, there would likely be no seating because that is the way the developer would probably want it. If there were requirements there would be choice where there had been none before. Since our adversaries were bewailing the plight of architects, the testimony carried a lot of weight. In May 1975 the Board of Estimate approved the new guidelines.

The guidelines had a salutary effect. The handwringing over their tightness proved unfounded. Once they were on the books the developers went along, quite equably. Over the ensuing ten years there was to be no complaint by a developer or architect over the basic guidelines.

Builders put in benches and chairs, they planted trees, and some went far beyond the minimum requirements in providing flowers and food kiosks and the like. The new zoning also encouraged the retrofit of existing plazas, and a number of hitherto dead ones were brought to life. The zoning guidelines were adopted by other cities, sometimes in such detail that they repeated the precise dimensions that had been derived from our New York prototypes. The formula for figuring the amount of sitting space to be required—1 linear foot for every 30 square feet of plaza space—was a back-of-the-envelope compromise between linear-feet people and square-feet people. It has been enshrined in countless zoning ordinances across the country and it works just fine.

So far, so good. Before long, however, some clouds appeared. The city's financial ratings slipped a bit, then a bit more. Soon the city was near bankruptcy. In highly publicized moves, a number of large corporations moved their headquarters to suburbia, and more seemed ready to join them. The building boom collapsed. From a level of 12,260,000 square feet in 1973, construction of office space fell to 360,000 in 1976.

The builders pled for help. They wanted to be able to build bigger and taller buildings. They wanted to build them on side streets as well as avenues. In addition to the financial problems they faced, builders had been running out of good sites. The eastern part of midtown had been so picked over that what was left were sites too small to build on profitably under construction rules. Builders might have concluded that what the market was saying was to go west. But they saw a simpler message. Change the rules.

The planing commission cooperated. Its urban design people were conceiving new kinds of bonuses: for through-block corridors, covered pedestrian areas, arcades, and atriums. They even gave extra bonuses for shops in atriums. By combining all these bonuses with development-rights transfers, zoning-lot mergers, and other techniques, developers could raise the floor-area ratio above 18. The bonuses, furthermore, applied to large sites as well as small ones: notably, the AT&T Building, the IBM Building, and the Trump Tower, the latter ending up at an f.a.r. of 21.6. More important than the increase in bulk, however, was a change in the review process. To rationalize the bulk there had to be.

There were two ways to get a project through. One was as-of-right. In this approach the developer hewed to the standard zoning provisions and asked no special favors or exceptions. This spared him appearing before review bodies. He didn't even have to call on the planning commission or the community board. If the building department found his plans in order, that would be that.

The other way was the special permit route. This way the developer had to go through a time-consuming review process. This was simplified somewhat as the Uniform Land Use Review Process, or ULURP. It set firm deadlines for each step of the review. In the notes at the end of this book there is a more detailed description. Suffice it to say here that the developer was offered a trade-off. He would have to submit to a series of negotiating sessions but he could ask for more of what he wanted—for example, more bulk.

Let us look at the pros and cons. The New York experience is by no means unique; the lessons it may afford recur in project review processes everywhere. To stick to the rules of the game? To be flexible and work things out case by case? The contentious history of review boards is a series of alternations between the two approaches.

Each has strong pros and strong cons. The as-of-right approach is rigid. It sets down beforehand, and in sometimes stupefying detail, the rules that must be followed: the minimum size of a plaza, for example, its maximum elevation above grade, and so on. It makes few distinctions for differences in site, and while it is meant to be objective, it does tend to produce the kind of design that the people who made up the rules like. In the case of the 1961 zoning, this was the free-standing tower set in open space, as the Seagram Building was.

But as-of-right has important advantages. For the developer there is certainty. Time is within his control. If he goes by the book he gets approval. The rules are clear and they are posted before the game begins. The homework has to be done by the planners before the regulations are drafted; they apply to all comers equally and they eliminate the red tape of the case-by-case approach. If the guidelines are found wanting, as they were with the plaza bonus, they can be amended.

The special permit approach offers much more flexibility. It allows planners to tailor design requirements to particular situations—often with a better fit to the intent of the law than to the letter of it. In the negotiating sessions, furthermore, improvements in the design can be suggested—and adopted—that would not have been under the as-of-right approach.

The planners have cards to play. The clock is ticking away on some high-cost borrowed money and the developer is anxious to expedite matters. The planners are in a position to suggest amenities and they usually push the developer quite hard in this respect—getting the developer to put in an extra escalator, for example, or public toilets on the ground floor.

But one trump card the planners gave up: the shield of bureaucratic procedure. No longer could they invoke as-of-right regulations to justify a hard-nosed stance. Under the special permit approach, as the developers well knew, the planners could bend the regulations and if necessary make up new ones to fit. To put it baldly, they could spot-zone.

In pressing for accommodation, the developer would have strong cards of his own. He would be helping the city's economy, creating jobs, increasing the tax base. Important people would be on his side. The pressures for acquiescence on the planners were considerable—from the mayor's office, from commercial groups, from leading businessmen, from anyone who cared about building a better city and did not want to see it hamstrung by bureaucratic nit-picking.

Such pressures are normal, and yielding to them was nothing new. What was novel was the way in which the yielding was rationalized as an advanced form of zoning sophistication. Take, for example, the atrium bonus. It was hedged with all sorts of conditions as to the impact of the building on its surroundings, and it could not be granted unless the planning commission made favorable findings on all of them. This it was very able to do, even under difficult circumstances. It simply declared the impact would be favorable.

The reductio ad absurdum of review is the city's Environmental Quality Review process. As a condition of approval, building projects must be certified as posing no significant adverse effects on the environment. Few major projects have been found to have adverse effects. Indeed, few have been found to have had *any* significant effects, adverse or otherwise.

How could this be so? The answer lies in who fills out the forms.

The principal investigative instrument is the Project Data Statement. Here are two of the questions, exactly as phrased:

1. Will project change in pattern, scale or character of general area of site, i.e—is the project different from surrounding development? __Yes __No

2. Will project change in demand for municipal services (police, fire, water, sewage, schools, health facilities, etc.? __Yes __No

The Trump Tower on Fifth Avenue was a case in point. Both questions were answered by a check mark in the "No" box. All of the other questions were given similarly favorable answers. And why not? The answers were filled in by the architect. There is no evidence that any independent investigation was made of these matters—such as a study of the shadows that might be cast. In due course, the environmental review process produced its determination: the project would "have no significant effect on the environment."

No significant effect. No change in scale. Wow. Fifty-five stories of glass. The board might well have said that yes, indeed, the building will affect its surroundings, but on balance the good will outweigh the bad. It might also have raised a question about the additional municipal services needed and the palpably silly statement that the building would require none. But the board said "no significant effect."

Getting planning commission approval of a project required much more effort. As an opening gambit a developer might come up with a fright plan. This would show the dreadful building he could put up under existing regulations if he was of a mind to. Since almost any other plan would be a great improvement, the planners would be in the happy position of being able to make helpful changes. And so they did. If lay critics still found the building dreadful, the planners would have a rejoinder. If you think this plan is bad, you should have seen the first one.

More often, the developer went for the big one right off. He had the architect design a building with every bonus possible and some possible new ones to get the building higher yet. The commission would demur. Part of the way up. But not all. In granting him his increase in bulk, accordingly, it could refer to the increase as a decrease. A builder, for example, starts out with a plan for a twenty-five-story building and presses for bonuses that will take it up to thirty-five stories. He ends up with thirty-two stories. Thus is the building "reduced" by three stories. The developer asked for the stars. The commission would only give him the moon.

The commission would draft special legislation to make the particular project legal, and lest it be thought spot zoning, it would be written as if it were of general applicability. There was not the grace of a wink. With great solemnity such legislation set forth the needs and benefits that the commission must find before giving approval. Invariably, the commission did so find. For his part, the developer was enjoined by the legislation to do a number of things that it was in his self-interest to do: obey all appropriate construction rules and regulations; hire security guards; keep the place clean. Lastly, he had to "conform the plan to the zoning"—a staggeringly redundant provision, the zoning having been written to conform to the plan.

As time goes on, a planner can come to identify with the project he is monitoring, and sometimes he can become a strong advocate of it. His own suggestions are incorporated into it. He has lived with it, often for a very long time. He sees the problems the builder and the architect face.

The common bond is the scale model of the structure. It can be entrapping. Once you start moving around those pieces of white cardboard, you partly possess a place; and in these minor manipulations of space there is a sense of larger control that is rather pleasing. It's like mapping a place; it is no more yours than it was before, but you feel that it is just the same.

One night, probably in some church basement, the builder and architect and the planner take the model before citizen members of the community board. Here are critics. And they act the part. For sheer rancor, unfair criticism, and rudeness, there is nothing like some of these public zoning meetings. One gets an idea of what a revolutionary people's court must be like. I've seen architects treated like brigands, lawyers interrupted with hoots and derisive laughter. It is a hell of an experience.

But stay the tears. The money and the power are on one side. The developer can bring in top experts. His lawyer will probably be one of the few people in the city who understands the zoning code. The experts may be given a critical reception by some of the members, but the board will usually have no counterexperts to refute them. The distinguished architect will probably be very skilled at the art of the presentation; most distinguished architects are, and board members appreciate this. Many have become connoisseurs of the art of the presentation, and they find the better architects tend to be the most disarming in their willingness to listen to board members' suggestions. Philip Johnson is a master at this. I don't know if any of the board members' suggestions ever ended up in the actual designs, but they certainly were gracefully received.

And then there are the models. Even the most truculent of board members can be entranced. The models look so clean and white, lit from beneath with a benign glow. If only buildings could be lit that

Scale models can be entrapping. Once you start moving around those white pieces of cardboard, you are hooked. Go on, says the architect, lift off the roof. Come into my parlor.

way, how splendid the city would be! And there are the movable roofs, just waiting to be picked up. You can look right down into the atrium. If you keep playing around with the model, you will soon be thoroughly hooked.

As they have gained in experience, the community boards have become less confrontational and more expert. They can still give developers a very hard time if they think the plan is bad. They are genuinely delighted, however, when a developer comes up with a well-designed one, and they can be downright polite. Their suggestions are often quite helpful and have led to substantial improvements in projects.

On major questions of size and shape however, the boards have no power. They do have some leverage, for the city's ruling bodies do not like to approve what the boards disapprove. In the end, however, the ruling bodies do approve. Since the boards anticipated this would be the case, they can be excused earlier hotfoots and catcalls.

To clinch approvals developers invoke "the numbers." No, a developer will concede, the project is not perfect. But it is the best possible set of compromises that could be arrived at. The numbers work out, albeit just barely. But change just one element and the whole thing will come apart.

Thus the intractability of John Portman's design for his Times Square Hotel. When he proposed it in 1969, the planning commission was delighted. It was pushing for the revitalization of the theatre district and it thought the hotel would be a fine catalyst. But many people disagreed. The project would require the demolition of three legitimate theatres, and this seemed a poor way to revitalize. Another problem was the design. With its street level dominated by vehicle roadways and parking access, with its sides lined with blank concrete, it constituted a virtual declaration of war on the New York street.

For one reason or another the project was delayed, and it was not until 1982 that construction began. Much had changed in the meantime; the design had not. Zoning now mandated retailing at street level and discouraged blank walls. But save for a few token changes, the walls remained largely blank. The architects would not budge. The planners did not effectively press them to, and so it was that the planning commission that sought a lively streetscape became the champion of a major contravention of it. In early 1986 the hotel opened with the 1969 design intact, like a gigantic mammoth frozen in the tundra.

The final issue in controversies is patriotism. Why are you do-gooders kicking the city? Why are you spitting on city hall? If the project is now jeopardized over some niggling little problem, everyone is going to lose. The bankers will pull out. Thousands of construction jobs will be lost. So will millions in extra tax revenues. The corporation that so wanted those zoning changes will move to Stamford. The developer will move to New Jersey.

It would serve them right. But civic officials rarely call such bluffs, especially when the city finances are in straits, as so often they are. A city in that stance is a developer's city, and a great many in the United States are exactly that.

To resist such pressures, planning commissions need support. They need the support of civic groups that will raise hell with them. In New York the groups that most strongly support planning, urban design, and preservation appear at public hearings to testify against commission proposals as often as for them, and they are usually most effective when they are against. Planners can be aggrieved with such friends but they can also see their usefulness. The countervailing pressure puts the planners in a better negotiating stance with developers.

In the review process the place to stake out is the middle of the road. Planners do this by directing developers' attention to the threats from the extremists on the flanks: from the do-gooders, Municipal Art Society groupies, Sierra Club types, smart-aleck public interest lawyers, and others who would be quick to spot any fault with the project, protest giveaways, demand strict observance of zoning regulations, and take other extreme positions. When planners cannot invoke credible threats of this kind, when they do not themselves feel the heat, it is a sign that civic groups have become too supportive and constructive and reasonable. That is when zoning and planning go to hell.

By 1980 it appeared that planning was indeed going to hell. Bulk was begetting bulk. The very anticipation of increases was making them self-fulfilling. When it became known that builders could get more bulk on a site than the zoning had allowed before, the fact got built into the price of the land. Most deals between developer and landowner were on a contingency basis: so much money if no zoning change sweetened the pot; so much if there was a zoning change. There was some speculative risk, to be sure; whatever the zoning, it was necessary that the project get the planning commission's approval. The market's assumption that it would be forthcoming was one of the more severe judgments made about the commission.

If the commission did balk at giving an increase, developers could plead hardship. Their public argument: they paid through the nose for the land on the expectation that they would get the extra bulk to justify the price they paid. If the city now goes back on its implied promise, it renders the deal unprofitable, and that means an unfair taking. It is a crass argument, but surprisingly effective.

In almost every case the planners waived the height and setback regulations. The 1961 zoning had specified that towers could cover no more than 40 percent of the lot and had to be set back from the street at least fifty feet. With big sites, developers did not mind this; with smaller sites, however, the setbacks meant their towers would be smaller and less profitable than they would like. The planners accommodated them. One member of the commission, Vice-Chairman Martin Gallent, protested the waivers. But they were the rule. Most of the towers approved in the late seventies covered more than 40 percent of the lot; in the Wall Street area, coverage went as high as 80 percent. And the buildings were a lot closer to the street than fifty feet. Some, indeed, rose sheer from the building line and kept going straight up— just like the Equitable Building that stirred New York into zoning in the first place.

As structures grew bigger, they put enormous speculative pressure on nearby sites. Indeed, the possibility of similar structures can doom the destruction of the buildings that are most important to save. Bergdorf Goodman and Saks Fifth Avenue are examples. Not only are they important stores, but their scale and their moderate height are vital to their surroundings. Bergdorf Goodman contributes to the amenity of the Pulitzer Plaza area by letting lots of sun fall in it, and its white limestone façade bounces enough secondary light onto Fifth Avenue to raise light levels several footcandles.

A twelve-story building occupying 100 percent of a site would ordinarily be an economical use of land and not so very far under the zoning limit—about three floors' worth. Any rise in that limit, however, greatly magnifies the attraction of the building. Developers pyramid their financing on a very small amount of their own cash, and any upward change in the extra floor space will be highly leveraged. This is the edge developers seek. If the zoning goes up from 15 to 18 f.a.r., the *extra* floor space potential doubles; at 21.6 it more than triples. The twelve-story building is now obsolete, worth more dead than alive. It was not the impartial working of the marketplace that endangered such buildings; it was the New York City Planning Commission and its permissive zoning.

One issue that was coming to the fore was the failure of some developers to provide the amenities they promised. With plazas so much the rule, planners were busy bonusing other off-street spaces— from sidewalk widenings to recessed sidewalks, to shopping arcades within buildings, to through-block circulation areas. This progression from street to interior culminated in the covered pedestrian area. Citicorp's dazzling court was a prototype, and the city urged developers to follow suit with atriums and gallerias.

New York would soon have been awash with atriums had not two of the new ones bombed very badly and very visibly. The builders pocketed the extra floors of rentable space, but they didn't put in the shops and things in the spaces where they promised they would. The commission said that this was really very bad of the builders but that at the time there was not much that it could do about it.

Sometimes the lack of shops and amenities was due to a change of ownership, with the new man saying he didn't know anything about any commitment and denying he was bound by it anyway. New York responded feebly when first confronted with such recalcitrants. But eventually enough fuss was raised by civic groups for the city to take action.

But how effectively? One problem in enforcement has been the lack of practical sanctions. The city can give a slap on the wrist or it can drop the atom bomb—revoke the developer's certificate of occupancy. This can mean giving the tenants the right to withhold rent, a measure so draconian as to be rarely invoked. One building owner was so obdurate, however, that the city did revoke his certificate of occupancy. This was for 2 Lincoln Square, a combination office building, residential tower, and regional headquarters for the Mormons. The building had been granted an extra six floors as a bonus for providing a landscaped off-street plaza. But all that was ever provided was an empty space. It was so bad that I periodically stopped by to update my photographic record of outstandingly bad spaces. I could always count on the place being dark, strewn with litter, bereft of benches and bereft of people. After the city acted in May 1983, there was an indication that the residential tenants might withhold their rents. Finally, in 1988, a deal was consummated by which the space would be taken over by the Folk Art Museum.

Sometimes the badness of a plaza is seized upon as reason for the worsening of it. A case in point is Grace Plaza, a big, barren slab of a place that was so inhospitable to people it came to be populated largely by drug dealers. The developer responded by putting up an iron fence. This was clearly against the commitment for which the developer had been given extra floors, and the planning commission forced the dismantling of the fence. The developer then retained a former head of the commission's urban design group. The plaza was a hopeless cause, the planner said. Why not fill it in with a two-story shopping mall?

The developer was enthusiastic. Well, he should have been. For failure of the plaza, he was set on the path to reward. The audacity of the idea garnered support, including that of Community Board Five. But the planning commission was aghast, as were civic groups, and the idea foundered. For years it remained a plaza in limbo. But a simpler solution may now be tried: make the place attractive. The Project for Public Spaces has drafted a plan that calls for, among other things, food kiosks, lots of chairs and tables, extensive programming of music and events.

Other cities have had similar problems. Cincinnati is one. In Fountain Square it has the finest square in the country, and it has been rightly concerned over what happens to the square's surroundings. For a developer who planned a hotel-office complex, the city spent $20.7 million clearing a site on the south flank of the square. In return the developer was to provide a glass-enclosed public space as an indoor counterpart.

What the city got was ten thousand square feet of nothing: no benches, no chairs, no tables, no snack facilities, no amenities save displays at Christmas. The mayor voiced his displeasure. So did the Urban Design Review Board. "The most vapid interior space with supposedly civic overtones I've ever seen in this country or elsewhere," said member David Niland.

The developer's people continued to thumb their noses. What they promised, they said, was an exciting place to walk through, not to sit in. Would guests of the Westin Hotel like to see riffraff sitting on benches? A group of civic leaders carted in some tables and chairs and staged a brown bag sit-in. The developer was unmoved. He would not put in seating. He still won't.

To repeat: in matters of zoning incentives and bonuses, what you do not specify, you do not get. And it better be in writing.

In the matter of zoning bonuses and incentives, what you do not specify you do not get.

The most flagrant nose-thumbing in New York was done by apartment house developers. They were awarded bonuses for providing parklike public spaces at the base of their buildings, but they customarily barred the public from using them. They even put up spikes on the ledges so that people would not sit on them.

In 1977, as a follow-through to the plaza legislation, the planning commission strengthened the zoning to assure both public access and retailing along the street frontage. Still developers thumbed their noses. Around the corner from where I live a developer put up a building with dummy storefronts instead of the real stores required by the zoning. He installed spikes on the ledges of the "park." The city has not so much as rapped his knuckles.

The cases I have been discussing are ones where the developer welshed. Most developers did not. With few exceptions, office building developers provided the stipulated amenities. But those exceptions were so visible and they festered so long that people got the idea the city was being had on every project. It was not, but the belief was to have as much to do with the disenchantment over incentive zoning as any other factor.

In the late seventies matters came to a head. One after the other, some very big buildings were started. The cumulative effect worried people—especially where the buildings were to be cheek to jowl, as on Madison Avenue. And where would it end? The planning commission had been granting so many special dispensations and rule changes that the two volumes of the zoning code had grown monstrously fat.

Civic groups were up in arms: park people, historic preservationists, architects, landscape architects. Newspapers and magazine articles scolded the commission. The commission itself berated the state of zoning. When a coalition of groups proposed a major study, a foundation offered to help with a grant if the commission would tackle the job. The commission accepted and in 1979 launched the Midtown Zoning Study.

As one of the people who had been beefing about the zoning, I was put on the spot by the commission as a consultant. My task: to evaluate the various incentive bonuses and the spaces they produced. Which were working? Which should be kept? Strengthened? Dropped?

As on the plaza study, I used time-lapse photography, observation, and simple head counting to check out the spaces. It was not difficult. The evidence was overwhelming. Most of the spaces were *not* working well—certainly not well enough to warrant the very generous subsidies given for them. Worse yet, in an ill-conceived effort to reduce "pedestrian congestion on the streets," the planners were bonusing people away from the streets.

Here are the principal spaces and what I found out about them:

Through-Block Circulation Areas: These were planner's spaces. The idea was to reduce pedestrian congestion on the sidewalks by providing spaces running through buildings. I checked all of such spaces and found that most of the people using them were going into the building. Remarkably few people used the passageways as a street to shortcut through. They preferred the real street, and even in the coldest weather. In January, during a period when 250 people an hour were using the Olympic Tower passageway some 4,500 people were using the parallel sidewalk of Fifth Avenue.

As for the relieving of congestion, there was no lessening of the flows on the side-street sidewalks. How could there have been? The through-block passages were not alternatives to the sidewalks, but connectors. Short of descending on the building from a helicopter, one could not traverse with connector without using the sidewalks.

Through-Block Networks: To promote networks of such corridors, the planners proposed that where a lot ran between two streets, the developer should provide a through-block passage and, where possible, line it up with any passages on the other side of the street. Such passages would be both mandated and bonused.

There were some partial networks already. One lay in the long blocks between Fifth and Sixth avenues in midtown. Most were within office buildings of the 1920s and 1930s—two hundred feet deep, with elevators and newsstands in the middle of the passage and, in some cases, retail shops lining it. To the knowledgeable, these have certainly been an amenity. One can zig and zag most of the way north from Forty-second to Fifty-third Street and be under cover about two thirds of the time. Most of the traffic is highly local: few people ever traverse the whole route; most will be en route to destinations within a block or so. Because of the unusual length of the crosstown blocks, the passages serve handily as shortcuts. But in total, as with most off-street flows, the number of people going through each passage will be small, averaging about 200 people per hour during off-peak hours. Were there more connections, better signage, and the like, however, there would undoubtedly be stronger flows. The question is how much of a price should be paid for them.

No price should be paid. It is entirely in order to require a builder to provide through-block passages in through-block buildings. Why bonus them to boot? The builder would be crazy not to provide such passages.

Arcaded Sidewalks: Arcaded sidewalks rank high in the literature of urban design and it is understandable that incentive zoning favored them. Europe provides many examples of successful ones—along the Rue de Rivoli in Paris, for example, where the arcade embraces the entire walkway between the buildings and the carriageway. The sidewalks bonused in New York are of a different form: an additional strip parallel to the regular sidewalk but recessed within the building or covered with a cantilevered roof. Thanks to the arcaded portion, the amount of space available for pedestrian movement is about doubled; and there is overhead cover against rain and snow. To spur developers to build continuous sequences of arcaded sidewalks, a special Lincoln Square zoning district offered floor-area bonuses to developers of buildings along Broadway if they would provide arcaded sidewalks, and several did so.

They did not work well. Nor have similar ones elsewhere. People are stubborn. The path they follow is set by the regular sidewalk, and if there are periodic widenings, they do not change course. As time-lapse studies show, they persist along the original track, and they do so even when the pedestrian flow is heavy.

Why shouldn't they? The pedestrians do not need the extra space, and to use it they would have to detour. There is no incentive for that. The overhead cover keeps out the rain; it also keeps out the sun and the light of the sky, and as a consequence arcaded sidewalks tend to be dark and gloomy. While it may be sacrilegious to say so, this is true of some of the dark, medieval passages of Italian cities.

And what happens when it rains? A surprising number of people keep right on going. If it really starts to pour, they will veer inward to gain cover; in a light drizzle, save for those who are going to go into the building, the majority will stick to the outer sidewalk.

One benefit arcaded sidewalks are supposed to provide is a better setting for retail shops and window shopping. Most arcaded sidewalks do feature retailing and that is to the good. But there is one great drawback. The extra space recesses the shops away from the main pedestrian stream. It is difficult to quantify the effect, but in walking by such places you will note that the shops lie at the edge of one's peripheral vision. All you have to do, of course, is turn your head and you'll see the shops. But not so many do so. Occasionally, you will see a passerby do a kind of double take and walk in toward a store to have a look. The fact that it took a conscious decision is a measure of lost potential. When the shops are right next to the passersby, there are first takes—many of them. There is an analogy here to the entrance to a park. When the entry is virtually part of the sidewalk, when it is easy to turn into, impulse use is frequent. So with window shopping. The best place for it is by the windows.

Shopping Arcades: Most of the city's shopping arcades were so poor it was almost unfair to cite them as prototypes: bleak corridors going from nowhere to nowhere, and nothing much in between. But let us consider the arcade at its best. Combining through-block circulation with retailing, it can produce a pedestrian amenity of strong drawing power. London's Burlington Arcade is the most cited example; the two best in this country are the arcades of Cleveland and Providence.

These were set up as commercial ventures. They still are, and the discipline of the marketplace has been a reason for their amenity. They have an excellent relationship with the street: high visibility, tightly scaled walkways, a strong sense of place—and all for sound economic reasons.

If they are economic, let developers build them. But no subsidy should be given. If the figures do not work without one, there is probably something wrong with the project, and the city would be better off if it was not built. By bonusing off-street shopping, the city is tilting the scales against on-street retailing.

Covered Pedestrian Areas: For the planners, the highest form of interior space was the atrium, or gallery, or galleria, or court, or, in the zoning language, covered pedestrian area. The Citicorp atrium was an important prototype. Just as the Seagram Building had helped shape the plaza zoning, Citicorp served as a kind of inventory of amenities for inside spaces. It had a roof to the sky, several levels of shops and restaurants, and lots of sitting and browsing areas, and it was well programmed with entertainment. It even had public rest rooms! Several other successful places came along: the Whitney Museum's sculpture garden in the Philip Morris Building; the garden and gallery of the new IBM Building.

In another chapter I go into the pros and cons of internal spaces: the issue of privatization; the distinction, or lack of one, between such spaces and suburban shopping malls. There is also the problem of success—setting in motion the destruction of the surroundings they so need as a foil.

The question at hand, however, was not whether atriums could be made to work well. Obviously, some worked very well. The question was whether or not they should be bonused. I believed they should not be.

The argument is not against atriums—or through-block areas, or arcaded sidewalks, or gallerias, as such. Here and there they can make sense, and if the voice of the marketplace tells developers they can make money from them, they will provide them. But should the provision be *public* policy? Whatever their merits, these spaces are an internalization of public space and a drain on the vitality of the street. This is not what planning should be about. The argument, then, is against paying developers to provide these spaces—against bonusing a hierarchy of spaces the denominator of which is that they are withdrawn from the street, and the ultimate success of which depends on withdrawing people from the street, as well.

Some spaces earned their way. The most truly public were plazas, and a number of them were well used and enjoyed, particularly those designed after the 1975 guidelines were laid down. It seemed in order to keep the plaza bonus—better yet, to go a step further and get developers to create small urban parks.

This was a born-again idea. When we were working on the 1975 plaza guidelines, we were uncomfortably aware that in some instances it would be better if developers did *not* provide plazas. As Sixth Avenue's string of plazas had demonstrated, the result could be a break in the continuity of the street wall and a surfeit of space. A smaller space better located would be much preferable.

Why not, someone suggested, give a bonus for just that—an off-site space? A developer with an avenue site could get his bonus if he would find a small site on a nearby side street, provide a Paley-Greenacre–type park, and maintain it. It would be a good deal for all concerned. The developer could transfer the unused air rights over the park to his building site, thereby getting his additional avenue space at side-street prices. The city would get a small park at the highest order of amenity, and without the burden of maintaining it.

We were still congratulating ourselves on this surefire idea when a snag developed. Several members of Community Board #5, which had jurisdiction over midtown, objected to the park idea. They thought it would be too good a deal for developers. They objected to just about everything else being recommended—except our goals, which they were for 500 percent, right down the line. With support like this, it looked as if the whole package of proposals would fail to pass the city's Board of Estimate.

To see to it that it would pass, then planning chairman John Zuccotti offered a compromise to Board #5. He would withdraw the urban park provision for further study and postpone any reintroduction to a later date. Board #5 accepted the compromise and resumed the fight against the proposals. Fortunately, this was the only real opposition and the Board of Estimate voted approval.

Now, in 1982, it was that later date. The timing was fortuitous. A small park just like that envisioned in the proposal had been provided by the International Paper Company as part of a building-and-plaza renovation. The park had everything plus the kitchen sink: gourmet food kitchen, chairs, tables, umbrellas, fountains, trees, sun, jazz, and lots and lots of people enjoying it all. There could not have been a better demonstration of the benefits of such a space.

Save for those for the plaza and urban park, I recommended that all the bonuses be dropped. Where a basic public benefit was concerned, it should not have to have a bonus dangled for the providing of it. It should be mandated. If a building has entrances on two streets, a person ought to be able to walk through, and without a bonus having been given the developer for vouchsafing the connection.

A lot of the bonused spaces are glorified lobby spaces. Developers and corporations have been quite willing to spend their money for impressive ones, and they should not have to be given incentives to boot. The same is true of stores at street level. This is vital for the blockfront, for the building's neighbors, for downtown in general, and building owners can make money by providing them. There should be no need to give them a bonus for doing so.

The need is the other way around: to mandate those amenities that should be mandated—stores, glass you can see through, newsstands, rest rooms, snack facilities. And places to sit. Why pay developers not to put spikes on ledges? Or to build ledges that are not so high you cannot sit on them? In Renaissance Italy, buildings were required to make some obeisance to communal usefulness. We should ask as much.

It would likely be given. Developers are a pragmatic lot. Once something gets on the books, that is that; they have other things to worry about than to refight old battles. During the 1975 hearings on

Developers are a pragmatic lot. Once a requirement is on the books, that is that. They have other things to worry about.

tighter zoning guidelines for open spaces, there was developer testimony that such additional amenities as more trees could tip a man into bankruptcy. But in all the time since then, no developer has ever raised objections to the requirements for seating and trees. Indeed, acceptance of most of the stiffer requirements has been so ungrudging that one feels a bit like developers whose buildings have rented out faster than they expected. The price must have been too low.

In their private strategy sessions, developers do not fret over exactions that are in the law. What they discuss is their fallback positions on optional items. What will they willingly give? What only as a last resort? Shall they hold out on that third escalator the planners want? Or throw it in early?

Moral: what you do not ask for, you do not get. Ask.

In 1982, the planning commission came through with a sweeping revision of midtown zoning. It asked a lot. It downzoned midtown, reducing floor-area ratios from a range of 18–21.6 to one of 15–18. On the West Side, where the planners wanted developers to go, ratios were left higher.

With two exceptions—those for plazas and urban parks—bonuses were dropped. The bonus for a plaza was reduced from an f.a.r. of 3 to an f.a.r. of 1. Leeway was left for atriums in special cases, and for arcades in the theatre district.

The planning commission got tougher about amenities. Instead of giving bonuses for them, it mandated them. Where a building fronted on two side streets, for example, the developer was required to provide a through-block connection. Since it would be stupid of him not to, the commission decided it should not give him a bonus to boot.

The commission mandated retail continuity along the street wall, with stores directly accessible from the street and with fronts of see-through glass. The commission mandated more and bigger trees. Instead of the skimpy saplings so often planted, the zoning specified trees of a minimum caliper of four inches, in gratings flush to grade, and with at least two hundred cubic feet of soil per tree. This meant that developers could not palm off little trees in tubs, which many liked to do so there would be more space underneath for cars. Now they had to dig.

Finally, the commission said it was going to swear off negotiated zoning. Skeptics had heard this before and were sure the commission would revert to its old ways. But it was as good as its word. In the years just after the passage of the revised zoning, most building projects in midtown went through as-of-right, with no changes asked or given.

But then, an exception here, an exception there, and negotiated zoning was back. The trouble was, the exceptions were for big buildings: City Spire, Saks tower addition, Coty-Rizzoli. Then there was the Coliseum project, exempt from any zoning at all since the city itself owned the site. It set the terms, too, and with an avarice unmatched by all but a few developers.

One school of thought holds that incentive zoning was a good idea flawed in execution. But the basic flaw has been in the process itself. If people who hold up standards then encourage departures from those standards, exceptions beget exceptions.

But the planning commission deserves kudos. It saw that the zoning had gone awry and it took steps to set matters right. But a question remains. How was it that the zoning got so very awry? One school of thought holds that incentive zoning was a good idea that was flawed in execution. Up to a point this may be true, but there will be no ad hominem argument here. The planners involved have been of top calibre; indeed, they made the city's urban design program the outstanding one in the country. Though there have been changes in the cast over the years, the same problems have kept coming up, and they have come up in other cities, too.

The basic flaw has been in the incentive zoning process. It was bound to go where it has. This is hindsight, to be sure, but there is a principle of some timelessness involved. If a standard is held up, and then those who held it up encourage a departure from that standard, a series of consequences is set in motion. The exceptions beget exceptions, and market pressures spiral up—pressures that confirm the trend and warp the judgment of those who should resist it.

But there is a contrary way of looking at it. Incentive zoning, it could be said, was a bad idea, but it was good it was tried. For there are pluses to count. The zoning has created many open spaces in the core of the city that would not otherwise have been created. It has prompted a marked improvement in the provision of places to sit, and more trees to sit under. It has prompted the creation of indoor public spaces, several of them of outstanding amenity.

The costs? The value to builders of extra floor space gained by bonuses has been huge—in the hundreds of millions of dollars. This of itself is not necessarily bad. What is far more important is what the public has been getting in return. That, unfortunately, has been too little. Some of the spaces have been well designed and well used; more have not.

But the larger costs of incentive zoning have been in the loss of the most basic of amenities—sun and light. It is a loss that is rarely counted. The stock apologia is that the shadows are "redundant"— that is, they fall in shadows already there, and if there are a few more to come, they aren't going to make any difference. But they will.

Fifteen f.a.r. is no magic figure, but it does seem a critical threshold as far as sunlight is concerned. It is when buildings go beyond this —to 18 f.a.r. and above, to forty and fifty stories—that the shadows grow so big, and the abandonment of the old height and setback requirements insures that the darkening will be accentuated. As I take up in the chapter on sun and light, it is not only the loss of direct sunlight that hurts, but of secondary light. For all practical purposes most of the light in midtown New York after 3 P.M. is reflected light, and it is the loss of this that is most keenly felt.

The losses are palpable. One of the sights that never should be is Paley Park in the dark in midafternoon. Even at the summer solstice, when the big buildings are in full sun, Paley is so dark the lights on the waterwall are turned on.

Do the amenities that were bonused offset the loss of sun and light? It is hard to quantify the loss and assign it a value, but what we see in front of us indicates that there is no fair offset. As a matter of logic, could there be one? A particular amenity does not compensate for the effects of the extra bulk of a building. These effects and the amenity are independent of each other. No matter how pleasant an atrium might be for those who use it, it does not itself temper the downdrafts induced by the tower. It does not temper the shadows cast by it. By making the shadows possible, indeed, the bonus may do more harm to some people than it does good to others. And suppose it wasn't even a good atrium? The offset concept is a sloppy one—rather like robbing Peter to pay Paul, but without conceding the robbery.

Another cost is the vitality of the street. In the name of freeing people from congestion on the sidewalks, planners have been bonusing them away from the sidewalks—to internal spaces that are public, but not quite public. It is a perverse kind of urban design, and the best thing about it is that in most cases it has not worked. It would be far worse for the city if it had.

Another question remains. Eventually the commission saw what had to be done. But why did it take so long to get around to it? Research was not the problem. Answering the key questions was largely a matter of going out on the street and looking; and this could have been done anytime. On the matter of the arcaded sidewalks, for example, it took about two days' work to determine that they were not working and why. Calendar time, however, was something else again. That was measured in years—twelve in the case of the arcaded sidewalks.

The problem is asking the questions. Some thirteen years elapsed after the plaza bonus was established before the commission got around to considering how the plazas were working out. The two days of work on the arcaded sidewalks could as easily have been done in 1972 as in 1982, and it would have been most helpful to the commission if it had been.

The time-lag problem is compounded by yet another kind of time lag. New York has been innovative in planning approaches, zoning especially, and other cities often follow its lead, sometimes borrowing not only the measure but the verbatim text of it. But not right away. They take their time too. So there are two time lags to add up, with the consequence that cities may adopt a New York measure just about the time New York is dropping it.

Incentive zoning has had no self-correcting mechanism built into it. In planning in general, there has been no systematic effort to find out what has been working and what has not been. Nor is there training for it in most schools of planning and design. It is odd that this should be so. Planning literature is so full of such terms as "evaluation," "monitoring," and "feedback" that one might assume they were imbedded in standard operating procedure. They are not. The Army has its inspector generals, municipal governments their comptrollers, corporations their management consultants. But planning bodies lack such instruments. You can read through all of the tables of organization, zoning texts, and comprehensive plans without finding a provision or a budget line for so much as one person to go out onto the street and look.

It is not because planners are uncurious or poor at observation. As individuals, some planners have a very keen eye for observation and they enjoy looking at the life of the place they are planning for. But it is extracurricular, on their own time. The busy work of planning has no room for observation, most certainly not if it could be of an adversary nature. One could volunteer, of course. Conceivably, a staff man might go up and say, Boss, that idea you pushed through is really bombing. Conceivably.

It is for want of sustained observation that the time lag between failure of an approach and recognition of it has been so awesomely long. Consider the major mistakes we have made in city planning and how long we clung to them. Did we have to wait for the dynamiting of the Pruitt-Igoe housing project in St. Louis to see that the design approach was wrong? For years evidence had been mounting that colonies of high-rise towers were no way to house families. Did we have to endure the evisceration of our center cities? The destructive effects of urban renewal were long before our eyes.

Some planners do go out and look. San Francisco's planners do a lot of walking and looking, and they have been assiduous in reexamining their zoning and development policies. Pittsburgh's planners studied how all the downtown spaces were being used, and they stiffened their requirements on the basis of what they saw. Here and there, undoubtedly, there might be a few more examples.

Often it is private groups that do the best observing. Some of it is

It is for want of observation that the time lag between failure of an approach and recognition of it has been so awesomely long. Did we have to wait for the dynamiting of Pruitt-Igoe to see that the design approach was flawed? Did we have to wait until our cities were eviscerated to question urban renewal?

quite professional: groups such as the Municipal Art Society of New York are forever putting an arm on architects and lawyers and various specialists to do work, and for free. But the laymen can be just as valuable. Being untutored in sophisticated planning analysis, they tend to ask simple questions and to do a lot of looking.

Let me conclude with three examples close to home. One is the downzoning of the Upper East Side. Neighborhood groups believed that the moderate scale of the side streets should be given real protection. So did the planning commission. A downzoning, however, would require detailed study of some two hundred blocks if it was to stand up. At the moment the commission had neither the budget nor the staff people to tackle the job. Halina Rosenthal, President of the Friends of the Upper East Side Historic Districts, said her people would do the job themselves. She organized a corps of volunteer observers. Block by block, they carefully recorded the heights of buildings, current use, and other data. At the end of five months they presented the completed report to the planning commission. It responded in kind. Within a few months the commission downzoned the midblocks of most of the side streets of the Upper East Side. Henceforth, buildings could be no higher than the width of the right-of-way, or sixty feet—the same proportion, by the way, the French laid down for Paris avenues in the 1600s.

Another example of citizen input is the case of the oversized spire. It came about because City Club president Sally Goodgold watched a softball game one day in Central Park. From the diamond she saw the cluster of towers going up by Carnegie Hall in a new perspective. One of the towers—City Spire—looked to her to be a bit higher than an existing building, the height of which she knew. And City Spire was not supposed to be that high. She mentioned the point to her fellow watchers. *New York Magazine* got wind of it and checked into the matter. Sure enough, the tower was too high—by twelve and a half feet. The city was shocked. Naughty. Naughty. It slapped the developer smartly on the wrist. He could keep the spire, but as penance he would have to build additional space for community dance groups to use.

A similar case was the overbuilt tower at 108 East Ninety-sixth Street. Genie Rice, head of the civic group CIVITAS, suspected that the developer was going to build it higher than the zoning allowed. Checking the official documents, she found that because of a misinterpretation of the zoning map the building was indeed going to go higher —by some twelve stories. The building department rescinded the permit. The developer appealed and proceeded to build the extra eight stories. CIVITAS was out for blood. The New York State Supreme

Court ruled that the stories would have to come down. Again the developer appealed, and the matter went to the appellate court. The court has not yet ruled. Whichever way, it is possible the developer will end up equitably: heads he wins, tails he does not lose.

These cases are too mixed up to yield a large moral. But they do reiterate a point. It is when civic groups and citizens become too supportive, too understanding, that planning and zoning go to hell. Matters don't get set right until they become impatient, angry, meddlesome; most important, when they go out and look.

17

SUN AND SHADOW

U.S. cities have been destroying their sun and light at an accelerating clip. But none has been doing it on such a massive scale, with more technical mastery, and with such a sophisticated set of urban design tools as New York City.

U.S. cities have been destroying their sun and light at an accelerating clip. But none have been doing it on such a massive scale, with more technical mastery, and with such a sophisticated set of urban design tools as New York City. And none, of course, have had such a big head start. For cities that still have some sun left, New York has many lessons.

The great building boom that began in the 1960s laid the groundwork but it did it incrementally, a building here, a building there. New Yorkers are very adaptable; year by year few noticed the loss of light. But the loss was great. Successive aerial photos show that by the mid-seventies there had been a dramatic increase in shadow area. There were still some empty spaces and low-rise buildings that let through patches of sunlight. But the great bulk of midtown was in shadow from midafternoon on.

Then the niches were filled in. On the side streets more of the limestone and brownstone buildings were demolished to make way for high-rise buildings; so, on the avenues, high-rise buildings to make way for higher-rise buildings. The game is not yet over. Fifth Avenue is still a gloriously lit street. A few low-rise blocks remain. But just the buildings now under construction are going to have profound effects.

The most pervasive loss has been of secondary light. The shadows of new buildings, it used to be said, fall on the shadows of old buildings and there is thus little lost. But this is not so. The shadows are compounded and there is a marked diminishment of light. The dark places get darker still. It is not just the loss of sun that is critical; it is the loss of sky overhead, of the light that makes the difference between being in shadow and being at the bottom of a well.

New York's course has been a regressive one. Under the old rules many tall buildings were built, such as the Empire State Building and the Chrysler Building. But they were relatively slim. The towers were set well back from the street and they covered only a part of the site. Now there are slabs, often with no setbacks at all, but rising straight up. Worse, some are so oriented that the effect, if not the intention, is a maximum blockage of sun. They do not knife into the sun; they sit broadside to it and cast huge shadows to the north.

As I noted in the chapter on incentive zoning, some of the lost sunlight was bonused away. A prime case in point is Paley Park on East 53rd Street. In 1970, a developer put up a speculative office building directly to the south of Paley Park. To gain additional bulk through incentive bonuses, the developer provided some open space and a through-block arcade. It provides a shortcut for pedestrians, several shops, and a nice visual approach to Paley Park—in shadow in midafternoon because of the building that went up higher because of incentive bonuses for the arcade.

To be fair, it should be noted that almost any office building that could have been built there would have blocked Paley's sunlight. But that is just the problem. Almost any new building could have been built there. The zoning provided no protection for the smaller-scale side streets. It would later, by which time most of the remaining sites would have been developed.

In New York, as in most cities, zoning did make provisions for sun and light. It outlawed the likes of the old Equitable Building, which rose straight up from the street. The ordinances prescribed an imaginary exposure plane sloping back from the streets; as buildings went higher, they had to be set back from this line so they would not violate it.

There is a parallel to the evolution of zoning in Paris. In the eighteenth century the city decreed that building heights be related to the width of the streets: low on narrow streets, higher on wider ones. Baron Haussmann continued the principle in his reconstruction. In succeeding years, the zoning was periodically modified; changes in the width-height ratios allowed the cornice line to go up a bit, and then a bit more. Next the area above the cornice line was expanded by mansarding, and then some more. Eventually almost as much bulk could be constructed above the old limit as below it.

The same kind of tinkering took place in New York in a much shorter time. Increasingly the planners modified the height and set-back regulations, and before long they waived them altogether. Sky exposure planes became truly imaginary. Out of reflex, developers still filed diagrams of them with plans that clearly violated them.

With sun tables, computer maps, scale models—and a touch of art—it is possible to derive far more light and less shadow from structures of a given size than is now the case. However, before taking up these techniques, let one point be reaffirmed. Given size is crucial. Big buildings cast big shadows. Bigger buildings cast bigger shadows. There is no optimum cutoff, but New York's original limit of 15 f.a.r. was a reasonable ceiling. Buildings of that density can cast plenty of shadow, but much of this is absorbed by street and avenue space. It is when the buildings go higher and fatter that real damage is done. When building heights are routinely increased to forty and fifty stories, the shadow impacts are greatly increased. For those on the receiving end the change is not one of degree; it may be absolute. They had sun; now they have none.

Big buildings cast big shadows. Bigger buildings cast bigger shadows.

What is needed is solar zoning. Given a sensible limitation on bulk, we can not only reduce materially the blocking of sunlight but increase the beneficent reflection of it. We can even manipulate and redirect it to places that had no sun before. In the process we may produce some new building shapes, eccentric and effective.

The most comprehensive approach has been the development of the solar envelope. The pioneer in this has been Ralph Knowles of USC. He has conceived the envelope as an imaginary container that would regulate development in terms of time as well as space. The conventional sky exposure plane puts upward and outward limits on the size of buildings. The solar envelope does too, but with the important difference that it tailors these limits to allow as much sunlight as possible to fall on other buildings.

The chief application so far has been for solar energy; zoning envelopes have been devised for residential construction so that each house will let plenty of sun fall on neighbors' rooftops and solar collectors. A number of cities in the Southwest have adopted solar zoning ordinances to this end. A great deal of legal and technical homework has been done on this kind of solar access, and there is reason to expect much wider application in the years ahead.

Most of the work to assure sun has been done in places where the sun is easiest to come by. Keeping suburban houses low is no great problem. What is far more difficult is the application of solar zoning to

cities. The work is only beginning. Knowles has been developing zoning models for parts of Los Angeles. The National Bureau of Standards has been funding some demonstration projects to explore solar
energy opportunities in such environments as suburban shopping centers and office parks. With the redevelopment authority of Baltimore,
it has been studying how the geometry of a low-rise commercial block
affects sun and heat and light.

Only lately, however, has attention been directed to solar access
in the center of the city. Not surprisingly, one of the best efforts has
been in a city far to the north, Canada's Calgary. Sitting as it does on a
high plateau at latitude fifty-one degrees north, it has a most disciplin-
ing climate. The winds are often fierce; the winter temperatures range
around forty below—lower when it really gets cold. But the sky can be
startlingly clear and there is lots of sunlight, the most of any Canadian
city.

It comes in at a low angle, however. This means that big buildings
can cast very long shadows. At the winter solstice, the Calgary Tower
casts a shadow eight blocks across downtown. Since Calgary has lately
been putting up more big buildings, it has problems it once had not.
But it has learned. For one thing, it has adopted stringent solar zoning
guidelines. For each street and avenue there are detailed prescriptions
of angles and planes that must be observed by builders to assure the
passage of sunlight. Solar zoning envelopes are shaped so that buildings to the south of public open spaces will fall within an angle of
thirty-seven degrees—the sun angle at 11 A.M. at the equinox.

The municipal government is practicing what it preaches. Its new
Municipal Building is tailored to the sun. On the sunward side, the
building is at its tallest: thirteen stories. From there it is terraced
down, a floor at a time, until it is three stories high. The angle is
thirty-seven degrees. This is enough to allow the sun to fall on the
open spaces beyond from 11 A.M. to 3 P.M. at the equinox, and for
most of the day in late spring and summer.

Another northern city put in solar zoning because of glare.
Thanks to a combination of low sun angles and some new glass-wall
towers, citizens of Seattle found they were squinting into reflected
sunlight a lot more than before.

A new Hilton Hotel brought matters to a head. The city's environmental review of the project had determined that the building
would have no adverse effects. But no sooner was it finished then the
effects became blindingly apparent. Its glass walls blasted light down a
key stretch of the interstate freeway leading into town; during morning rush hours in winter, the sun came in at such a low angle that it
was reflected directly into drivers' eyes. Slowdowns led to massive
traffic jams.

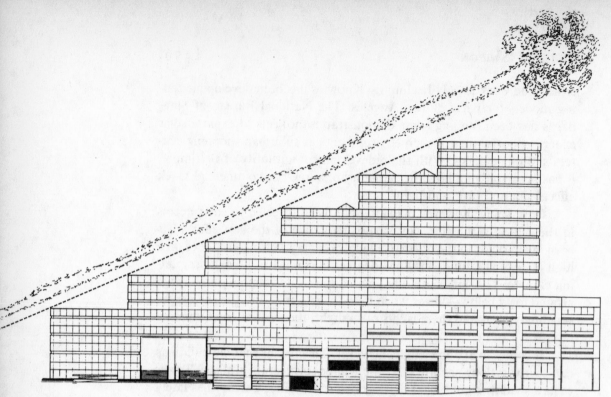

To maximize the passage of sunlight, Calgary's new city hall is sloped down at an angle of thirty-seven degrees.

These reflections could have been predicted had anyone thought to do so, and in 1978 the city council passed a law requiring that henceforth such matters be thought of. All proposed construction must be reviewed to see what adverse impacts there might be from light and glare, and these must be mitigated by redesign.

Few cities have had effective height limitations and stuck to them. Paris did, in the seventeenth century, but it later blew its advantage by cheating above the cornice line. Flexibility has been the problem. Developers and architects—and the real estate market—can adjust to almost any level, so long as it is the level, and no monkey business. It is the anticipation of adjustments and exceptions and wavering municipal wills that send land prices higher, and, in turn, the buildings.

But one American city had a very successful height limitation: Philadelphia. It was successful because it was arbitrary. In the words of planner Edmund Bacon, "A major line, unprecedented in history, created not by law but by consensus. It is the line above which no building has risen." It is the height of William Penn's statue atop City Hall: 491 feet.

There was no legal basis for this figure, no rationale based on floor-area ratios or sky exposure planes or such. It was just that it seemed supremely right that the tallest building in the city be its city hall, that it be in the very center of the city, and that it be crowned with a statue of the city's wise founder.

And 491 feet is a lot of feet—enough for forty stories—and a very comfortable limit for several generations of builders. (Height figures of Philadelphia office buildings indicate that few of them had been pressed up against the limit.)

In 1985 developer Willard Rouse proposed a complex that would breach the limit, and considerably so: two towers, one of 826 feet, another of 700 feet. The low alternative would be three towers of 491 feet—within the limit, but bulkier.

There was a big civic outcry. But there was also support for the high buildings. Many Philadelphians said it was time the city shed its stodgy image, that it would be good to have some really big buildings, as New York did. It would serve notice that Philadelphia was big time now, not a sleepy Quaker town.

Mayor Wilson Goode held a two-day hearing and listened to just about everybody with an opinion. Then he came out for doing away with the William Penn statue limitation. The tacit consensus was over.

They had a good thing going for them. And they lost it.

Sun is money. To be able to take away so many units of sunlight is the other side of the coin of being able to put up that many more feet of commercial space. An architect can modify this equation somewhat by the way he configures the building. But the key factor is bulk. To repeat: big buildings cast big shadows. Bigger buildings cast bigger shadows. And make more money. Unless the city has rigorous guidelines for bulk and sun and light—and the mettle to stick to them—money will win out over sun.

The case of Dallas is instructive. As one official put it, Dallas has not been in the business of discouraging developers. It has had no effective guidelines for sun and bulk and height. As a consequence a new park space in the center of downtown was in jeopardy from the day it was completed. This was Thanksgiving Square, a triangular-shaped space that was mostly in full sun, even in winter.

Across the street to the sunward, a site was cleared. It was for a very tall slab building, titled, as is so often the case, for that which it would defile. Thanksgiving Tower, it was called. Businessman Peter Stewart, the moving force behind Thanksgiving Square, commissioned sun studies by a local engineer. They showed that the building would cast far more shadow than it had to. The tower was going to be laid broadside to the sun. That is why the shadow would be so big, and at the midday time when sun was so needed (except in July and August, when it was not). If the building were canted so that it sliced into the

Greenacre Park in full sunlight. Thanks to an easement and some preemptive buying, the full sunlight should continue.

sun, there would be far less shadow. But the developers would not change the plans by so much as an inch. Nor would the city government pressure them to do so. The tower went up. It cast big shadows, just as the studies indicated that it would.

The indefatigable Stewart, eyeing other vulnerable spaces, asked the city to adopt a tough sun-and-shadow ordinance. The city liked the idea. The developers did not. The matter rests.

Of all the cities, New York has been far and away the leader in the trading of sun for bulk. In the 1961 zoning resolution it set a floor-area ratio of 15. This was based on happy medians of past experience and was not a bad base. At fifteen or below shadows were tolerable, much of them being absorbed by the street. But as the ratios went higher—eventually to 21.6 in some instances—the shadow effects went up more than proportionately. As we noted in the chapter on zoning, bulk begot bulk, and in the quest to pile up yet more floors, developers grew increasingly heedless of the impacts on their surroundings. And so, what was worse, did the planners.

In the case of the chromium palace two parties were joined in culpability. The building in question was to be big and squat and rise sheer from the street. Bad enough to begin with, it gained yet more bulk as bonus was piled on bonus: arcade bonus, atrium bonuses, zoning-lot merger, waiver of height and setback regulations, air-rights transfer from an adjacent landmark.

The project would have gone through as planned had it not been for one side effect. Someone found out that the height had gone up so much that the building would shadow Greenacre Park a block and a half away. The shadowing was, to be sure, inadvertent. The planners did not know the building would cut off sunlight that way. They did not want to know. They did not do any homework to find out. The architect did not know. His diagrammed shadows fell on white space, no park or other buildings being indicated. The planners did concede that there was a park. But they said the shadow would be redundant, falling on another building's shadow. The planning commission approved the project.

It was the last straw. On this one the community-board people and civic groups decided to go down fighting. They went before the city's final tribunal, the Board of Estimate, and asked it to overrule the planning commission and deny the bonus for the extra bulk. And they came with their homework done, complete with sun studies and computer printouts. Redundant my eye. There would indeed be shadows—at least two or three floors' worth and at just the wrong time. In an unprecedented move, the Board of Estimate rescinded the atrium bonus and ordered the building height reduced by three stories.

The planning commission was stunned. The developers were

stunned. So were other developers. There had been a tacit understanding that this was not the way things were supposed to work. The madder they got, the more they turned their ire on the very planning commission that had tried so hard to be more than fair to them.

In its 1982 revision of midtown zoning, the planning commission renounced the likes of the chromium palace. It reintroduced height and setback regulations in a novel way. To assure plenty of "daylighting" as well as sun, consultants Michael Kwartler and Alan Schwartzman developed a two-tier approach; one prescriptive; the other, performance. The aim is the same in both cases; to have buildings so shaped that they allow a satisfactory amount of open sky above and daylight below.

Architects can take their pick. The prescriptive route is as-of-right; it sets forth detailed height and setback standards, which, if followed, will result in the desired amount of daylighting. If the plan conforms to these standards, it is approved.

The first approach measures causes; the second measures effect. The architect evaluates the amount of light his proposed building would block. With daylight evaluation charts, he plots the amount of daylight as it would be perceived in several locations. The scene is divided into imaginary squares. By counting the squares where light would be blocked and those where it would not, the architect can figure the percent of daylight that would be let through.

Seventy-five percent is passing. If it is that or more, the building will be approved, however the architect arrived at his solution. The score can be further improved by increasing the reflectivity of the building surfaces and thus the amount of light sent back to the street.

So far, most architects have opted for the prescriptive approach. The other is more complicated but not as complicated as it first seems. With the advent of computer mapping, architectural offices can quickly make the computations for counting squares of daylight and such data. Some already have cranked the necessary equations into their tapes.

One figure that should be cranked into New York computers is twenty-nine degrees east of true north. Let me disgress a bit to explain why. The street grids of most cities are laid out on cardinal points of the compass, and main streets tend to run due north-south or east-west. New York's grid is different, and a good thing for the city that it is. The commission that was appointed to determine the future street system met in 1811. They decided on the rectangular grid. It was the cheapest for building construction, the commission said, much preferable to fancy circuses or ovals as in Europe.

In fitting the rectangular grid to the shape of the island, the commission had to angle it somewhat. The north-south avenues did not point to true north, but twenty-nine degrees to the east of it. The fortuitous result is an optimum sun pattern for the streets. Since the north side of the blocks are angled a bit to the east, they receive several hours of early morning sun. The small side streets get sun during most of the morning and during mid- and late afternoon. (The houses on them get it right up to sunset if they have bay windows extending far enough outward.) The avenues get full sun at the height of the promenade, around 1 to 2 P.M. It is, in short, a most happy union of sun and grid.

There has been some backsliding. When the city has sponsored the development of sites it owns itself, it has proved the most avaricious of developers, not only tolerating great bulk but demanding it. Huge shadows have promised to be the consequence spawning a new round of ingenious rationalizations. One is the shadowless building. Sun diagrams of these show the outlines of shadows that would have been cast were not the spaces already shadowed by somebody else. Speed shadows are another variant. For these the sheer height of the structure is cited as an ameliorating factor—its shadow is so leveraged that the top of it races across the cityscape. Public opinion has hardened significantly against the supertowers; and so, perhaps, has the office space market.

Of U.S. cities, San Francisco has been the most zealous in guarding its sun. Not so long ago it had been complacently lax. It had set the maximum floor-area ratio for buildings at fourteen and it offered incentive bonuses with which developers could make them bigger. That they did, with towers and pyramids, and the citizenry became alarmed. The most dreaded of prospects, "Manhattanization," loomed ahead.

Environmentalists agitated for a referendum, and in 1979 they got an anti–high-rise measure put on the ballot. It called for reducing the maximum building heights to 200 feet or twenty floors in the core downtown area, lower in the adjacent downtown areas—80 to 130 feet.

By a narrow margin, the measure failed. But the momentum did not. The planning commission undertook a major overhaul of its incentive zoning and its bulk and height regulations. Building heights were reduced to a maximum of 550 feet, and maximum floor-area ratios and bonuses where sharply pared.

In 1984 another anti–high-rise measure, Proposition K, was put on the ballot. It would ban any building that would shadow parks and public open spaces. One thing it had going for it was a visible outrage.

It had manifested itself in Chinatown a decade earlier. This was the construction of the Pacific Telephone Building, a twenty-two story high rise of unparalleled ugliness, and one of the worst of my collection of blank walls. It was not only dreadful to look at, it cast a shadow that fell on much of St. Mary's Square at lunchtime most days of the year.

Then, in 1982, a few blocks away, the tiny Chinese Playground was threatened by a prospective 140-foot-high condominium tower. A team from Berkeley's landscape architecture program went to the planning commission and demonstrated exactly how many hours of sunlight would be lost if the tower were to go up. The team also demonstrated how such building proposals could be forestalled in the future. They had drawn up maps that showed solar "fans," a set of imaginary planes calculated to correspond exactly with the angles of the sun—low angles stretching east to embrace the morning sun, somewhat steeper for the midday sun from the south, and low again toward the west for the afternoon sun.

The commission adopted this approach. It lowered allowable building heights around the playground to preserve its sun. Encouraged by this step, community groups went a step further and proposed that this kind of solar zoning be applied citywide. The matter was put to the voters in June of 1984. It was approved by a three-to-two margin. And just in time. Passage halted several high-rise towers near Union Square.

18

BOUNCE LIGHT

So far we have been dealing with measures to curb shadows. But there are many more positive aspects to be explored. The same big bad buildings that are cutting off light to one area can reflect it to another. The potentials for such bounce light should be explored; so, too, should spotlighting techniques for redirecting the sun into dark places that never had it before. The prerequisite is a thorough microclimatic study of the effects of new buildings on their surroundings. This review should be done by the planning commission or by an independent body on its behalf. It should not be left to the architects.

On technical matters, planning bodies usually accept the data given them by the architects and developer. They do not have the budget to do their own studies or commission them. So they're grateful for the data, when they should be just a bit suspicious, and they usually adopt them as their own in the final statement of findings. Sun studies are a case in point. It's not that they are slanted—not deliberately, anyway—it's just that they can be grossly inaccurate. Three that I examined recently were not only in error but palpably so. One had true north 6 degrees to the west of true north. Another, by one of the biggest firms, had shadows falling on abstract space, with no indication as to what buildings, if any, were in their path. A third had late afternoon sun at 340 degrees; the sun itself gets only to 270 degrees when it calls it a day.

In none of these instances did the review bodies spot the error. If the studies had shown the sun setting in the east, the review bodies probably would not have spotted the error. There is something in the process that militates against it. Too much faith and trust proved troublesome for San Francisco's planning commission. One of the worst shadows was the product of a building that the architect's study indicated would be exemplary. When it proved otherwise, the planning commission came in for a lot of criticism, and it resolved never to make the same mistake again. Luckily, across the Bay in Berkeley there was just the kind of body the planners could turn to for help.

With a grant from the National Science Foundation, the late Donald Appleyard had created the Environmental Simulation Laboratory. One of his first studies was of the view from the road. Over a room-sized topographical model of Marin County he suspended a 16mm camera. With a computer-driven mechanism the camera could be instructed to move along a given route at any simulated speed. Thanks to a periscope attachment to the lens, the camera would record the scene from the driver's-eye viewpoint.

The technique was to be highly useful in studying the street-level effects of San Francisco's sun and density problems. With a large model of the city inherited from its world's fair, Appleyard and successor Peter Bosselmann tested various alternatives: the sun and light patterns as they existed, at they would be if heights were increased or decreased; the effects of different setback limits. And these were not static examples. With astonishing verisimilitude, the camera would take one on an eye-level walk or brisk drive in a car.

As I noted in the previous chapter, these simulations helped San Francisco's planners come up with new and tougher height and bulk requirements. They were also helpful in reviewing particular projects developers wanted to put up. More times than not, the simulations showed that the buildings would cast more shadows than they were supposed to or had to. The simulations also showed that with some adroit revisions the buildings' shadows could be substantially mitigated. Some architects screamed and yelled at first, but they came around.

The laboratory's equipment is expensive but the basic job can be done without fancy hardware. Bosselmann demonstrated this when he came to New York to lend a hand on a study of Times Square. The Municipal Art Society of New York feared that zoning of the area was likely to be disastrous. It asked Bosselmann if he could do a quick study with simple instruments. He could. He created large-scale cardboard models of all existing buildings, with their facades made of color prints of the actual buildings and signs. Additional models incorporated different design possibilities. The models could be moved at table height, and by shifting them one could see what the alternative effects would be—on the vistas up Broadway and Seventh Avenue, on the galaxy of signs behind Duffy Square.

Several points became strikingly self-evident. Ordinary office buildings would make a mediocre hash of the place. Zoning that recognized the unique attraction of it would not. City officials and planners were fascinated by the exhibits—models, as we have noted, are entrapping. Whether the city will heed the particular lessons is a question. A larger one, however, is whether it will heed the general lesson and set up its own evaluative center.

Planning commissions are the logical bodies to do this. But they have not done so and are not likely to. They are receptive to evaluations, even critical ones, but they do not like to originate them. There must be something in intragovernmental protocol that inhibits them from doing so. In any event, if the job is to be done, it will have to be through an independent center of some kind.

Such a center would be staffed and equipped to apply a wide range of techniques. It would do sun studies using the models and before-and-after methods pioneered by Berkeley; it would do computer mapping of sun and shadow patterns as practiced by several architectural firms, most notably by Skidmore, Owings, and Merrill. The center would do wind-tunnel testing to determine the drafts a building might induce and the measures that would modify them. It would also study the winds generated by nature and some microclimatic defenses. More cities than Chicago are windy cities but few do anything so rudimentary as to provide seating sheltered by windbreaks. Bus shelters are minimal measures, being designed more for the display of advertising than for the comfort of people. There is so much that could be done in the way of experimentation: berms in the right place, glass windbreaks and deflectors, sun niches and wind traps. Save in supercold places, like Calgary, planners and designers have not done much to explore the possibilities.

The center could also evaluate the use—and nonuse—of existing buildings and spaces. It was to demonstrate how simply this could be done that I set up the Street Life Project. My hope was that the planners would not only adopt our findings but adopt the techniques and develop their own in-house capability. Pittsburgh's planning department did a study comparable to our plaza study and made excellent use of the findings. As far as I know, however, the only full-time evaluation being done today is that by the Project for Public Spaces.

It would help if the center had a university connection. Its board should be representative of various interests affected: planners, architects, landscape architects, developers, community leaders, and, ex officio, the chairman of the planning commission. Foundation support would be vital. While the center could be partially self-supporting through fees from the city and other clients, it should have financial independence. It must be able to ask its own questions, not merely

We need independent centers staffed and equipped to check out the microclimatic effects of major projects—and early enough in the game to change plans for the better.

Smaller cities do not have the bulk and density problems of the biggest cities. That is their good fortune. They still have some sun to save.

respond to others! Its best research tack will be exploring new possibilities—new ways of making microclimates more benign, sun and light more pervasive.

Smaller cities have good reason to set up similar evaluative centers. They do not have the bulk and density problems of the biggest cities, but that is their good fortune. They still have a lot of sun to save. Proportionately, the cost of an environmental simulation setup would be higher for them, there being fewer clients and buildings for splitting the bill. But the cost could be moderate just the same.

Some of the most effective sun-study techniques have been developed for use by community planning boards. Professor Brent Porter of Pratt Institute makes small-scale cardboard models of a particular area of the community. He then places these on top of a kind of sundial diagram. For a light source he uses the sun. He takes the models outside, then twists and tilts them until the shadow of a small stick intersects the line denoting the desired time—2 P.M., for example, on December 22. The shadows cast by the models will approximate those that would be cast in actuality. Porter has also developed comparably simple techniques for charting an area's wind shadows. For a community board of Manhattan's Upper East Side he and a group of his students did a complete microclimatic study of wind and sun effects. They found a strong correlation between the two. The big buildings that blocked a lot of sun tended to be the ones that also had fierce downdrafts at their bases.

Study technology, to repeat, is not a problem. High tech or low, there are all sorts of ways to answer the questions. It is the asking of them that is the critical step. And the process must be dynamic, with answers prompting follow-up questions. How much sunlight, for example, will the building pass on to its neighbors? This is the stock question and will be answered with shadow diagrams.

But there is a more important question, and one that is rarely asked. How much sunlight *could* the building pass on? Answering this will require imagination. Height and setback regulations may assure a certain amount of open sky above; they do not necessarily assure a satisfactory amount of sunlight—or light derived from it.

If we had to deduce the passage of the sun from the clues that most new towers afford, we would conclude that the sun rises in the east, goes full circle, and comes back east to set. But it does not. It sets in the west. No additional research is needed on this point.

Take a look at the way most buildings are sited and configured. If we had to deduce the passage of the sun from the clues these buildings afford, we would have to conclude that the sun rises in the east, traverses a full circle, and comes back to the east to set. Many buildings show the same face to every direction, as if the sun fell uniformly on all sides. North, south, east, and west: there is often no difference between the side that faces south and the one that faces north.

The sun does not set in the east, it sets in the west, and it only traverses 180 degrees. No additional research is needed on this point.

If you want to maximize the amount of sunlight passing over a building, you should configure the mass so that it slopes down toward the north. This is the thrust of Calgary's zoning. Ordinarily, however, few buildings are configured in this fashion. Indeed, they are just as apt to be configured in reverse. A big new residential complex puts the lowest part on the southern end of the site, the highest on the northern, thereby reducing the amount of sun falling on the row houses to the northwest. The complex has been acclaimed for its sensitive design.

Had the question been raised early, and forcibly, the mass could have been configured to better effect for all concerned. The same would have been true in the case of the too high hat. Out of sheer inadvertence an architect put a "high hat" structure for his elevators and water tanks to the rear of his tower. Had the question been raised he would have realized that this positioning provided the extra feet that would shadow a key public open space. Had it been to the front there would have been no extra shadow. But the question was not raised in time. Thus the epitaph. We never thought of it.

So that it is thought of, all proposed buildings should be subjected to a rigorous study of their microclimatic effects on their surroundings: wind-tunnel tests of models, not just to determine the sway up top, but the drafts down below; sun studies to determine the shadows cast, the light reflected, and where and when; the light that is lost because it is just out of reach and need not be. There are many positive aspects to explore.

One of them is bounce light. Big buildings can send back many footcandles of light. Sometimes they send it at the wrong angle to the wrong places—as with Seattle's glare. But sometimes the effect can be quite beneficent. New York's Citicorp Building, for example, is a notable bestower of light—so much so that trees on one receiving block have been growing faster than before. Citicorp's reach has been long range. On late afternoons in spring it reflected sunlight all the way to the west side of Fifth Avenue between Fifty-seventh and Fifty-eighth, some seven blocks away. That is, until the IBM Building went up.

Paley Park benefited. Shortly after it had lost much of its sunlight to a building to the south, a building went up to the northeast. One side of it was a solid expanse of black brick. When the sun fell on this wall, however, a surprising amount of light was bounced to the southwest—and to Paley Park. It bestowed a soft fill light—that is, until an intervening building went up.

Urban design guidelines sometimes rule out open spaces with northern exposures. I think this is a mistake. A southern exposure is preferable, to be sure, but spaces without one should not be ruled out. Thanks to bounce light, they can enjoy sunlight vicariously. A case in

To maximize the amount of sunlight that a building lets by, the mass should be configured so that it slopes down toward the north. There are few such buildings.

point is Grace Plaza in New York. It is a bum plaza, but lack of light is not the reason. The building across the street to the north gets full sun in the afternoon and sends a lot of it back to the plaza.

Such effects have been largely accidental. In very few cases did the architects anticipate them and in no case that I know of were they deliberately planned. Easley Hamner, associate of Hugh Stubbins on the Citicorp project, says they were concerned over possible lawsuits from buildings to the south. In Texas there had been suits by building owners aggrieved over the extra air-conditioning load caused by reflected sun from glass buildings. No such problems appeared likely for Citicorp and no design changes proved necessary. As it turned out, most of the reflections work to good effect.

Why not plan them? A surface reflects back light at an angle equal to that with which it received it. If you know one, you can figure the other, and *seriatim,* successive bounces that might be good to plan. We get many of these bounces willy-nilly; we might as well determine the where and when of them.

We can also determine the quality of the light. Building materials are the key factor. The glass walls that have become so much the rule may cut down heat transmission into the building, but the light that they reflect is harsh. The glass sends sunlight back the way it came: in parallel rays. It is a highly concentrated light in time as well as in space. Depending on the azimuth and the altitude of the sun, a black glass building can be a blast of light or a big black void.

Porous surfaces such as brick or limestone act differently. They reflect far more light; white-painted masonry, for example, has a reflectivity factor of .85 versus .12 for dark glass. But the light is benign. It does not glare. Instead of reflecting the sun back in parallel ways, porous surfaces break up the rays and diffuse them. For urban design this has two good consequences. The light is evenly reflected by the buildings that it falls upon and they are the easier to look at for this. Some of them fairly glow.

Just as important is the light reflected into other areas. It can be very pleasant. Fifth Avenue in the Fifties is a splendidly lit place, and one reason is the prevalence of limestone and travertine in the facades. The play of light on these surfaces is reflected on their surroundings and the street and the people on it, and a pleasant and flattering light it is. Like good restaurant lighting, the effective light comes from the side, not overhead, and it washes away flaws. (Advice to ladies: if you want to be discovered looking your very best, be on the west sidewalk of Fifth Avenue between Fifty-fifth and Fifty-seventh around four-thirty in the afternoon on the vernal equinox.)

If you look to the sources of these lighting effects, you realize how great an asset are the light-colored buildings, such as Bergdorf Goodman. You see, too, how well the newly cleaned St. Patrick's Cathedral illumines the streets around it, and how vital to its light, in turn, are the low-rise limestone buildings that flank the promenade to Rockefeller Plaza.

More than aesthetics are involved. In taking footcandle readings along Fifth, I have found that although the readings of the sky vault overhead are fairly consistent, there are marked variations in the light received at eye level. These variations are due principally to the materials in the facades: the limestone of Cartier's; the black glass of Olympic Tower. One expands the light; the other swallows it up.

The planners are now requiring that any new building on Fifth Avenue be of light-colored masonry along at least 20 percent of its frontage up to the first setback. Better yet, zoning encourages a more general use by giving architects extra daylighting credits for light-colored materials. Other cities should be taking similar steps. If they do nothing more than get architects to lay aside that black glass, they will be worth the while.

Facades are not the only places for reflective materials. Interiors of blocks, the orphans of so much development, could profit by bounce light. Just the light reflected by one slab of a building's backside could make a significant difference. The same is true of many residential blocks. Brownstone rears are not pretty, but if those on the north side are painted buff or white, they will do wonders for the interiors of the blocks.

There is another question to be asked. Is there some sunlight that could be intercepted? Yes, if you look for it. But this is not usual procedure. Most sun-and-shade diagrams are in plan. Where there is a plaza, for example, the diagrams will show the portions that are in shadow and those that are in sun at a given time. The view will be literally a black-and-white one. Sun here and shadow there and that's that.

Thus are opportunities obscured. If you look at the same place in section you will see angles at which the sun falls. The floor of the plaza may be receiving no sun at all, but above it the sun may be coming in at an angle that puts it about twenty feet above the center of the plaza. And it keeps going. There is nothing on the plaza to intercept it, to reflect it. But if there were some foliage up there—say, a thirty-foot-high honey locust—there would be sunlight. It would be partial—a tiny fraction of the space. But what a difference that fraction can make! The diffused and dappled light that filters through can be very pleasant, and persuasive.

To capture such opportunities it is important to plan for large trees—really large trees, eight-inch caliper minimum—and this means making sure the planting beds are large and deep. This can be difficult. New plazas and small parks are often built atop underground garages, and spaces for cars are given priority over trees. It's tough enough to get space for them in the planning stage. It is virtually impossible after the concrete is poured.

Another way to borrow light is by direct projection. This is similar to bounce lighting but uses highly directed light aimed at specific targets. To give an illustration let me sketch a hypothetical situation. A small center-city park has lost most of its sunlight. Worse yet, it is now so surrounded by new buildings that there is precious little daylight, let alone sun. A new office tower, however, offers hope. When it is finished, there will be a direct line of sight from its roof to the small park.

Could not some of its light be projected to the park? Something such as a mirror would burn the park users to a crisp but the use of highly reflective panels might work well. It would not take many of them to send a substantial amount of light. The setup could be computer controlled to track the sun for maximum effect in the park— including the backlighting of a much liked statue in the center of the park.

Farfetched? Yes, but no more so than some of the building features that architects have been coming up with. The prismatic glass of Der Scutt's Trump Tower, for example, shoots light in almost an infinity of directions. Whether planned or not, these buildings are manipulating light. It would make sense to anticipate what the effects will be —and what better effects there could be.

The new field of solar optics suggests one of the possibilities. The pioneer in this is scientist Michael Duguay, now of Bell Laboratories. In a 1977 experiment he demonstrated that it was practical to capture sunlight with a "sun-tracking coordinator," project it through a small hole in a building, and then pipe it down into the interior spaces of the building. It is the sort of thing that Leonardo could well have invented; most of the elements are ancient: mirrors, gears, lenses, and, most basic, a knowledge of where the sun will be at any given time.

The University of Miami is applying this approach in the design of its new civil engineering building. In a scheme that resembles a Rube Goldberg drawing, ten heliostats have been placed on penthouses on the roof; through a system of mirrors and lenses, sunlight is funneled down into the working area. Over time, the captured sunlight should cut their electric bill considerably.

On the market now are computer-controlled mechanisms that track the sun and reflect its light to interior workplaces. The same principle could be adapted to the supplemental lighting of exterior spaces. Reflective panels up high could be geared to bounce light down into spaces that have been darkened from on high—such as Paley Park. Panels might be used with polarizing filters, to moderate the light transmitted according to the light received. Tricky business, to be sure, and there could be the devil to pay in damage suits if the mechanisms got out of whack. But what a show there could be! Laser beams are fine, but nothing is better than the sun itself, and we do not need high tech to make the most of its possibilities.

The ancients were more resourceful than we. In his *The Poetics of Light* architect Henry Plummer has described how the most stirring power of daylight has come with its painting of time. "Buildings from ancient Egyptian temples to the chapel at Ronchamp," he writes, "have been able to catch hold of passing time, overcoming the deadening inertia of fixed forms through structures choreographed to lyrically mutate under flights of sun. Textures are hardened and softened by shifting angles of rays, shadows lengthen and brush across surfaces, while colored beams lance into the darkness."

If only we think of them, there are all sorts of things we can do to bend light and reflect it to felicitous effect: a slight canting of a facade to catch the late afternoon sun across it; a panel of white canvas up high to light the dark part of a small park; a spire such as that of the Chrysler Building, which glints at you wherever you are and makes you fell the better for it. We need more follies like this.

There are all sorts of things than can bend light and reflect it to felicitous effect: a canting of a façade to catch the late afternoon sun across it; a panel of white canvas up high to light the dark corner of a small park; a spire like that of the Chrysler Building, which glints at you wherever you are and makes you feel the better for it. We need more follies like this.

19

SUN EASEMENTS

The zoning approaches we have been discussing, let it be conceded, are something of a bribe. Instead of requiring sunlight as a right, we have been wheedling it. We have been asking developers to block the sun only partially instead of completely and have been richly rewarding them for their avarice in doing so. The process has become so outrageous that a kind of zoning-speak has arisen to legitimatize it. Thus, when a developer seeks to add eight more stories and the planning commission grants him four, the increase in bulk is announced as a reduction in bulk. When a developer has a site next to a city park, are his allowable bulk and height restricted? Just the opposite. He is allowed to waive height and setback regulations, increase the height and bulk, and dump his shadows onto the park. This is a provision of "Park Improvement District" legislation.

Sunlight should be a right, not an amenity that is nice to have, and the police power should be used to assure it. The courts will not go this far, however. There is a point beyond which use of the police power is deemed a taking of property without fair compensation. A government cannot use the police power to compel a benefit, the courts hold. If it wants it, it has to pay for it.

In time, the courts may come to look on sunlight as more of a right. Much will depend on how successfully citizen and environmental groups push the concept. The recent legislation in San Francisco and the upholding of it in the courts is encouraging in this respect.

In the meantime there are some other avenues that should be pursued. Even if we take the narrow view of sunlight—as a benefit—

we will find that the ability of public agencies to deal with it has been considerably strengthened. They can buy sunlight. They can rent it. They can give tax credits for it. Such notions may sound odd, but it is in this hazy area between rights and benefits that some interesting opportunities lie.

One way to purchase sunlight is through a solar easement. You buy from a house owner a binding agreement that he will not add anything to his house that would block the passage of sunlight to yours. Led by Colorado, in the last few years a number of states have passed statutes expressly authorizing solar easements. The purpose is to assure sun for solar energy collectors. The easements must be very explicit. They must state the angles at which the easement extends over the property to be protected, how much the property owner to the sunward is to be paid for abiding by the easement, and how much he is to pay for violating it. The compensation feature disturbs some observers. They reason that while easements might be inexpensive in ranch country, they might be prohibitively expensive in more urban areas.

There is another approach and it avoids compensation. The model for this is New Mexico's statute, which was subsequently accepted as the basis for California's and Minnesota's statutes. These statutes invoke the who-was-first principle of Western water-rights law, or Doctrine of Prior Appropriation. The statutes provide that the first man to install a solar collector has first call on the sun and will continue to. Those who subsequently build in the area must not encroach on his "solar window"—the path of the sun to his roof.

It is quite a conferral. The original idea of water-rights law was to assign priorities to the use of a natural resource during temporary periods of scarcity. Under the solar legislation, the man who first stakes a claim to the resource is awarded it permanently. As far as his neighbors to the south are concerned, he is in the catbird seat—so much so that he could seriously impede subsequent development and impair their property rights.

There is not enough experience yet for firm conclusions, but I would guess that the easement approach will prove sound, if limited, and that the prior-appropriation approach will not. I would also guess that the easement approach will prove most useful in conserving sunlight for sunlight's sake and that its main application will be in cities.

A related approach is air-rights transfer. Coupled with landmark designation, this has been very useful in taking the development pressures off historic properties. Under New York City's statute—the stiffest—the city can designate a building as a landmark, or a group of them as a historic district. By so doing, the city can enjoin the owner of a landmarked building from making alterations without the city's approval. The protection of sun and light is incidental, but it is most certainly a major effect.

No compensation is involved. But there is a sweetener for the owner. He can sell the unused air rights above the building to the owner of a contiguous property, who, in turn, can add these to the amount of floor space he is entitled to build on his own property. (Exception: Under New York law, buildings in historic districts are not eligible for air-rights transfer.)

The ability to transfer air rights was noted by the Supreme Court when it upheld the city's Landmark statute in the Grand Central Terminal case. The owner, Penn Central, complained that the city's designation of the terminal as a landmark deprived it of the ability to earn a reasonable return. The Court disagreed. It noted that Penn Central was able to sell its air rights for quite considerable sums. In one transaction it sold 75,000 square feet to Philip Morris for $2 million; with these rights Philip Morris increased the size of its building by three and a half stories.

Private sales of air rights have been used similarly. An example is the felicitous deal arranged by the Church of Sweden on Manhattan's Forty-eighth Street. The church was only five stories high in an area zoned to allow for taller buildings. The developer of an office building that was to go up right next door to the church had an idea. If he bought the church's air rights he could make sure that his right flank was protected, and that some horrible day the windows of his building would not be blocked off by a tower rising on the church site. He would also have rights to add a good many additional square feet to the amount already permitted for his building.

The church was agreeable. It had paid only $570,000 for its building back in 1978. Now it would not only get to keep the building, it would pocket $990,000 for selling the air rights to the empty space above it. (N.B.: The St. Bartholomew's case worked out very badly, but one reason was the failure of the church to explore the possibilities of selling its air rights. It figured it could make more money if it became codeveloper and put up a tower on part of the site.)

Air-rights transfer has been hemmed in by the requirement that transfer be to contiguous sites—that is, next door, across the street, or catty-cornered. To expand the program, it has been urged that air rights be able to "float." As in the transfer-of-development-rights programs for agricultural areas, the rights would be leapfrogged to "receiving sites" some distance away. Such transfers do pose some tough problems. The main one is the effect added bulk will have on the area to which it is transferred. What should be the cutoff points? Who determines the boundaries of the sites? Such determinations require a review board with a highly expert staff, stonewall resistance to political pressures, and great wisdom. One would like to find such a body.

There is another problem. It is in the word "transfer." With air rights the additional building potential is not curbed. It is moved somewhere else, and these shifts can sometimes do more damage in one place they they prevent in another. With an easement, however, the additional building potential is not shifted; it is severed. There is no potential to shift. The donor yields his right to built additions, deface the property, or whatever it is the easement specifies, and it is done for perpetuity. The easement "runs" with the property and is binding on all subsequent owners. This is why easements stand up where zoning does not; and the commitment to the long term is crucial to the tax deductibility of gifts of easements.

The most successful application of the principle has been with conservation easements. They have been used most often with farms and rural land in the path of development. The easements provide that the landowner will not build additional houses on the area covered, chop away hillsides, cut down stands of trees, dam creeks, suffer billboards, or otherwise foul up the property. The easements are for perpetuity. They "run" with the land and are binding on all subsequent owners.

Easements do not necessarily cover all of a man's property. One of the most helpful lessons learned in the early easement programs was the desirability of tailoring easements to the land. One portion of a property might be well suited to development. With the idea in mind of developing it on the cluster principle, the owner might be willing to donate easements on the creeks, the draws, the wetland meadows, and the woods that are so vital to the beauty of the landscape—and so enhance the portions that are developed. There has been a great deal of highly imaginative negotiating along these lines: by local land trusts, conservation commissions, the Nature Conservancy, and others. (Tops: the Brandywine Conservancy in my home county—an extraordinarily ingenious program for so conservative an area.)

Looking back, I think we were much too slow to realize how relevant these rural easement strategies were to the city. The first application was in the form of facade easements. They were especially useful for preserving the exteriors of historic buildings. Historic preservationists carried the ball on these programs. Local governments eventually got around to passing landmark statutes with teeth and establishing commissions to enforce them, but until they did, easements were a first line of defense.

There were other potentials to be explored. In 1970 several of us set up the New York Landmarks Conservancy, Inc. The city already had an excellent statute and a landmarks preservation commission. We thought a lay group such as ours could be helpful in supporting the commission, needling it, and doing a number of things the commission could not—such as buying old buildings and recycling them, or conserving the scores of buildings and blocks that did not rate landmark status but were nonetheless of architectural or historic significance.

One of our first ventures was the acquisition of facade easements on such buildings—brownstones, limestones, old commercial structures with fronts intact. Donors would often approach us. They were impelled by a feeling for their old buildings; they were also impelled by the realization that a facade easement could be entered as a charitable deduction on their income tax.

We would hammer out the terms of the easement with them. Basically, it would stipulate that there were to be no structural changes in the exterior of the building save by our permission. We were particularly concerned with what was visible from street level. The owner had to pledge to keep the exterior in good shape and to advance a sum to offset some of the expenses the Conservancy would incur in the administration of the easement. The valuation of the easement for tax purposes was up to the building owner and his assessor. In all cases, owners received a substantial tax reduction from the IRS, though by no means all that some of them asked for.

There were bugs to be worked out. In the beginning we were nowhere near tough enough in setting conditions and enforcing them. The amount of legwork and monitoring was great and there were contingencies we had not anticipated. (In the protracted case of the rooftop Jacuzzi we learned that visibility from the street was not always a satisfactory guideline; we were threatened with legal action by people who lived above the rooftop.)

But the program was working. Thanks to the shakedown period, we had our procedures ironed out. We were not happy with the term "facade" and felt that "conservation easement" would be a better one. We prepared brochures and promotional material and got ready to launch a selling campaign.

Then in 1980, Congress passed an act changing tax treatment of easements. In a few sentences it threatened to put us out of business.

The act came up with a tight definition of "architectural and historic significance." Henceforth, it would mean properties that were (1) listed on the National Register of Historic Places; or (2) certified as being of significance within a required historic district. To put it another way, the act restricted easement protection to properties that were already protected by other means. It ruled out our program.

Or did it? We noted that the act left conservation and scenic easements relatively unscathed. It was generally assumed, of course, that these applied to rural and suburban spaces. But there was nothing in the act that restricted them to rural and suburban spaces. The wording of the IRS guidelines for the implementation of the act would be critical.

The more we thought about it, the surer we were that our facade easements really were scenic easements—certainly so in their effect. But we had to make the point. Whatever the architectural or historic significance of the buildings, we had to establish that their greatest benefits were in the conservation of the landscape. The *urban* landscape.

My idea of a good time is not a session with the Internal Revenue Service but we thought it might be wise to pay a call. We went to Washington to see Stephen Small, the IRS official who was drafting the regulations for the implementation of the act. We told him of our concept. His first reaction, understandably, was skepticism. Good try, fellas! But he gave us a fair hearing. As we discussed the benefits of light and air, scale, relief from urban closeness, he saw a strong case for urban landscape easements. He said he would try to broaden the regulations to include them.

He did. The final regulations were published in January of 1986 and they included all the points necessary for urban landscape easements. Here are some of the criteria the regulations include for defining a view as "scenic":

> "The openness of the land (which would be a more significant factor in an urban or densely populated setting or in a heavily wooded area).
> "Relief from urban closeness. . . .
> "The degree to which the land use maintains the scale and character of the urban landscape to preserve open space, visual enjoyment, and sunlight for the surrounding area."

Small thought it would be important that our first urban easement pack a maximum of benefits. Greenacre Park did that and more: sunlight, trees, flowers, waterwalls and fountains, mothers with their babies, young lovers, older people in the autumn sun—everything but the flag.

We went over the property maps for a likely donor. Across the street, we found, was a four-story building owned by a prominent real estate man and civic leader, Seymour Durst. We asked him if he would consider giving an easement. He said he would. There ensued some unusually thorough discussions between the lawyers for Durst, the Greenacre Foundation, and the Conservancy. At length, on December 24, 1986—the day before Christmas—Mr. Durst deeded the easement.

Mr. Durst's building is not high enough to shadow Greenacre.

The point of the easement is to keep it that way; secondly, to prevent assemblage of a tower that would shadow it. By remaining low, furthermore, the building contributes to the ambiance and moderate scale of this pleasantly tacky block.

The potentials of an urban easement program are tremendous. Development values are dear indeed in the city but they can be harnessed to good effect. As rural programs have demonstrated, stripping the development values from one part of a property can increase the values on another part. Cluster development makes good use of this principle.

In the city a large measure of protection can be achieved with relatively modest curbs on additional development. Think of a row of brownstones. They are, let us say, four stories high for the most part and make a fine light guard for the blocks around it. It would be much easier to solicit easements from the owners if the heights were not frozen. Some of the owners, quite likely, may have been thinking of adding a small penthouse or greenhouse atop the roof. And why not? Sun studies might show that no sun would be blocked if the structure was mansarded back from the cornice line and sloped at the rear to keep the sun angles clear.

Low-rise buildings are the obvious ones for an easement program, both for enjoying the sunlight passed through by others and for passing it on themselves. But medium-rise buildings can qualify too. Many a neighborhood block enjoys almost full sun because there are a number of the conventional six-story apartment buildings of the 1930s. They are not much to look at with their fire escapes, but during most of the year they do not block much sun; more important, they preempt the sites from being used for big new apartment buildings that would.

Even very big buildings can be involved in easement projects. Let us say that a corporation has a tower and small park that it would like to protect as much as possible. Across the street is a site that has been assembled for another big tower. In the usual course of events the tower will go up, take away most of the sun, and that will be that. You cannot make an omelet, it will be said, without breaking some eggs.

It is obvious that an easement that would have required the new building to be much smaller would have cost tens of millions—as much as half the value of the big building. But so draconian an easement would not have been necessary. Let me return to the example of Paley Park. It is excruciating to watch the path of the sun as it comes to the towers to the south. During a key part of the afternoon the sun comes very close to not being blotted out. But it is blotted out, and Paley Park is much darker for it and will be for year after year after year.

A relatively small shift in the placement of a tower can make a critical difference in the amount of sun that falls on a space and the timing of it. The case of the Dallas tower is an example. But rarely are such situations anticipated. People will invest large sums in the creation of key open spaces but take no steps to secure their southern flanks. They fail even to hypothesize the adversities.

It is so easy to do so. The sun is most reliable, and with some rudimentary measurements it is possible to calculate just where the shadow limits of possible new construction would be. The pastor's office is an example. Bordering a small park is a parish house two stories high. The board of directors of the park would have liked to purchase an easement from the church that would keep the parish house two stories high. That way no additional shadows would fall on the park. The church balked. The pastor, it was learned, wanted an office built for him atop the parish house.

Sun studies indicated that if a structure about eleven feet high was positioned at one end of the parish house, no additional shadows would fall on the park. An easement defining these limits would be agreeable to the church, and for a sum far less than a no-construction-at-all easement.

Easements can be useful in purchase-and-sale-back projects. Once again Greenacre Park is an exemplar. Its northern exposure was getting clogged up with buildings. This did not affect the sun but it did cut down on the sky vault above and the feeling of openness. But there was one chink in the building mass to the north. It was the rear of the Real McCoy's Bar and Grill. It was only three stories high, and above it was a window to the sky.

The bar and grill was purchased by a friend of the park for $1 million. It was tidied up a bit, had an easement put on it constraining any further development, then was put back on the market. It was soon sold, for $1 million. If you are ever in Greenacre Park, look up at the waterfall, the small fire-escape building beyond, and the patch of blue sky above. It is there because it was not taken for granted.

20

THE CORPORATE EXODUS

The out-migration started slowly. The first to move was General Foods, to White Plains in 1954. Ten years later IBM moved out, to Armonk. Then Olin, to Stamford. In 1970 the momentum picked up. A few corporations headed for the Sunbelt. Most headed for the suburbs, to Connecticut's Fairfield County in particular. By 1976 over thirty major corporations had moved out of New York City, and more were leaving—including one of the biggest, Union Carbide. Office vacancy rates were climbing. With the city on the edge of bankruptcy, it looked as if a full-fledged rout was in the making.

High time, many people said. Even New Yorkers joined in the reprehension. Couldn't blame Union Carbide, the New York *Times* editorialized; the city had let it down. Dr. George Sternlieb, director of Rutgers' Center for Urban Policy Research, who had been prophesying such events, fairly chortled at their arrival. "It takes a man who's been shot in the head a while to realize he's dead," Sternlieb observed. "New York may not realize it, but if you look at the numbers it's clear that New York is dead."

But the rout did not come off. The bad news about New York had been so bad that a classic bottom was being formed. Any corporation that had not yet decided to leave probably would not leave. The ones who had left had long before signaled their intentions. In our research on public spaces we had found an early warning indicator. It was the corporation's own building. Often it would give an advance tip that the corporation was not long for the city.

Union Carbide's headquarters on Park Avenue was on such. This sleek black building was on the Skidmore, Owings, and Merrill's best, and it was superbly located. In operation, however, it bristled with distrust of the city. Large strips of empty space bordered its sides and fronts, and with nary a bench or a ledge for anyone to sit on. Guarding entry was a corps of guards. It should have come as no surprise when the company announced in 1976 that it was forswearing the city and would move to Danbury, Connecticut.

Union Carbide's timing was not very good. The mass exodus was just about over. Preposterous as it may have seemed then, the bad news was peaking just as the city's competitive position took some decided turns for the better. Overseas business had become a great stimulant; there was an influx of foreign firms, especially in finance. International divisions of corporations were expanding and it was in New York that they were doing it. A number of firms that had earlier contemplated leaving the city had second thoughts. Philip Morris announced it would stay. So did Pfizer. New York's troubles were by no means over, but there was to be a respite, and time for mulling over some lessons.

One thing had become clear. While the relocations were touted as economic measures, they were in fact very costly, and for more parties than the corporations. Let us follow the Union Carbide case. At 270 Park Avenue it had a fifty-three-story building with 1.2 million square feet. It sold it for $110 million, or $92 a square foot—a fire-sale price for such a building at such a location, and a great coup for the buyer, Manufacturers Hanover Trust Company. It sold its previous headquarters, a smaller building, for $161 million, or $333 a square foot.

Union Carbide's new headquarters would be slightly larger than the old one: 1.3 million square feet. It would cost $190 million. To link up with the highway system, a freeway section and cloverleaf had to be constructed, the cost to be borne by federal taxpayers.

The design, by Kevin Roche and John Dinkeloo, was a handsome one and in horizontal terms matched the highly centralized management structure of the company. Some observers were surprised. They thought the company would take advantage of the move to shift to a looser, more contemporary organizational set up, with more autonomy for the divisions. But it did not, thereby producing, in the words of one critic, a monument to the 1950s.

In any event, it was far away: some ninety miles from New York and in an area not well served by mass transportation. Relocation costs were heavy: $40 million. Of thirty-two hundred employees, about seven hundred lived close enough to the new site not to have to move. About twelve hundred did have to move and find new homes and schools, and the company subsidized their moves. About twelve hundred people refused to move and left the company.

At the time of the move housing was in short supply in the Danbury area—in particular, housing affordable by middle-income people. The move itself put housing further out of reach for people who would work there. So they made do. They commuted, and for a number, the commutes were long indeed.

In varying degrees other office growth areas have suffered similar imbalances. Housing is not where the office jobs are, and vice versa, and the new-town ideal of one's working within walking distance of one's home was never further from reality. In the fox-hunt country of New Jersey's Morris and Somerset counties, new office complexes are bringing many white-collar clerical workers to a beautiful countryside. But for daytime use only. Not to live there. Physically, there is plenty of room for new housing, and eventually most of the remaining farms and estates will go, and there will be housing. But it will be long in coming and probably very dear. Arcadia will ever be receding.

In the meantime another steep price is being paid. Traffic. It is the prime problem that the office growth areas face and it is hard to see how there can be any substantial relief for years to come. The highways were laid out for other settlement patterns, other kinds of journeys, and they do not match with the mixed, all-directions traffic spawned by office centers. Wherever you want to go in these areas, there never seems to be a direct route. You zig and you zag, stop for interminable lights, turn right for one route, left for another. The freeways aren't so bad; it's the mishmash between them that is awful.

Engineers cannot solve this problem. It is essentially governmental. How many more access points to allow on a given stretch of highway? Should developers be assessed the cost of overpasses? Should there be overpasses? Should there, for that matter, be more projects? In whose township? There are few regional bodies with teeth to make the tough decisions. Until there are, stay on I-95. Leave it and you are in trouble.

In the downtowns as in the countryside, companies are befouling the surcease they sought. Greenwich, Connecticut, now has over 2 million square feet of office space, much of it in the downtown area. For most employees, however, there is no mass transit that is practical for them. They must drive, and via a street system that was laid out in the 1700s. Five o'clock can be a memorable experience. For the executives the geography is fine; some have homes only a few miles away. Those who head north to the woods and the estates have only a few miles more. But most employees do not live in Greenwich. They head south—for Exit 5 of the New England Thruway and, after they get on it, some of the densest traffic on the Eastern Seaboard.

In both Greenwich and Stamford the stations are only a few blocks away from many of the headquarters. But only a minority of employees appear to use them. Possibly because of the need for a car trip at the other end of the line, the majority make the whole trip by car.

Is it for such factors that companies have moved? They cite transportation as one; they cite tax differentials; they site office costs, availability of trained people, and other tangible factors. Sometimes, as at Pfizer, the various factors have been ranked by computer studies and then given weightings by each of the executives. Location consultants, such as The Fantus Co., have been retained by companies to advise them whether they should move or not, and if so, to where. Detailed comparisons have been drawn up to measure the relative merits of locations A, B, and C.

Such studies have been impressive. The boilerplate alone has sometimes been as thick as a phone book. But what the studies have mainly proved is that tangible factors have little to do with the moves.

It is the intangibles that have been the key. "Environment" is the umbrella term. Shorn of euphemism, here is what executives mean by it: (1) The center city is a bad place: crime, dirt, noise, blacks, Puerto Ricans, and so on. (2) Even if it isn't a bad place, middle Americans think it is and they don't want to be transferred here. (3) To attract and hold good people we have to give them a better environment. (4) We have to move to suburbia. Thus Union Carbide, concluding a two-year study: "The long term quality-of-life needs of our headquarters employees" were the overriding factors.

Self-serving piety has been characteristic of the moves. Not for the brass; not for the company; it has been for their people that they have moved, and for their life-style needs.

It's a wonder executives keep a straight face. Life-style needs of employees? Companies don't have to spend all that money researching them. They don't have to compare area A with area B and area C. All they have to do is look in the phone directory. Where does the boss live? That is where the company is going.

And that is where they went. During the height of the exodus I made a location study. I plotted the moves of all the major corporations that had moved from New York to the suburbs and beyond over the previous ten years. By checking old phone directories, street maps, and registers of executives, I plotted the home locations of the chief executive officer and his fellow top executives at the time the decision was made to move. Then I plotted the location the company moved to.

The correlation: of thirty-eight corporations, thirty-one moved to

Where should the company move to? Companies don't have to spend all that money researching. They don't have to compare area A with Area B and Area C. All they have to do is look in the phone directory. Where does the boss live? That is where the company is going.

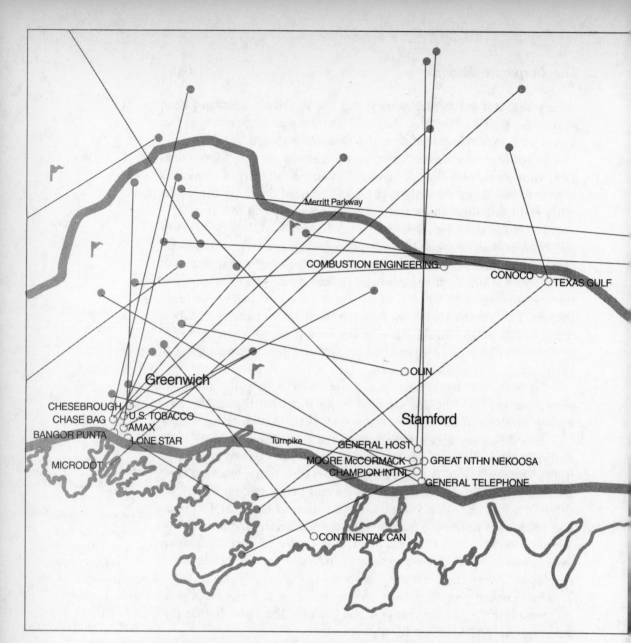

Merritt Parkway

COMBUSTION ENGINEERING

CONOCO

TEXAS GULF

OLIN

Greenwich

Stamford

CHESEBROUGH
CHASE BAG   U.S. TOBACCO
BANGOR PUNTA   AMAX
                   LONE STAR   Turnpike   GENERAL HOST
MICRODOT   MOORE McCORMACK   GREAT NTHN NEKOOSA
                                                     CHAMPION INTNL
                                                                            GENERAL TELEPHONE

CONTINENTAL CAN

Networking at work. Of thirty-eight companies that moved out of New York City to better quality-of-life needs of their employees, thirty-one moved to the Greenwich-Stamford area. Black circles show where the chief executive officers lived at the time the move was planned; white circles show where the new headquarters was subsequently located. Average distance from the CEO's home: eight miles.

a place close to the top man's home. Average distance: about eight miles by road.

The geographic concentration was extraordinary. The heartland was in Greenwich—specifically, in a circle about four miles in diameter, bounded on the east by the Burning Tree Country Club and on the west by the Fairfield Country Club. Within it were no fewer than twelve chief executive officers.

And where did most of their companies move to? Greenwich and environs.

This was hardly a chance distribution. As a check I plotted the home locations of the top executives of ninety-five corporations that had not moved from New York. Rather than being concentrated in a few spots, they were widely distributed over the metropolitan area, with about a quarter in New York City itself.

Companies say the top man's preference becomes a factor only after the basic decision to move has been made. The facts suggest the reverse: that it is a prime motivating factor from the beginning. The coincidence is too great to be rationalized otherwise. Obviously something other than objective analysis had been at work in the Greenwich cases. Peers had been at work. The place was rife with chief executive officers, and it was in the locker rooms of those golf clubs that the most important location research may have taken place.

If executives wanted to take their people to the suburbs, that was their prerogative. But would it be good for the company? Very much so, said the executives, and they had glowing stories to back them up. Certainly not, said urban loyalists, and they had stories, too. The test, of course, would be performance. Later, some astonishing data would become available, but at the time there was not too much to go on. I made year-to-year earnings comparisons but most of the moves had been too recent for firm conclusions to be drawn.

Several points were clear, however. Some kind of cyclical process had been at work. A number of companies had shown a predisposition to move and this appeared to have been linked to the company's stage of life. Move-out companies tended to be big companies, near the top of the Fortune 500. They tended to be technically oriented, with a high quota of engineers in management. The companies were heavily capitalized and self-sufficient enough not to need banks as much as they did earlier. Most started out in small cities or towns elsewhere, moved to New York, and were now moving once again, away from the city.

Whatever the impulses for the moves, most executives seem to be pleased with them. They have a strong psychic investment in being pleased, of course, but most of the middle management people appear to be pleased also. They like the pleasant surroundings and the time saved in commuting—which has generally been used for more time at the office than at home. (The usual arrival hour is nearer 8 A.M. than 9.) As for the hustle and bustle of the city, people who have just moved out may miss it at first; after a while they do not. Whatever they are missing, they are happily unaware of what it is.

And there may be the rub. Migrations are a self-proving proposition, and if executives are happy, it is in part because the moves tend to screen out people who would not be. Some people, among them the most able and aggressive, refuse to go out, and they join other companies. Some who do go out find the atmosphere deadening and leave.

Most people adapt. The rural environment is easy to adapt to. Physically, there is much space, pleasantly arranged. Individual officers and workstations tend to be larger than their counterparts in the city—vastly so in the case of some top executives' offices. There are attractive common areas. Outdoors there may be shaded walks and picnic areas.

Corporate campuses are quiet places. Outside the loudest noise is the sound of the lawn sprinklers, the hum of traffic on the nearby parkway.

These places are quiet places. What one notices at first is the stillness. Outside, the loudest noise heard is the swish of the water sprinklers on the lawn, the muffled hum of the traffic on the nearby parkway. Except at 8 and 5, not many people are to be seen coming and going. At outlying campuses some executives may stroll around the buildings. At General Electric there are "one-turn" men and "two-turn" men. Most of the time, however, there is little activity outdoors.

The pace is slow, visibly so. Both migrants and visitors remark on how much more slowly people seem to move. To some this is a healthy lack of hassle—a relaxed, low-stress atmosphere that is good for clear thinking. To others, it is torpor.

"They walk slower," says a nonmigrant executive. "They talk slower. They think slower." The charge is expressed in other ways— "dry rot," "gone to seed." It is a biased charge, to be sure, but it is one that companies should hear. "It's not right for guys to have such big offices," says an executive whose office size is disciplined by city costs. "It gets to a person after a while. They're big frogs out there and they're getting out of touch." Executives of migrant firms sometimes wonder themselves. It's not that they themselves will go slack, they say; they had their formative years in a tougher clime. But what about the younger men? "They're the ones I worry about," says one senior executive. "There's just too damn much contentment. Over the long run the move is going to be bad for this company."

These are subjective matters. One aspect that is not is self-containment. Headquarters, even those in the center of towns, have little connection with their surroundings. They are elements of a car culture: one arrives by car and leaves by car, and there is not much interchange with the outside world in between. Within the headquarters a range of services makes the outside unnecessary. These are particularly bountiful in outlying campuses. At Beneficial Management's corporate village in Peapack, New Jersey, a pleasant grouping of low buildings is arranged around a courtyard and bell tower. There are outdoor dining areas, dining rooms within, shops, health facilities; the garage is laid out so that one drives to an underground space and takes an elevator to within a few feet of his office.

Even in downtown locations, headquarters are self-sufficient. In

Italian village campus: Beneficial Management Corporation, Peapack, New Jersey.

Stamford there is a broad boulevard lined with them. But it is not much walked upon. There appears to be little human traffic between the separate headquarters. Employees do visit the huge shopping mall across the way, but not so many that the sidewalks are ever too busy. Or that the traffic lights have to be timed to give the pedestrian a break. He has to press a button to get on the waiting list.

What Stamford has made is an architectural park. The buildings, by some of the country's most noted architects, form a series of detached exhibits, several mounted on podiums. Only one has a street-level presence: Champion International's, designed by Ulrich Franzen —it has an outdoor plaza and a branch of the Whitney Museum on the ground floor. A number of the others do not have any pedestrian access at street level at all; their entry points are up above, on the upper levels over the parking garages.

People in suburban campuses share a problem. People don't go out to see them very much. This is evident in the visitors' parking areas, the layout of which clearly anticipated far more of them than have been turning up.

Campus location or downtown, headquarters people share a similar problem. People do not go out to see them very much. Traffic at checkpoints, such as gatehouses and security desks, is light; so is the parking in the area reserved for visitors, the provision of which clearly anticipated far more of them than have been turning up.

Executives of companies contemplating a move are wary on this point. They have heard about the low visitor rates. But they believe they have enough clout that people will go out to see them. So people will: people with something to sell to the company; people with accounts to service; people who are less important than whomever they are going to see. Nobody drops in. The visits are planned visits, and as the companies' how-to-get-there booklets indicate, these can take some effort. ("After exiting from the Merritt at #38, turn right onto Middle Ridge Road and continue to the third stoplight . . .")

Some would-be visitors balk, and they are apt to be the important ones. "They even sent a limousine in for me," recalls a top antitrust lawyer. "They said I should prepare the case out in White Plains. One visit was enough. I said no, they could send the executives in to me. We'd rent a suite at the Barclay and go over the case there. And that's what we did."

The problem is not just the infrequency of the visits but the character of them. When senior executives have to travel out to see senior executives of an outlying company, they can be keenly aware that a measure of coercion is involved. They don't like this. One executive told me of a journey he and two fellow executives had to make to a company with a New Jersey campus. They went out because they had to; the New Jersey company had a process they badly wanted to license. "We had to go out twice," he said. "They really stuck it to us. There they were in the big chairs. It was like a court and we were serfs. We felt silly, frankly. It was a bad place to do any negotiating in."

Another man's home territory is not the best place to bargain with him, especially when the trip out is itself an obeisance. Truly critical negotiations are best done informally, on common meeting grounds equally accessible to both parties. These the city has in abundance—clubs, restaurants, building lobbies, street corners. These places are the heart of the city's intelligence networks, and a company that cuts itself off from them loses something that no electronic system can ever provide.

Some companies have tried to compensate for the isolation by using consultants more. Many experts have been earning their per diems by traveling out to brief company people and shoot ideas back and forth with them. One executive summed it up in a word. What, I had asked him, gesturing to the empty visitors' parking lot, did they do about visitors? "We hire them," he said.

Executive of outlying companies do go back into town periodically, and the companies would like to have them see more people when they do. "We encourage them to schedule their contacts more tightly," says one executive. "No wasted time on purely social stuff; no long lunches with old college buddies." Which is to say, no surprises: no chance encounters, no unexpected points of view.

There has been some relocation work back to town. Companies are quite touchy on the matter, but many of their people are commuting to the city for their key work: keeping in touch. This is especially the case with people in communications. You can't work the room if you are not there. Some of the intown offices that companies have kept are now more crowded than they were before. General Electric's former headquarters building on Lexington Avenue has more GE people working in it than when it was headquarters. Some companies that kept no space have reestablished their presence with "regional" offices and with hotel or apartment suites.

In some respects, the moves to suburbia have spurred contact. Plane travel to company outposts has been rising—some companies have been enlarging their private fleets—and executives have been spending as much if not more time on the road than before. Within the new headquarters, furthermore, some of the predominantly horizontal layouts have led to more interchange than in the vertical structures of the city. This is especially noticeable around lunchtime, as people congregate in the dining rooms and common areas.

But these are internal contacts, company people talking to company people. There is a price to pay for this inbreeding and the farther away from the mainstream a company goes, the more vulnerable it is to it. Every large organization has within it tendencies to turn inward on itself. Moving to suburbia intensifies these tendencies.

The moves are acts of withdrawal and the buildings convey it. Many of the new structures are curiously defensive in design, as if the problem were too many outsiders trying to get in rather than too few. A number of companies are sited on steep hillsides, like forts. One, then American Can, had a sort of Goldfinger's castle with an entrance that opened for executives' cars, like a portcullis. General Electric has a gatehouse for screening people before they drive on to the headquarters itself, where a designated employee will receive them.

No bag ladies, no winos, no oddballs assault their landscaped ramparts, yet the companies seem every bit as obsessed with the threat of them as they were back in the city. Guards are all over the place. There are elaborate TV surveillance systems. With their long, white cameras, slowly rotating, they are as much to be seen as to see. So too the master consoles in the lobby, with their banks of small TV screens and blinking lights. They are the most impressive design element of many lobbies and the spiritual centerpiece of them.

The companies say they want people to come. Their buildings say no.

After the 1976 departures the outward movement slowed to a trickle, averaging about two firms a year. Then in 1986 the pace picked up: four moved out and several others announced they were going to: Exxon, J. C. Penney, Mobil, AT&T. As in the midseventies, the news thoroughly alarmed the city. This time, many said, the city really had had it.

There was a widespread disposition to see the move-outs' side, and to see their departure as a damning indictment of the city: its high taxes, crime, and stress and strain. The moves had been preceded by exhaustive study of all factors, the firms emphasized, and certainly this must have included the experience of the previous move-outs. It was generally assumed that they had done very well in their suburban campuses, and in financial as well as environmental terms.

But had they? When I did my 1976 study, not enough time had elapsed to draw valid conclusions. But now ten years had gone by and there was hard data. To follow up, I tracked the performance of the 38 companies that had moved out and 36 that had not, and by that most hard-boiled of measures, the valuation of the marketplace.

The first discovery was that seventeen of the thirty-eight move-out firms had lost their identity. They had been bought out, raided, or merged, and in no case as the dominant partner. That left twenty-two companies. For each I traced the stock valuation for the eleven-year period December 31, 1976, to December 31, 1987. The average increase was 107 percent—somewhat better than the 93 percent increase of the Dow-Jones Industrial Average.

What about the companies that had stayed in New York? The results were downright startling. For the thirty-six major corporations that stayed the average increase was 277 percent—over two and half times the increase of the move-outs.

Assigning cause and effect is difficult. There are just too many variables. It could be that the sojourn in suburbia did dull reflexes, as some prophesied it would. But it could also be argued that the companies were the better for having moved and would have fared worse had they not moved.

I think the die was cast well before the companies moved out. The impulse seems to have been internal, the consequence of cyclical changes within the companies, and independent of the city and its problems. In a word, they were not doing very well. Some had grown old and fat and slow. Several had identity problems. (American Can got out of the can business entirely, changed its name to Primerica, and went into finance.) To paraphrase Dr. Johnson, if a company is tired of New York, it is tired.

Understandably, companies that were unhappy became unhappy with the city. Frequently they telegraphed their intentions by citing somebody else's complaints; the recalcitrant yokel was a favorite. When the companies finally did announce, it was with a vengeance. The leave-takings were acts of renunciation, a turning of the back to the past. The sheer mechanics of the migration, the planning studies, and the design work promised to be a shot in the arm. And so it was— for the top management group, at any rate, if not for the underlings who were unable to pick up roots and join the move. Sorry about that.

Another study revealed a wide disparity between the performance of move-outs and that of stayers. In a 1980 assessment for the Regional Plan Association, Regina Belz Armstrong analyzed three kinds of firms: those that stayed in New York City; those that moved to the suburbs; those that moved out of the region entirely. The factors she checked were productivity, profitability, and growth.

Of the twenty-three companies that had moved to the suburbs in the period 1972–75, the majority had profitability lower than average for companies in their industry in the region, and the growth rate was only a half that of the others. The twenty firms that had moved out of the region had performances moderately below average for their group.

As in my study, firms that remained in New York City did very well, some spectacularly well. The average value of output and profit per dollar of labor input increased much faster than both the regional and national average, and faster yet than the average of the move-out firms.

Spanish village campus: Las Colinas, Texas.

Costs? Both studies are illuminating on this score. At the top of the list of reasons advanced for moving out has been the cost of New York. They are indeed high, and for a range of things: for a house, anywhere; for commutation; for schooling. High too are costs of office space, it being more expensive to be at the crossroads than up a back road.

But costs are relative. What is the payoff? What is the profit earned from the lower costs? The expenditures for housekeeping are far less important to a balance sheet than profitability and performance. On this score, both studies speak loudly. The lower costs enjoyed by the move-out companies did not correlate with excellent performance. The higher costs of the New York companies did.

There will probably be more move-outs. More companies will be growing older and fatter, and as a normal consequence they will leave. This will be painful for the cities they leave, especially when the moves come in bunches, as they seem to do from time to time.

They too are losing back-office work to their suburban office parks, and sometimes they lose headquarters as well. When firms move South and Southwest, furthermore, they will not necessarily move to a downtown. J. C. Penney did not. To the discomfiture of Dallas it moved all the way from New York, not to Dallas, but to the town of Plano. Some Dallas leaders were incredulous. Plano?

On balance, the center city is competing rather well. The office jobs that it has been losing have been mostly in the big, aging companies—the ones most likely to head for suburbia and to bomb when they do. The new-job increases have been mostly in newer, smaller firms. They are local companies, most of them, but as Jane Jacobs has observed, local economies are where it all starts. The small companies need access to a wide range of specialized services and people. They cannot have this in-house. They are not big enough. They cannot have this out in some isolated location. They need to be in the center—or as close to it as rents and space will permit.

Turnover is brisk. Many will fold, but here and there some of the companies will become big companies. Eventually, some of them may defect to the suburbs, but in their dynamic years they will thrive in the city. So, at least, our comparison study would indicate. As a group, the companies that competed in the city proved to be tougher and more profitable than the companies that did not—and by an impressive margin. The crossroads, it would appear, is a very good place to be.

21

THE
SEMI-CITIES

I first saw Dallas thirty years ago on the ride in from the airport. There, rising abruptly up from the cotton fields, was a great cluster of towers: bold, assertive, declarative.

Today Dallas has many more towers and they are taller and lit up. But that's not what you see first. Driving in from the airport or coming down from the north, you see a series of towers grouped around the cloverleafs. There is the Las Colinas development, with a skyline so imposing that people take it for Dallas. But Dallas itself is farther back, upstaged and somehow diminished.

Trends are writ large here, but the same kind of development is taking place in metropolitan areas everywhere. Mega-centers, mini-downtowns, growth corridors, urban villages, technoburbs: no one has yet come up with a satisfactory euphemism, or epithet. Partly, this is because the development is something of a bastard form, without a unifying ideology. The new-town movement of the sixties had a very coherent set of aims; the physical vision was coherent too, and if it failed, it went down with philosophy intact. The current growth, by contrast, is quite free of utopian constraints.

It is eminently opportunistic and it takes many forms. Some of the development consists of clumps of towers; some of low-rise build-

ings in parks; some of high-rise corridors. But most have several denominators. They are adjacent to or near a highway interchange; there
is a shopping mall in the complex or nearby; transportation is by car,
not only to and from but within; there are acres of parking, both at-
grade and multilevel; there is a hotel with an atrium, a health club,
and a conference facility (with, inevitably, "state-of-the-art audiovisual
support"); there is meticulous landscaping; connections to airports are
provided—indeed, some of the developments are airport cities themselves, so convenient for converging executives that they may bypass
the real city entirely.

Some of the growth is at the far edge of the metropolitan area.
North of New York City, development has pushed beyond Westchester
County to Putnam County. Several large farms along Route 22 have
been converted into large mixed-use projects, and most of the rest of
the farms have been acquired for the same purpose.

Some of the development has been close to the center city and
clearly at the expense of it. Outside Detroit, the suburb of Southfield
has been transformed into a gigantic office park and now has more
office space than all of downtown Detroit: 21 million square feet versus 15 million.

The most spectacular examples of growth have been in New
Jersey, and not surprising for this "corridor" state, they have been in
the form of corridors. Dr. George Sternlieb, director of Rutgers' Center for Urban Policy Research, has studied eight of them. Their
growth, he has found, has not been at the expense of New York City
but of New Jersey's older industrial cities, such as Trenton and New
Brunswick. They sorely need more jobs, white-collar and blue-collar.
They are not getting them. The blue-collar jobs are diminishing; the
white-collar ones are in the corridors.

The most interesting corridor is the strip along Route 1 by
Princeton. The first settler was RCA. Back in 1942 it set up the David
Sarnoff Research Center. In form it was fairly conventional: a large
three-to-four-story building that looked like a nice factory. While it
was compact, it did foreshadow subsequent development by being set
in a large expanse of green space.

It was Princeton University that set the character of the Route 1
development. It had had the foresight to assemble almost 3,000 acres
of prime land on both sides of the highway. Unlike RCA's unitary
pattern, Forrestal's dispersed low-rise buildings over a wide swath,
most spaced well apart from others and some tucked away in the
woods. A roster of prime tenants signed up—among them, IBM and
more of RCA. A Scandinavian firm set up a conference center and a
restaurant that made local news by having good food. North and
south of the Forrestal campus other developers started office com-

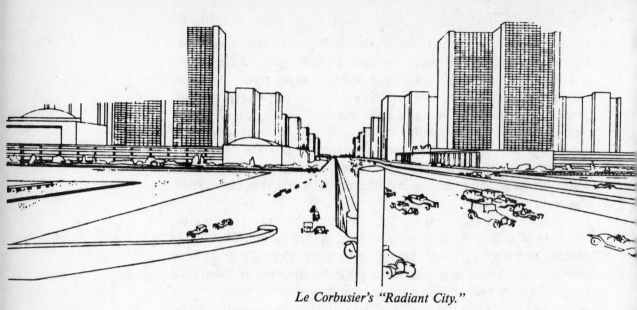

Le Corbusier's "Radiant City."

plexes. By 1987 there were over 25 million square feet of office space in the 5-mile strip by Princeton, and what undeveloped land was left was already spoken for.

The tie with Princeton has been merchandised to a fare-thee-well. Initially, there was a lot of talk about synergy and cross-fertilization and how stimulating for both corporate and academic people the fraternization would be. It turned out that there wasn't any to speak of. The university people stick very much to the university. Still, the propinquity remains a selling point. Across still-open fields you can see the spires of Princeton from Route 1, and a grand sight they make, almost theatrical in their proclamation. Surely values are being transmitted. Or so at least one would gather from the promotional materials; in the Route 1 world they depict, there are cloistered spaces and tweedy intellectuals mingling with young managers.

One Princeton asset definitely has been transmitted: 08540, zip code of the town. As is increasingly the custom with post offices, Princeton's main one has been moved out of town to a suburban location—in the middle of the corridor. For good measure, the zip code has been stretched to embrace most of the firms in it.

These are not corporate headquarters; they tend to go it alone and set up their own separate campuses. In the Princeton area, for example, are the headquarters of Merck and of the Educational Testing Service, with their own separate estates. The corporate moves to the kind of centers we are discussing are primarily of white-collar back-office personnel. Merrill Lynch is an example. It has set up two campuses in the Route 1 corridor. One of them contains a trading room for mutual-fund accounts, but the bulk of the work is in data process-

Crystal City, Virginia.

ing, and the like. The centers also attract branch-office operations—for insurance companies, Bell system units, and such. The service very small firms, including one-man operations. The Carnegie Center complex has an "Executive Center" facility providing part-time rental of office space, access to conference rooms, and typing and photocopying services.

As in similar areas elsewhere, the labor market in the Route 1 corridor is tight and it is likely to get much tighter. In 1981 there was 5 million square feet of office space; by 1987 there was 25 million going on 30 million. Trained white-collar people are in short supply, secretaries and data processing people especially. Trenton and New Brunswick have no pool. They have people who need jobs but it is blue-collar jobs they need. For all the growth in the corridors the lower-income people are being more distanced from this white-collar world than ever.

Keith Wheelock, president of Dun & Bradstreet's location division, told a group of corridor executives that it was the Greenwich-Stamford situation all over again: too much new office space for too few people with too little housing. The best advice they could give people planning to move into the Route 1 corridor, he said, would be simple. Stay away.

Another reason would be the traffic. Along the Eastern Seaboard there is no experience to match a late afternoon drive on Route 1. It is a succession of stoplights, cars backed up in the right-hand lane, and interminable waits. The staggering of work hours has helped some. Overpasses can help too; they make it less difficult for people to get in and out of their campuses from Route 1.

But that is only the beginning. Route 1 does not go where most people want to go. Soon they have to get off it and that is as difficult as getting onto it. For there is no dominant direction to the flow. The pattern of settlement is pure New Jersey: a road pattern laid down in Colonial days, going this way and that and with few clearly defined places along the way. This is one of the reasons mass transit offers little promise for this area: it needs to tap strong concentrations of people to be economical and the densities along Route 1 are much too low.

There is a good side to this. While the settlement pattern may be diffuse, it is comely. There is a wealth of early 1800s frame houses, and many Victorian gingerbread ones. The area is well wooded and there is a surprising amount of farmland left open. Around Princeton and to the west is estate country; along the Lawrenceville Road, an unusually attractive series of mansions and stables and winding drives. Then there is Princeton itself.

But this is all rather irrelevant to people who work on Route 1. The executives and lawyers and Wall Street people who can afford the fine housing do not work on Route 1. The people who do are lucky if they can afford the most modest of the tract houses in the Route 1 area. At the minimum they need a $50,000 income and there are few houses on the market at this range.

In East Brunswick, "entry level" houses come on plots averaging 55 by 100 feet; they have three bedrooms and between 1,100 and 1,700 square feet of space. They sell for $140,000 to $170,000. The next step up would be houses on wider lots—90 by 100—a two-car garage, and maybe a basement. They sell for $160,000 to $195,000. Further away from Route 1 home buyers may find houses somewhat less in price. But even in the rural places, or what were rural several years ago, there are no bargains. The drives from Route 1 will be getting longer.

Executives are not disturbed. In the Sternlieb study, the heads of the companies along the growth corridors said that highway access and the cost of land were the major factors that influenced their location choices. The availability of affordable housing for their employees was nearer the bottom of the list. As they were aware, few of their employees—14 percent—lived in the municipality in which the company was located. Sorry about that.

This is a far cry from the new-town model and its vision of people walking to work. The model was unrealistic, however, and in its way retrogressive; it minimized the great advantage of a metropolitan area —wide access to jobs—and prescribed what in essence would be a kind of company town. But there was one aspect of the model that was quite progressive: walking itself.

There is not much of it in the new complexes. Whether it is a physical or a cultural phenomenon, the outermost limit for walking there seems to be around 800 to 1,000 feet—about the distance between the anchors of a shopping mall. Even short of this, however, people will hop into a car for a short trip, the reflex being more important than the actual distance. They can do this in cities too, so it can't be blamed all on suburbia. To repeat a forecast: if Americans could widen their walking radius by only 200 feet, there would be a revolution in U.S. land use.

But there would have to be some structural changes. There would have to be places to walk. This struck me very forcibly on a journey from Princeton to a meeting on Route 1. It was a beautiful day; I had plenty of time, so I walked. Along the still-bucolic Washington Road the path was soggy but challenging, and I managed. When I came up to Route 1, however, the path vanished. There was no way across—no legal one anyway. I finally made a dash for it, cars honking at me. On the other side was a brief sidewalk. It vanished as Route 1 went through an underpass. I squeezed along one side, inches from a roaring mass of cars and truck-trailers.

When I arrived at the meeting I was greeted with incredulity. *Walked? From Princeton?* People came up to ask me about it. They thought I was some kind of nut.

I was, but an unrequited urge for walking may be harbored by more people than one would think. To get an idea of the recreation mix that should be planned for, developer Alan Landis of Carnegie Center had anthropologist Setha Low of the University of Pennsylvania study several suburban complexes. She found that of all sports the most favored was walking, after lunch especially. She also found that there were no places to walk safely. It had to be on the roads; there were neither paths nor pavements. It hadn't occurred to the developers and architects to provide them.

Carnegie Center has applied the lessons. There are many paths and alternate paths and places to pause. There is an attractive outdoor dining place and a lagoon to circle. Distances are marked. Knowing how far you're walking, apparently, is an incentive. I've noted this at some headquarters' campuses. At GE's in Connecticut, for example, executives may tell you whether they are a "one-turn" or a "two-turn" man—a turn around the building complex being roughly a quarter of a mile.

It helps if there is a place to walk *to*. The most ambitious effort along Route 1 in this respect is the Forrestal Village project. It is a relatively high density cluster of buildings and it is laid out in a fairly tight urban form. There are some mall-like interior spaces, but what sets the character of the place is its streets—comfortably small, of pleasant scale, with continuous retail frontage—and that fine old institution, the office over the store. The initial tenant mix is strong on upscale specialty shops, perhaps too much so. Eventually there will be 125 shops, plus a day-care center able to handle two hundred children. There is a Marriott Hotel and a conference center. "A one stop village," its developers say, "that gives you access to just about everything you need or want every day of your life."

Not quite. It is a fine village center but for one thing. It is a village center without a village. No homes abut it. No schools pour forth their children. Perhaps in time, now vacant spaces will bring housing to the center's edges. Currently, however, no one lives within normal walking distance of the center. It won't seem like a real village until they do.

Looking at the not-quite-villages, one is reminded of how good a model is the conventional town. With its grid and its center it is not only a comely and efficient form of development, but an excellent base for expansion. Towns in the range of fifteen thousand to twenty thousand population, for example, can handle a population increase of as much as 50 percent by extending the grid two to three blocks on each side. Most have not done it this way, unfortunately, and the increase has been splattered over far more open land than there was land in the town. But in most cases the town is still the center.

Most of the new growth areas lack the anchor of a town, or even of a semicenter. They are a strung-out series of elements that are for the most part unrelated to each other and that do not encourage the kind of interaction that is the hallmark of an urban center. They are accessible only by car; even within their boundaries the car is dominant.

Ten acres are being used to do the work of one. Compared to conventional suburban sprawl, the corridor pattern is of moderately high density. But only in comparison. By any urban standard, it is very low density, and that is the source of many of its problems. As the corridor's sprightly newspaper, *Route 1,* has editorialized: "The trouble is not too many people, but too few."

The tightest pattern is that of Carnegie Center. It does not string its buildings along a road but clusters them around central open spaces. In one of the first complexes to be completed there are a pond, bridges, paths, and an outdoor café. Between the clusters there is open space, and on the far side of the tract a large swath has been set aside as a greenbelt. Even if the acreage of the larger spaces is not counted, the ratio of building space to open space is small.

In the first part of Forrestal Center to be developed, the ratio is infinitesimal. Buildings are sited far apart from one another and there are vast stretches of intervening green. In degree, this emphasis on low density and abundant landscaping was a reaction to a horrible example. Down the road is half-mile stretch of Route 1 that is virtually a caricature of roadside America: diner, tacky stores, movies, motels, garish signs. Understandably, the Forrestal people wanted to go emphatically in the other direction.

So did the local governments. Zoning ordinances were redrafted to lock the door on strips. Following the Forrestal model, zoning now called for low densities in new development. Floor-area ratios for office parks were set at an average of .25—a very low ratio indeed. Generous buffers of open space were required, as well as vast amounts of concrete roadway to connect everything up. If you calculate the footprints of the actual buildings, the floor-area ratios average out to around 2 or 3. In relation to the number of buildings this is sprawl—high-class sprawl, perhaps, but sprawl nonetheless.

Visually, the payoff is disappointing. Twenty years ago, when research parks and corporate campuses were making their appearance, they seemed models of planning and design. Their low densities were especially praised. Now that they are becoming the rule, second thoughts are occurring.

The open space is inefficiently used. Too much of it is institutional: vast lawns setting off the corporation's logo; interminable stretches of unrelieved greenery. Some of the landscaping, let it be said, is exemplary; Forrestal is especially noteworthy for its great trees, many with small signs to identify the species.

But remarkably little personal use is made of the open space. Usually, open spaces work best along their edges and along watercourses. This is where there are the most benefits. But these depend on how many people experience them. On this score, the bulk of the open space is undiscovered country—many square miles in the center of tracts that no one sees, except from a plane.

One is reminded of the Year 2000 Plans of the sixties, which decreed vast swaths of open space. They foundered, for they were impractical. Abstract open space is unsustainable. So, in time, will Route 1 itself demonstrate. Open space, like development, needs the discipline of function. Use it or lose it.

There is one development in the corridor that is an exemplar in this respect. It has a wealth of open spaces; they connect with one another; they are enjoyed day in and day out by a great many people, and on foot. Yet the development density is much greater than in the Route 1 developments. I refer to the campus of Princeton University. Its floor-area ratio is .75 for the main campus. Yet for all the infilling that has taken place, the open spaces do not feel cramped. The very enclosure the buildings afford makes the spaces congenial in scale. Pathways provide fine linkages. And people walk.

What to do? It might not be a good idea to replicate the town of Princeton, but the idea of towns is gaining currency as a new approach. Samuel Hamill, director of the Middlesex Somerset Mercer Regional Council, believes that further growth ought to be concentrated in centers, not strips, and that the New Jersey town is the best model to follow.

Whatever the answers, the mess has become so visible that it is forcing people to think of steps they would not have thought of ten years ago. There is growing sentiment, for example, for highway districts empowered to levy assessments for highway improvement and access to benefiting properties. Leaders in the Route 1 corridor area are cooperating with the state planning commission in the preparation of a statewide plan. Among the approaches being favored is the creation of regional bodies with review power over major developments.

The sticking point in such programs is the degree to which the regional body could override the local governments. New Jersey's are as local as they come, and some would undoubtedly fight any veto power. So would many developers. Even so, a regional body could wield considerable power. The Hudson River Valley Commission was given limited powers; it could only delay a project, not veto it. It turned out, however, that the power to delay was often tantamount to the power to veto. Additional months of high-interest money could make developers see the light and could be further leveraged by not setting the meter ticking on review until full data were supplied by the developer. Experience with California environmental commissions indicates similar persuasiveness in the review process The essential is a staff with a high degree of expertise and the ability to come up with constructive counterplans.

But it is very late in the game for the likes of Route 1. Much can be done with newly applied tools, such as development-rights transfer, greenway networks, cluster development. But most of the major land use decisions have been made, and while there will be more growth to shape, the character of it is not apt to change very much. There will probably be some infilling, and a somewhat tighter pattern within new developments. But basically Route 1 will probably be more of the same: an automobile-dominated strip of low-density development.

Similar growth areas may also be beyond metamorphosis. King of Prussia, west of Philadelphia, should be a city by now; it is astride the junction of three major highways and has enough office, research, and shopping space to be a rather good-sized city. But it has not become a city—not even a town. It remains a collection of parts, accessible by highways and separated by them.

There is a growth area in the United States that is going the other way. It is Bellevue, Washington, twenty miles east of Seattle. Only ten years ago it seemed the epitome of the car suburb, with a smattering of office towers and parking lots for a downtown. But then, starting about 1978, the leaders were jolted into taking stock, one reason being the threat of a huge shopping mall beyond the city limits. Quite literally, Bellevue was at a fork in the road. They had to decide, and sooner than later, what kind of place they wanted it to be.

They decided that Bellevue should be a city. The activity shouldn't be off by some interchange, they asserted as they killed off the mall. It should be in the center: a very walkable one, with many shops and restaurants and pleasant outdoor spaces.

That is what is coming to pass. The central business district that Bellevue is building does not sprawl; it has a tight pattern of development with well-defined edges. Within the core of the CBD, developers can put up buildings with a floor-area ratio as high as 8 by providing bonusable amenities—up to 10 by providing specified public spaces. Beyond the CBD, however, developers must build low, with the maximum floor-area ratio a meager .5. This represents a clear public decision to concentrate and direct development rather than simply let it happen.

Thanks to the rules of the game, developers are not leapfrogging over empty spaces but are filling them in. Downtown, as a consequence, remains quite compact—an easy walk from one side of it to the other. That is not to say people do walk that far; when I was last there I did not see a surfeit of walking. Bellevue people insist that there is indeed more walking and that within the past two years the increase in walking in the core area has been quite noticeable. Because of the concentration, there are more people there and more amenities to prompt them to walk.

They believe the very structure of downtown is likely to induce more walking. Bisecting downtown is a central pedestrian corridor. At one end there is an attractive shopping mall; at the other, a unique transit center, with lots of seating and overhead cover. Developers along the corridor contribute segments to it, and via incentive zoning, bonuses are given to provide a rich townscape of trees, handsome paving, lighting, and canopies to temper the Northwest's drizzle. At likely gathering places, small parks are being similarly provided, and with all the amenities a good urban space ought to have.

Bellevue has also begun a large central park. Several years ago a fifteen-acre school site became surplus. In many a city a rapacious city hall would have sold it off for a massive development. Bellevue bought it from the school district and held a national competition to select a winning design. The first elements of the park were opened in mid-1987 and have already been discovered by strollers, joggers, and brown baggers. It is even getting use at night.

The car is being tamed. Instead of more parking, the city is mandating less. New buildings used to have to provide a standard five spaces per thousand square feet of office space. This has been cut to three spaces. To pinch matters further, commercial parking lots and garages are forbidden in the CBD. About half of all new employees working in downtown will have to join car pools or take a bus to get there.

Urban design guidelines favor a strong and attractive street wall, with frontages out to the building line rather than recessed away from the pedestrian flows. Taking a leaf from New York's code, Bellevue mandates retailing—street-level retailing—along the corridor and principal streets. The shops must be directly accessible from the street; shopping arcades buried within buildings do not get bonused. The glass of the shop fronts must be see-through glass. Blank walls are illegal.

The city would like to get some people living in downtown. It has a clean slate in this respect. There has been no gentrification in Bellevue, for there has been no old stock of housing to gentrify. To stimulate builders, the city is giving special incentives for residential construction in two districts. One complex now going up combines shops at street level with terraced apartments atop.

While Bellevue is firm on where it wants to go, its basic plan on how it gets there is open ended. Most large-scale complexes, by contrast, are usually designed all at once, and even if they are to be constructed over a long time span, the plans are end-state plans, complete to the last phase. This has two consequences. One is homogeneity. The small units of a very big complex are generally less attractive then the small units of a moderate-sized complex. Just why this would be so is difficult to determine, but the differences are visible.

Another consequence is the freezing of design against change. Such plans admit of no second thoughts, no course corrections to incorporate lessons learned in the first phase. Life insurance companies' giant housing projects have been a case in point. Most of the West Coast ones started off with a mixture of high-rise towers and a series of two-story duplexes grouped around garden courts. The courts rented out fast; the towers slowly. The market was fairly shouting, but as subsequent phases were built, the proportion of units was not altered.

There was no provision for such flexibility. Eventually a tight housing market bailed out the towers and there was no lesson left to heed.

How will Bellevue fare? Its approach is so much against the grain of present suburban patterns that optimism must be tempered. The new-town movement seemed promising too and it proved to be unrealistic. My hunch is that Bellevue is going to work out well, not so much out of step as ahead of it. It will prove thoroughly practical, says Mark Hinshaw, principal urban designer for Bellevue. There are similarities with the new-town ideal, he notes: the emphasis on pedestrian movement and scale, public transportation. But in one key respect, Bellevue is wholly different. It is a city and it wants to be a city. There is none of the antiurban bias that flawed some new-town designs, nor is there the inclination to the picturesque and to an excessive purity and order. Bellevue's downtown, says Hinshaw, is shaping up as intense and urban. Even discordant, he said hopefully.

It is ironic that an erstwhile suburb should be taking this tack. As we will see in the next chapter, a large number of U.S. cities are taking an almost diametrically opposite one. To compete with suburbia, they are going suburban.

22

HOW TO DULLIFY DOWNTOWN

The lines are getting blurred. Suburban office centers are imitating the center city. The center city is imitating suburban office parks. This may be overstating the point but a real question is being posed. Where will the center go? There are two contrary trends. On one hand there are cities that are tightening up their downtown, reinforcing the role of the street, and in general reasserting the dominance of the center. But a growing number are going in the opposite direction. They are loosening up the structure; gearing it more to the car; taking the pedestrian off the street, and retailing too. They are doing almost everything, indeed, to eliminate the structured advantages of the center they inherited.

As a way of distinguishing which camp a city is in, I have prepared a checklist of eight questions. No one city scores yes on all eight, but quite a number score high. Conversely, some cities score very low. There seems to be a strong tendency to go decisively in one direction or in the other.

1. Was much of downtown successfully razed under urban renewal?
2. Is at least half of downtown devoted to parking?
3. Have municipal and county offices been relocated to a campus?

4. Have streets been de-mapped for superblock developments?
5. Have the developments included an enclosed shopping mall?
6. Have they been linked together with skyways?
7. Have they been linked together with underground concourses?
8. Is an automated people-mover system being planned?

The higher the score, the more likely the city is to be one that has lost its ego, its sense and pride of place, its awareness of where it has come from and where it is going. It is a city with so little assurance that it is prey to what could be billed as bold new approaches, and to architectural acrobatics of all kinds.

Small and medium-sized cities seem particularly vulnerable. Their downtowns, for one thing, are more subject to the dominance of the freeway then are very large ones. The latter may have staged their antifreeway revolts while they were still short of evisceration. Many smaller ones never did rebel and, for their compliance, had much of their center destroyed. A cloverleaf in a small city can chew up a much larger proportion of downtown than a cloverleaf in a big one, and it can wreak more damage to the fabric of the center.

The most vulnerable are the cities that have lost their ego, their sense of place and pride. They are patsies for quantum leaps and architectural acrobatics.

In other ways smaller cities face a tougher challenge then big ones. For structural reasons, they are more hurt by the competition of outlying shopping malls. With smaller cities, the distance from downtown to the interchanges and their malls is apt to be no more than three to five miles. In some cases, cities whose boundaries embrace some of suburbia have allowed developers to build their malls within the city limits—and have rued the day they foolishly did so. The retailers that are left in downtown have been hurt; the last department store may be about to close up or has already done so. One of the saddest sights is the boarded-up windows, especially so when they front on a pedestrian mall with no one in it.

Smaller cities tend to have quite low densities in their downtowns. It is not because they have a low overall population; some villages that draw on a limited population have relatively high densities. The problem is the distribution of people. Whatever the total number in the metropolitan area, the number in downtown is the crux. In many cases there are simply not enough people to make the place work right.

Big cities, by contrast, tend to have many more people in downtown, both in absolute and relative terms. Thanks to the pedestrian flows they generate, it is difficult to design an open space that won't work. It has been done, but more often than not the space is bailed out by the high numbers of passerby and the law of averages.

When I first visit a city, I like to make a quick check of foot traffic at the 100 percent corner at midday. If the flow per sidewalk is at a rate less than one thousand people per hour, the city is beyond gimmickry. It has lost its engine.

Many cities compound their problems by the way they distribute what people they do have. They fail to concentrate. Instead, they diffuse. They spread over a large area what would work were it concentrated in a small one. Pedestrian malls are an example. Some have worked well—the malls in Boulder, Colorado, for example, and Tampa, Florida. Many have not. There are a number of reasons for failure—one regional shopping mall too many, for one—but the principal reason has been too much space for too little activity. Some cities have very broad rights-of-way—especially in the West, where streets are sometimes a hundred feet across. Take away the cars and the places look empty. There is a vacuum and it is not filled by rock gardens and play sculpture. The breadth of the area is so great that one side of the street is out of impulse distance of the other. Sometimes you can't even read the lettering on the stores on the other side.

I have yet to see a pedestrian mall that would not have been better if it had been a block or so shorter.

There is too much length as well. When cities gear up for a pedestrian mall, they like to shoot the works and go for one that's six to eight or ten blocks long. It is too many. Few cities can sustain a mall of that size. I have yet to see a mall that would not have been better if it had been several blocks less. Three blocks is not a bad limit, as several cities have found when they ran out of funds for a longer one.

Another kind of diffusion is the creation of new downtown centers away from the center. Land assembly is often easier and cheaper on the edge of downtown, and sometimes there is a very large open site available. If a satellite downtown is built there, proponents say, in time there will be development of the space between, and the two downtowns will be united.

But they probably will not. Kansas City provides an example. Its Crown Center complex is located about twelve blocks from downtown; it covers eighty-five acres and is almost a downtown in itself. But not quite. Nor has downtown moved toward it. In the intervening space there has not been much development. Many Kansas City people believe the city would be much better off if the two downtowns were one.

Even a few blocks can be a divisive distance. Columbus, Ohio, provides an illustration. It has a fairly tight downtown core anchored in part by the state capitol and its fine grounds. The Nationwide Mutual Insurance Company put up a large headquarters building about four blocks from the core and later joined a hotel to it with an overhead walkway. They seem an entity distinct from downtown, and the gap between them and the core remains.

Downtowns work best when they are compact. It is remarkable indeed how many have a core no more than four blocks square.

It is not linear distance that is critical, but continuity. Downtowns work best when they are compact; it is remarkable, indeed, how many good downtowns have a core that is no more than about four blocks square. If an activity is located adjacent, it becomes part of the core. If it is a store, the other stores work for it. But if you leapfrog new activities beyond the core, the continuity is broken. In Dallas, one of the reasons City Hall Plaza is underused, people will tell you, is how far away it is from downtown. But it isn't; it is in fact quite close —only three blocks from Main Street. But it seems much farther. There is a sharp break in continuity as high rise abruptly gives way to low rise and to those great separators, parking lots. Until there is substantial infill the plaza will continue to feel too far away.

In choosing a site for a stadium or convention center, cities more often than not go for an outlying site. It seems more economical. Access will likely be via freeway, so the site will be convenient for at least one quadrant of the metropolitan area. But the center would be the better choice. As St. Louis and Pittsburgh would attest, a stadium that is in or close to downtown reinforces the life of the center, and it draws on a broader area.

Arguments against a central location are based on the car. Will there be enough parking? This was one of the big questions in the controversy over the site selection for Seattle's convention center. One site was on exposition grounds beyond downtown; another on the edge of downtown. The last possibility was to deck over a freeway smack in the middle of downtown. It would be next to another decked-over facility, Freeway Park, and would be itself an attractive element of downtown, with terraces, roof gardens, shops, and open-air cafés. At a key public meeting, the site selection committee listened to seventeen convention center experts testify. To a man, they were against the downtown site. At the outlying location, they said, there would be plenty of room to marshal the buses that would be necessary to transport people from the downtown hotels to the outlying site. As for all that glass, and roof gardens and shops, forget it. A sealed box is what's needed. The committee took a deep breath and voted for the freeway site. And for a structure with lots of glass and roof gardens and shops.

The pitfalls we have been discussing so far involve the diffusion of downtown. A worse one, however, is in the other direction. It would encapsulate downtown. If you cannot beat them, some cities have come to think, you might as well join them. So they look to the instrument of their decline for salvation and welcome the construction of a suburban shopping mall in downtown. And they give away the store to get it.

While it will be self-contained, it will affect the surrounding area very substantially. For one thing, a street will likely have been demapped by a compliant city so that the mall can stretch over more space. Like its suburban model, the city mall will be car oriented and

Second-level systems can split a city: upper level for the middle class, street level for blacks and people who have to use buses.

will require vast amounts of parking. The price of a downtown mall usually includes the demolition of more of downtown to make way for more garages.

Another price, we have noted, may be a second-level walkway system. They start innocuously enough—a bridge from a garage to an office building, for example. But these things grow, and grow some more, until eventually there will be a whole system complete with stores and services. As a result, there will be two cities: an upper-level one for white middle-class people; a street-level one for blacks and lower-income people.

A further consequence may be a high blank-wall quotient. For a second-level system to attract the most people, it will be deemed helpful if the street level is made to attract fewer. A Gresham's law sets to work. As the dullification proceeds, windows are boarded up and what was good gets replaced by the bad. Blank walls breed blank walls.

The worst discontinuity is parking. It is usually ugly, though it need not be. Parking structures can be oddly pleasing in their geometry. Their blankness at street level can be offset with stores. Parking lots can be planted with trees and shrubbery. The blight of parking lies in what is not there. People. Activity. Function. The daytime storage of vehicles is not a highest and best use but it is treated as if it were.

In some American cities so much of downtown has been cleared for parking that there is now more parking than there is city.

In some American cities, so much of the center has been cleared to make way for parking that there is more parking than there is city. And quite literally too. Some cities, such as Topeka, Kansas, have gone so far as to reach a tipping point. If they clear away any more of what's left, there would not be much reason to go there and park.

A first step to liberation would be a reduction in the additional amounts of parking required. Communities are not as demanding about this as once they were but they still indulge the parker to an excessive degree, smaller cities in particular. For new office buildings from three to five parking spaces are required for each thousand square feet of office space and garages must be within or adjacent to the office building. The result is a series of very short garage-to-office trips and a lower level of overall pedestrian activity.

What would happen if additional parking was not provided? In New York, the South Street Seaport brought approximately 300,000 square feet of retailing to its site and it is jammed with customers. Not one additional parking space has been provided. Some people take the subway; some, the bus. The bulk, mostly office workers, walk to the place.

So far, the only hopeful action has been *not* adding more parking. Before long, we may actually start cutting it. It might make economic sense. In their zeal to woo the car, developers and municipalities grabbed off some of the best-located parcels of downtown. Indianapolis is an example. This is a good city with a fine centerpiece in its Monument Square. But so much of the surrounding area of downtown is given over to parking that it is hard to envision further progress without some garage clearance. The demolition of the Pruitt-Igoe houses in St. Louis was a symbolic event. So might be the first demolition of a bunch of downtown parking structures. There is a lot of valuable land under that concrete.

The explosion will be some time in coming. In cities most dominated by parking lots and parking garages a key civic issue is the lamentable lack of parking. Let me cite Dallas again. In has the highest ratio of parking spaces to office space in the country. But studies continually call for more parking, and at moderate cost.

This visitor, who marveled at how plentiful and inexpensive parking was in Dallas, participated in a survey touching on the problem. With the help of two newspapers I drafted a set of questions to be put to citizens. Question number one: is there enough parking in downtown? Answers: NO. NO. NO. AND MUCH TOO EXPENSIVE. Question number two: how far is it from where you park and where you work? Answers: average distance about two and a half blocks.

Two and a half blocks. And short blocks at that. Experience in other cities is similar. Supply has so conditioned demand that parking has become an end in itself, with people in a bondage to it more psychological than physical. But suppose, just suppose, that Americans were to extend their walking radius by only a few hundred feet. The result could be an emancipation of downtown. Parking could be pushed outward and this would take an adverse pressure off downtown. Instead of being sequestered for the storage of vehicles, prime space would be released for positive activities. The price? Parkers would have to walk about five minutes more than they do now—and better off for it they would be.

Curbside parking is more wasteful of space than ever. Parking parallel to the curb, which chews up the least, is becoming a lost skill. Many people under thirty have become so used to the head-in parking of suburban shopping malls that they are unable to cope with any other kind. A number of cities have had to switch from parallel to head-in for this reason.

Rights of way are a great potential source of prime space. A surprising amount of roadway space is not used for the movement of cars but for nonmovement, and with lots of redundant space. As a number of comely projects have demonstrated, these bits and pieces of space are often superbly located and they make excellent park and sitting places. The same recycling of space that frees up a vehicle lane for additional sidewalk space makes for not only a more

If Americans would widen their walking radius by only two hundred feet, there could be a revolution in U.S. land use.

amenable street but one that functions more effectively for transportation.

In our wastefulness, in sum, lies opportunity. The disinclination to walk more than a few blocks; the oversupply of badly used vehicular space; the low supply of pedestrian space, well used or ill; the usurpation of the center for automobile storage—the litany of our bad ways is almost cause for rejoicing. There is really a great deal of space in the city if we have the wit to see it. And put it to better use. As can be said of Lexington Avenue, in the most crowded place there is plenty of room.

23

TIGHTENING UP

Most American cities started with a compact layout. Usually it was the maligned grid, with blocks in the range of two hundred by three hundred feet. As many cities are coming to believe, they were right the first time. The tight grid and short blocks may be rigid, but the pattern maximizes pedestrian activity, and it provides many of those best of spaces, street corners.

Grids often run counter to the topography, and due to the accidents of early settlement patterns there are sometimes two grids: one going one way, one going another. In what may have been a case of a drunken surveyor, a Southern city has two parallel streets that come to a point.

It is the property of a grid to make departures from it interesting. William Penn's Philadelphia is a model of symmetry, with four public squares equidistant from each other. But among the features that are so liked today is a great diagonal cut through the grid for a City Beautiful–movement parkway. Also liked are the parts of the grid that should be clearly obsolete: the very narrow streets and alleys south of Market. They make a fine pedestrian area.

The board of commissioners that plotted the island of Manhattan in 1807 liked the grid. They explicitly rejected ovals or circles or other fancy European modes. They said the important thing was to stimulate commercial development, and the pattern that was best for that was the grid. So they laid out a grid, and virtually all grid too, there being little provision for parks or public squares. These had to come later.

But the commissioners did fasten on one felicitous touch. Most grids have been based on the points of the compass. Not Manhattan's. The island runs on a bit of a slant. The commissioners wanted to maximize the development potential, a tendency still very much alive today. So they fitted their grid to the slant, not to the compass. As a result, the supposed north of the city's north-south avenues is actually twenty-nine degrees east of true north. It so happens that this is near ideal for letting the sun fall on three exposures, including about an hour and a quarter of sun early mornings on northern facades. Generations of brownstone dwellers have been in the commissioners' debt.

San Francisco is another example. As has been frequently observed, they were out of their minds to lay a grid on top of this hilly place. But it seemed to work, and when earthquake and fire leveled the city they went right back to the grid. It still seems to work.

It is not the grid, however, that is important so much as compactness. Curves and oblique angles can work as well in this respect as right angles and rectangles. The eccentric street pattern of the tip of Manhattan was laid out by the Dutch in the seventeenth century. It still works. The streets are too dark; they are too narrow. Cars have trouble negotiating them. So the cars stay away. Pedestrians dominate. On Nassau Street they more or less took over the roadway even before cars were banned.

Boston is similarly perverse. If you wanted to design a street pattern for pedestrian movement you could hardly come up with anything better than the ancient twists and turns of the financial district. Ahead of their time, they tip the scales in favor of the pedestrian over the car. Bostonians are aggressive pedestrians, and when cars get slowed down on a winding street they will often bully them to a dead stop. Lately Boston has banned cars from some of its main shopping streets, and the pedestrian activity has been prodigious. But the die had already been cast.

I am biased because I gew up in the area but I do think that of all centers, Philadelphia's has cohered the best. There are many possible reasons: surveyor Thomas Holmes, Edmund Bacon, the placement of the Schuylkill; whatever the cause, center city development has not been scattered, but concentrated within a two-mile rectangle, river to river. The center is precisely where it was planned to be and in the middle is the magnificent Second Empire pile of masonry that is City Hall—upstaged by a building higher than William Penn's hat, but still a compelling symbol. One thing about Philadelphia: you know where you are.

Another legacy is the short block. In many U.S. cities, older ones in particular, blocks fall in the range of two hundred to three hundred feet, and a workable arrangement it has proved to be. Some cities, however, feel that it has been a disadvantage. Downtown is too chopped up, they feel, too unsuited for vehicle traffic. There are too many intersections, too many traffic lights to stop for, too few broad thoroughfares. Such cities welcome developer proposals to de-shorten the blocks by eliminating a street or two and thereby creating a super-block.

They should count their blessings. Small blocks make for good pedestrian downtowns. As planner Ron Ubagh points out, "The smaller the blocks and the greater the number of narrower streets, the better the downtown environment. The traffic is spread out more and there can be a nice degree of compatibility between pedestrians and vehicles."

The grid systems were very adaptable to the streetcar lines and to the expansion of the lines to the suburbs. The original suburbs mixed the grid with curving roads and parkways—particularly so if the Olmsteds had anything to do with it. But the settlement patterns were relatively cohesive; near any one stop there would be enough people to make a stop worthwhile. Many of our newer outlying areas not only lack mass transit service; they lack the pattern of development that makes it economical.

Older cities are well geared for mass transit. They have the concentrations of people that make mass transit work; more to the point, they have mass transit systems. Some of the subway systems are rickety, produce enormous deficits, and have been losing riders as fares rise. But they are systems in place, and while the costs of rehabilitating them are great—$3 billion for New York's—their costs are far less than the costs of new subway systems.

From a cost point of view a particularly welcome development has been the rediscovery of the trolley. A number of cities that tore up the tracks after World War II are now putting in systems. They're not called trolleys anymore, but "light rail" and cities like to emphasize their high-tech aspects. Sacramento has just inaugurated the first leg of a projected 18-mile line. A car on this line looks very much like a trolley running down the middle of the street. To Sacramento people it is futuristic, and they are delighted with it. "A pivotal step," says Mayor Jane Rudin, "taking Sacramento into the twenty-first century."

Compared to heavy-rail systems, costs can be quite tolerable. With a capital investment of $86 million, San Diego used an existing right-of-way to fashion a 16 mile line running from the Mexican border to the center of town. The cars are double-jointed German ones, painted a fire-engine red, and when they come down the street you perk up.

More futuristic are the people movers. These are systems featuring single cars operating on overhead tracks. They are completely automated, like some airport systems, and have the same sepulchral voices telling you to stand clear of the doors. Whether they make much sense is a question.

In one respect they are quite retrogressive. For years the standard rendering of the city of the future included monorails and gleaming white pylons. The monorail cars were suspended from their structures; people movers ride atop theirs. Either way, however, the structures are a problem. As New York found out, at great cost, overhead structures can have a devastating effect on the street, and differentials in property values will reflect this. And the structures will not look white and clean for very long. As with the undersides of elevated expressways, their end state is likely to be dirty, gray concrete.

People movers do not marry well with other forms of transit. In addition to its new Metrorail system, Miami now has a people-mover system. It traces a 1.9-mile loop around downtown. And that is that. At one point it comes by the Metrorail but the two do not connect. Their gauges are different. So around and around and around the people mover goes.

Heavy or light, a problem of the newer rail systems has been their route structures. Disproportionately, they best serve the high-income people who least need mass transit, and they poorly serve the blacks and low-income people who need it the most. Washington, D.C., for example, has an inner-city population that is mostly black. The people who ride the Metro are predominantly white, and high-income white at that. (73 percent of riders, according to a recent survey, earn $25,000 a year or more.)

In most cities mass transit means bus transit. Sometimes it is very bad. Miami, which has not bought a new bus in seven years, has notably poor service, with only half the size fleet it needs for its present routes. New York can't seem to buy buses that work, and a large number of its drivers can't drive passably; instead of easing to a stop they jam their way to it. But some cities have excellent systems: new equipment well maintained, frequent schedules, sheltered bus stops, skilled and courteous drivers. Atlanta is one such city. It is also embarking on a subway system, and though it does not need one right now it figures that it will later—at which time its good bus system will make a fine feeder system.

Costs of mass transit can be prodigious. Some parts of the new systems have cost far more than the traffic warrants; even established systems have racked up huge bills for improvements. There are more factors to be considered. In computing costs and benefits, however, one of the greatest boons of a mass transit system is not considered at all. It is what the mass transit system makes unnecessary: vast acreages of parking. By reducing the dominance of the car and the parking lot and the parking garage, the systems reinforce the integrity of the center. Mass transit makes a pedestrian downtown possible. Crank in

One of the greatest boons of mass transit is what it makes unnecessary: the leveling of downtown for parking.

this benefit and such environmental benefits as clean air and lessened congestion—not to mention aesthetics—and mass transit begins to look like a bargain.

Infill; Outreach

The function of the center for which compactness is most vital is retailing. Stores thrive best when they are cheek by jowl, concentrated within a relatively small area. So they were once. In the sixties and seventies, however, many cities lost this compactness. The decline of downtown retailing left a legacy of empty storefronts and those most depressing of sights—boarded-up department stores and movie theatres with blank marquees. The loss of stores was bad enough, but worse was the break in continuity. In total, there may still have been a good number of stores, but they were so scattered that in any one block there was not the density to make it work right.

The market had contracted, but the space had not. Cities with enough stores to fill about ten blockfronts had retail districts with sixteen or more and, consequently, many gaps. Cities would be far better off if they could compress their retail districts.

Gainesville, Florida, is an example. Its downtown has lost stores to the suburbs but it still has enough to make a thriving downtown. But it is not thriving. The stores are spread out over a retail district that is much too big for what is in it. Per block there are too few stores, too few within supporting distance of others. A new and used bookstore that would be an asset for any city is not in downtown at all but in a shopping strip on the edge of town. What communities like Gainesville need is a sort of urban renewal in reverse. It is diverting to imagine the reconstruction that could be accomplished with a giant helicopter to squeeze things up. And get that bookstore back where it belongs. Such resorting is not a practical course, perhaps, but at the very least cities could stop moving out in the other direction. When they plan a pedestrian mall, as we have noted, almost invariably they stretch it out far beyond the capacity of the retail base to sustain it.

Infill is what cities should be up to. If a city can find the right tenants for the prime vacant spots, even a marginal shift could make a big difference—and in the appearance of downtown as well as dollar volume. But there is usually no entity to bring this about, and opportunities go begging.

Downtown needs more stores but what it needs most is more kinds of stores—specialty stores in particular. But the retail mix is generally a matter of happenstance, and with too many mismatches between stores and the market. There may be, for example, a plethora of shoe stores or women's clothing stores, at which the shopping malls excel, but no first-rate men's shop, at which malls do not excel. There may be a furniture store but no fabric shop; a photographer's studio, but no full-line camera store. Sometimes even the staples are missing. One time I went looking for aspirin in Boulder, Colorado. It was a most attractive downtown. On the pedestrian mall there were people ambling about, some sunning on the grass, some reading, one playing a guitar. There were nice outdoor eating places. There were many shops. I could buy books and records, handcrafted leather goods, oil paintings. There was a gazebo with homemade ice cream. But no aspirin. Not one store stocked it. The restored Victorian hotel did not have any. At length I did what millions of Americans do. I got in the car and drove to the shopping mall.

Shopping mall managements do not wait for good tenants to show up. They go out after them. Downtown people should do the same.

For infill there has to be outreach. Shopping mall managements do not sit and wait for good tenants to shop up. They go out after them. Downtown people should do the same. Frederick, Maryland, has a fine breadth of stores and has outcompeted not one but two large shopping malls. An activist mayor has led a search operation and induced a well-balanced mix of stores. There is nothing showy in downtown Frederick; but there is store after store, good ones, and not a vacant front.

One of the longest outreaches began in Albuquerque, New Mexico. A leading banker wanted a first-class food operation for Albuquerque. The one kind of restaurant the city had never had was a traditional Japanese one. An emissary was dispatched to Tokyo. He came upon a Japanese millionaire who was entranced with the idea. The result: Restaurant Minato.

Good specialty operations do more than fill a gap. They widen the demand. An example is the emergence of the West End Historic District in Dallas. Fifteen years ago it consisted of some defunct breweries, factory buildings, and warehouses. It was slated for razing, to make space for parking. Then, in 1975, it was declared a historic district by the city, and some imaginative architects and entrepreneurs began recycling it. Today the district is a lively mixture of stores and offices and restaurants—thirty-five of them at last count, more than there were in all of central Dallas before. And there is variety: some are very good and very expensive; some are for the family trade; and some are of the raffish kind that marks Dallas' slow retreat from Calvinism. The district is fun to go to and it has had a strong impact on people's perception of downtown. There *is* a downtown, many now believe, and those who would earlier have located the center of Dallas out at a freeway interchange are now apt to place it in the center of Dallas.

Some cities are trying to compete with the shopping malls by copying the physical form of them. What they should be copying is the centralized managements of them: their ability to coordinate tenant selection, promotion, leasing, and market research. The malls, of course, have the great advantage of ownership; cities do not. But short of ownership there is much that cities can do to beef up their retailing, and the various downtown associations have been badgering them to do more. They have been pressing for the establishment of public-private entities that could be invested with some of the management functions of the shopping malls, such as tenant selection and location —that is, infill and outreach.

In some cities, business improvement districts have been set up with the capacity to initiate improvements and levy assessments on the benefited properties. In New York the largest such district has been set up by the Grand Central Partnership, a consortium of corporations and building owners who want to see an upgrading of this somewhat tacky area. One hundred and twenty-four property owners are included. Each contributes to the kitty an amount proportionate to his total floor space, at a rate of 10¢ per square foot. Billings are $5 million a year. With these funds the partnership will supplement the city's services with additional services and activities.

As a first step it commissioned Ben and Jane Thompson to do an inventory of the area's pluses and minuses and how the area might be improved. The result is an unusually thorough analysis and an unusually imaginative agenda. An erstwhile retailer himself (Design Research Stores), Thompson has put special emphasis on the retail potential of the area.

In a number of small cities the Main Street program of the National Trust for Historic Preservation has established a number of similar entities. To date, no district has been set up with sweeping powers, such as condemnation. But there is movement in that direction. In Maine, legislation has been passed to authorize development districts—public bodies with authority to enter into leases and cancel them for nonperformance.

One of the finest examples of centralized management is the business district of State College, Pennsylvania. Few small cities anywhere have so dense and thriving a mix of stores, services, and restaurants. The retailing is continuous along the principal streets; there are no gaps or vacant storefronts. The streetscape is basic Pennsylvania. The main movie theatre remains unconverted. It shows movies. There are lots of people on the street—even at night.

It helps, of course, to have thirty-five thousand students on the other side of the main street. But there is a larger market too: forty thousand people live in the town or nearby. There are two outlaying

Some cities are trying to compete with the shopping malls by copying their physical form. What they should be copying is their centralized managements.

shopping malls, but downtown has been strengthening its position as the true center of its region.

One reason is Sidney Friedman. He owns a major percentage of the stores and restaurants and offices in the town. A soft-spoken real estate man, he began his entrepreneurial career by opening a bicycle rental agency when he was a freshman at the college. Twenty years ago he began acquiring stores in downtown. The place was dying. Major stores were closing down or moving out. The movie theatre, known to students as "The Armpit," was barely operating. There were rumors that the venerable State College Hotel might be demolished.

Friedman bought the hotel. He had become engaged to his wife in its Corner Room. This was a second-story pergola of great if dowdy charm—perched, it so happened, over the 100 percent corner. Friedman proceeded to buy other properties. At the time he had no particular strategy in mind, but he worked his way into one store by store. "I realized there was no sense in my going after J. C. Penney or Kmart," he says. "They're too big for downtown. We do best with specialty stores, top-of-the-line men and women's wear, gift shops, delis, ethnic restaurants, nightclubs."

Friedman will not rent to fast-food franchises. "I could get fifteen to twenty dollars a foot from them versus ten for a local man," he says. "But I prefer to have local ownership. Fast-food outlets just aren't right for downtown."

To keep the right mix of tenants, Friedman goes out looking. At Altoona there was an especially good men's store. Friedman convinced the owner to locate a branch in one of his alleys. It now does a bigger business than the base store.

Friedman is keen on alleys and small stores. He is particularly proud of Calder Way, an upgraded alley that previously had been lined with dumpsters and the backsides of stores. He had the stores turn a face to the alley, and on its other side he constructed a line of "split level" stores—the two levels doubling the whammy of the frontage and helping light the place at night.

Friedman does not have the clout that shopping mall managements have. The local zoning board does not lie down for him. Other property owners may move in opposite directions—such as renting to Burger King, Roy Rogers, and Wendy's. But Friedman has set the pace for this lively community, and the fact that he did it without unique powers or clout makes the lessons all the more relevant to downtowns everywhere.

24

THE CASE FOR GENTRIFICATION

What our center cities have needed most is more people living in the center. If only, the hope has been voiced, younger people would come back to the old neighborhoods and fix them up, what a boon it would be. Here and there a few heartening precedents could be spotted. When I worked on the *Fortune* series on "The Exploding Metropolis" in 1957 we were able to run a portfolio of attractive blocks in various cities. These were mostly upper-income places, however, and from the market studies we did it was hard to see any substantial shift back to the center city.

One large reason was the kind of housing offered. The kind most in demand were the row houses of Georgetown and Brooklyn Heights. These were clearly out of reach for most people but they did provide strong cues for design and marketing of new housing. They were not heeded. The federal Title I urban redevelopment projects were just getting under way, and in scale and spirit they were the diametric opposite of the old blocks. With little variation from city to city the process was the same; not only were blocks razed, but streets as well, and huge superblock projects grouped colonies of high-rise towers in abstract green space.

A terrible mistake was being made. These bleak new utopias were not bleak because they had to be. They were the concrete manifestation—and how literally—of a deep misunderstanding of the function of the city.

By such measures as tenant satisfaction, crime rates, and maintenance it should have been evident that the high-rise towers were proving much less suitable for families with children than low-rise units. But the momentum was unstoppable. In New York City the project format became so imbedded in the rules that it was difficult to build any public housing that departed from it. And it was a photogenic format. What on the ground looked like dirty, gray concrete gleamed white against cloud-filled skies in architectural photographs. Particularly attractive were the photos of the Pruitt-Igoe project in St. Louis.

But cities—older cities especially—had a great asset: a plentiful supply of old housing. The houses were not of the quality of the red-brick Federal houses of Georgetown or Brooklyn Heights. They were ugly, many of them: brownstones, for example, the felicities of which took a lot of time to appreciate. Most of the housing was in bad shape, much of it foreclosed. But this proved a blessing. Some sites actively promoted their rehabilitation. Baltimore, for one, set up a "homesteading" program with its stock of tax-foreclosed properties; to buyers who would pledge to fix them up the city would sell the houses for a nominal sum. The result has been some very attractive neighborhoods. One, the Otterbein houses, is a very Baltimore place and with front steps as white as any in the city.

Pittsburgh is another city that has had homesteading programs. It started with a "Great House Sale," in which it put fifty-eight city-owned houses up for sale at one hundred dollars apiece to people who would rehabilitate them. Since then prices have gone up; it has been selling abandoned properties to homesteaders for three hundred dollars apiece.

By and large, however, the people who have been rehabilitating old neighborhoods have been doing it without much help from government—sometimes despite government. The federal government subsidized suburbia with FHA-guaranteed mortgages but offered no such help for rehabilitating city houses. The Department of Housing and Urban Development did have some demonstration programs, including one for "new towns in town." It was, if anything, too well meant. It was thoroughly suburban in its assumptions and was so laden with antidensity, anticity provisions that it was bound to founder.

Banks and insurance companies were not much help either. Banks would withhold mortgage financing from areas being rehabilitated until the rehabilitation was largely completed and financing no longer so needed. Then they would lend. Insurance companies were often so chary of older neighborhoods that obtaining adequate fire and liability policies was extremely difficult and costly.

Cash was the big problem. When banks did offer mortgage financing there was a sizeable gap to fill. The home buyer usually had to put up about 30 percent of the purchase price in cash, and raising it took some doing. Money for the actual renovation was hard to come by too. Rates on second mortgages were astronomical and the terms too short.

Despite the difficulties, the rehabilitation movement gained force. There was common sense to it. The neighborhoods might have looked shabby with their Perma-Stone facades, broken windows, and vacant lots. But with them went an infrastructure of streets and utilities and urban services substantially intact. For a fraction of any pro rata replacement cost, the home buyer was acquiring a share of this urban base.

In the eyes of these beholders the old houses acquired a beauty that had not been so discernible before. There was, for example, a considerable shift in aesthetic judgments on the brownstones. They used to be drab, dark, and monotonous—indeed, ugly. But then, with no physical change to speak of, they changed. They became fine examples of the Italianate style, their stoops a graceful evocation of the urban rhythm. To paint over the brown, as remodelers did earlier, was sacrilege. If, as in Park Slope, the brownstones were twenty-four feet or more wide, had parquet floors and stained glass, they became objects of veneration. Even the basic eighteen-footers—the tract houses of their day—commanded respect. And rising prices. People who bought them thought they were getting a tremendous bargain. As the real estate market was subsequently to demonstrate, they were indeed.

Good news? You would think so. But many people do not think so. Invoking that dread term of urban affairs, they say it is "gentrification," and those who hailed the possibility of a middle-class revival of neighborhoods are unhappy now it has become a reality. They say that it is elitist; that it has been at the expense of the poor; that the displacement of them by middle-class people has broken up once stable neighborhoods and ethnic groups. There is not a conference on city problems that does not ring with protestations of guilt over gentrification. Shame on us for what we have done.

The gentrification charge has had an inhibiting effect on government support. Let me go back to one of the first cases. In the 1969 *Plan for New York City,* the planning commission hailed the brownstones revival with enthusiasm. "If brownstoners have done what they have done in the face of major difficulties," the plan said, "it is staggering to think of what could be done if the difficulties were removed." To that end, it proposed

- municipal loans or mortgage guarantees for one- and two-family homes.
- a revolving fund to bridge the gap between the price of the house and a conventional mortgage.
- long-term loans for renovation work.
- municipal second mortgages for twenty years at regular mortgage rates.
- temporary tax abatement on house improvements.

The proposals were not supported. They were criticized, and by many of the civic activists that had been expected to support them. Elitism, they charged. The great reservoir of brownstones was in Brooklyn—many square miles of it—but to judge from the criticisms, the brownstone movement was something fomented by a small coterie of smart-aleck Manhattan liberals and quiche eaters. (This was before the term "yuppies" was invented.)

What displacement? And when? The gentrification charge is very misleading. Check the year-by-year changes in neighborhood households and you will find very few cases of direct displacement; that is, a renter going out the door as a homeowner comes in. Low-income renters are frequent movers; 40 percent of the renters in a city neighborhood will move. Of all moves, the Department of Housing and Urban Development has estimated, only 4 percent are caused by displacement. When there is displacement, furthermore, it comes early in the game, usually well before the home buyers arrive.

The "gentrification" charge implies that the chief threat to housing for the poor is the upgrading of neighborhoods. The problem is the opposite. The chief threat is disinvestment. And the worst culprit is the federal government.

What causes it? The implicit assumption of the gentrification concept is that the chief threat to housing for the poor is the improvement of neighborhoods. The problem is the opposite. The chief threat is the deterioration of neighborhoods. The poor are not being hurt by middle-class investment. They are being hurt by disinvestment—by landlords and owners who let buildings go to rot, who walk away from them, who torch them. More units have been lost through abandonment in the Bronx alone than have been provided by brownstone rehabilitation in all of New York City.

The worst case of disinvestment is the federal government public housing program. The number of units constructed each year has been falling precipitously: from 68,500 in 1978 to 1,426 in 1985. The condition of units is worsening; by law the rent cannot be more than 30 percent of the family's income but local housing authorities are having trouble holding the line. Maintenance has suffered—and lately to such an extent that more units are being lost than built. Our public housing program needs an overhaul in policy and design. What it needs most, however, is a fair amount of money.

Rehabilitation programs are proceeding well and they are doing it without displacement. As part of its "Landmark Rehabilitation" program, Savannah, Georgia, is restoring 1,200 units in its Victorian district and will rent 600 of them to low-income blacks. In Kansas City the Quality Hill redevelopment is restoring what is left of a former gold coast by rehabilitating old structures and infilling with new three-story row housing. During the staged construction the project has been able to house most of the people who were on the site earlier.

Harlem might one day be an example. It has already suffered disinvestment and displacement. It is, in fact, underpopulated, having lost almost a third of its population since 1970. Much of the tenement housing is burnt out. But Harlem has great advantages. It is well served with mass transit; it has broad, tree-lined avenues and excellent access to parks. There are many cleared sites for new housing; there is a fine stock of brownstones, some blocks of which, such as Striver's Row, have been kept in excellent shape.

In the country as a whole, let it be noted, the market for rehabilitated center-city housing is a small one. Most of the data available indicate that the prime prospects are people already living in the city. Next are people who normally would go to the suburbs but who have elected to stay in the city for one reason or another. This is probably the swing sector and could be enlarged were the supply of units increased and the cost not. About a third are people who have been living in suburbia; a considerable proportion of them are empty nesters, whose children have grown up and moved away. All in all, it has been estimated, house sales in rehabilitated city neighborhoods number no more than 100,000 units a year.

These few people, however, can have a profound impact on the center city and the perception of it by others. Since the base is so small, a relatively small addition can carry a lot of leverage. In Denver, for example, another twenty-seven hundred people would double the downtown resident population. Such additions will not jam the bars and put hordes on the streets at night. Like their counterparts in suburbia, city residents are homebodies. But their presence does make a difference, and a very healthy one. In Charlotte, North Carolina, the NCNB bank sponsored a town house development that is only five blocks from the center of downtown. People *walk* to work from it. They also agitate for more retailing and services, more activity at night. Of such steps is a center revitalized.

Cities-within-cities, alas, are still being built. They are usually very large—often on clear tracts, such as obsolete freight yards, that give architects and developers the blank slate they would be better off for not having. The projects are sufficient unto themselves; the surrounding neighborhoods are not in the province of their planning. For

Cities-within-cities go with very large, clear tracts, like freight yards, which give architects and developers the blank slate they would be better off for not having.

urban services the projects provide bits and pieces within: a gourmet food shop, a simulation of a raffish pub. A recent example is Presidential Towers, a middle-class development in Chicago. Writing in *Inland Architect,* Catharine Ingraham hails it as ersatz city. "The idea that one can imitate the diversity of cities in isolated developments by bringing together desirable pieces of the urban fabric has taken hold of city planning. Paradoxically, the more one imitates, or extracts things from the vernacular city, the more artificial the results seem. The development stands as a bulwark against the very diversity that it capitalizes on."

But there are some good prototypes. There have been for some time, which makes the bad ones all the less understandable. Here and there, year after year, residential projects have been built that are of reasonably high density, eminently economical, of pleasing scale, and thoroughly urban. They do not date.

One of the best contemporary models is St. Francis Square in San Francisco. With its town-house groupings, interior open spaces, and private patios, it is one of the pleasantest neighborhoods you will see anywhere. It was built for low- and middle-income people twenty-five years ago. To repeat a point: a design that is well conceived for a time and place tends to be timeless. We should not have to search hard for such lost lessons. They are all about us.

25

RETURN TO
THE AGORA

Will the center hold?

What you see can make you doubt it. Ride the freeways and you see the consequence of a weakening center. You see a mishmash of separate centers, without focus or coherence. Taken by themselves, some of the components are well done, but it is still a mishmash that they add up to. And it is hard to see how it can do anything but worsen.

The decentralization trend that is sending the back-office work of the center to the suburbs is strengthening. The computers have already made the move. Cities can argue that it would make much more sense to locate these functions within the city, with its services and its transit network—in low-cost Brooklyn, for example, rather than Manhattan. Few corporations are buying the argument: it's either the center or the suburbs.

The cities of the northeastern and north-central states seem to have been hit particularly hard. A succession of demographic studies have argued that they have had it, that they are "aging" and functionally obsolete, being geared to a declining manufacturing economy and with an overpriced labor force—and that, in any event, they are in the wrong latitude. The message is clear. Go to the South and the Southwest. The cities in those regions, runs the argument, are expanding vigorously, offer lower taxes, lower-cost housing, a more tractable labor force, and a quality of life unmatched by the cold North.

But the Sunbelt cities are having their problems too. One reason taxes have been relatively low is that they have been postponed, as has been investment in infrastructures. Oil revenues are no longer taking up the slack. The spectacular population growth of some of the cities has been due in large part to the annexation of neighboring communities, but cities are running out of places to annex. They have no mass transit to speak of and are as much hostage to the car and the freeway as they are their beneficiaries. Quality of life? Migrants from the rolling green landscapes of the North have some environmental surprises in store. Those mild winters have a price.

But regional comparisons need not be invidious. The presumed decline of the aging cities of the North is belied by some significant countertrends. To a large extent, the movement to the Southwest has been a movement of maturing products and processes. Many of the Southwest's manufacturing plants will soon age too: a year there is as long as it is anywhere else. In the meantime, some presumably over-the-hill cities up North have been doing surprisingly well.

But regional differences are not as important as regional similarities. As economist John Hekman has pointed out, it is not regions that grow old, but products. They have a life cycle of their own, and they go from innovation, through development, to maturity and standardization. At each stage the resources needed by the manufacturer change, and this can prompt him to make some large geographic moves.

This is what has been happening in the moves to the Southwest. Hekman points to the computer industry as an example. "Highly sophisticated products and production processes tend to be located in the main centers of technology, like Boston, New York, Minneapolis, and, more recently, Dallas and Palo Alto." The manufacturing of peripheral items and knockoffs of systems tend to be scattered elsewhere. They do not need high technology so much as lower production costs. The Southwest has the edge on lower production costs of standardized items. New England, however, has a strong edge in its technical and research base for the development of new processes. In the birthrate of new firms, Massachusetts is second only to California.

The Middle Atlantic states are not doing so well. State and local governments in such areas often concentrate on subsidy and restriction to keep old industries from moving out. Hekman thinks that this is the worst possible mistake and that what they ought to be concentrating on is the nurturing of new firms with a strong technological base. "The key to beating the product cycle and industrial migration," he says, "is not in keeping the industries at home, but in replacing them with new industries."

The work of economist David L. Birch of MIT points to similar conclusions. Through detailed studies of job creation in a cross section of American cities, he found that most cities lose about the same percentage of their job base each year—about 8 percent on average. This is a normal consequence of entrepreneurial activity. "The culprit in declining economies," says Birch, "is not job losses but the absence of new jobs to replace the losses . . . Development strategies aimed at holding a thumb in the dike would appear to be as futile as telling the tide not to go out."

My study of the migrations from New York City provides further documentation. There was not a great deal that the city could do to stop them. To a large extent, the causes of the companies' moves were internal, the consequence of cyclical changes within the company and its industry, and were independent of the city and its pros and cons. To say that such moves are normal is not cheering to the city's defenders, but it is not all bad news. As the market-valuation comparisons demonstrated, the companies that moved out tended to be lackluster performers. The companies that stayed in the city were outstanding performers.

The city, of course, does not want to lose any companies, mediocre or not, but it most probably will lost more. Yet there are favorable aspects to the turnover. The jobs the city is losing are predominately in the older and bigger companies, and the ones that are not doing very well are the ones most apt to pack up the whole company and leave town. The jobs the city is gaining, by contrast, are predominantly in the newer and smaller firms.

The jobs the city is losing are mainly in the older and bigger companies. The jobs the city is gaining are mainly in newer and smaller companies.

In a study of San Francisco's experience between 1972 and 1984, Birch found that small firms were creating the new jobs. Larger firms with 100 employees or more, were shedding jobs. Company age was a factor too: firms less than four years old produced a net gain of 30,597 jobs over the period, but those twelve years old or more had a net loss of 13,382 jobs.

New York has been enjoying similar gains. In 1986 it has a net gain of 64,000 office jobs and about the same was expected for 1987. Some of the gain has come from the expansion of local firms, most markedly in financial services. This expansion has been so buoyant as to be unsettling and has absorbed most of the space vacated by the move-outs. Firms moving into New York, including several from the Sunbelt, have brought jobs. What in time may prove the most fruitful source are the jobs created through the start-up of entirely new companies.

Conventional economic development programs concentrate on hanging on to big firms with tax abatements and other defenses. Like Hekman, Birch believes this is bad strategy. It does not meet the needs of the growth sector, and it does not do much that is effective for the nongrowth sector. Characteristically, tax abatements come on strong in the boom periods, when they are least warranted. New York has been a patsy in this respect many times. Corporate gratitude for such favors, it has learned, is a nonfactor. But the game goes on. Sponsors of big office projects press for concessions and threaten to pack up and go to Stamford if they don't get them. If the city calls their bluff, they will probably stay. If they do go, it will serve them right.

The belief that major office projects are the prime source of new jobs dies hard. Most cities have assumed that they are and have equated office building construction with the city's economic vitality. But the growth is in firms that are priced out of the tower market. They need older, somewhat beat-up quarters off to the side but not too far from the center.

"Office tower developments," Birch argues, "is not job development. It may, indeed, be something of a deterrent. The kind of firms that can afford the $35 a foot are the ones that are not producing new jobs. To make way for the tower, however, older buildings are being demolished which are affordable by the small firms which do produce new jobs."

If the number of people who can afford the high rents of the towers is diminishing, how come so many new towers are being built? It is not because of any excess of demand. Office vacancy rates across the country have been rising for some time. The impetus for construction has been financial. It has been driven by a huge supply of investment capital. What the markets give they can take away.

New York City is especially vulnerable. One of the reasons it fared well in the creation of office jobs in the mid-eighties was the prodigious growth of the financial services sector. But what markets can help create they can take away. The contraction in jobs following the 1987 crash was severe. It could get much worse.

On balance, however, the shift of jobs and people has been favorable for cities. What is most encouraging is where the growth has been taking place. The gain in jobs has been greater than the loss of them, and the gains have been mainly in newer and smaller firms—the kind where future growth is most likely to come from.

It is true that the ablest, best-performing corporations are the ones which stay in the city and that those which leave tend to be the less able. But the city cannot rejoice over this. Ill advised or no, the defecting companies take a lot of jobs with them, and the psychological hurt is perhaps the most telling.

Even the corporations that stay are moving some jobs to the suburbs. They are the more routine jobs, but the city is understandably upset to see them go. And the movement will probably continue. Headquarters remaining in the city are getting leaner; in some instances, the headquarters consist of some office suites and a handful of top executives, with the great bulk of the organization out by the freeways.

With or without a downturn, the center city may start losing more office jobs than it is gaining. But this would not necessarily be a catastrophe. Only twenty years ago, critics were jumping on the city for having too many people in it, in the center most of all. A behavioral sink, they called it, and preached the horrors of urban density. If the city now loses some density, it hardly seems fair to whack it for that, as some observers do. They would have it both ways and interpret any additional outward movement as further evidence of the city's malaise—terminal malaise.

Only twenty years ago critics were jumping on the city for having too many people in it. If now it loses some, it hardly seems fair to whack it for that.

Will this come to pass? Let us return to the Route 1 corridor and its counterparts. As we have already noted, they are supplanting the center city for white-collar work. Will they supplant it as the center as well? Some people believe so. They see these new areas as the true wave of the future—not just another kind of suburb but a new city itself. A forceful expression of this diagnosis is Robert Fishman's *Bourgeois Utopias.* "In my view," he writes, "the most important feature of postwar American development has been the almost simultaneous decentralization of housing, industry, specialized services, and office jobs; the consequent breakaway of the urban periphery from a central city it no longer needs; and the creation of a decentralized environment that nevertheless possesses all the economic and technological dynamism we associate with the city." In sum, all the advantages of the center without it—the city without tears.

How can this be? What makes this best of both worlds possible, says Fishman, is technology—specifically, "the advanced communication technology which has so completely superseded the face-to-face contact of the traditional city." It has generated urban diversity without urban concentration.

But there has been a price: scatteration. Fishman concedes that the "technoburbs," as he calls them, are a bit of a mess and will probably remain so for some time. But he believes that eventually they will be set right by regional planning and advanced traffic technology.

A premise of this optimism is that there are a good many options still open. But are they really? It is easy to overlook how preemptive early development patterns can be. In most of the new growth areas the formative decisions have already been made. There is an analogy here to the residential development of the countryside. The early subdivisions often set the character of subsequent growth long before the main body of suburbanites had arrived. In many metropolitan areas the die was cast as early as the fifties. By then, the farmers had sold off their key frontage land on the county roads; the streams had been riprapped or buried in pipes; the wooded ridges had been shaved. The names of the subdivisions had foretold the future: they were customarily named after the natural features they were about to obliterate.

But there was much hopeful talk of shaping new growth patterns. The sixties was a time of "Year 2000" plans, which were full of bold possibilities to consider: enucleated growth points, linear developments, rings of satellite communities, and the like. At countless clinics and conferences, people weighed the pros and cons of the various alternatives. It made people feel good, these exercises in ordered choice, and they went about them as solemnly as though the choices were in fact there to make.

The most celebrated was the "wedges and corridor" plan for the Washington metropolitan area. It called for channeling growth into spokelike corridors and conserving the bulk of the land in great wedges of green open space. It was a bad plan actually, the key tracts of the green wedges having been bought up by developers. But the plan persisted for some time as the region's best hope, planners preferring to go to hell with a plan than to heaven without one.

It does not follow that the new growth areas cannot be helped by regional planning. It is very much needed, late in the game though it may be. But it is hard to conceive of any drastic changes in the patterns or the lack of them. Once the freeways are built, the interchanges sited, and the malls anchored in place, future choices are constrained and not very much can be done to change matters.

There are palliatives, to be sure: jug handle turnoffs at exits of research parks, overpasses to improve access to malls, new frontage roads, additional limited-access stretches, or entirely new highways. But such measures can be extremely costly and the application of them made the more difficult by the pervading lack of centrality. There is no dominant direction. The traffic flows go every which way, and the mediation of them calls for yet more concrete.

So there are problems, the decentralizers say. But is there any real alternative? Yes, there is: the town. It was invented several millennia ago and has persisted as a remarkably consistent and useful form.

Let me cite West Chester, Pennsylvania, my hometown. It has a number of the advantages of such towns. For one thing, the settlement pattern is compact and efficient. It was laid out in the classic grid bestowed on southeastern Pennsylvania by surveyor Thomas Holme. There is a fine and complete stock of housing; ranging from single-family detached to double houses and row houses.

All of the houses are within walking distance of the center of town. That does not mean people actually walk the whole distance. They are Americans. But they could if they had to.

Downtown is intact. Back in the 1950s the town fathers turned down urban renewal—whether from torpor or foresight, no one is sure. But as a result the center was spared demolition. A few individual buildings were torn down that should not have been: such as the Turk's Head Hotel, the town's original one. But thanks to some cranks and preservationists the best old buildings stand, and by standing, have gained a new functionalism. The banks are an example.

Out by the interchanges there are drive-in banks. West Chester has *walk*-in banks. You walk right in off the street. You don't need a car to gain admittance. The architecture of the two leading banks is contextual. They have white marble Greek temple fronts. They say *bank*.

There was a clear edge between town and country, a boon that was fated to disappear. Another portent was the construction by James Rouse of the Exton Square Mall, five miles north of town. For a while it looked as if it was going to knock off West Chester's downtown. Mosteller's Department Store closed down and so did several other stores.

Rouse had said that a town such as West Chester could compete very well with malls in specialty retailing and restaurants. That is the way it has worked out. Several specialty shops have been doing well, and one, Jane Chalfant's, is outstanding. There are good places to eat. The Quaker Tea Room on East Gay Street was taken over by a French couple and reopened as La Cocotte. The Borough Hall was converted into a restaurant. So was part of the old Sharples Separator Works.

Lawyers are the principal industry of this county seat. They are located one next to another and form a stable constituency for downtown. The Chester County Courthouse itself is quite declarative. Its clock steeple and the five-story Farmers and Mechanics Building are the high points of town. You see them from far away when you are on the eastern approaches and the sight of them is oddly reassuring.

I feel very much as Russell Baker did about his Main Street. "When you stood on Main Street," he wrote, "you could tell yourself,

The sense of place
that a town can give is
important for those
who live beyond the
town. A well-defined
center can give
coherence to a whole
countryside.

'This is the center, the point on which all things converge,' and feel the inexplicable but nonetheless vital comfort that results from knowing where you stand in the world and what the score is . . . On the shopping mall, people know they are standing not at the center, but somewhere vaguely off toward the edge of a center that has failed to hold."

The sense of place that a town can give is most felt by those who live within it. But is is also important for those who live beyond. A well-defined town with a tight core can give coherence to a whole countryside. It's a better place to live *in* if there is someplace to go *to*.

There is also reason to expand a town on its periphery rather than leapfrog development way beyond it. The town is an efficient model. Had West Chester been extended in the fifties and sixties about two blocks on each of its sides, some thirty years of growth could have been taken care of handily. It was not. Political realities being what they are, the expansion required several hundred square miles of land and umpteen thousand miles of utilities.

I'm not suggesting that what happened was all wrong. Some of the developments were well handled, the cluster developments especially. The county did a number of things right, such as acquiring regional parks. Thanks to an outstanding easement program, the loveliest stretches of the Brandywine were saved from development. The fact remains, however, that had more of the expansion been contiguous to the town, the end result would have been more amenable as well as more economic. So would it have been for many other towns across the country.

And so it could be in the new growth areas too. While it is too late for major shifts in direction, the application of the town principle could help tighten up a pattern that badly needs it. There has been some progress along these lines, as in the creation of combined shopping, hotel, and office centers at Forrestal Village. But the best precedent, as I noted earlier, has been Bellevue, Washington, and the transformation of an incipient office park into a city.

It is the genius of the
Center City that it is
not high-tech. As far as
essentials are
concerned, it has little
more than did the
agora of ancient
Greece.

For those who see the suburban growth areas as the cities of the future, the key word is "technology." They have a point, but it is one that should be stood on its head. It is the genius of the center city that it is *not* high-tech. What is remarkable, indeed, is how little technology it does use. There are elevators, telephones, Xerox machines, and air-conditioning. But that is about it. The really fancy stuff is out on the periphery.

Socially, the city is a very complex place. Physically, it is comparatively simple. For the business of the center, it must have streets, buildings, and places to meet and talk. As far as essentials are concerned, it has little more than the agora of ancient Greece.

I am going to quote from R. E. Wycherley's fine study of the agora. It is not straining an analogy to see in the history of the agora some lessons for cities today. The parallels are considerable, especially so in the surprising turn the agoras finally took.

It began in a simple way: "A fairly level open space was all that was needed," writes Wycherley. "A good water supply was important and satisfactory drainage. A roughly central site was adopted, since the agora had to provide a convenient focus for city life in general and for the main streets . . . The same free space sufficed for all kinds of purposes. Here the people could assemble to be harangued; the only equipment needed was some sort of tribune for the speakers, and possibly seats for men of dignity."

As time went on, buildings were added. There would be a council house for magistrates. The stoa, or open colonnade, served as a general-purpose structure and eventually became the frame for rows of shops. The agora was a good place through which to amble: there were rows of trees for shade (plane trees mostly) and a number of convivial places at which to stop (the fountain house, for example, or the wine shops).

"No clear line," writes Wycherley, "was drawn between civic centre and market. The public buildings and shrines were in the agora; meat and fish and the rest were sold in the same agora." Booksellers had their stalls, and so did bankers, known as men-with-tables. "Marketing 'when the agora was full,' i.e., in the morning, must have been a noisy and nerve-racking business. The fishmongers had a particularly bad reputation; glared at their customers; asked exorbitant prices."

The agora was a sociable place. People would drift from spot to spot, pausing to chat under the plane trees or by one of the fountains. To some observers—Aristophanes, for one—these were vulgar, undesirable fellows. He saw no good purpose served whatsoever by "idlers," such as Socrates. Nor did Aristotle. Like some modern planners, he wanted the various functions separated out and contained. He recommended that there be two agoras—one for ordinary commerce and the other of a religious nature, free of idleness and vulgar activity.

"But the Greeks thoroughly mixed up the elements of their lives," Wycherley points out, "and for better or worse this fusion is clearly seen in the agora." It is seen physically too, for the agora was part of the street network of the city; it was not enclosed or segregated from the rest of the city but vitally linked with it.

Then, about the third century A.D., the agora began to lose its centrality. With the advent of the enclosed peristyle court, the agora was secluded from the city around it, eventually with complete enclosure. "There was a greater tendency," says Wycherley, "to plan the main agora square as a whole on this principle, to make it an enclosed building turning in on itself. City life had lost something of its old quality, and the agora had a less vital part to play, a less intimate relation with all the varied activities of the community . . . When the agora became a mere building, however grand, this meant a certain disintegration of the city."

The withdrawal and seclusion of the agora is uncomfortably similar to the direction so many cities have been taking. It does not follow that they, too, will decline, but the warning signals are worth heeding. As in Greece, many a city is moving its key public space out of the street system; it is moving the space away from the true center, putting walls around it, and making it a structure turned in on itself. For good measure, cities are adding two separators the Greeks did not have, concourses and skyways. The only encouraging note is how badly the megastructures have fared. A few more bankruptcies among such projects, and cities might conclude that they were doing something wrong.

The agora at its height would be a good guide to what is right. Its characteristics were centrality, concentration, and mixture, and these are the characteristics of the centers that work best today. Physically, there are vast differences, but in the gutty, everyday life of the street they would probably be remarkably similar. I would give anything to be able to mount a time-lapse camera atop a stoa and film the life of the agora. I would be especially interested to see if there were a considerable number of 100 percent conversations in the middle of the pedestrian flow. I would think there would be; people do not stand that way except in places where they feel comfortable. In such places, the idle gossip that so annoyed Aristotle and annoys many people today often becomes vulgar, noisy, and argumentative, but it is the true currency of the city—word of mouth.

Is word of mouth obsolete? Electronics has not dampened our love of talking. Go out to the corporate headquarters that relocated in suburbia, and you will find plenty of word of mouth there. They would go balmy if there weren't. The only trouble is that it is primarily company people talking to company people. To the disappointment of these companies, nowhere near as many people have been coming out to see them as they expected.

Increased communications and travel have not obviated face-to-face interchange; they have stimulated it. There are no reliable figures on the point, but there does seem to have been a large increase in conferences, meetings, focus groups, sensitivity workshops, and other forms of talk, the whole serviced by a league of expediters and facilitators. Outlying locations are often favored. Many meetings are convened at airport motels, which shows you how far people will go to be face-to-face.

But the city is still the prime place. It is so because of the great likelihood of *un*planned, informal encounters or the staging of them. As I have noted, street corners are great places for this. They are also great for bargaining, with no party having an advantage over the others. I have watched scores of executive groups going through their elaborately casual postlunch goodbyes, and I have to marvel at the deftness with which someone will finally get them all to the point. Elevator lobbies are good places too; so are clubs and restaurants, which provide excellent opportunities for working the room.

It is because of this centrality that the financial markets have stayed put. It had been widely forecast that they would move out en masse, financial work being among the most quantitative and computerized of functions. A lot of the back-office work has been relocated. The main business, however, is not record keeping and support services; it is people sizing up other people, and the center is the place for that. This is true of most of the major financial markets of the world. With few exceptions, they remain right where they started out.

The problems, of course, are immense. To be an optimist about the city, one must believe that it will lurch from crisis to crisis but somehow survive. Utopia is nowhere in sight and probably never will be. The city is too mixed up for that. Its strengths and its ills are inextricably bound together. The same concentration that makes the center efficient is the cause of its crowding and the destruction of its sun and light and its scale. Many of the city's problems, furthermore, are external in origin—for example, the cruel demographics of peripheral growth, which are difficult enough to forecast, let alone do anything about.

What has been taking place is a brutal simplification. The city has been losing those functions for which it is no longer competitive. Manufacturing has moved toward the periphery; the back offices are on the way. The computers are already there. But as the city has been losing functions it has been reasserting its most ancient one: a place where people come together, face-to-face.

More than ever, the center is the place for news and gossip, for the creation of ideas, for marketing them and swiping them, for hatching deals, for starting parades. This is the stuff of the public life of the city—by no means wholly admirable, often abrasive, noisy, contentious, without apparent purpose.

But this human congress is the genius of the place, its reason for being, its great marginal edge. This is the engine, the city's true export. Whatever makes this congress easier, more spontaneous, more enjoyable is not at all a frill. It is the heart of the center of the city.

Let me append a methodological note.

I have tried to be objective in this book, but I must confess a bias. In comparing notes with fellow observers, I find that I share with them a secret vice: hubris.

Observation is entrapping. It is like the scale models architects beguile you with; start lifting off the roofs and you gain a sense of power. So it is with the observation of a place: once you start making little maps of it, charting where people come and go, you begin to possess the place. You do not possess it, of course. The reality continues to exist quite independent of you or any thoughts you may project onto it. But you *feel* you possess it, and you can develop such a proprietary regard for it as to become pettily jealous if anyone else arrogates it.

A further temptation beckons. As time goes on, you become familiar with the rhythms of the various street encounters: 100 percent conversations, prolonged goodbyes, reciprocal gestures, straight man and principal. Now you can predict how they are likely to develop and, by predicting them, get the sense that you are somehow causing them as well. They are your people out there. Sheer delusion, of course, but there is nothing so satisfying as to see them all out there on the street doing what you expect they should be doing.

Three men at the corner are in a prolonged goodbye. One of them is slowly rocking back and forth on his heels. No one else is. At length, the man stops rocking back and forth. I chuckle to myself. I know that in a few moments another of the men will take up the rocking motion. Time passes. More time passes. No one budges. More time passes. At length, one of the men shifts his weight; slowly, he begins rocking back and forth on his heels. I am very pleased with myself.

APPENDIX A

DIGEST OF OPEN-SPACE ZONING PROVISIONS
NEW YORK CITY

In 1961 New York City enacted a zoning resolution that gave developers a floor-area bonus for providing plaza space. For each square foot of plaza space, the builder was allowed 10 feet of additional commercial floor area. The requirement of the plazas was that they be accessible to the public at all times. That, as it turned out, was about all they were.

The 1975 amendments required that plazas be *amenable* to the public as well, and laid down specific guidelines for insuring that they would be. The guidelines are presented here in slightly abridged form.

1975 ZONING AMENDMENTS

Seating

There shall be a minimum of 1 linear foot of seating for each 30 square feet of urban plaza area, except that for urban plazas fronting upon a street having a grade change of at least 2.25 feet in 100 feet or for through-block urban plazas, there shall be minimum of 1 linear foot of seating for each 40 square feet of urban plaza area.

Seating shall have a minimum depth of 16 inches. Seating with backs at least 12 inches high shall have a minimum depth of 14 inches. Seating 30 inches or more in depth shall count double provided there is access to both sides.

Seating higher than 36 inches and lower than 12 inches above the level of the adjacent walking surface shall not count toward meeting the seating requirements.

The tops of walls including but not limited to those which bound planting beds, fountains, and pools may be counted as seating when the conform to the dimensional standards above.

Movable seating or chairs, excluding seating of open air cafes, may be credited as 30 inches of linear seating per chair.

No more than 50 percent of the credited linear seating capacity may be in movable seats which may be stored between the hours of 7 P.M. and 7 A.M.

Steps, seats in outdoor amphitheaters, and seating of open air cafes do not count toward the seating requirements.

For the benefit of handicapped persons, a minimum of 5 percent of the required seating shall have backs.

Planting and Trees

At least one tree of 3.5 inches caliper or more shall be planted for each 25 feet of the entire street frontage of the zoning lot. They shall be planted with gratings flush to grade in at least 200 cubic feet of soil per tree, with a depth of soil at least 3 feet 6 inches.

Trees within an urban open space: For an urban plaza 1,500 square feet or more in area, 4 trees are required. For an urban plaza 5,000 square feet or more in area, 6 trees are required. For an urban plaza 12,000 square feet or more in area, 1 tree is required for every 2,000 square feet, or fraction thereof, of urban plaza area. Where trees are planted within an urban open space, they shall measure at least 3.5 inches in caliper at the time of planting. They shall be planted in at least 200 cubic feet of soil with a depth of soil of at least 3 feet 6 inches and be planted either with gratings flush to grade, or in a planting bed with a continuous area of at least 75 square feet exclusive of bounding wall, and at a maximum spacing of 25 feet apart.

Planting: When planting beds are provided, they shall have a soil depth of at least 2 feet for grass or other ground cover, and 3 feet for shrubs.

Retail Frontage

Except for that portion of a sidewalk widening along a narrow street, at least 50 percent of the total frontage of building walls of the development fronting on an urban open space, or fronting on an arcade adjoining an urban open space, exclusive of such frontage occupied by vertical circulation elements, building lobbies, and frontage used for subway access, shall be allocated for occupancy by retail or service establishments permitted by the applicable district regulations, but not including banks, loan offices, travel agencies, or airline offices. In addition, libraries, museums, and art galleries shall be permitted. All such uses shall be directly accessible from the urban open space or adjoining arcade.

Lighting

Urban open spaces shall be illuminated throughout with an overall minimum average level of illumination of not less than 2 horizontal foot candles (lumens per foot). Such level of illumination shall be maintained throughout the hours of darkness. Electrical power shall be supplied by 1 or more outlets furnishing a total of 1,200 watts of power for every 4,000 sq. ft., or fraction thereof, of an urban open space area, except for a sidewalk widening.

Circulation and Access

An urban plaza shall be open to use by the public at all times, with direct access from an adjoining public sidewalk or sidewalk widening along at least 50 percent of its total length of frontage. Along the remaining length of frontage, in order to allow maximum visibility from the street to the urban plaza, no wall may be constructed averaging higher than 36 inches above nor at any point higher than 5 feet above curb level of the nearest adjoining street.

The level of an urban plaza shall not at any point be more than 3 feet above nor 3 feet below the curb level of the nearest adjoining street.

Where there is a grade change of at least 2.25 feet in 100 along a portion of a street fronted upon for a distance of at least 75 feet by an urban plaza with an area of 10,000 square feet or more, the level of such urban plaza may be at any elevation which is not more than either 5 feet above or below curb level of the nearest adjoining street. Along the length of frontage not required for access, no wall higher than 36 inches above the level of the urban plaza may be constructed.

Where an entry to a subway station exists in the sidewalk area of a street on which an urban plaza fronts and such entry is not replaced within the urban plaza itself, the urban plaza shall be developed at the same elevation as the adjacent sidewalk for a distance of at least 15 feet in all directions from the entry superstructure. Such urban plaza area around a subway station entry shall be free of all obstructions.

Where an entry to a subway station is provided within the urban plaza itself, stairs shall have a minimum width of 10 feet.

An urban plaza or portion of an urban plaza extending through the block and connecting 2 streets which are parallel or within 45 degrees of being parallel to each other shall have a minimum width of 40 feet.

Any portion of a building wall adjoining such urban plaza for a length greater than 125 feet shall be limited to a maximum height of 85 feet above the urban plaza level, and above such height the building shall be set back not less than 15 feet from the urban plaza boundary, provided that such restriction shall not apply to any building wall adjoining an urban plaza which urban plaza has a minimum width of 75 feet.

Access for the Physically Disabled

There shall be at least 1 path of travel to each of the following:

- the major portion of the urban open space
- any building lobby accessible to the urban open space
- any use that may be present on, or adjacent to, the urban open space

Such paths shall have a minimum width of 5 feet, except where specific provisions require a greater width, free and clear of all obstructions.

Ramps are to be provided alongside any stairs or steps for such paths. Ramps shall have a minimum width of 36 inches, a slope of not greater than 1 in 12, a nonskid surface, and, for open-edged ramps, a 2-inch-high safety curb. At each end of a ramp there shall be a level area, which may be public sidewalk, at least 5 feet long.

All stairs or ramps within such paths shall provide handrails. Handrails shall be 32 inches high, have a midrail 22 inches high, and shall extend at least 18 inches beyond the stair or ramp ends.

Where stairs are used to effect changes of grade for such paths, they shall have closed risers, no projecting nosings, a maximum riser height of 7.5 inches, and a minimum tread width of 11 inches.

Food Facilities; Permitted Obstructions

Urban open space shall be unobstructed from its lowest level to the sky except for the following obstructions, which are permitted only in urban plazas and open air concourses, but not permitted in sidewalk widenings: any features, equipment, and appurtenances normally found in public parks and playgrounds, such as fountains and reflecting pools, waterfalls, sculptures and other works of art, arbors, trellises, benches, seats, trees, planting beds, litter receptacles, drinking fountains, and bicycle racks; open air cafes; kiosks; outdoor furniture; lights and lighting stanchions; flag poles; public telephones; temporary exhibitions; awnings; canopies; bollards; and subway station entrances which may include escalators. Kiosks, open air cafes, and open air amphitheaters and ice-skating rinks which charge admission may be placed within the area of an urban open space upon certification by the Chairman of the City Planning Commission and the Board of Estimate to the Commissioner of Buildings.

Where a kiosk is provided, it shall be a 1-story structure, predominantly of light materials, such as metal, glass, plastic, or fabric which does not exceed 150 square feet in area.

Where an open air cafe is provided it shall be a permanently unenclosed eating or drinking place, permitted by applicable district regulations, which may have waiter or table service, and is open to the sky except that it may have a temporary fabric roof in conformance with Building Code.

An open air cafe must be accessible from all sides where there is a boundary with the remainder of the urban open space.

An open air cafe may occupy an aggregate area not more than 20 percent of the total area of the urban open space.

No kitchen equipment shall be installed within an open air cafe. Kitchen equipment may be contained in a kiosk adjoining the open air cafe.

An open air cafe qualifying as a permitted obstruction shall be excluded from the definition of floor area.

Outdoor eating services or uses occupying kiosks may serve customers on urban open space through open windows.

For wheelchair users, where drinking fountains are placed in an urban open space, at least on fountain shall be 30 inches high, be hand and foot operated, and display the International Symbol of Access.

Maintenance

The building owner shall be responsible for the maintenance of the urban open space including, but not limited to, the confinement of permitted obstructions, litter control, and the care and replacement of vegetation within the zoning lot and in the street sidewalk area adjacent to the zoning lot.

Performance Bond

Prior to obtaining any certificate of occupancy from the Department of Buildings, the building owner shall provide to the Comptroller of the City of New York, a performance bond or the City securities to ensure the mandatory tree planting, movable seating and the litter-free maintenance of the urban open space including the replacement of such trees and movable furniture during the life of the development.

In the event of a failure in the required performance, the Chairman of the City Planning Commission shall notify the building owner in writing of such failure and shall stipulate the period of time in which the building owner has to correct the failure. If the failure is not corrected in the stipulated time the Chairman may declare the building owner in default in the required performance, and the City may enforce the obligation by whatever means may be appropriate to the situation, including letting contracts for doing any required planting, installation or maintenance and paying all labor, material and other costs connected with such work from the bond or City securities the building owner is required to provide.

Plaque

A plaque or other permanent sign shall be displayed in a prominent location on any urban open space for which a bonus is granted. Such sign shall indicate number of trees, and number of movable chairs, and any other features whose listing may be required by the City Planning Commission, the name of the owner and whomever he has designated to maintain the urban open space.

Existing Plazas

For plazas built prior to this amendment, kiosks and cafes may be placed within the area of the plaza upon certification by the chairman of the City Planning Commission and the Board of Estimate that such uses would promote public use and enjoyment, stabilize desirable uses in the surrounding area, are part of a general improvement including more seating and landscaping, and that the uses will be maintained by the owner.

Other Provisions

Location and orientation: Southern exposure is required wherever possible. To protect the continuity of the street wall, the frontage a plaza can occupy is restricted when there are other large spaces nearby.

Proportional restrictions: To discourage strip plazas, width of plazas must not be less than a third of the length.

Open-air concourses: These apply to spaces adjacent to subway stations and were written with the proposed Second Avenue subway in mind. They call for a sunken plaza at mezzanine level of no less than 4,000 square feet nor more than 8,000. At street level there should be walkways at least 20 feet wide, and, space permitting, a street-level plaza.

APPENDIX B

MANDATING OF RETAILING AT STREET LEVEL

In the 1975 tightening of requirements for open-space bonuses, the New York City Planning Commission took a first step toward banning blank-wall frontages. It required that as a condition of the bonus at least 50 percent of the frontage on the plaza be devoted to retail uses.

In the 1982 revision of midtown zoning, the commission went further. It required that all of the frontage on retail streets be used for retailing, whether there was a bonus or not. Stores had to be accessible from the street, and the glass fronts had to be of transparent glass.

Below is the commission's "plain English" explanation, and the abridged text.

81-42 Retail Continuity along Designated Streets

The vitality of retail commercial streets depends upon a continuous row of retail establishments which can draw pedestrian shoppers along the length of the street. Areas occupied by open space or non-retail uses can interrupt the flow of shopping pedestrians and impair retail activity along nearby frontages. The provisions of this section are designed to protect the retail activity along designated streets by restricting ground floor occupancy to those commercial uses which will enhance the existing retail character.

Abridged text:

81-42 On designated retail streets . . . a building's street frontage shall be allocated exclusively to [retail, personal service, or amusement] uses . . . Museums and libraries shall be permitted . . . Store fronts for the permitted ground floor uses shall be not more than 10 feet from the street line or, where an arcade is provided with supporting columns at the street line, not more than ten feet from the supporting columns.

In no event shall the amount of street frontage occupied by lobby space or entrance space or a building entrance recess exceed 40 feet.

81-142 On wide street frontages in underlying C5 commercial districts, at least 50 percent of a building's street wall surface shall be glazed and transparent at ground floor level.

New York City Planning Commission, *Midtown Zoning* (New York: 1982). (Available from the commission at 7 Lafayette Street, New York, N.Y. 10007.)

NOTES

Chapter 2. The Social Life of the Street

p. 8   The ordinary encounters of everyday street life can be filmed quite unobtrusively. One way is to shoot from afar with a telephoto lens. This perspective is all right for tracking shots and pedestrian flows. But it is all wrong for most street activity. For that you should get up close, and the closer the better. Facial expressions, hand gestures, feet movements: you want to move in for these. The problem, of course, is to do this without your subjects' being aware of your interest. But on a busy street they usually pay you no heed. To keep it that way, I find that it is important not to hold the camera up to eye level and point it at them. I mount a spirit level atop my cine cameras. If I look down at it, the camera cradled in my arms, I can be reasonably sure the subjects are properly framed. I use a very wide angle lens to assure this—and to give me enough depth of field for good focus. I stand off to one side and try to keep the people at the edge of my peripheral vision. I never look at them directly. If they catch you doing this they are on to you immediately—and you are affecting that which you are studying. Jan Gehl's continuing studies of Copenhagen's street life showed a significant increase in activity. Between 1968 and 1986, the center city population declined 33 percent. The number of pedestrians using the area, however, increased 25 percent. There was a qualitative improvement too. People were not only coming to the center more frequently; they were staying longer when they came.

p. 10   An excellent study of waiting behavior has been carried out by Professor Hidetoshi Kato and some of his students at Tokyo's Gakushuin University. The waiting place: the plaza in front of Shibuya Station, Tokyo, with the statue of faithful dog Hachiko. Hachiko was the pet of a Professor Uneo. Every morning Hachiko would go to the station to see his master off, and every evening he would return to greet him. One day Professor Uneo died and did not come back. Day after day Hachiko would go to the station to greet him. People were touched by this loyalty. Hachiko became famous. People contributed money to have a statue of him placed outside the station. It became the leading rendezvous place of Tokyo.

Professor Kato mounted a time-lapse camera above the square and recorded the daily activity. His students interviewed the people who were waiting for someone. People were consistent in their choice of places to wait, the number-one location being slightly off-center from the statue. People were consistent also in their bench use. As with New York sitters, those who sat for long periods were strongly outnumbered by those who sat for short periods—but the long-termers accounted for the great bulk of the available seat minutes. Averaged elapsed time of waiting was thirteen minutes during the day, nine in the evening. The Japanese are very punctilious and can exhibit considerable annoyance when waiting overlong. Americans are more casual about this, but then they are more casual about turning up on time.

Most of the waiting is requited, but sometimes it is not. To Professor Kato the square is theatre: "This is the place," he says, "where young lovers say hello to each other at 5 P.M. and say good night at 9 P.M. This is the place where the drama begins and the drama ends. Happy stories and sad stories."

Hidetoshi Kato, "A Study of Waiting Behavior," in *A Comparative Study of Street Life: Tokyo, Manila, and New York,* Hidetoshi Kato, Randolph David, William H. Whyte (Tokyo: Gakushuin University, 1978).

p. 11   Our counts showed a fairly consistent distribution of people by size of group. At Seagram Plaza the proportion of people alone averaged 38 percent; the proportion in groups, 62 percent. People in pairs, 38 percent; in threesomes, 12 percent, in fours or more, 12 percent. At the Exxon Plaza the proportion alone was 47 percent; in groups, 53 percent. People in pairs, 34 percent; in threesomes, 11 percent; in fours or more, 8 percent. Counts were of people sitting, with the exception of standees who were part of a sitting group.

Low percentages of people in groups are an indication something is wrong. The steps of the New York Public Library, which had been a popular place for sitters, had a level of only 33 percent in groups in 1974. The place was infested with drug dealers. Since then the flanking terraces have been reclaimed with food kiosks and chairs and tables. The percentage of people in groups is back around 50–60. On the streets of midtown New York the percentage of pedestrians who are in groups runs about 60.

W. R. Berkowitz's study of group percentages in various countries indicated that of people on main avenues, 61.6 percent in Turkey, Iran, Afghanistan were in groups of two or more; 61 percent in England; 56.8 percent in Sweden; 51.4 percent in Italy; 48.9 percent in the United States.

W. R. Berkowitz, "A Cross-national Comparison of Some Social Patterns of Urban Pedestrians," *Journal of Cross-Cultural Psychology* 2: 129–144.

p. 11   An exchange in the New York *Times* has prompted an excellent definition of schmoozing. In an article on the subject, writer William Geist had said it was the same as kibitzing. Not so, said Morton Weinfeld, chairman of the sociology department of Montreal's McGill University. In a letter to the editor (July 19, 1987) he observed that "to schmooze is to engage in a relaxed, amiable, meandering conversation. Good schmoozing is an egalitarian, collaborative effort. Kibitzing is competitive, more like repartee. A needle here, a bon mot there, a quip, a put-down, a non sequitur are the kibitzer's stock in trade. Indeed, the kibitzer is a parasite who lives off the schmoozer."

p. 15   David Efron, *Gesture, Race, and Culture* (Mastor: The Hague 1972) 94–107, 121–30; excerpted in *The Body Reader,* ed. Ted Pelhemus (New York, Pantheon Books, 1978).

A tentative study of some of the spatio-temporal and "linguistic" aspects of the gestural behavior of Eastern Jews and Southern Italians in New York City, living under similar as well as different environmental conditions.

Chapter 3. Street People

p. 26   It is in order to be as unobtrusive as possible, but in studying a particular place—such as Lexington Avenue in the Upper Fifties—the regulars spot you very quickly. If you are frank with them and explain what you are up to, they can be quite helpful. On Lexington we ended up knowing a larger number of regulars than we expected to be there: proprietors of small stores; haircutting establishments, and their hawkers and handbill passers; bus dispatchers, traffic people, various shills and messengers—even several of the "six lovely conversationalists" who used to lean out the third-floor window of the Lexington Rap Club. Street vendors could be a problem. They tend to be very suspicious, particularly of people with cameras. Dope dealers are the worst. You never can be sure who is a dope dealer and who isn't. In some areas, if you film in any direction you are quite likely to film a dope transaction, whether you realize it or not. The dealers do not like this at all. In Bryant Park, which they long regarded as their territory, it was risky to even carry a camera.

p. 26   A salute is in order. When we started observing people on the streets of Tokyo, we found that an avid observer had been doing the same thing fifty years before. He was Wajiro Kon, a noted ethnologist of indefatigable curiosity. He charted the daily flows of students as they went to school and back; he charted the character of the crowds at various places, with a detailed breakdown of their dress, apparent age, and occupation. He noted how many people were in groups (75 percent on Ginza streets), and how far they walked. He even plotted the locations of suicides in Hibaya Park.

Wajiro Kon, *Kogengaku: Studies of the Past and Present* (1930; reprint, Tokyo: Domesu, 1971). In it Kon used the word "modernologio," or studies in modernology, to describe his work.

p. 27   The importance to street vendors of helpers and allies is noted in Randolph David's fine study of Manila's street life: "In addition to the police the practical problems of vending are the simple problems of surviving a particularly slow and boring day without falling asleep, of getting a quick meal, or using the toilet while one's wares continue to be on display. For all these needs, a companion is needed. And, indeed, it seems standard policy for vendors to go at least in pairs. Unavoidably, a number of vendors will not be able to bring a companion. In such cases, fellow vendors tend to assume the responsibility for assisting one another. We have observed that, for instance, ambulant vendors effectively play the role of companion to many of their static and semi-static counterparts."

p. 38   An interesting part of Judge Aspen's decision in *Friedrich v. Chicago* concerned break dancing. As in New York, so in Chicago break dancing surfaced as a fad in 1983. Everywhere one looked, it seemed, young blacks were staking out large swaths of sidewalk and doing acrobatics to music—loud music. Some of them were terrible: a few inept people jumping up and down to a portable tape player. But some were really quite talented and put on a show that attracted large crowds. It was these crowds, Judge Aspen noted, that caused most of the mischief.

But break dancing peaked in 1984 and is now performed only sporadically. This raises a question. If break dancing was the only major threat to public safety and if it has largely disappeared, why then the ordinance? In a section that could be subtitled "Much Ado About Break Dancing," Judge Aspen tackled the question:

"If it is true that breakdancing has gone the way of the hula hoop and is a faded fad, then perhaps the frequency of large audiences has substantially fallen . . . Thus, if the City chooses to renew the ordinance next year, it would be well advised to consider the passing of the breakdancing phenomenon in its evaluation. If it has passed, and if—as the evidence showed—most other performers attract only small crowds, the constitutional underpinnings of the ordinance may have vanished for future years."

Friedrich v. City of Chicago, 619 F. Supp. 1129 (N.D. Ill. 1985), *vacated* F 2d, (7th Cir. November 25, 1986) Judge Marvin E. Aspen.

Chapter 4. The Skilled Pedestrian

p. 56   Erving Goffman has given us the best definition of the pedestrian compact: "City streets, even in times which defame them, provide a setting where mutual trust is routinely displayed between strangers. Voluntary coordination of action is achieved in which each of the two parties has a conception of how matters ought to be handled between them, the two conceptions agree, each party believes this agreement exists, and each appreciates that this knowledge about the agreement is possessed by the other. In brief, the structural prerequisites for rule by convention are found. Avoidance of collision is one example of the consequences."

Erving Goffman, *Relations in Public* (New York: Harper Colophon, 1972), 17.

p. 58   For gauging pedestrian speeds, the simplest and most accurate technique is to follow pedestrians with a stopwatch over a set distance and note the elapsed time. New York's avenues are conveniently laid out for this, the north-south blockfronts running 200 feet from building line to building line. On Fifth Avenue at mid-morning on a mild day, men will traverse the 200 feet in 40 to 42 seconds on average—about 300 feet a minute, 3.4 miles an hour. The range of speeds is broad, running from 32 to 60

seconds. (As noted elsewhere, the traffic lights are timed for drivers'
convenience, going red just as the pedestrian arrives at the crosswalk.)

p. 57   A number of studies bear out the pedestrian's inclination to the direct
route. In one such study sociologist Michael Hill tracked 250 pedestrians
on routine trips. The overwhelming majority followed at least-distance
route. Women tended to take a more complex route than men; younger
people than older people.

     Michael R. Hill, Department of Sociology, University of Nebraska
Proceedings of the Third Annual Conference on the Pedestrian; Boulder,
Colorado; 1983.

p. 57   Passing technique, one of the cooperative behaviors Goffman cites, is the
subject of an interesting study by psychologist Michael Wolff. On New
York's Forty-second Street he and a female associate took turns approaching pedestrians. They would focus on a pedestrian moving on a
straight-line collision course in the middle of the flow. Some of the pedestrians would not chicken, thus forcing a confrontation. But most made
way. The median yielding distance was about seven feet in low-density
situations, five feet in high. "A common behavior," says Wolff, "especially between members of the same sex, was not total detour and avoidance of contact, but a slight angling of the body, a turning of the body
and an almost imperceptible side step—a step and slide. When a pedestrian executed a step-and-slide, he did not move out of the path of the
oncoming pedestrian to totally avoid contact or bumping; for a clear
'pass' to occur, the cooperation of the other pedestrian was required and
given. People with bags and packages made less effort to accommodate."

     Michael Wolff, "Notes on the Behavior of Pedestrians," reprinted in
People in Places: The Sociology of the Familiar, eds. Arnold Birenbaum
and Edward Sagarin (New York: Praeger, 1973).

p. 57   Eric Knowles notes that studies of movement in crowded situations tend
to treat pedestrians as multiples of the basic one-person unit. This obscures the fact that a pair of pedestrians may act differently than two
individual pedestrians. When an oncoming pedestrian indicates that he is
going to pass directly between a pair, the pair will resist giving way and
may mutter expressions of displeasure.

     Eric S. Knowles, "Boundaries Around Social Space: Dyadic Re-
sponses to an Invader," *Environment and Behavior* (December 1972).

p. 64   Psychologists Mark and Helen Bornstein have plotted the relationship
between the size of a city and the speed of its pedestrians. Over a two-
year period they checked the speeds of pedestrians in fifteen cities and
towns in six countries in Europe, Asia, and North America. At each
place they measured off a fifty-foot stretch along the principal street.
Then they timed the pedestrians who were walking alone and unencumbered. They chose sunny days with moderate temperatures, and periods
when there was little congestion. At the end of two years they plotted the
data on a chart with two scales: one for the population of the city; the
other for the pedestrian speed average. The relationship between the two
was remarkably close; the more populous the city, the faster people
walked. Comparisons of places within a country indicated that city dwellers walked significantly faster than their smaller-town compatriots.

Mark H. Bornstein and Helen Bornstein, "The Pace of Life," *Nature* (February 19, 1976).

p. 65   We used several techniques for checking speeds of pedestrians. One was to film them as they traversed a block. Our best perch was a fifth-floor balcony overlooking the east blockfront of Lexington Avenue between Fifty-seventh and Fifty-eighth streets. This was an extremely crowded place, with all kinds of obstacles and diversions. By tracking pedestrians one at a time we could, with considerable precision, gauge their speeds at any point in their trip and record the retards and accelerations. This was especially useful when we were studying the influence of window displays, obstructions, and the like.

p. 63   In his studies of pedestrians in Copenhagen, Jan Gehl found that in cold weather pedestrians averaged one hundred meters in 62 seconds. This is brisk going, equivalent to two hundred feet in 37 seconds.

p. 62   How harmful is a fast pace? Robert V. Levine and Kathy Bartlett of California State University, Fresno, investigated the relationship between pace of life and the incidence of coronary heart disease in six countries. For pace of life they measured walking speeds in central business districts, the accuracy of public clocks in banks, and the promptness of postal workers in fulfilling requests for stamps. As expected, cities in the more economically advanced countries had the fastest pace; cities in the least developed, the slowest. Within countries, walking speeds were higher in the bigger cities than the smaller.

One hypothesis did not prove out. Pace failed to correlate with coronary heart deaths. In this respect, Japan was the clear winner. It has the most accurate clocks, the fastest walkers, the promptest postal workers. It also had the lowest incidence of coronaries. Overload, to twist a point, may be good for you.

One oddity: in the tests of how long it took postal workers to fill an order for stamps, the United States did very well, with an average time of 26.7 seconds. And New York City was included in the study!

Robert J. Levine and Kathy Bartlett, "Pace of Life, Punctuality, and Coronary Heart Disease in Six Countries," *Journal of Cross-Cultural Psychology* (June 1984).

Chapter 5. The Physical Street

p. 69   Why not have expandable sidewalks? Traffic engineers have been inventive in shifting roadway space to match changes in vehicle flow, instituting counterflow lanes at peak times. But little has been done for pedestrian flows. They are as swingy as vehicle flows; furthermore, there are potential fits between the two. On Lexington Avenue, for example, the chart of daily pedestrian flows traces a characteristic central business district pattern: three peaks—A.M., midday, and P.M.—with the highest volume at midday. The vehicle flows, by contrast, trace a saucer pattern, with the low points coming at the pedestrian high points. If the whole right-of-way was at grade, it would be possible to expand the sidewalk space at noon by moving markers out five feet or so thus contracting the vehicle space accordingly. At 2 P.M. the markers could be repositioned. Outlandish? The present imbalance in supply and demand certainly is.

p. 76   Based on his study of Copenhagen's pedestrians, architect Jan Gehl figured that a flow rate between ten and fifteen people per meter of walking
width per minute is a good density range for a street. Per foot of walkway
this translates into three to five people per minute—just about halfway
between Fruin's seven people and RPA's two. If there is a happy medium,
this is about where it lies.

Chapter 6. The Sensory Street

p. 79   To study Lexington is to realize how significant can be the *non*movement
of pedestrians. Most pedestrian studies scant this, being primarily concerned with the journey from A to B. They do not tell us much about
what happens between A and B—or the fact that sometimes the pedestrian never gets to B at all. To chart the incidents of the journey, we made
a series of tracking shots of people walking north on a Lexington block
front. Here is what happened to ninety-five of them: sixteen went into one
of the stores on the block; one turned around and walked back south; two
stopped for a midblock conversation lasting five minutes; seventy-six
completed the journey, with an average elapsed time of fifty-eight seconds
—slow compared to speeds on duller, less busy streets. What the pedestrian walks by can materially affect this pace. As they passed the florist's
stand, some people slowed, then made up for lost time by accelerating as
they came to the dull facade of the Manufacturers Hanover Trust.

The vexations of city officials in keeping order are much like those of
their counterparts in medieval England. In his book *Street Life in Medieval England* (Oxford, 1939) G. T. Salusbury-Jones tells how earnestly
they tried to keep traffic moving on the main streets. They were frus-
trated by the narrowness of them, the encroachments, such as pens and
stalls, and they were especially annoyed by the shod cart and its metallic
banging. They also had a problem with pigs; they liked the street because
it was so full of refuse.

Streets were very noisy: There were bells of all kinds constantly
ringing; the crying of wares; the sound of wooden galoshes; craftsmen
banging away in their stalls, which were open to the street; the clatter of
shod cart wheels. Not until noon, at the "schenche," or noon-drink, was
there a respite.

p. 87   My research in Japan was limited to three visits. The first was in 1975,
when a group of planners and designers from New York met to compare
notes with officials of that estimable bureaucracy, the Tokyo Metropolitan Government. The meeting was sponsored by the Japan Society of
New York and the International House of Tokyo. In 1977 Professor
Hidetoshi Kato of Gakushuin University set up a workshop to plan comparative research on the street life of New York, Tokyo, and Manila. The
principals were Professor Kato, Professor Randolph David of the University of the Philippines, and myself. Assisting were Margaret Bemiss
and Rebecca Irwin. The study was published in 1978: *A Comparative
Study of Street Life: Tokyo, Manila, New York.* Gakushuin University
1978.

In 1981, in connection with a symposium organized by the *Yomuiri
Shimbun,* I visited Japan again and followed up on our previous studies
of Tokyo's pedestrian life.

p. 87   While the Chuo-Dori sidewalks did draw the most people, the center of the street was fairly active. Because of its breadth it induced promenading, much as the Madison Avenue closing had. Family groups walked three and four abreast. Children appeared to be setting the pace, with the parents affecting to be just tagging along. As our film record showed, the children seemed to be leading in the direction the parents wanted to follow. There was a high degree of convergence on the many food vendors, a large proportion of which were employed by the department stores.

p. 87   The Madison mall was a case of myth destroying reality. One of the charges levied at the mall was its presumed attraction for undesirables. The place was overrun with them, merchants said. In an effort to resuscitate the mall, Mayor John Lindsay invited merchants and others to a breakfast meeting and had me show our film record of the mall activity. There was a flautist and several off types visible in the footage of the opening-day crowds, but thereafter the scene was one of utmost respectability. But some merchants still would not believe what they saw. One accused me of doctoring the film.

Other mall projects did go through, however. Nassau Street in the Wall Street area, so crowded as to be in fact a mall, was made a regular one. Fulton Street in Brooklyn was closed to all but bus traffic and was spruced up with canopies and benches and other amenities.

Chapter 7. The Design of Spaces

p. 112   Architect Philip Johnson on seating at Seagram:
"We designed those blocks in front of the Seagram Building so people could not sit on them, but, you see, people want to so badly that they sit there anyhow. They like that place so much that they crawl, inch along that little narrow edge of the wall. We put the water near the marble ledge because we thought they'd fall over if they sat there. They don't fall over; they get there *anyhow*."
Interviewer: "Well, it's the only place you *can* sit."
Philip Johnson: "I know it. It never crossed Mies' mind. Mies told me afterward, 'I never dreamt people would want to sit there.'"
John W. Cook and Heinrich Klotz, *Conversations with Architects* (New York: Praeger, 1973).

p. 121   As with car parkers and other users of space, long-term users account for the bulk of the available seat minutes of a place. At the IBM garden, for example, close-up analysis of sitting patterns at three tables revealed that from 12:30 P.M. to 7 P.M. there was a total of fifty-six sitters, accounting for 1,077 seat minutes. Average stay: 19 minutes. Median stay: 17 minutes. Of the fifty-six sitters, seventeen accounted for 54 percent of the total seat minutes.

At the IBM garden the tables are fixed to the floor. But the chairs are not. Most people sit next to the tables but some move the chairs somewhere else. This affords a good indication of what would likely be the preferred locations for additional chairs and tables. The chair movers,

like beach-umbrella people, tend to locate just beyond the existing locations. Few leapfrog out to a distant spot.

p. 121   An annoying variant of the fixed seat is the airport arrangement of rows
of chairs bolted together. An armrest is often provided, not so much for
comfort as to defeat efforts to stretch out—as one might wish to do if he
missed the red-eye special. Robert Sommer sees airport seating arrangements as part of an institutional failure to recognize the social aspects of
airports. They seem deliberately designed, he says, "to eliminate conversation among passengers. The rows of seats are placed back-to-back or
arranged classroom style facing the counter where the ticket agent plays
the role of teacher . . . To see most waiting rooms one would never
know coat racks had been invented . . . Some people come to the airport alone, but a sizeable number arrive with family, friends, and business
associates. To see them sitting dumbly side by side in the shiny plastic
chairs is saddening."

Robert Sommer, "Megaports," *New York Times*, March 3, 1974.

p. 123   Lincoln Center provided another lesson in seating. Dry seating is better
than wet. Lincoln Center had lots of ledge space around its many tree
planters, and it was the right height for sitting. At just the times when it
was most needed, however, it was interdicted to human use. At noon the
sprinkler heads imbedded in the planters cycled on, spraying the ground
cover, the ledges, and any people foolish enough as to be sitting on them.
After about an hour the sprays would cease, and if the sun was shining,
the ledges would be almost dry enough to sit on after the matinees began.
The functionary who was in charge of such matters was prevailed upon
to shift the spraying times, and thus was the amount of seating available
at the Center quintupled, albeit for a limited time. As is the case in such
situations, however, don't bet against the house. Offsetting the increase in
ledge seating, the functionary sequestered the supply of movable chairs in
the cellar areas, thereby preventing their use by undesirables and members of the public.

p. 128   The Commissioners of Central Park told Frederick Law Olmsted to put a
fence around it. He responded vigorously:

"It is not desirable that the outer park should be separated by any barrier
more than a common stone curb from the adjoining roadways. It is still
more undesirable in the interest of those who are to use it that it should
be separated more than is necessary from the interior park . . . The
trees which grow upon it are used in design as part of the scenery of the
main park, adding to its beauty, attractiveness and value. The scenery of
the main park should much more be made to add to the beauty, attractiveness and value of the outer park. As far as it is practicable the two
should be incorporated as one whole, each being part of the other."

As for iron fences:

"I consider the iron fence to be unquestionably the ugliest that can be
used. If on the score of utility, it must be used then the less the better, and
certainly where used, it should not be elaborated and set up on high,
and made large and striking as if it were something admirable in itself,

and had better claims to be noticed that the scenery which it crosses and obscures."*

p. 129   Another amphitheater pattern like that of Rockefeller Plaza is provided by the Citicorp Building in New York. Its sunken plaza has two levels, and bordering it at street level above are sittable ledges. During a summertime luncheon concert we noted the distribution of 400 people. In the lowest part of the plaza there were 80 people; on the first flight of steps up, another 80; on the next level the main steps, 90; on the street level ledges, 150 people.

The distribution of people at the sunken plaza of the First National Bank of Chicago is similar. At a time when there was total of 800 people sitting, our counts showed that 45 percent were sitting on the lower plaza; 15 percent on the first flight of steps up from it; 40 percent on the upper flight and mezzanine level. On the surrounding sidewalks a constantly changing cast of onlookers looked down at the scene.

Our findings meshed with those of a study by Professor Albert Rutledge and a group of his students of the department of landscape architecture of the University of Illinois, Urbana. Using basic "pen and pencil" methodology, in a short period of time he came up with a fine evaluation of the plaza and a set of recommendations that could make it work better. "First National Bank Plaza: A Pilot Study in Post Construction Evaluation" (Urbana, June 1975).

Chapter 8. Water, Wind, Trees, and Light

p. 134   A fine study with strong emphasis on climatic aspects of urban space is Don C. Miles with Robert S. Cook, Jr., and Cameron B. Roberts, *Plazas for People* (New York: Project for Public Spaces, 1978). Based on an analysis of Seattle spaces, the study shows the shortcomings of the standard plaza format in places where there is a good bit of rain and wind. It proposes designs sensitively tailored to these realities.

To chart the relationship between climate and the voluntary activity on an open space, a photographic record was made of a plaza of Virginia Polytechnic Institute at various times. This was then related to temperature, insolation, wind speed, and humidity. The correlation was very strong and afforded a basis for predicting probable levels of activity.

Dean R. Bork and Whit Watts, "Research: Climate and Behavior," *Landscape Architecture* (July/August 1985).

p. 136   Some architects do not like trees much, big trees in particular. They upstage the elevations of the architect's building. It was for this reason that one of the largest plazas in the country was planted with small, scraggly trees. They would not mar one's view of the building.

Architects who exact such underplanting are committing visual error. In a static view—such as that of an architectural photograph—a tree can block out a part of the view. In a moving view, which is the way we more often perceive spaces and structures, trees do no block out the view.

* Excerpts from a letter to the Board of Commissioners of Central Park, April 1960. Frederick Law Olmsted, *Forty Years of Landscape Architecture: Central Park,* edited by Frederick Law Olmsted and Theodora Kimball (Cambridge, Mass.: M.I.T. Press, 1975).

As with the shutter of a movie camera, the succession of intermittent views is constantly revealing.

Another source of visual error is the plan view. Those round stamps that denote trees can seem to block out a view, when in fact the trees do not do so on the ground. This confusion was a factor in the competition for the redo of Boston's Copley Square. One feature of the existing square that the jury hoped contestants would leave intact was a lovely bosque of linden trees. Most of the contestants eliminated the bosque. Principal reason: it would block the line of sight of a key diagonal. But it would not. The understory of the lindens, now twenty years old, is high enough to clear the view from one end of the diagonal to the other, and a lot else besides. In the winning design of landscape architect Dean Abbott, the lindens stay. And for the first time there will be places to sit under them.

p. 137   Some transportation engineers do not like trees. The trees can wreak havoc with underground utilities; they take up valuable space that vehicles could put to better use. The bigger they are, the more trouble. So they go. Even in Paris, as Norma Evenson relates in her account of the street widenings of the 1950s and their decimation of the city's great legacy of street trees. Avenues that previously carried a double row of trees on each side were reduced to one row on each side, and many streets lost all of their trees.

Norma Evenson, *Paris: A Century of Change* (New Haven, Conn.: Yale University Press; 1979.).

Chapter 9. The Management of Spaces

p. 142   One objection to outdoor cafés is that they have become a cliché, gazebos especially. It was not always thus. Some years ago architectural renderings of ideal squares and plazas almost always featured outdoor cafés, Paris-style kiosks, a hurdy-gurdy man, and children holding balloons. This was OK fashion, possibly because in actual life such amenities were absent. Now that cafés are becoming more of a reality purists are less tolerant of them. In a design competition for the possible redoing of Grace Plaza in New York, 260 entries from design schools were submitted. Of these, only 6 included anything as rudimentary as chairs or tables, and only 1 of these made the finals. Several noted architects on the jury commented favorably on the relative absence of such "banal" features. No proposal was adopted. The plaza remains one of the worst plazas in the city.

Chapter 10. The Undesirables

p. 156   For a perceptive study of teenage "undesirables" see Nancy Linday, "Drawing Socio-economic Lines in Central Park: An Analysis of New York's Cultural Clashes," *Landscape Architecture* (November 1977). Back in 1973 we were asked by then Park Commissioner Richard Clurman to undertake a study of the troubles at Bethesda Fountain. It had become the central rendezvous for Hispanic teenagers, and there were problems with dope and vandalism. One of our best observers, Nancy Linday, spent a summer there as part of the scene. She found that the place was one of the few where the teenagers were welcome, and most of them were making good use of it, however raucous they might seem to the tourists who came to gawk at them. Among her recommendations: enlist the teenagers in programming and maintenance; make more use of their leaders as "mayors."

p. 156   "Undesirables" were one of the reasons the proposed Madison Avenue mall was beaten down. During the two-week trial of it our cameras recorded what went on. The film showed clearly that the people who used the mall were the people who worked and shopped in the area. But some retailers saw "undesirables." If the place had been overrun with angels they would have see undesirables. While I was talking to one shop owner, she noted two young women in blue jeans writing things on pads. "There they are!" said the shop owner, pointing to two of our observers.

p. 158   The Project for Public Spaces has used direct observation and time-lapse photography for a series of studies of key open spaces, ranging from Harlem's 125th Street to visitor centers of the National Park Service. It has been most effective in retrofitting problem spaces. One was the Exxon Minipark in New York City. It had been invaded by dope dealers, and the management had reacted by putting up a high fence. The dope dealers were delighted; the fence made it easier to them to dominate the place. The PPS recommendations were based on the proposition that the best way to ward off adverse uses was to make the place all the more lively and useful for people in general. Among the changes made: more alfresco food facilities, tables, chairs, music, and entertainment. The place has been doing very well ever since. A twelve-minute video is available on this study and reports on a range of studies. Project for Public Spaces, 153 Waverly Place, New York, N. Y. 10014.

p. 161   In an excellent study for the upgrading of Lincoln Center's concourse center and shops, consultant Paco Underfill made special note of the ladies' room. It was the same size as the men's room and, like most ladies' rooms in public places, had a line outside it at peak times. He recommended that it be at least doubled in size, a preferable ratio being 2½ to 1. This has not yet been done. Paco Underhill, "Vive la Différence," Express (1984).

p. 162   An oddity in the plans for some office buildings are the plans for the equipment floors. The equipment is mostly for air-conditioning and heating; otherwise the floors are empty and thus do not count as part of the developer's quota of allowable commercial space. On one plan I saw recently there was a full-size men's room and a full-size women's room. Since no one save a few engineers would ever visit the floor, the provision did seem wasteful. But was it? Someday, perhaps, the developer might find that he didn't really need that equipment floor. Maybe it could be used for offices. With rest rooms already in place.

Paris, birthplace of the *vespasienne,* is trying out a new style of comfort station. Instead of the traditional cylindrical structure for men, there is an oval-shaped, fully enclosed structure and it is for either men or women. It contains a washbasin and toilet. When the patron closes the door on leaving, a self-cleaning and disinfecting process is automatically started.

Chapter 14. Megastructures

p. 207   In a biting critique of megastructures, William G. Conway, a former associate of architect John Portman, has noted the baneful effect they can have on the spaces between them. In "The Case Against Urban Dinosaurs" (*Saturday Review* May 14, 1977), Conway holds that these controlled environments reveal the architect's hostility to the city he professes to save. In Atlanta, says Conway, "the five huge architectural jewels in the South's queen city are transforming her crown into fool's gold. This reverse alchemy is laying waste the downtown *between* the megastructures. In so doing it obeys the laws of economics now ignored by the project sponsors and by the city officials who clamor for more megastructures without first knowing the effects of those already constructed."

p. 214   Titles of articles on Renaissance Center, in chronological order:

> "Megastructures for Renewal: A Strong Visual Form, High Densities and Citizen Participation Are Proposed for a Megastructure with Promise for Renewal Areas," *Architectural Forum* (June 1967).
>
> "Soaring Costs Threaten Huge Center for Downtown Detroit," *New York Times,* April 2, 1975.
>
> "Flawed Fortresses: Residential-Business Towers of the 1960's Yield to Separate, Coordinated Structures," *The Wall Street Journal,* May 19, 1978.
>
> "Detroit's Symbol of Pride Is in the Red," *New York Times,* November 1, 1981.
>
> "The Ren Cen: Owners Plan Large Scale Redesign," *Detroit Free Press,* April 24, 1985.
>
> "Ren Cen Will Get a Friendlier Look," *Detroit News,* May 1, 1985.
>
> "Detroit's Symbol of Revival Now Epitomizes Its Problems," *New York Times,* September 1, 1986.

p. 214   Commenting on Boston's Lafayette Place, in the Boston *Globe,* architectural critic Robert Campbell really let fly: "One doesn't quite know where to begin in castigating this lemon. From the outside it is ashen and depressing almost beyond credibility. Its worst side is its east-facing front, the side you see from the financial district. Connoisseurs of architectural disaster should position themselves carefully two or three blocks back from Lafayette Place on Bedford Street to savor its full impact.

"Any important building should offer its energies and its trust to the street. Instead, Lafayette Place turns a gray shoulder to the street, looking more like a prison than a row of storefronts. Its blank walls and locked doors are an insult to the city and its people . . . Lafayette Place is a suburban mall dropped into the middle of a city, an inward looking building with all its life hidden inside and nothing but blank walls facing toward the world around it." Robert Campbell, "The Very Complex Lafayette Place," *Boston Globe,* September 3, 1986.

p. 217   An internal space you can find your way around easily is the Mayfair shopping mall in Coconut Grove, Florida. Architect-developer Kenneth Treister designed it to have clear orientation cues. He did not, for one thing, have symmetrical walkways, as is usually the practice. Each walk-way is different from the others: corridor widths vary; so do colors and the heights of ceilings. Signage is not consistent, but changes from shop to shop. All this uniqueness does make for some visual busyness but it is pleasant. And you do find your way around.

Chapter 15. Blank Walls

p. 222   A notable blank wall is the one recently built for the Los Angeles County Museum of Art. It takes the wicked pen of Manuela Hoelterhoff to do it justice. Writing in *The Wall Street Journal* (December 15, 1987), she says, "The original complex by William Periera, recently deceased and rarely admired, featured pavilions leading off from an open, stepped and ele-vated courtyard on Wilshire Boulevard. These pavilions wouldn't have won a beauty contest but in their own leprous little way made friendly gestures to the park behind and the sky above . . . A simply immense wall has been put up along Wilshire. It hides the Periera complex and new building, but it is also about as inviting as Lenin's tomb. This sepul-chral expanse is penetrated by a very steep ceremonial staircase, and you might feel rewarded in your effort if the embalmed remains of the chiefs of Atlantic Richfield, the building's biggest sponsor, were there to greet you at the top."

p. 227   For text of no-blank-walls retailing legislation, see Appendix B. Further requirements for street-level retailing are being incorporated into the zon-ing for the theatre district. Developers will have to have retailing on their side-street frontage as well as their avenue frontage. Stores will have to take up at least half of the side-street frontage and be no more than forty feet wide. The planners hope this will spur more theater-related uses, such as instrument shops, costume shops, and the like.

p. 227   San Francisco's planning department puts strong emphasis on retail con-tinuity. For commercial districts it provides that retail uses be the pri-mary uses of the ground floor. "Space fronting on pedestrian rights-of-way should be principally devoted to windows, display space and other uses which are of interest to pedestrians, except for required door entries. Blank walls should be allowed only if circumstances indicate no feasible alternative."

p. 228   An example of citizen concern over blank walls was the reaction to one aspect of the plans for Toronto's Eaton Centre. It promised to be a hand-some atrium complex with lots of glass. But along one side, on Yonge Street, it was going to present a largely blank wall. Yonge Street had become raunchy but it remained high in the affection of many citizens. The architect was asked to open up more access to Yonge Street and get some storefronts on the street. He did so. The Centre has been a popular success, and while the Yonge Street part is somewhat tacky, it is a lot better than a blank wall.

Chapter 16. The Rise and Fall of Incentive Zoning

p. 236   It might be helpful to set down the ways developers can get projects through when they want exceptions to what the zoning regulations say they should do. "Special permit" is an overall term and, as here used, refers to a number of procedures: granting of special permits by the planning commission for projects; rezoning for individual projects; review of projects for discretionary bonuses, such as for atriums; landmarks; special-district zoning; granting of exceptions by the Board of Standards and Appeals.

Basically, there are two routes. One is through the Board of Standards and Appeals. This is used when the developer asks for a variance on the grounds of hardship. He will plead that there are special circumstances that will prevent him from making a fair profit under the existing rules. He may have run into an unusual bedrock formation that will require a lot of extra blasting. The only way he can keep from going broke on the project, he says, is to add six more floors over what the zoning allows. The board will give him a hearing. It will be attended by members of civic and neighborhood groups, and more times than not they will testify against granting the variance. Not so many years ago, more times than not the board would grant the variance. Lately it has been tougher.

If the developer cannot plead hardship he will go the route of the Uniform Land Use Review Procedure. This was adopted in 1976 to cut the amount of time it took to get a project through under negotiated, case-by-case zoning. ULURP, as it is inelegantly termed, starts when the developer submits his project to the planning commission for review. When it certifies that the application is complete, it sends it along to the local community board. The board has sixty days in which to review the project, hold public hearings, draft its comments, and send them back to the planning commission. Within its sixty days it further reviews the project, holds a hearing, and then votes to approve or disapprove. The matter then goes to the Board of Estimate, the city's ruling body. It too has sixty days. Finally, after its hearing, it votes. At any stage of the game the time can be shortened. It cannot, however, be extended.

p. 236   A good thing about hearings on city planning matters in New York City is the fine eighteenth-century chamber they are held in at City Hall. The corridor outside is the key part. Milling about will be civic activists holding court; zoning lawyers and their principal opponents, deep in gossip; regulars whose principal occupation is testifying at hearings; leaders of delegations that have come to testify; staff members of the commission lobbying for their measure. The congestion is intense, and functional: if you stand in one spot, a slight rotation will bring you abreast of just about everybody in planning.

Inside the chamber, the straight-backed benches will be filled with people who have come on behalf of various measures or their defeat. Whatever the time, the proceedings will be running an hour or two hours behind schedule. On the dais will be members of the board or, more likely, their stand-ins. Whichever, several will be holding whispered conversations with one another; there will be much passing of notes. Assistants will be coming and going for brief consultations. One or two on the dais may actually be listening to whoever is testifying. At the three-minute mark, time will be called. The testifier may be incredulous. It seemed only a minute. A board member may ask a question of him or simply thank him for his helpful testimony and ask that he give any written statement to the clerk. In either event the testifier will usually be treated with politeness. As well he should be. Everything has already been decided.

p. 239   Review boards are patsies for good renderings, in part because most renderings are awful. The blues, for example, are customarily a shade far bluer than any sky would be; the greens far greener than any lawn. Backgrounds are airbrushed into a neutral fuzz, when the oil tanks and railroad tracks would actually look better. Given an artful rendering, however, review boards can be surprisingly uncritical, and rarely do they question the veracity of the scene. Noting this, a puckish designer in Louisville decided to test the limits of believability. In a rendering of a proposed pedestrian mall, he pictured an attractive, luminous light standard glowing about twelve feet off the ground without a column or support of any kind. It just floated. Further along the mall he had a lady leading a lion on a leash. During all the many hearings and discussions of the plan, no one ever questioned the floating light or the lady leading the lion.

p. 243   There has been a growing tendency to use plazas as office building addresses and to name them for an avenue that the building is not on. (e.g., Park Avenue Plaza, which fronts on Lexington). Paul Goldberger has suggested that the ultimate step might be demolition of the Plaza Hotel, its replacement with an office tower and plaza. It would be called Plaza Plaza.

Chapter 18. Bounce Light

p. 274   International Daytracking Systems Inc. of San Diego markets systems comprised of roof-mounted mirror units. Sunlight is electronically tracked, then guided down through ducts to ceiling-mounted diffusers.

Another reflective device is the Philadelphia "busybody." This consists of two mirrors joined at an angle and positioned outside a second-story window so one can see what mischief is taking place on the street outside. This venerable principle could be used to bring spaces partially hidden from the street into view and to increase their apparent depth.

Chapter 19. Sun Easements

p. 276   This outrageous provision for rewarding developers who build next to parkland is part of the general zoning of New York and can be applied throughout the city. Section 74-851 *New York City Zoning Resolution.*

Chapter 20. The Corporate Exodus

p. 294   The comparison study is based on two groups: (1) major industrial firms that had left New York City for a suburban headquarters location prior to 1977; (2) major industrial firms that had their headquarters in New York City prior to 1977 and stayed there. Period of comparison: December 31, 1976, to December 31, 1987.

Initially, the suburban group numbered thirty-nine firms. There was a rather severe attrition, however, with seventeen of the firms being dropped because they had lost their identity through merger or acquisition.

The New York City group was more stable. Of the initial thirty-nine, only two were dropped because of merger or acquisition.

Earlier in the research on this book I had computed the relative performances for the decade 1976–86. As time went on—and the market suffered a crash—I extended the study to include 1987. It did not make much difference. For the ten-year period, the suburban firms averaged an increase of 107 percent; the city firms, 303 percent. For eleven years the respective averages were 107 percent and 277 percent.

Chapter 21. The Semi-Cities

p. 303   Walking is a nonconforming use in many other interchange areas. The King of Prussia complex at Valley Forge is an especially aggravating example. Except at great risk it is impossible to cross from one side to another on foot. Most people, of course, drive there, so they have no problem. But if one is stranded there without a car, as I have been, there is a problem. How does one get out? I asked the clerk at the George Washington Motel. Rent a car, he said. There was a Hertz at the Schuylkill interchange. But how to get to *it?* There was no taxi on hand. No bus service. No pedestrian ways. Hugging the concrete retaining walls of the cloverleaf, I made my hazardous way to the Hertz place. And rejoined American society.

Chapter 22. How to Dullify Downtown

p. 311   The country's outstanding developer of regional shopping centers says that most cities of 300,000 or less should never have had to see a regional shopping center. If they have, he says, it's their own fault. James Rouse, at a Conservation Foundation meeting on cities: "One of the problems in revitalizing the old city is that its retail is spread over too wide an area to create a marketplace, and the stores don't pull for one another. I would stress the importance of a city's aggregating those things which can support and reinforce each other. The central city ought to be the most exciting marketplace in the whole region."

BIBLIOGRAPHY

Chapter 1. Introduction

Calhoun, John B. "The Role of Space in Animal Sociology," *Journal of Social Issues,* 1966, Vol. 22, No. 4, 46–58.

Lofland, Lyn H. "Social Life in the Public Realm: A Review Essay," prepared for the *Journal of Contemporary Bibliography,* 1987.

Mumford, Lewis. *The Culture of Cities.* New York: Harcourt Brace, 1938.

The editors of *Fortune, The Exploding Metropolis.* Garden City, N.Y.: Doubleday & Co., 1957.

Chapter 2. The Social Life of the Street

Ashcroft, Norman, and Albert E. Scheflen. *People Space: The Making and Breaking of Human Boundaries.* Garden City, N.Y.: Anchor, 1976.

Bakeman, R., and S. Beck. "The Size of Informal Groups in Public," *Environment and Behavior,* September, 1974.

Barker, Roger. *The Stream of Behavior.* New York: Appleton-Century Crofts, 1963.

Birdwhistle, Ray L. *Kinesics and Context.* Philadelphia: University of Pennsylvania Press, 1970.

Brower, Sidney. "Streetfronts and Sidewalks," *Landscape Architecture,* July 1973.

Ciolek, Matthew T. "Location of Static Gatherings in Pedestrian Areas: an Exploratory Study." Canberra: Australian National University, 1976.

Dabbs, James M., Jr. "Indexing the Cognitive Lead of a Conversation." Paper: Georgia State University, 1980.

———, and Neil A. Stokes III. "Beauty Is Power: The Use of Space on a Sidewalk," *Sociometry,* 1975, Vol. 38, No. 4.

Efron, David. *Gesture, Race, and Culture.* The Hague: Mastor, 1972; excerpted in *The Body Reader,* Ted Pelhemus, ed., New York: Pantheon Books, 1978.
    A tentative study of some of the spatio-temporal and "linguistic" aspects of the gestural behavior of Eastern Jews and Southern Italians in New York City.

Gehl, Jan. *Pedestrians.* Copenhagen: Arkitekten, 1968.

———. *Life Between Buildings.* New York: Van Nostrand Reinhold, 1987.
    This book, first published in Copenhagen, is one of a series of studies by architect Gehl that have had a major influence on design and planning in Scandinavia. The patterns of pedestrian life he has observed and the recommendations he has made are highly applicable to American cities. So too are his techniques for studying people—quite objective, but strong on imagination and humor. They are also a primer on the use of photography as a research tool. A splendid piece of work.

Goffman, Erving. *Behavior in Public Places.* New York: Free Press, 1963.

———. *Relations in Public.* New York: Harper & Row, 1971.

Goldberger, Paul. *The City Observed: A Guide to the Architecture of Manhattan.* New York: Vintage Books, 1979.

Hall, Edward T. *The Hidden Dimension.* Garden City, N.Y.: Doubleday & Co., 1966.

———. *The Silent Language.* Garden City, N.Y.: Doubleday & Co., 1969.

Heckscher, August, with Phyllis Robinson. *Open Spaces: The Life of American Cities.* New York: Harper & Row, 1977.

Henley, Nancy M. *Body Politics.* Englewood Cliffs, N.J.: Prentice-Hall, 1977.

Jaffe, Joseph, and Stanley Feldstein. *Rhythms of Dialogue.* Academic Press, 1970.

Lofland, Lyn H. *A World of Strangers: Order and Action in Urban Public Space.* New York: Basic Books, 1973.

Lynch, Kevin. *The Image of the City.* Cambridge, Mass.: M.I.T. Press, 1960.

McPhail, Clark, and Ronald T. Wohlstein. "Using Film to Analyze Pedestrian Behavior," *Sociological Methods and Research,* Vol. 10, No. 3, 1982.

Moudon, Anne Vern, ed. *Public Streets for Public Use.* New York: Van Nostrand Reinhold, 1987.

Proshansky, Harold M., William H. Ittelson, and Leanne G. Rivlin, eds. *Environmental Psychology: Man and His Physical Setting.* New York: Holt, Rinehart & Winston, 1970.

Sennett, Richard. *The Fall of Public Man.* New York: Alfred A. Knopf, 1977.

Sommer, Robert. *Personal Space.* Englewood Cliffs, N.J.: Prentice-Hall, 1969.
    In this country, psychologist Sommer has been the outstanding exponent of direct observation of the impact of design on behavior, himself a fine observer and walker.

Webb, Eugene J., Donald T. Campbell, Richard D. Schwartz, and Lee Sechrist. *Unobtrusive Measures: Non-reactive Research in the Social Sciences.* Chicago: Rand McNally, 1966.

Chapter 3. Street People

Booth, Charles. *Life and Labor of The People in London.* London and New York: McMillan & Co. Ltd., 1902.

Boyle, Wickham. *On the Streets: A Guide to New York City's Buskers.* New York: New York City Department of Cultural Affairs, 1978.

David, Randolph. "Manila's Street Life: A Visual Ethnography." In *A Comparative Study of Street Life: Tokyo, Manila, New York,* Hidetoshi Kato, William H. Whyte, and Randolph David. Tokyo: Gakushuin University, 1978.

Fried, Albert, and Richard L. Elman, eds. *Charles Booth's London.* New York: Pantheon, 1968.

Nager, Anita R., and W. R. Wentworth. *Bryant Park: A Comprehensive Evaluation of Its Image and Use with Implications for Urban Open Space.* New York: Department of Parks and Environmental Psychology, program of the City University of New York, 1976.

Salisbury, G. T. *Street Life in Medieval England.* Oxford, 1984.

Suttles, Wayne D. *The Social Order of the Slum.* Chicago: University of Chicago Press, 1968.

Whyte, William H. *Analysis of Bryant Park: Recommendations for Action.* New York: Rockefeller Brothers Fund, 1977.

Chapter 4. The Skilled Pedestrian

Drummond, Derek. "Pedestrian Traffic in Downtown Montreal," School of Architecture, McGill University, Montreal.

Fruin, John J. *Pedestrian Planning and Design.* New York: Metropolitan Association of Urban Designers and Environmental Planners, 1971.
A pioneering work on the levels-of-service concept as applied to pedestrians and the spaces they use.

Goodrich, Ronald. "Pedestrian Behavior: A Study of the Organization of Co-optive Behavior in Public Places." Paper, 1976.

Milgram, Stanley. "The Experience of Living in Cities: A Psychological Analysis," *Science,* 167 : 146L–68; 1970.

Whyte, William H., with Margaret Bemiss. "New York and Tokyo: A Study in Crowding." In *A Comparative Study of Street Life: Tokyo, Manila, New York,* edited by Hidetoshi Kato. Tokyo: Gakushuin University, 1977.

Wolff, Michael. "Notes on the Behavior of Pedestrians." Reprinted in *People in Places: The Sociology of the Familiar,* edited by Arnold Birenbaum and Edward Sagarin. New York: Praeger, 1973.

Chapter 5. The Physical Street

Appleyard, Donald. *Livable Streets.* Berkeley, Calif.: University of California Press, 1981.
Pioneering study by an outstanding researcher on the impact of different levels of vehicular traffic on neighborhoods.

Brambilla, Roberto, and Gianni Longo. *A Handbook for Pedestrian Action,* 1977.

———. *The Rediscovery of The Pedestrian,* 1977.

———. *Banning the Car Downtown,* 1977.

———. *American Urban Malls,* 1977.

The preceding four reports were published by the Institute of Environmental Action, in association with Columbia University, New York. They are for sale by the Government Printing Office, Washington, D.C., 20402.

Gruen, Victor. *Centers for the Urban Environment*. New York: Van Nostrand Reinhold, 1973.

Knack, Ruth Eckdish. "Pedestrian Malls: Twenty Years Later," *Planning*, December 1982.

Lewis, David, ed. *The Pedestrian in the City*. New York: Van Nostrand Reinhold, 1965.

Malt, Harold Lewis. *Furnishing the City*. New York: McGraw-Hill, 1970.

Federal Highway Administration. *Proceedings of the Fourth Annual Pedestrian Conference*. Washington, D.C.: Government Printing Office, 1985.

Pushkarev, Boris S., and Jeffery Zupan. *Urban Space for Pedestrians*. Cambridge, Mass.: M.I.T. Press, 1975.
This study for the Regional Plan Association of New York is the most extensive ever done on pedestrian needs, and while based primarily on New York City, it has lessons for all cities. It is technically noteworthy for its use of aerial photography to chart pedestrian flows.

Rifkind, Carole. *Main Street*. New York: Harper & Row, 1977.

Rudovsky, Bernard. *Streets for People: a Primer for Americans*. Garden City, N.Y.: Doubleday & Co., 1969.

Chapter 6. The Sensory Street

Bring, Mitchell T. "Narrow Village Streets Enliven a Crowded Kyoto," *Landscape Architecture*, June 1976.

Clay, Grady. "Why Don't We Do It on the Road?" *Planning*, May 1987.

Cullen, Gordon. *Townscape*. New York: Van Nostrand Reinhold, 1962.

Fleming, Ronald Lee. *Facade Stories*. Cambridge: Townscape Institute, 1982.

————, and Lauri A. Haldeman. *On Common Ground: Caring for Shared Land from Town Common to Urban Park* Cambridge, Mass.: M.I.T. Press, 1982.
Excellent guide to the maintenance and management of town and city spaces.

Fleming, Ronald Lee, and Renata von Tscharner. *Place Makers: Public Art That Tells You Where You Are*. Cambridge, Mass.: Townscape Institute, 1981.

Jackson, J. B. *Discovering the Vernacular Landscape*. New Haven, Conn.: Yale University Press, 1983.

Jacobs, Allan B. *Looking at Cities*. Cambridge, Mass.: Harvard University Press, 1985.

Lynch, Kevin. *The Image of the City*. Cambridge, Mass.: M.I.T. Press, 1960.

Sommer, Robert. *Farmers' Markets of America*. Santa Barbara, Calif.: Capra Press, 1980.

————, and Marcia Horner. "Social Interaction in Co-ops and Supermarkets," *Communities*, June-July 1981.

Valeri, Diego. *A Sentimental Guide to Venice*. Milan: Aldo Morello.

Venturi, Robert, Denise Scott-Brown, and Stephen Izenour. *Learning from Las Vegas*. Cambridge, Mass.: M.I.T. Press, 1972.

Chapter 7. The Design of Spaces

Carstens, Diane Y. *Site Planning and Design for the Elderly.* New York: Van Nostrand Reinhold, 1985.

Clay, Grady. *Alleys: A Hidden Resource.* Chicago: Planners Bookshop, 1978.

Davies, Stephen, and Margaret Lundin. "Department of Corrections," *Planning,* May 1987.

Edney, J. J., and N. L. Jordan-Edney. "Territorial Spacing on a Beach," *Sociometry,* 37:92 L4 1974.

Fein, Albert, ed. *Landscape into Cityscape: Frederick Law Olmsted's Plan for a Greater New York.* New York: Van Nostrand Reinhold, 1967.

Friedberg, M. Paul, with Ellen Perry Berkeley. *Play and Interplay.* New York: Macmillan Co., 1977.

Hix, John. *The Glass House.* Cambridge, Mass.: M.I.T. Press, 1981.

Linday, Nancy. "It All Comes Down to a Comfortable Place to Sit and Watch," *Landscape Architecture,* November 1978.

Lyle, John T. *Design for Human Ecosystems.* New York: Van Nostrand Reinhold, 1985.

Panero, Julius, and Martin Zelnik. *Human Dimensions and Interior Space.* New York: Whitney Library of Design, 1979.

Project for Public Spaces. *Designing Effective Pedestrian Improvements in Business Districts.* Chicago: American Planning Association, 1982.
Also available from Project for Public Spaces, 153 Waverly Place, New York, N.Y. 10014, 212-620-5660.

Project for Public Spaces. *User Analysis: An Approach to Park Planning and Management.* Washington, D.C.: American Society of Landscape Architects, 1982.

Project for Public Spaces, "What Do People Do Downtown? How to Look at Main Street Activity." Paper, National Main Street Center, National Trust for Historic Preservation, Washington D.C.

Ramati, Raquel. *How to Save Your Own Street.* Garden City, N.Y.: Doubleday & Co., 1981.

Spirn, Anne Whiston. *The Granite Garden: Urban Nature and Human Design.* New York: Basic Books, 1984.

Trancik, Roger. *Finding Lost Space: Theories of Urban Design.* New York: Van Nostrand Reinhold, 1985.

Zimmerman, Hans Bernd. "Study of Social Patterns on Brooklyn Heights' Esplanade." Paper, Graduate Center of the City University of New York.

Chapter 8. Water, Wind, Trees, and Light

Buti, Ken, and John Perlin. *A Golden Thread: 2500 Years of Solar Architecture and Technology.* New York: Van Nostrand Reinhold, 1980.

Environmental Simulation Laboratory. *Sun, Wind, and Comfort.* Berkeley, Calif.: University of California Press, 1984.

Evenson, Norma. *Paris: A Century of Change 1878–1978.* New Haven: Yale University Press, 1979.

Fitch, James Marston, *American Building: The Environmental Forces That Shape It.* 2d edition. New York: Schocken Books, 1975.

Nash, Jeffrey E. "Relations in Frozen Places: Observations on Winter Public Order," *Qualitative Sociology,* Fall 1981.

Van Valkenburgh, Michael. "Water: To Freeze on Walls," *Landscape Architecture,* Jan.–Feb. 1984.

Zion, Robert. *Trees for Architecture and the Landscape.* New York: Van Nostrand Reinhold, 1968.

Chapter 9. The Management of Spaces

Art Work Net Work. *A Planning Study for Seattle.* Seattle: City of Seattle, 1984.

Beardsley, John. *Art in Public Places.* Washington, D.C.: Partners for Livable Places, 1982.

Crowhurst-Lennard, Suzanne. "Towards Criteria for Art in Public Places," *Urban Land,* March 1987.

Crowhurst-Lennard, Suzanne H., and Henry L. Lennard. *Public Life in Urban Places.* Southampton, N.Y.: Gondolier Press, 1984.

Davies, Stephen, and Margaret Lundin. "Department of Corrections," *Planning,* May 1987.

McNulty, Robert H. *The Economics of Amenity.* Washington, D.C.: Partners for Livable Places, 1985.

Page, Clint, and Penelope Cuff, eds. *Negotiating the Amenities: Zoning and Management Tools That Build Livable Cities.* Washington, D.C.: Partners for Livable Places, 1985.

Project for Public Spaces. *Managing Downtown Spaces.* Chicago: APA Planners Press, 1986.

Public Art Fund. *Ten Years of Public Art.* New York: Public Art Fund, 1982.

Sommer, Robert. *Farmer's Markets.* Davis, Calif.: University of California, 1982.

Snedcof, Harold R. *Cultural Facilities in Mixed Use Development.* Washington, D.C.: Urban Land Institute, 1985.

Chapter 10. The Undesirables

Becker, Franklin D. "A Class-conscious Evaluation: Going Back to Sacramento's Pedestrian Mall," *Landscape Architecture,* October 1973.

Newman, Oscar. *Defensible Space: Crime Prevention Through Urban Design.* New York: Macmillan Co., 1972.

Chapter 11. Carrying Capacity

Calhoun, John B. "The Role of Space in Animal Sociology," *Journal of Social Issues,* 1966, Vol. 22, No. 4, 46–58.

Milgram, Stanley. "The Experience of Living in Cities: A Psychological Analysis," *Science,* 167:1461-68. 1970.

Chapter 12. Steps and Entrances

Archea, John, Belinda Collins, and Fred I. Stall. *Guidelines for Stair Safety.* Washington, D.C.: National Bureau of Standards, 1979.

Blondel, François. *Cours d'architecture enseigne dans l'Academie Royale d'architecture.* Paris, 1675. De l'imprimerie de Lambert Roulland. Avery AA 530 B 625.

Fitch, James Marston, John Templer, and Paul Corcoran. "The Dimensions of Stairs," *Scientific American,* Volume 231, No. 4, 1975.

Goldberger, Paul. "Cavorting on the Great Urban Staircases," *New York Times,* August 7, 1987.

Templer, John, principal investigator. *Development of Priority Accessible Networks: An Implementation Manual.* Manual prepared by the U. S. Department of Transportation. June 1980.

Chapter 13. Concourses and Skyways

Brown, David, Michael MacLean, and Pieter Sijpkes. "The Indoor City," *City Magazine,* Fall 1985.

Dillon, David. "Dressed for Success," *Dallas Morning News,* November 1, 1987.

Drummond, Derek. "Redesign of Plaza Reflects PLM's Diminished Stature," *Montreal Gazette,* June 18, 1988.

Greenberg, Kenneth. "Toronto: Streets Revisited," *Public Streets for Public Use,* Anne Vernez Moudon, ed. New York, Van Nostrand Reinhold, 1987.

Jacob, Bernard. *Skyway Typology.* Washington, D.C.: AIA Press, 1984.

Miller, Nory. "Evaluation: The University of Illinois Chicago Circle Campus as Urban Design," *American Institute of Architects Journal,* January 1977.

Pangaro, Anthony. "Beyond Golden Lane: Robin Hood Gardens," *Architecture,* June 1973.

Pastier, John. "To Live and Drive in L.A.," *Planning,* February 1986.

Ponte, Vincent. "A Report on a Sheltered Pedestrian System in the Business Center." Report prepared for the City of Dallas, 1979.

Ponte, Vincent. "Reflections on the Pedestrian System," *Urban Design International,* Fall 1986.

Villecco, Marguerite. "Urban Renewal Goes Underground," *Architecture Plus,* June 1973.

Chapter 14. Megastructures

Brown, David, Michael MacLean, and Pieter Sijpkes. "The Indoor City," *City Magazine,* Fall 1985.

Jacobs, Allan B. "They're Locking the Doors to Downtown," *Urban Design International,* July/August 1980.

Oney, Steve. "Portman's Complaint," *Esquire,* June 1987.

Wolf, Peter. *The Future of the City: New Directions in Urban Planning.* New York: Whitney Library of Design, 1974.

Chapter 16. The Rise and Fall of Incentive Zoning

Barnett, Jonathan. *Urban Design as Public Policy.* New York: Architectural Record Books, 1979.

Cook, Robert S., Jr. *Zoning for Downtown Urban Design.* Lexington, Mass.: D. C. Heath and Co., 1980.

Evenson, Norma. *Paris: A Century of Change,* New Haven: Yale University Press, 1979.

Huxtable, Ada Louise. "Stumbling Towards Tomorrow," *Dissent,* Fall 1987.

———. "Structural Gridlock," *New York Times,* June 2, 1980.

Kayden, Jerold S. *Incentive Zoning in New York City: A Cost-Benefit Analysis.* Cambridge, Mass.: Lincoln Institute of Land Policy, 1978.

Chapter 17. Sun and Shadow

Bosselmann, Peter, et al. "Sun and Light for Downtown Streets." 1983 Institute of Urban and Regional Development, University of California, Berkeley.

———. "Sun, Wind and Climate." 1984.

Buti, Ken, and John Perlin. *A Golden Thread: 2500 Years of Solar Architecture and Technology.* New York: Van Nostrand Reinhold, 1980.

Knowles, Ralph L. *Sun Rhythm Form.* Cambridge, Mass.: M.I.T. Press, 1981.

San Francisco Department of City Planning. *The Downtown Plan: Proposal for Citizen Review.* San Francisco, August 1983.

———. *The Downtown Plan.* San Francisco, 1984.

Chapter 18. Bounce Light

Bosselmann, Peter. "Experiencing Downtown Streets in San Francisco." In *Public Streets for Public Use,* edited by Anne Vernez Moudon. New York: Van Nostrand Reinhold, 1987.

Nazar, Jack L., and A. Rengin Yurdakul. "Patterns of Behavior in Urban Public Spaces." Paper: Department of City and Regional Planning, Ohio State University. 1987.

Plummer, Henry, "The Strange Rejuvenating Beauty of Radiant Things." *Architecture,* October 1987.

Chapter 19. Sun Easements

Small, Stephen J. *The Federal Tax Law of Conservation Easements.* Alexandria, Va.: Land Trust Exchange, 1987.

Whyte, William H. *Conservation Easements.* Washington, D.C.: Urban Land Institute, 1959.

Whyte, William H. *The Last Landscape.* Garden City, N.Y.: Doubleday & Co., 1968.

Whyte, William H. "Urban Landscape Easements." Paper: Land Trust Exchange, Alexandria, Va., 1988.

Chapter 20. The Corporate Exodus

Armstrong, Regina Belz. *Regional Accounts: Structure and Performance of the New York Region's Economy in the Seventies.* Bloomington, Ind.: Indiana University Press, 1980.

Birch, David L. "Job Patterns and Development Policy," *PLACE,* February 1982.

Gaffney, Mason. "The Synergistic City," *Real Estate Issues,* Winter 1978.

Hekman, John S. "Regions Don't Grow Old; Products Do," *New York Times,* November 4, 1979.

Sternlieb, George, and James W. Hughes. "The Changing Demography of the Central City," *Scientific American,* April 1980.

Chapter 21. The Semi-Cities

"An Action Agenda for Managing Regional Growth," Middlesex Somerset Mercer Regional Council, Princeton, N.J., December 1987.

Corbusier, Le, *The City of Tomorrow and Its Planning.* New York: Dover Publications, 1987.

Fishman, Robert. *Bourgeois Utopias: The Rise and Fall of Suburbia.* New York: Basic Books, 1987.

Hamill, Samuel, Jr. *An Action Agenda for Managing Growth.* Princeton, N.J.: Middlesex Somerset Mercer Regional Council, 1978.

Jackson, Kenneth T. *Crabgrass Frontier: The Suburbanization of the United States.* New York: Oxford University Press, 1985.

Miles, Don C., and Mark L. Hinshaw. "Bellevue's New Approach to Pedestrian Planning and Development." *Public Streets for Public Use,* edited by Anne Vernez Moudon. New York: Van Nostrand Reinhold, 1987.

Sternlieb, George. *Patterns of Development.* Piscataway, N.J.: Center for Urban Policy Research, 1986.

Sternlieb, George, and Alex Schwartz. *New Jersey Growth Corridors.* Piscataway, N.J.: Center for Urban Policy Research, 1986.

Chapter 22. How to Dullify Downtown

Clay, Grady. "Why Don't We Do It in the Road?" *Planning,* May 1987.

Davidson-Powers, Cynthia. "Play Ball!" *Inland Architect,* November/December 1986.

Kowinski, William Severini. *The Malling of America.* New York: William Morrow, 1985.

Lancaster, Hal. "Stadium Projects Are Proliferating amid Debate over Benefit to Cities," *The Wall Street Journal,* March 20, 1987.

Muller, Edward K. "Distinctive Downtown," *The Geographical Magazine,* August 1980.

Pastier, John. "To Live and Drive in L.A.," *Planning,* February 1986.

Redmond, Tim, and David Goldsmith. "The End of the High-rise Job Myth," *Planning,* April 1986.

Redstone, Louis G. *The New Downtowns.* New York: McGraw-Hill, 1976.

Ubaghs, Ron. "Viewpoint," *Planning,* January 1988.

Chapter 23. Tightening Up

Armstrong, Michael W., and Bob Kemper. "Who Owns Downtown State College?" *Centre Daily Times,* February 9, 1986.

Barnett, Jonathan. *The Elusive City: Five Centuries of Design, Ambition and Miscalculation.* New York: Harper & Row, 1986.

Jacobs, Jane. *The Death and Life of Great American Cities.* New York: Random House, 1959.

————. *The Economy of Cities.* New York: Random House, 1969.

————. *Cities and the Wealth of Nations.* New York: Random House, 1984.

Lindsey, Robert. "Sacramento Finds Trolley Is a Symbol of the Future," *New York Times,* April 5, 1987.

Moudon, Anne Vernez, ed. *Public Streets for Public Use.* New York: Van Nostrand Reinhold, 1987.

Webb, Michael. "A Hard-nosed Developer Proves the Experts Wrong," *Historic Preservation,* April 1984.

Widner, Ralph R. "Revitalizing Downtown Retailing," *Urban Land Institute,* April 1983.

Von Eckardt,Wolf. *Back to the Drawing Board: Planning Livable Cities.* Washington, D.C.: New Republic Press, 1970.

Chapter 24. The Case for Gentrification

Goodman, John, Jr. "People of the City," *American Demographics,* September 1980.

Horstman, Neil W. "Proud Savannah," *PLACE,* May/June 1987.

Ley, David. "Gentrification: A Ten Year Overview," *City Magazine,* 1986.

Von Tungela, Jim. "Where Will Maudie Move Next?" *Preservation News,* July 1983.

Young Professionals and City Neighborhoods. Boston: Parkman Center for Urban Affairs, 1978.

Chapter 25. Return to the Agora

Bacon, Edmund. *The Design of Cities.* New York: Viking Press, 1967.

Birch, David L. *Job Creation in Cities.* Cambridge, Mass.: M.I.T. Press, 1981.

Cooper-Hewitt Museum. *Cities: The Forces That Shape Them.* New York: Rizzoli, 1982.

Dubos, Rene. *So Human an Animal.* New York: Charles Scribner's Sons, 1968.

Hekman, John S., "Regions Don't Grow Old; Products Do," New York *Times,* November 5, 1979.

Jackson, J. B. *The Necessity For Ruins.* Amherst, Mass.: University of Mass. Press, 1980.

Price, Edward T. "The Central Courthouse Square in the American County Seat," *Geographical Review,* January 1968.

Redmond, Tim, and David Goldsmith. "The End of the High-Rise Jobs Myth," *Planning,* April 1986.

Sitte, Camillo. *City Planning According to Artistic Principles.* New York: Random House, 1965.

Thompson, Homer A., and R. E. Wycherley. *The Athenian Agora.* Princeton, N.J.: American School of Classical Studies at Athens, 1972.

Tillich, Paul. Quoted in *The Metropolis in Modern Life,* edited by R. M. Fisher. Garden City, N.Y.: Doubleday & Co., 1955.

Wycherley, R. E. *How the Greeks Built Cities.* Garden City, N.Y.: Doubleday Anchor, 1969.

INDEX

Unless otherwise indicated, all streets, buildings, parks, areas, and other places included in this index are located in New York City.

INDEX

Olmstead, Frederick Law, 128,
172, 358–59
Olympic Tower, 245, 273
Omni International (Atlanta),
206
101st Street, 5, 103
Open spaces
hours of use, 153
incentive zoning, 250, 251
New York City zoning, 343–
45
passersby, 130
public entertainment, 151–
52
relation to street, 128–31
sitting space, 126–28
sunlight, 132–34
trees, 135–37
water, 137–40
winter use, 134
Oppenheimer, Herbert, 235
Orthodox Jews
schmoozing, 14
Osaka (Japan), 89
Otterbein houses (Baltimore),
326
Outdoor cafés, 142–43, 346
Outdoor eating, 142
Outreach, 322–23
Overstreet Mall (Charlotte,
N.C.), 203–4
Oviatt Building (Los Angeles),
214

Paley Park, 100, 105
food vendors, 143
light, 252, 271
movable chairs, 122
relation to street, 130–31
security, 159, 161
steps, 187
sunlight, 132–33, 257
waterwall, 140
Paris (France), 95, 149, 246,
257–58, 260, 360, 361
Park Avenue, 109, 115, 285
Parking, 6, 71–74, 136, 171–
72, 308, 310, 313, 314
Parks
carrying capacity, 172
electricity, 151–52
food facilities, 143
incentive zoning, 248–49,
250
security, 158, 159
shadows, 276
sun traps, 134

water, 137–40
Passing
pedestrians, 21–22, 57, 58,
353
Pauls, J. L., 183
Pauses
speech, 17
window shopping, 84
Peachtree Plaza Hotel
(Atlanta), 112
Peapack (New Jersey), 290–91
Pedestrian areas, covered,
247–48
Pedestrian congestion, 7, 245
Pedestrian flows, 6
arcaded sidewalks, 246–47
Bryant Park, 160
and conversations, 8–9
plazas, 109
and sitters, 166
Pedestrian malls, 102, 357
downtown, 312
Madison Avenue, 87
retail base, 321
Tokyo, 87–88
Pedestrians
Los Angeles, 216
major cities, 22–23, 216
skills, 56–57, 353–55
and streets, 68–78
walking speeds, 64–67, 353–
55
Pedestrian traffic
city layout, 318
and conversations
separation from vehicles,
193–94, 198–99
street entertaining, 37–39
and vendors, 141
Penn Central, 278
Pennsylvania Station, 186, 189,
191, 194
People movers, 311, 319–20
"Percent for art" programs,
148, 150
Performance bond, 347
Perimeter space, 127
Peters, Ray, 34–35
Petit, Philippe, 32–33
Pfizer, 285, 287
Philadelphia (Pennsylvania),
61, 145, 260–61, 317
Philip Morris, 285
Philip Morris Building, 162,
177, 211, 248, 278
Picasso, Pablo, 148
Pickpockets, 50–51

Pike Place Market (Seattle),
150
Pimps, 53, 54
Pink Flamingos (Calder), 146
Pioneer Courthouse Square
(Portland), 152–53
Pitchmen for causes, 49–50
Pittsburgh (Pennsylvania),
151, 253, 313, 326
Place Ville Marie (Montreal),
175, 176, 194, 195, 197–
98
Plan for New York City (1969),
327–28
Plano (Texas), 297
Planters, tree, 136
Planting beds, 136, 342
Plazas
and art, 145–58
badness of, 243
carrying capacity, 172
and climate, 133–35, 359
design and use, 104–31
electricity, 151–52
food facilities, 143
grass, 124–28
ground-floor fronts, 227
incentive zoning, 229, 232–
35, 248, 250, 252
location of, 108–9
New York City zoning, 343–
45
passersby, 130
relation to street, 128–31
security, 159, 163–64
sitting space, 114–23, 124,
136–38
standing patterns, 107–8
sunlight, 132–34
trees, 136–37
undesirables, 158
vendors, 142
water, 137–39
Plummer, Henry, 275
Police, 27–30, 53–54, 141
Polshek, James Stewart, 186
Ponte, Vincent, 198–99
Pools, 139
Porter, Brent, 270
Portland (Oregon), 75, 87,
139, 152–53
Portman, John, 215, 216, 217,
220, 240
Presidential Towers (Chicago),
330
Prices, land, 241
Primerica, 295